Adapting Instruction for Mainstreamed and At-Risk Students

— SECOND EDITION —
Adapting Instruction for Mainstreamed and At-Risk Students

JUDY W. WOOD
Virginia Commonwealth University

Merrill, an imprint of
Macmillan Publishing Company
New York

Maxwell Macmillan Canada
Toronto

Maxwell Macmillan International
New York   Oxford   Singapore   Sydney

Cover photo: © Larry Hamill 1991
Editor: Ann Castel
Production Editor: Sheryl Glicker Langner
Art Coordinator: Lorraine Woost
Cover Designer: Cathleen Norz
Production Buyer: Pamela D. Bennett

This book was set in Palatino by Monotype Composition Company, Inc. and was printed and bound by Book Press, Inc.
The cover was printed by New England Book Components.

Macmillan Publishing Company
866 Third Avenue
New York, NY 10022

Macmillan Publishing Company is part of the
Maxwell Communication Group of Companies.

Maxwell Macmillan Canada, Inc.
1200 Eglinton Avenue East, Suite 200
Don Mills, Ontario M3C 3N1

Library of Congress Cataloging-in-Publication Data
Wood, Judy W.
    Adapting instruction for mainstreamed and at-risk students / Judy
W. Wood.—2nd ed.
        p.   cm.
    Rev. ed. of: Adapting instruction for the mainstream. © 1984.
    Includes bibliographical references (p.   ) and index.
    ISBN 0-675-21421-1
    1. Handicapped children—Education.   2. Socially handicapped
children—Education.   3. Mainstreaming in education.   I. Wood, Judy
W.   Adapting instruction for the mainstream.   II. Title.
LC4019.W66   1992
371.9'046—dc20   91–30665
                                                                              CIP

Printing: 1 2 3 4 5 6 7 8 9   Year: 2 3 4 5

To my sons Eddie, Scott, and Jason

Preface

The first edition of this text was developed in response to the "new reality." Hawisher and Calhoun (1978) referred to this reality as "the integration of mildly handicapped students into the general education program of the public schools" (p. 1). This reality is now seeing the end of its second decade come to a close. It has been a reality that students with disabilities have won the right to be served in regular education. However, another "new reality" has emerged. Serving these children has not been easy, and many students with disabilities still today sit in regular education classes but remain unserved. Our system has learned that the physical placement of students in a mainstreamed setting does not guarantee that they will be successful. We have learned that the instructional process must be modified as well. For the needs of these children to be met, a second "new reality" must be developed.

The second edition of this text focuses with more detail on the specific instructional needs that students are experiencing in regular education settings. It expands the model for mainstreaming the whole child, which was introduced in the first edition. The model focuses on providing appropriate instruction and a risk-free environment for all students. The model, expanded for this edition, is divided into four parts. Part One, Mainstreaming: Overview and Assessment, provides the reader with an overview of the legislation that established the backbone of services for students with disabilities, presents a model for assessing students, and discusses the importance of sharing the educational responsibility for all students. Part Two, Adapting the Environment, begins to structure the foundation of the intervention process. The socio-emotional, behavioral, and physical environments are each presented with interventions and suggestions for making each environment appropriate for students. When these environments are in place, we can look to Part Three, Adapting Planning and Teaching. This section provides practical suggestions for teachers for systematically adapting instruction. A format for adapting the lesson plan is presented and followed throughout the next four chapters. Ideas for adapting teaching techniques, content, and media are provided in a functional format. Part Four, Adapting Evaluation and Grading Procedures, looks at a model for adapting tests and alternatives to grading. These two chapters, in addition to the four chapters in the planning and teaching components (Part Three), are favorites among inservice educators.

Over the past decade, this model has been successfully implemented within classrooms across the country. Previously discouraged students are becoming self-assured and their unique needs are being met.

I hope that through this text each reader will learn many new ways to help all students. I ask all educators in my workshops across the nation to make a commitment to take one thing from the workshop—and, I hope, many new ideas—and make a difference in the life of one child. I hope that each reader will do the same with this text. In turn, I make a commitment to my readers to continue to make a difference in the lives of children. Thank you for reading this text. Please feel free to contact me if you have any suggestions that will make the third edition more practical.

Acknowledgments

Appreciation is extended to all educators and service providers, inservice and preservice, who strive daily to make the world a better place for all children, youth, and adults.

I am indebted to the reviewers who provided valuable comments and suggestions: Carol Chase Thomas, University of North Carolina at Wilmington; Melanie B. Jephson, Stephen F. Austin State; Yona Leyser, Northern Illinois University; and Julie Jochum, Bemidgi State University. I appreciate so much your many long months of toil in helping me produce a text worthy of my readers.

Over the course of this text, I have been blessed with wonderfully talented editors, Marianne Taflinger, Vicki Knight, and my present editor, Ann Castel. Each I thank. A special thanks to Ann who saw a need for this second edition and who has worked so diligently with me. To my production editor, Sheryl Langner, to my copy editor, Linda Belew, to my art coordinator, Lorry Woost, and to the staff at Merrill, an imprint of Macmillan Publishing, thank you. It is always a great pleasure to work with each of you.

I am most appreciative to my friends and colleagues without whose support and faith in our mission this text would have not been a reality. Andrea Lazzari provided technical assistance, chapter contributions, and expertise. Her talent is immeasurable and her friendship greatly appreciated. Jennifer Kilgo, my good friend of many years, continues to support me professionally and personally through this endeavor. The positive influence, expertise, and unconditional friendship shared by Andrea and Jennifer are greatly appreciated. A special thanks to Terry Overton who so graciously and professionally contributed Chapter 2 to the text. Without the continued support of my friend Debra Gibson, this edition would have been an impossibility. She continues to believe, even in the darkest moments. Thank you for a decade of friendship. Dr. Paul Wehman, who saw the possibilities over a decade ago, I thank you. He continues to mentor, support, and provide friendship in all that I do. His influence on my career cannot be measured.

Other very special people have had a great impact on this edition. A special thanks to Beverley Watson, Jane Dean, and Dollie Thomas for the expert typing of the manuscript. Thanks to: Gretchen Funderburg and Courtney McCabe for tending to every detail, no matter how large or small; Joe McLain, a very talented artist, for his wonderful sketches for this edition; Kathleen Causey for the graphics, for her desire for perfection, and for her positive influence on this mission; and Ruth Dickinson for her continued support.

Our profession is filled with great educators. Many have touched my life. Jenean Hall has made a major impact on my work and on the lives of so many children. My good friend, Les Jones, continues to stand beside me and for his love and support, thank you. Greg Robinson saw the difference that our mission makes and has supported, encouraged, and challenged me to continue. Great teachers, Marta Rosbe, Nancy DePue, Frances Lee Browder, Nancy Flick, Lynn Estep, Judy Goodwin, and Phoebe Clarke, have made a difference in so many lives, specifically my sons'. Thank you for paving the road to success for so many.

I express my appreciation to other professionals who have made a tremendous contribution to our profession. To Dr. Frank Tota, Faye Pleasants, Judy Gorham, and Bob Seiff of Roanoke City Public Schools, Roanoke, Virginia, I extend my gratitude for allowing field tests to occur within the system and for having faith in my vision before anyone else believed. To Cherritta Matthews, my good friend, thank you for allowing me to field test throughout your state. You have made a difference in the lives of so many. To Mary Margaret Salls, Marjie Sanford-Jordan, Amelia Jenkins, Nora Nielsen, Luke Martin, and Donroy Hefner, all of Austin, Texas, a personal thanks for your continued enthusiasm. To Deborah Bowman, my friend of many years, thanks for your friendship and for your help. To Dr. John O'Bannon, a caring healer, thank you for the years of physical support and for being my friend. A special thanks to Norman and Mary Parish for their many years of personal support.

Two educators have been a significant influence in my career. Dr. Joe Parks of Austin, Texas, saw how my work fit into his vision to make life better for children. A very special thanks to this great educator for believing and doing. Dean Gary Rush, University of Tennessee at Martin, my true friend for over two decades, I can never repay. Thank you for seeing the possibilities, for providing a way, for supporting when life looked dim, and for your continued unconditional love and support.

Life has given me so many friends who come and go throughout the years. However, a few, no matter the distance, provide a lifetime of love. I continue to acknowledge my childhood friends, Len Hughes, Kay Christian Morse, and Buster Bounds for always being in my life.

To my best friend, sister, strongest life influence, and most faithful supporter, Sandra Foutz, thank you for your love and for being my net. To my mother, Ercyle Walker, my father, Ford Walker, whose influence lives on, and my brother, Ford Walker, II, thank you for providing the foundation and for your love.

Each of my texts and all of my works are dedicated to my best friends and sons, Eddie, Scott, and Jason. Without their unconditional love and support, my life would be impossible. They continue to share me with others, encourage me when times are hard, and provide me with the greatest of life's blessings—children's love. I thank each of you for being so special. I am so proud of you in all that you do, for showing others that all things are possible for those that believe, and for believing in me. . . . This second edition is lovingly dedicated to each of you.

Contents

CHAPTER THREE
Mainstreaming: A Shared Responsibility   67

CHAPTER SIX
Adapting the Physical Environment

PART THREE
Adapting Planning and Teaching   185

CHAPTER SEVEN
Adapting Lesson Plans   187

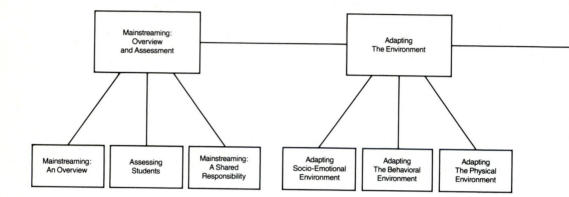

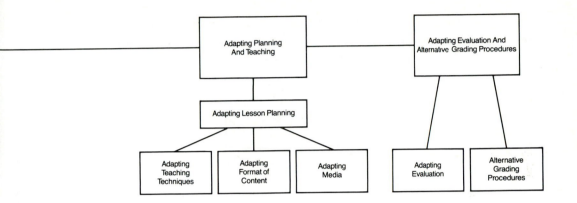

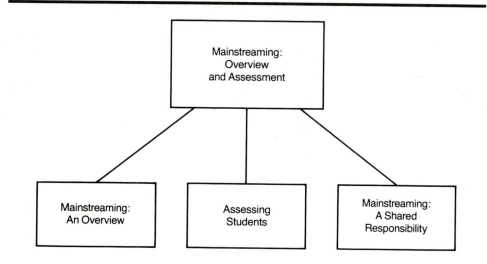

PART ONE

Mainstreaming: Overview and Assessment

Part 1 of the text includes three chapters: "Mainstreaming: An Overview," "Assessing Students," and "Mainstreaming: A Shared Responsibility." These three chapters provide the legal basis for mainstreaming, take the reader through the assessment process, and emphasize the importance of sharing the responsibility for the education of mainstreamed and at-risk students.

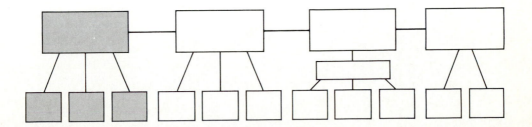

CHAPTER ONE

Mainstreaming: An Overview

Judy W. Wood

Andrea M. Lazzari

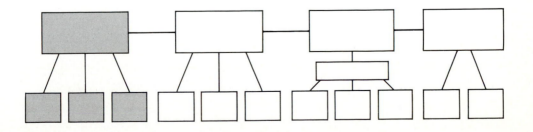

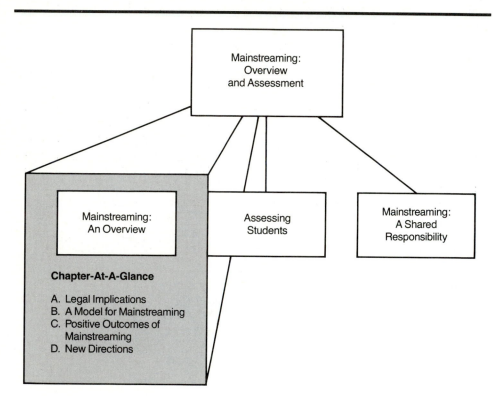

Chapter-At-A-Glance

A. Legal Implications
B. A Model for Mainstreaming
C. Positive Outcomes of Mainstreaming
D. New Directions

In 1975, landmark federal legislation began a national movement which provided students with disabilities the right to an education with their nondisabled peers. This movement, coined as mainstreaming, became the impetus for numerous changes in education. Preservice standards at the university and college levels were modified, state certification requirements were altered, and inservice education topics began to change. Public schools were presented with new challenges. Students with disabilities, previously served in self-contained classes or denied a public education altogether, were now knocking on the doors of regular education classes. As the doors began to open, and the special student took a seat in the regular class, other problems surfaced. Regular education teachers realized that they needed additional skills to teach these students. Special education teachers found that their roles had to expand from providing direct services to children in self-contained settings to working as consultants with regular educators, at times even team teaching with their colleagues. Special education students were now faced with a curriculum totally different from that to which they were accustomed and, frequently, students with disabilities were not meeting success in the mainstream of education. Parents were presented new roles of advocating for the child within regular education. They now had to become knowledgeable not only of their rights and those of their children, but also in curriculum of regular education. Many questions were raised for which there were no easy answers: Why is my child failing? What can be done? Whose responsibility does this become?

The year 1975 was a good year. As the year rung in, changes in education were on the threshold. At last, students with disabilities would have educational rights equal to those experienced by other children. Yet, soon to be noticed was the fact that, although the right to an equal education was made available, the education was not always appropriate.

This text focuses on adapting instruction for students with disabilities; that is, those students with mild mental disabilities, emotional problems, or learning disabilities. (See Table 1.1 for general information about these groups of students). Although this text emphasizes students with mild disabilities, its guidelines for instruction can be applied to all students who are experiencing problems within the education system. These students may be slow learners, students at risk, or any child who is having difficulty. Educators will also find that the ideas presented may be used with all children ongoing within the instructional process. Chapter 1 provides an overview of mainstreaming (a) starting with reviewing the legal implications, (b) describing a model for mainstreaming, (c) reviewing the positive outcomes, and (d) looking at new directions.

LEGAL IMPLICATIONS
The Movement to Mainstream

Initially, the mainstreaming movement was a direct result of an effort to protect the rights of students with disabilities and make life as normal as possible for

Table 1.1
Categories of Students with Mild Disabilities

Category	Percent of School Enrollment*	General Characteristics**
Students with Learning Disabilities	4.73%	Average or above-average IQ; may be below grade level
		Exhibit problems in spelling, writing, punctuation, grammar, and/or arithmetic
		Difficulties with oral expression or receptive language
		Poor general coordination
		Hyperactivity (excessive movement)
		Hypoactivity (lack of activity)
		Withdrawn
		Lack organizational skills
		Difficulty remembering today what they knew yesterday
		Low frustration levels
		Poor self-esteem
		Visual and auditory problems
		Difficulty remembering facts, figures, abstractions
		Difficulty asking for assistance
Students with Emotional Disturbances	0.95%	Difficulty with environmental conflicts such as fighting, bullying, violating rules
		Hyperactivity (overactive, impulsive)
		Anxiety disorders
		Inability to learn that cannot be explained by intellectual, sensory, or health factors
		Inability to build or maintain satisfactory interpersonal relationships with peers and teachers
		Inappropriate types of behaviors or feelings under normal conditions
		A general pervasive mood of unhappiness or depression
Students with Mental Retardation	1.68%	Low self-image
		Not well accepted by nondisabled persons
		Exhibit failure sets

Table 1.1
continued

Category	Percent of School Enrollment*	General Characteristics**
		Establish goals lower than their abilities
		Locus of control is extrinsic
		Difficulty with social skills
		Work better with concrete concepts than with abstractions
		Difficulty with short-term memory
		Difficulty organizing information
		Difficulty transferring learned information
		Will not achieve expected levels
		Function 3 to 4 years behind normal peers
		Benefit from a functional curriculum
		Slow in learning
		Difficulty paying attention
		Difficulty remembering what they have learned

* *Note.* Data from U.S. Department of Education (1987). To assure the free appropriate public education of all handicapped children, *Ninth annual report to Congress on the implementation of the Education of the Handicapped Act*, Washington, DC: U.S. Government Printing Office, p. 5.
** These students may have one or a combination of the listed characteristics. This list is not inclusive.

them. These concerns for students' rights began to grow in the early 1950s, developed rapidly throughout the 1960s, and reached legal fruition in the 1970s. The 1980s presented a decade of change, confusion, and new direction. In the 1990s, change focused on definition of terminology, and laws are being passed that extend the initial rights past the parameters of the public schools.

The civil rights movement of the 1950s, which pursued equal opportunities across racial boundaries, began to enter the arena of public education. The 1954 U.S. Supreme Court decision *Brown v. Board of Education of Topeka* ruled that school segregation violated the 14th Amendment, thus setting a precedent for equality in education for children with disabilities. Basically, the question that arose was, "If a free public education cannot be denied based on race or creed, can it be denied based on disabilities?" At the close of the decade, in 1958, the Council for Exceptional Children (CEC) began to support the National Association for Retarded Children (currently known as the National Association for

Retarded Citizens [NARC], founded in 1950) in seeking legislation for training special education personnel. These two groups proposed a reorganization of the U.S. Office of Education to meet special education demands and seek more appropriate services for the disabled. The Office of Education created the Division of Handicapped Children and Youth in 1963, thus meeting the demands of advocacy groups. The division later became the Bureau of Education of the Handicapped and is now the Office of Special Education and Rehabilitative Services.

The Elementary and Secondary Education Act (ESEA) of 1965 further supported the movement for services in special education by providing federal monies to the states for economically disadvantaged children and for the disabled. In 1970, federal services began to expand rapidly when Public Law 91–230, the Elementary and Secondary Education Act Amendments, became law and recognized disabled and exceptional children as a special needs target population. Society was beginning to acknowledge that humane treatment and educational opportunities were necessary for disabled children (Haring, 1978).

At the same time legislation supporting persons with disabilities was passed, several major suits brought by dissatisfied parents were decided. For example, in the 1967 landmark decision *Hobson v. Hanson*, Judge Skeely Wright ruled that the tracking system used to place children was discriminatory. In 1972, the Pennsylvania Association for Retarded Citizens (PARC) filed a class action suit against the Commonwealth of Pennsylvania concerning the right to education for disabled children. The PARC charged that the state was violating the equal protection and due process rights of children with mental retardation when it allowed a school psychologist to recommend that a child be excluded from school based on the inability of the school to serve the child. In the consent agreement, a three-judge federal court ruled that all children with mental retardation must receive a free public education and appropriate training. Additionally, the judges ruled that all previously excluded children had to be identified and evaluated by local school districts, a reevaluation of all children in special education had to be initiated every 2 years or when change of placement was considered, and parents who were dissatisfied with their child's placement had a right to a hearing. *Mills v. Board of Education* was also decided in 1972 in favor of handicapped children's rights: the judge ruled that children with handicaps had the right to an education and that the term *handicapped* included all physical, mental, or emotional handicaps, and not just mental retardation.

Section 504 of the Rehabilitation Act of 1973, Public Law 93–112

Attention to the individual rights of persons with handicaps continued to grow. Section 504 of the Rehabilitation Act of 1973, Public Law 93–112, made provisions to prevent the exclusion of any handicapped person from vocational programs receiving federal funds and, in 1974, Section 111a of Public Law 93–516 amended the Rehabilitation Act to require any recipients of federal funds to provide equal employment services for persons with handicaps.

From 1950 to 1975, then, litigation brought about by advocacy groups built a framework for the educational future of persons with disabilities. As laws were passed, educational opportunities began to open for children with disabilities, and the basic individual rights of these children soon became a major national concern in public education. As litigation continued, the need grew for a federal mandate that would have significant ramifications for the education of children with disabilities. This movement culminated in Public Law 94–142, The Education for All Handicapped Children Act, which President Gerald Ford signed into law on November 29, 1975.

Public Law 94–142, The Education For All Handicapped Children Act of 1975

Recognized as a landmark in legislation for education, The Education for All Handicapped Children Act basically provides a free public education for individuals with disabilities. According to the Council for Exceptional Children [CEC] (1989), Public Law 94–142 has four major purposes:

1. To guarantee the availability of special education programming to handicapped children and youth who require it.
2. To assure fairness and appropriateness in decision-making about providing special education to handicapped children and youth.
3. To establish clear management and auditing requirements and procedures regarding special education at all levels of government.
4. To financially assist the efforts of state and local government through the use of federal funds. (p. 2)

Major Components of the Law

Public Law 94–142 has had a tremendous impact on our education system. "Whom must we serve?" "When must we serve?" and "How must we serve?" are all issues that have surfaced since the passage of the law. Basically, the law has five major components that affect the classroom and instruction. A brief discussion of each of these components follows to provide a better understanding of the law and its implications. These are:

- A right to a free appropriate public education (FAPE)
- Nondiscriminatory evaluation procedures
- Procedural due process
- Individualized education programs (IEPs)
- Least restrictive environment (LRE)

By law, all children are guaranteed a *free public appropriate public education* at no expense to parents or guardians. Historically, many children with disabilities were denied this basic freedom; as a result, they received no education, were charged tuition for private services, or were unable to obtain any type of services. The passage of Public Law 94–142 established the fundamental right of a free appropriate public education for children with disabilities. Initially, this right was afforded to children with disabilities from age 3 through 18 as of September 1, 1978. Incentives were provided for states to extend the availability of this right from age 3 to 21 by September 1, 1981. Subsequent legislation provided additional incentives for states to extend this service from birth to 21 years of age by 1991. Students with special needs can no longer be denied the right to attend school. They must be provided an education equal to that of regular students and the support services necessary for an education.

Attempting to eliminate errors in the classification and placement of children with disabilities, Public Law 94–142 provides procedural safeguards. Historically, evaluation procedures were limited and frequently discriminated against a child's culture or physical or perceptual disabilities. The establishment of *nondiscriminatory evaluation* procedures in the law requires that testing and evaluation materials and procedures used for the evaluation and placement of children defined as disabled must be selected and administered so as not to be racially or culturally discriminatory (*Federal Register*, Vol. 42, pp. 42496–42497). The law requires that, at the minimum, all state and local educational agencies ensure that:

1. Trained personnel administer validated tests and other evaluation materials and provide and administer such materials in the child's native language or other mode of communication.
2. Tests and other evaluation materials include those tailored to assess specific areas of educational need and not merely those designed to provide a single general intelligence quotient.
3. Trained personnel select and administer tests to reflect accurately the child's aptitude or achievement level without discriminating against the child's disability.
4. Trained personnel use no single procedure as the sole criterion for determining an appropriate educational program for a child.
5. A multidisciplinary team assess the child in all areas related to the suspected disability.

Procedural due process extends the basic rights of all U.S. citizens to children with disabilities and their parents. Due process provides certain procedural safeguards to guarantee fairness during educational evaluation and placement:

1. Written parental permission is necessary before a child can be evaluated for special education services.
2. Written parental permission is necessary before special education placement, and this permission may be withdrawn at any time.
3. Parents have the right to examine and question all relevant records on their children.
4. Parents have the right to request an independent evaluation of their child's present level of performance.

5. Confidentiality must be maintained.
6. Parents and school authorities have the right to a due process hearing and the right to present evidence, call and confront witnesses, and have a lawyer present during the hearing.
7. Parents and school authorities have the right to an appeal.

The *individualized education program* (IEP) refers to a written education plan that must be developed annually for all children with disabilities receiving special education and/or related services. Functioning as a road map for instruction, the IEP is the one safeguard parents have to ensure that their children receive instruction designed to meet their unique educational needs. Prior to placement of a child in a special education program, a selected committee holds an IEP meeting to write and sign the IEP. The committee is composed of a representative of the school system, the child's teacher, one or both of the child's parents, the child, if appropriate, and other individuals at the discretion of the parent or school system. Even though the IEP is revised every year, the IEP team may be reconvened at any time. A complete and updated assessment of the child is required at least every 3 years.

From state to state and locality to locality, the format of the IEP may vary. However, certain basic components appear on all IEPs. A fundamental knowledge of these components will assist the regular classroom teacher not only in instructing the child with disabilities in the mainstream, but also in understanding the total special education program. Table 1.2 contains basic information about all the components common to IEPs.

When developing a student's IEP, it is important to keep in mind that it represents only a *written* description of a student's total educational program. The actual program, when carried out, stretches far beyond the limits of the written document. While an examination of an IEP may reveal that it includes all of the required components, this does not necessarily mean that the document constitutes an appropriate educational program for that child—one that has the potential for meeting that student's individual learning needs.

A review of existing IEPs reveals three areas that commonly need more detailed information: (a) the specification of the amount of special education and/or related services, (b) a description of the student's present level of performance, and (c) a statement of the goals and objectives (P. J. Raskopf, personal communication, November 20, 1990). A closer look at each of these three sections can help IEP team members develop IEPs that are more directly related to students' individual learning needs.

Vagueness is a common shortcoming in the section of the document specifying the amount of special education and/or related services. A simple notation of "daily" or "weekly" does not reveal the true amount of services a student is to receive. Use of descriptors such as "two 30-minute group sessions per week" or "a minimum of 4 hours per week, every week, not to exceed 6 hours, as indicated by student's needs" will leave no question as to the amount of services the student is to receive and also will help when monitoring IEPs for compliance.

Table 1.2
Components of an IEP

Component	Description
Present level of educational functioning	Information obtained from norm- or criterion-referenced tests; gives actual level and skill at which a child is functioning
Annual or long-range goals	Projection of how far teachers think a child can progress during school year; each present level of educational functioning will have a projected annual goal
Short-term instructional objectives	Objectives, written in behavioral terms, listing the intermediate steps between the present level of performance and the annual goals
Beginning and ending dates	Projected dates for initiation of services and anticipated duration of services
Objective criteria and evaluation procedures for short-term objectives	Statement of criteria and evaluation procedures for completion of short-term objectives
Special education services	Type of specific service the child is receiving
Related services	Any service outside of special education required for appropriate education
Regular classroom participation	Curriculum areas and amount of time each day the student will spend in regular classroom
Projected dates for assessment	Must be reviewed at least annually by IEP committee to determine whether short-term instructional objectives are being achieved
Committee members present	Must be signed by all committee members
Parental signature	Parents present at IEP meeting are asked to sign IEP at their discretion

It is important to remember that the amount of special education and/or related services indicated on a student's IEP should reflect the student's needs and should not be dictated by administrative convenience or limits imposed by professionals' caseloads. For example, if a secondary student needs speech-language therapy twice weekly but the speech-language therapist visits the high school only once a week, services should be scheduled to reflect the student's needs, with modifications made in the therapist's schedule as necessary. Likewise, the dates when services are to be initiated should not be modified to accommodate waiting lists. If a student is found to need a particular service at the time an IEP is written, the student should begin to receive that service as soon as possible, that is, a few days to 1 week after the IEP is written. In some instances, the IEP team may decide that it is in the best interest of the student to delay initiation of services, as in the case of a major program change to be initiated close to a long school holiday, but such cases should be an exception to standard practice.

One critical guideline to keep in mind when writing a *description of a student's present level of performance* is that it must be described adequately and accurately. In this section of the document, standardized tests as well as performance and observational data should be described in language that all IEP team members, including the parents, can understand. Thus, it is helpful to report standard scores in age or grade equivalencies whenever possible and to translate terms such as *cognitive level*, *auditory processing*, or *peer interaction* into familiar terms. A frequently observed weakness in this section is that of focusing on the student's deficits rather than presenting a balanced view of a student's strengths, as well as areas targeted for growth or improvement. This is perhaps the most important area for parental input into the IEP. Since parents observe their children in many different situations and in response to many different individuals, their input is essential to ensure an accurate and realistic description of the student. The importance of developing a realistic description of the student is underscored by the fact that this description will be the basis of the goals and objectives, which in turn will provide a blueprint for lesson plans for classroom activities. If the goals and objectives are based on an inadequate or inaccurate description, it is unlikely that they will be effective in identifying and meeting a student's unique learning needs.

While the *goals and objectives* written on IEPs are usually adequate, weaknesses are frequently found in the specification of the evaluation criteria and the procedures and schedule that will be used to determine whether goals and objectives have been met. One signal that evaluation criteria may not be delineated appropriately is the use of the same criterion for every objective on a student's IEP. A "95% or greater accuracy rate" may be ideal, but it may not be realistic for the skills involved in each objective or it may not be the easiest or most logical means of measurement. Similarly, if each evaluation procedure on an IEP reads "teacher-made test," the student may not be given an opportunity to demonstrate accomplishments in various ways. As discussed in greater detail in Chapter 11, there are a variety of valid means of assessing student performance, and these should be reflected in each student's IEP. If the evaluation schedule reads "end of school year" for each objective, this may not take into account that a student's timetable for acquiring skills across curriculum areas may vary significantly. Again, this may serve as a red flag indicating that the IEP has not been individualized. In summary, for an IEP to be effective in meeting a student's needs, each stated objective should be matched with individualized evaluation criteria, evaluation procedures, and a timetable for evaluation.

The least restrictive environment (LRE) clause of Public Law 94–142 places responsibility on the school district to educate children with disabilities in the same settings and programs as nondisabled children to the maximum extent appropriate. The child's needs as indicated on the IEP determine placement in the least restrictive environment, which may vary from child to child. The concept of the least restrictive environment is based on the premise that many creative alternatives exist to help the regular educator serve children with learning or behavior problems within the context of a regular class setting.

Thus, since the 1975 passage of Public Law 94–142, children with mild disabilities have moved from being almost totally excluded from regular classrooms to being almost totally included. Although attempts to amend and weaken the law occurred in 1981, pressure from advocacy groups defeated such efforts. The rights of children with disabilities to a free and appropriate education in the least restrictive environment remains guaranteed by law.

Public Law 99–457, Education of the Handicapped Act Amendments of 1986

Numerous sections of the 1975 P.L. 94–142 law were amended when President Ronald Reagan signed into law The Education of the Handicapped Act Amendments of 1986. Provisions of these major amendments include:

- All the rights and protections of P.L. 94–142 (EHA, Part B) were extended to children with disabilities ages 3 through 5 years in school year 1990–91. To support the achievement of this objective, the prior Preschool Incentive Grant program (P.L. 94–142, Sec 619) was revised to reflect authorization of a dramatic increase in the federal fiscal contribution for this age group.
- A new state grant program for disabled infants and toddlers (ages birth through 2 years) was established for the purpose of providing early intervention services for all eligible children as defined by the legislation. This program appears as a new Part H of the existing Education of the Handicapped Act (EHA).
- The proven components of the EHA, Part C, early education authority were retained and refined to maximize support toward achieving the objectives of the new early intervention and preschool initiatives. (CEC, 1989, p. 12)

Public Law 99–457, unlike other amendments, focuses not only on the child with disabilities but also on the family. This law shifts from a child-centered, single-agency planning effort to a family-focused, multidisciplinary planning effort. Among the required components of Part H, the Individualized Family Service Plan (IFSP) is of paramount importance to the child and family. Specific concerns that must be addressed in this family-tailored plan include:

- A statement of the child's present levels of physical development, cognitive development, language and speech development, psychosocial development, and self-help skills, which is based on professionally acceptable objective criteria.

- With the concurrence of the family, a statement of the family's strengths and needs related to enhancing the development of the child.
- A statement of major outcomes expected to be achieved for the child and family; the criteria, procedures, and timelines used to determine the degree to which progress is being made; and whether modification or revisions are necessary.
- A statement of the specific early intervention services necessary to meet the unique needs of the child and the family to achieve the outcomes, including the frequency, intensity, duration, and method of delivering the services, and the payment arrangements, if any.
- Other services and the steps that will be undertaken to secure those services.
- The projected dates for initiation of the services and anticipated duration.
- The name of the case manager who will be responsible for implementing the IFSP and coordinating the agencies. (Hale, 1990, pp. 14, 17)

Public Law 101–336, The Americans With Disabilities Act of 1990

A major breakthrough for persons with disabilities, The Americans With Disabilities Act (P.L. 101–336) was signed into law in the summer of 1990 by President George Bush. This law prohibits discrimination against any persons with disabilities and has four major focus areas:

1. Employers cannot discriminate against a person with disabilities who can perform the essential functions of the job. Employers must make reasonable accommodations for employees with disabilities unless it would create an "undue hardship," "requiring significant difficulty or expense." The law takes effect for businesses with 25 or more employees in July, 1992, and for businesses with 15 or more workers in 1994.
2. Transportation must be accessible. New buses must be lift-equipped unless the manufacturer does not supply this. Localities must provide alternative transportation if persons with disabilities are unable to use fixed route service.
3. Buildings that are being built must be accessible for wheelchairs. Older buildings with barriers should have them removed if this is "readily achievable."
4. Telephone companies must have relay assistance to voice telephones for those with hearing or speech impairments available within a 3-year period. (*Visual News*, 1990, p. 1)

Public Law 101–476, Education of the Handicapped Act Amendments (EHA) of 1990

In October, 1990, President Bush signed into law the EHA Amendments, which reauthorized discretionary programs and made certain changes to several parts of the Act. A major change set forth in this legislation was the renaming of the

EHA as the Individuals with Disabilities Education Act. Other significant changes include:

1. The addition of two new categories of disability: "Autism" and "Traumatic Brain Injury."
2. The addition of a definition of "transition services" and added requirements on the IEP to address this service.
3. The addition of definitions of "assistive technology device" and "assistive technology service."

Perhaps the most significant change brought about by these amendments is the change of emphasis in terminology from "handicapped children" to "children with disabilities," both within the EHA and other laws that refer to the EHA (National Association of State Directors of Special Education, 1990).

Over the past 40 years, legislation has molded a blueprint for providing services to all children who are having difficulty within their educational programs, as summarized in Table 1.3. The following model provides instructional and placement options for all students, specifically those students for whom it is found to be absolutely necessary to assess for possible special education placements.

A MODEL FOR MAINSTREAMING

Models for the integration of students with disabilities into regular class settings or for reentry into the mainstream fill the professional education literature. A basic assumption is that a student with disabilities is placed into a model displaying an array of educational placements ranging from the least restrictive to the most restrictive. Another basic assumption of many of the models is that a student will be placed into an alternative setting for varying degrees of time during the school day. The model in Figure 1.1 focuses instead on the numerous instructional options that can be found within regular education. The regular education class functions as the *home base* for all children regardless of the difficulties they might be experiencing. The emphasis is to provide different instruction within the regular class or close to its parameters rather than different physical placement.

As seen as Figure 1.1, ideally, all children begin school with a regular class placement. On the left side of the model, four options are available within the regular class setting for all students. The right side of the model presents six options available to a student when the options on the left do not work, and only after the student has been through the formal assessment procedures (Chapter 2). A brief discussion of each step in Figure 1.1 follows.

Regular Education Class Placement

All students should begin their educational experience within a regular education class unless extenuating circumstances make this an educational impossibility. Some young children with disabilities or those who are significantly developmen-

Table 1.3
Decades of Change Milestones for Legal Implications

Decade	Milestone	Implications
1950s	Brown v. Board of Education of Topeka (1954)	Set the precedent for equality in education for children with disabilities
1960s	Division of Handicapped Children and Youth established (1963)	Extended the demands of advocacy groups
	Elementary and Secondary Education Act (1965)	Supported the movement for services in special education by providing federal monies to states
	Hobson v. Hanson (1967)	Ruled that the tracking system used to place children was discriminatory
1970s	Public Law 91–230, The Elementary and Secondary Education Act Amendments (1970)	Recognized disabled and exceptional children as a special needs target population
	Pennsylvania Association for Retarded Citizens v. Commonwealth of Pennsylvania (1972)	Ruled that all children with mental retardation must receive a free public education and appropriate training; re-evaluation became necessary; and rights to a hearing became law
	Mills v. Board of Education (1972)	Ruled that children with disabilities had the right to an education
	P.L. 93–112, Section 504 of the Rehabilitation Act of 1973	Made provisions to disallow the exclusion of any person with disabilities from vocational programs receiving federal funds
	P.L. 94–142, The Education for All Handicapped Children Act of 1975	A landmark in legislation for children; provided a free, appropriate, public education for all individuals with disabilities
1980s	P.L. 99–457, Education of the Handicapped Act Amendments of 1986	Extended provisions of P.L. 94–142 to children with disabilities ages 3–5; established a new state grant program for infants and toddlers with disabilities (0–2) and their families
1990s	P.L. 101–336, The Americans With Disabilities Act of 1990	Prohibited discrimination by employers against persons with disabilities; addressed accessibility of public services, accommodations, transportation, and telecommunications
	P.L. 101–476, Education of the Handicapped Act Amendments of 1990	Changed name of EHA; added new categories of "autism" and "traumatic brain injury;" added "transition services" to IEP requirements and new definitions of "assistive technology"

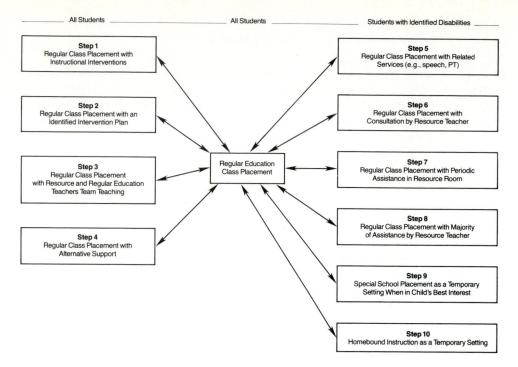

Figure 1.1
Instructional/Placement Options for Children (J. Wood)

tally delayed are located and identified during their preschool years and will receive direct intervention or support services during that period. The vast majority of children who are at risk educationally may go unnoticed until the elementary years.

Traditionally, if a student experienced noticeable difficulties academically or socially within regular education, the child would be identified as disabled and the long process to find an appropriate placement would begin. Many times, the student would continue to experience failure until a placement decision was made.

Educators now realize that we cannot afford to lose this precious time with students. Educational problems can and should be addressed within the regular class prior to formal assessment, which often becomes unnecessary as a result. Steps 1 through 4 of the model form viable alternatives for the regular education teacher to pursue and investigate for each child prior to formal assessment.

Step 1: Regular Class Placement With Instructional Interventions

In Step 1, at-risk students remain in the regular class with their peers, and the teacher informally assesses the problem, providing an appropriate intervention. Chapters 2 and 3 provide information on the teacher's role in the process of informal assessment. Frequently, adaptations or interventions of teaching technique, materials, or testing procedures within the regular classroom provide all the adjustments a student needs to succeed. As teachers make Step 1 a natural component of their instruction, they will find that referring for formal assessment will be reserved for students with more severe difficulties. The remainder of this book amplifies Step 2, that is, providing a model for adapting the learning environment through modifications of planning, teaching, and evaluation. When teachers have exhausted their repertoires of interventions, it may become necessary to seek help from their building support team members.

Step 2: Regular Class Placement With An Identified Intervention Plan

In Step 2, the teacher seeks assistance among peers for the child who is at educational risk. Within the assessment process, this step is called *prereferral*. The prereferral process is a step within the educational system by which a teacher can go to a team of peers, discuss a child who is experiencing difficulty within the class, and, with the team's help, develop an intervention plan for the child. Currently, 34 states require that a prereferral process be used in all local school districts (Wood, Davis, Lazzari, Sugai, & Carter, 1990).

Step 3: Regular Class Placement With Resource and Regular Education Teachers Team Teaching

Step 3 is rapidly becoming a preferred option for helping all children within regular education classes. Traditionally, the resource teacher remained in the special class and was not allowed to teach a student unless that student had been identified as having a disability and had a valid IEP. Educators are now realizing that a valuable resource—the special education or resource teacher—is not being utilized. Programs are now being implemented whereby the regular and resource teachers work collaboratively within the regular class setting, with both teachers helping all students. Instructional interventions are used during this step, with both teachers sharing the responsibility for educating all children.

Step 4: Regular Class Placement With Alternative Support

In Step 4, at-risk students may move out of the regular class to receive additional services. Some models bring these services, provided in reading and math for students performing in the bottom quartile, into the classroom. Chapter 1 is a commonly used alternative. A visit to the guidance counselor, school nurse, or school psychologist also helps support many children. In some areas, a foster grandparent program brings senior citizens into the school for reading or one-on-one time, benefitting both the students and the volunteers.

Regular educators may continuously use Steps 1–4 to provide educational options for students who have difficulty with traditional education. When these alternatives have been exhausted, the formal assessment process may become necessary, leading to Steps 5–10.

Step 5: Regular Class Placement With Related Services

P.L. 94–142 defines *related services* as those that are necessary to assist the child to *benefit* from special education (*Federal Register*, 1977, Sec. 121.550). Related services include physical therapy, occupational therapy, guidance counseling, and speech-language therapy. Students must formally be identified as in need of any related service. At times, the related service will be provided as a support to services provided by a special education or resource teacher. In other cases, such as a student with a language delay, a related service may constitute the student's primary and only special education service and be provided as an adjunct to a regular class placement. The student may leave the regular class for a short period at varying times to receive a related service, or it may be delivered in the regular class. Regardless of type of service, the student's home base remains in regular education.

Step 6: Regular Class Placement With Consultation by Resource Teacher

In Step 6, the special needs student receives regular class instruction with nondisabled students. This step does not involve resource room placement. However, when the student with disabilities is experiencing instructional or behavioral problems, the regular class teacher can summon the special education resource teacher for instructional adaptation and modification suggestions. The special education teacher can then prescribe educational alternatives to regular class instruction. Thus, the special student receives services without being moved to a special class setting.

The clear advantages of resource consultation include less obvious labeling of students, less stress on teachers, and less crowding of special education classrooms. For example, even though students with disabilities must be screened, evaluated, and placed for special education consultation services, they remain more "like" than "different" because they are still integrated with their peers in the regular class setting. In addition, the overworked regular classroom teacher has a support teacher to assist with the instructional modifications. Finally, keeping students with disabilities on consultation whenever feasible keeps special class space available for those students in definite need of such placements.

This step within the model also serves as a phasing-out option for students who have previously received instruction from the resource teacher outside the regular class. The consultation step is a popular choice for students who need a label to receive services, while teachers observe carefully to ensure that they can succeed without direct support.

Step 7: Regular Class Placement With Periodic Assistance in Resource Room

Other situations require that a student with disabilities, although still in a regular class setting, receives part-time services in the resource room. For example, a student may need special assistance in reading or require extra time for social studies. The adaptations and modifications in the appropriate instructional program for these students require a more concentrated effort by the special resource teacher. In this step of the model, the student may go to resource room for as little as one class period a day or for as much as half a day. The student's IEP dictates the amount of time to be spent as well as the subjects to be studied in both the resource room and the regular classroom. The main difference between Steps 6 and 7 is that in Step 6, the student never leaves the regular classroom for instructional purposes, whereas in Step 7, the student may leave for one to several periods per day.

Step 8: Regular Class Placement With Majority of Assistance by Resource Teacher

For varying reasons, both academic and nonacademic, some students with disabilities may need intense instruction or attention by the special education resource teacher. This instruction may occur in either the regular class setting or a special class setting. The intensity of the student's needs and the preference of the parent and/or student may dictate the specific locations where services will be provided. Integration of the student occurs as much as feasible.

Step 9: Special School Placement As a Temporary Setting When In Child's Best Interest

This point in the continuum reflects a change in emphasis from the student with mild disabilities to the student with more severe difficulties. A student served at this step needs a more concentrated program because the regular class setting, even with modifications and adaptations, fails to meet the instructional needs of the child. This service option should be viewed as only temporary while every effort is made to return the child to the regular class setting.

Step 10: Homebound Instruction As a Temporary Setting

Sometimes, children need to receive educational services at home. A child recovering from surgery may need such services for only a short period of time, whereas a more seriously ill child may require homebound instruction for an extended period. In any case, a visiting teacher travels to the student's home and provides instructional services; occasionally, a school uses a two-way communication system when services are required for an extended period of time. This approach, if used during school hours, provides contact between child and classroom, between child and teacher, and between child and peers, thus providing a simulated educational environment for the disabled student.

Model Summary

An array of service options presently is available for all children served within the schools. Services that historically were available only for a student with an identified disabling condition are now open to any child experiencing instructional difficulties. Equally important, opportunities that were at one time available only for the nondisabled student are now obtainable for students with special needs as well. Educators are beginning to see that they must share the responsibility for the education of all children. Professionals and parents speak of integrating special students; however, if special students are never segregated, integration will become unnecessary—they will never have left the mainstream!

The mainstreaming movement has had a paramount effect on the education of all children and has established new roles for both regular educators and special educators. With this movement now entering the end of its second decade, the field of education is experiencing many new directions: many positive outcomes of mainstreaming, a focus on at-risk students, and a movement labeled the *regular education initiative*.

POSITIVE OUTCOMES OF MAINSTREAMING

Whether students are integrated back into the mainstream of regular education or helped to remain in the mainstream, many positive outcomes result. Regular students, special students, and educators all benefit from this *new reality*.

One positive outcome of the mainstreaming effort is that regular education students receive a realistic view of a heterogeneous society. In addition, they learn that they can help others, and they learn how to help others. Many students serve as peer tutors or buddies for students with disabilities in their classes. A mother once related that she inadvertently learned that her son was serving as a buddy to a student with hearing impairments. When she asked her son why he had not mentioned what he was doing he replied, "I never thought that it was a big deal." When all students learn that helping others is a natural process in life, everyone benefits. As regular students begin to accept others who may be different from them, they also learn to accept differences within themselves.

Many students in today's schools are at risk. These students, for one reason or another, have not been identified as in need of special services, were found ineligible for special services, or their special services were phased out. The new reality provides great benefits for this population, since all educators are learning how to provide interventions for all students. Meeting their needs more adequately reduces the risk of dropping out of school becoming their only option.

Special students have reaped great benefits from the mainstreaming effort. However, remaining within regular education from the beginning has even greater rewards. Reentry is always difficult and becomes unnecessary if the student never leaves the regular class setting. Remaining in the regular class reduces labeling, allows bonding and friendships to develop, and serves as a modeling process. Special students belong in mainstreamed environments from the start to avoid having to earn a place within the social structure of the class. Additionally, regular students can serve as models for appropriate social behaviors and provide academic support.

Educators, both regular and special, benefit from regular class placements for special students. Mainstreaming back or remaining in the mainstream of regular education has produced a role for all educators. Special and regular educators can learn from one another as they share their expertise and special skills.

Prior to the passage of P. L. 94–142, universities trained regular educators to teach only those children who presented no obvious learning difficulties. Children with learning problems were quickly and quietly scurried off to special class settings. But with the pendulum swinging from segregation to integration, the regular class teacher must now exhibit competencies required for special instruction as well as those required for regular class instruction.

Many states mandate training of regular educators in special education competencies. Special education teachers no longer serve a few children in isolated environments. Today, they frequently work side-by-side with regular educators, sharing the responsibility for the education of all children. In addition to their roles of assessing or prescribing, special education teachers must focus on communication and human relations. Chapter 3 will expand on this new role of shared responsibility.

The role for the college educator is also changing as a result of the movement of mainstreaming students into regular education settings. With substantial and steady numbers of students with disabilities receiving services in regular classes, teachers frequently do not possess the knowledge and skills to meet their needs, due to the absence of training in special intervention strategies during their own preservice coursework (Wood, 1989). General educators report a lack of training at the preservice level to work with students with disabilities (Flynn, Gack, & Sundean, 1978; Johnson & Cartwright, 1977; Middleton, Morsink, & Cohen, 1979). The educational reform movement has spotlighted the need to improve teacher training at the preservice level, charging institutions of higher education with training teacher educators in specific strategies for educating students with disabilities, including "how to work with students with disabilities within the context of the regular education curriculum, how to assist students with disabilities in becoming involved in the school's social network, and the development of effective pedagogy" (National Council on Disability, 1989, p. 57).

The lack of adequate training and preparation to meet the needs of main-streamed students is not, however, unique to regular educators. As evidenced by results of a 1989 national survey conducted by the Department of Professional Development of the Council for Exceptional Children (CEC), special educators have similar training needs. This survey was sent to a random sample of CEC members to determine their preferences for topics, materials, and formats for professional development training. Respondents were presented with a list of items and asked to rate each item on a 4-point scale in response to the question, "Is this a topic that I need to know more about?" The *top item* identified as a training need by the 855 respondents was "Adapting instruction for special education students in the mainstream" (E. Byrom, personal communication, September 28, 1990; CEC, 1989).

NEW DIRECTIONS

The At-Risk Population

The mainstreaming movement has opened many doors of opportunity for another vast and frequently overlooked population of students, those at risk for school success. Additionally, new issues have surfaced in education. New directions within education have been forged and have made a profound impact on the system. One strong new direction is that of programming for the vast numbers of students who are identified at risk for educational failure.

Consider the following statistics:

- Of the approximately 3.5 million babies born in this country each year, over 7% have congenital anomalies that involve genetic, physical, or biological defects (Peterson, 1987).
- Over 23% of children age 3 and under are poor. During the early years, which are crucial to development, nearly one fourth of all U.S. children lack medical, nutritional, and early-learning resources (Reed & Sautter, 1990).
- More than 12.6 million U.S. youngsters—nearly 20% of all children under the age of 18—are poor (Reed & Sautter, 1990).
- It has been estimated that 100,000 to 200,000 cocaine-exposed children are being born each year, many of whom will later need special learning environments (Rist, 1990).
- Over 1 million children are abused or neglected by their parents each year and, for every case of child abuse that is reported, two additional cases go unreported (Winters, 1985).
- More than 25% of all high school seniors in the U.S. do not graduate (Olson, 1987).
- In the three decades from 1956 to 1986, the suicide rate in the U.S. among the 15–24 age group increased from 4.5 to 12.3 deaths per 100,000 (Guetzloe, 1989).
- A 1989 national survey revealed that at least 3 million Americans are homeless and that families with children comprise the fastest-growing segment of the homeless population (National Coalition for the Homeless, 1989).

What are the implications of these overwhelming statistics for educators? Even a cursory glance at these figures soundly shatters the image of the rosy-cheeked student who cheerfully beckons to us from the back-to-school advertisement—a student who is healthy, carefree, well nourished, and supported and nurtured by two loving parents. Today, as a result of demographic shifts and changes in societal rules and practices, the face of the student population is changing. Students at risk for educational failure comprise the fastest-growing student population. As such, they are the focus of growing concern among a cross-section of regular and special educators, in both rural and urban settings (Council of the Great City Schools, 1988; Helge, 1989a).

But exactly how is a student placed in the at-risk category? Must a student belong to one or more of the statistical groups noted above to be considered at risk? Historically, other labels have been used to identify this same population: culturally deprived, marginal, underprivileged, low-performing, low-achieving, remedial (Presseisen, 1988). While there is no clear consensus regarding an exact definition of students at risk, current definitions have been extended beyond those factors imposed solely by poverty or cultural deprivation. Helge

Table 1.4
Characteristics Associated With At-Risk Students

Substance abuse
Involvement with crime
Suicide attempt/depression/low self-esteem
Child abuse (physical, emotional, verbal and/or sexual)
Poverty
Child of alcoholic or substance abuser
Child in a dysfunctional family system
Illiteracy/English as a second language
Migrant
Disabling condition
School dropout
Sexually active/pregnant
Minority and poor
Health problem
Performance significantly below potential
Residence in a rural or remote area

Note. From "Rural (At-Risk) Students—Directions for Policy and Intervention" by D. Helge, 1989b, *Rural Special Education Quarterly, 10,* p. 10. Copyright 1989 by *Rural Special Education Quarterly.* Adapted by permission.

(1989b) identified 16 characteristics most frequently associated with at-risk students (Table 1.4). Typically, students will be involved with one or more of the conditions, which are frequently related to one another.

The Iowa Department of Education (1989) has adopted a broader definition of the at-risk student as follows:

> Any identified student who is at risk of not meeting the goals of the educational program established by the district, not completing a high school education, or not becoming a productive worker. These students may include, but are not limited to, dropouts, potential dropouts, teen-age parents, substance users and abusers, low academic achievers, abused and homeless children, youth offenders, economically deprived, minority students, culturally isolated, those with sudden negative changes in performance due to environmental or physical traumas, and those with language barriers, gender barriers, and disabilities. (p. 20)

As displayed in Table 1.5, this definition includes three distinct categories of at-risk students, as identified by specific, observable criteria.

Although differences exist in the type and number of factors that may be used to place a student in the at-risk category, a conservative estimate of the percentage of students who are seriously at risk for school failure is one fourth to one third of the total school population (Frymier, 1989). In rural areas, the prevalence of at-risk students may be even higher, with some rural states such

Table 1.5
At-Risk Categories and Specific Criteria for Identification

Not Meeting Goals in Education Program	Not Completing High School	Not Becoming a Productive Worker
Low achievement scores; below the 30th percentile or 2 years or more behind	Pregnancy	No identified career interests
Inability to cope with a full class schedule; low grades in one or more classes (below grade "C" or 2.0 on a 4.0 scale)	Teen parent	Course selection is highly random, leading toward no specific post-school training or career choice
	Dropout	
Poor attendance; missing 1 day per week	Culturally or geographically isolated; not able to interact with students of a different race or socio-economic background	No reasonable career plans upon graduation or beyond graduation
Suspended or expelled 2 or more times		No specific plan for post-high school training
Lack of friends	No extracurricular involvement	
Dislike for school; frequent mention of not belonging	Substance use or abuse; unhealthy physical appearance	Low motivation to seek employment
Sudden negative changes in classroom performance or social interaction	Inability to adjust to transition steps in the education process (elementary to junior high/middle school, or junior high/middle school to high school)	Inability to keep employment; unacceptable work behavior
Poor organization of study habits; can't find homework, lacks necessary materials		Unfamiliarity with and inability to use community service agencies
Inability to pay fees, lunch tickets, transportation, materials	Homeless	Low aptitude/skills for competitive work
	Frequently tardy	
Limited English proficiency	Transient (moves from school to school—within and outside the district frequently)	
Disabled and not succeeding as expected after being given support services by special education staff	Suicidal tendencies	
Difficulty meeting long-term goals	Negative peer influence (social crowd of dropouts, delinquents, and/or poor achievers)	
Low motivation to complete assignments	Victim of overwhelming peer harassment	

Note. From *Guidelines for Serving At-risk Students* by Iowa Department of Education, 1989, Des Moines, IA: Author. Copyright 1989 by Iowa Department of Education. Adapted by permission.

as Wyoming reporting that as many as half of their children could be classified as at-risk (Helge, 1989b).

The effects of individual risk factors and combinations thereof will differ from one student to another. However, the earlier children are exposed to conditions that place them at risk, the greater the likelihood of a long-term negative effect on their development and academic achievement. Children who enter the public school system without a grasp of basic concepts and self-help skills and with limited abilities to listen, attend, and follow directions will begin to lag behind the achievement levels of their peers by the end of their kindergarten year. Without early detection and intervention, this discrepancy in ability and performance will continue to grow.

The body of research on the positive effects of preschool education in preventing later scholastic failure among children at risk (Schweinhart & Weikart, 1980; Mitchell, 1989) leads to the inescapable conclusion that high-quality, comprehensive early childhood programs must be made available to all children, especially those who are disadvantaged and/or at risk. Funding is a critical factor in accomplishing this end. With the exception of Head Start, which continues to be funded with small annual increases, federal support for early childhood programs has declined in real dollars over the past decade. Some states, however, have begun to develop and fund programs for young at-risk children and many state departments of education are beginning to initiate prekinder-garten programs in local public school districts. More recently, federal interest in early childhood programs appears to have been renewed somewhat, as evidenced by the creation in 1988 of Even Start, a joint parent-child education program with the dual goals of improving adult literacy and providing education to children from age 1 to 7 (Mitchell, 1989).

The importance of establishing and maintaining programs for young at-risk children to prevent later academic failure and school dropout cannot be overemphasized. Still, the need to continue similar efforts beyond the preschool years is also critical. No longer can early childhood educators (Grades K–3) in public schools rely on curriculum approaches and methods designed for students with enriched backgrounds. As increasing numbers of children exposed to one or more risk factors enter elementary school, techniques must be available to identify and meet their unique needs. For many children, this will entail educating their parents along with them. For others, specialized instruction blending approaches from regular early childhood education, special education, and compensatory education will best meet their needs. For all children, early identification and intervention are key factors that will increase their chances of school success as they progress through the upper elementary grades.

As students enter middle school, critical factors in adolescent development (e.g., development of coping skills and dealing with issues of identity, indepen-dence, self-esteem, and self-image) may become unduly complicated when a student already is affected by or becomes involved with one or more of the risk factors listed in Table 1.3 (Helge, 1989a). Because of societal pressures and the compounded nature of many risk conditions faced by adolescents, curricular modifications are needed at the middle and secondary levels to meet the changing needs of students. A greater emphasis on life skills, including training in problem solving, interpersonal communication, and the development of coping skills can help all students to meet and overcome the challenges of daily living imposed by risk factors.

Educators can no longer work in isolation in their attempts to provide interventions for the magnitude of problems facing at-risk children and youth. Nor can they be expected to bear the full burden of overcoming social and economic inequities with limited personnel and fiscal resources (Reed & Sautter, 1990). It is critical for educators to form partnerships with parents and community leaders in accessing community resources (e.g., community mental health agencies, comprehensive community health services) and developing in-house resources (e.g., after-school care, family literacy training) to help overcome the multitude of problems associated with at-risk conditions.

When the growing statistics for at-risk groups are considered along with the increasing numbers of individuals, families, and communities affected by one or more risk conditions, it becomes clear that no school, classroom, or teacher can escape the influence of these risk conditions. All educators, including regular and special education teachers and administrators, must develop new strategies to serve heterogeneous student populations and meet the diverse needs of at-risk students in the regular education environment. Out of the need to develop alternatives for all children and reduce the labeling process, a second new direction began to develop—the regular education initiative.

The Regular Education Initiative (REI)

REI Defined

The regular education/special education initiative goes by many names— collaborative teaching, cooperative teaching, supported education, prereferral intervention, mainstream education, and, most commonly, the regular education initiative (REI) (Miller, 1990; Robinson, 1990). The REI calls for a restructuring of special and general education to create a partnership among educators from both disciplines to better serve all students. Typically, the REI focuses on two groups of low-performing students—those identified as mildly disabled and those at risk for school failure due to disadvantaged economic or social backgrounds. If carried out in its purest form, the REI would result in a "seamless web" of education services in which all students would receive individualized services in the regular education environment without a need to label or give special designation to any student (Robinson, 1990). Ideally, the REI will result in the joining of effective practices from special, regular, and compensatory education to establish a general education system that is more inclusive of students with special learning needs (Reynolds, Wang, & Walberg, 1987).

Historical Framework

The REI most likely began at the local level as teachers, administrators, and parents began to realize the shortcomings of a segregated special education system. It was legitimized in a 1986 policy statement by Madeleine Will, then-Assistant Secretary for Special Education and Director of the Office of Special Education and Rehabilitative Services of the U.S. Department of Education (Robinson, 1990). Some criticized Will's statement as a reflection of Reagan-Bush economic policies that were aimed at decreasing federal support for education. Yet the proposal served to focus national attention on the lack of an interface between regular and special education (Kauffman, 1989; Robinson, 1990). Since that time, professional educators have debated at length over the relative strengths and weaknesses of the REI.

Impetus for Reform

Numerous factors served to fuel the REI movement. Proponents for reform (Anderegg & Vergason, 1988; Gersten & Woodward, 1990; Kauffman, 1989; Reynolds, Wang, & Walberg, 1987; Robinson, 1990) charged that:

1. Special education had become a "dumping ground" for students who were not truly disabled but, rather, difficult to teach.
2. A lack of consistency was evident in defining categories of students with disabilities, especially for the category of learning disabilities. This resulted in a great discrepancy between and within school divisions and states regarding which students were eligible for special education services.
3. Unnecessary barriers were created that excluded students with special needs from becoming fully integrated into school and community life. This served as a disadvantage to students both with and without disabilities.
4. There was a lack of compelling evidence of the validity of categories and other special education requirements in promoting expected educational outcomes.
5. Educators were disenchanted with tracking systems in general. Special education was viewed as one of the most rigid tracks.
6. There was a lack of standardized curriculum in pull-out programs (e.g., resource room). In cases where such a curriculum was used, it was not linked to the core curriculum used in the regular classroom.
7. Requirements for excessive and oppressive paperwork existed without evidence of direct benefit to the students served.

Restraining Factors

Not surprisingly, the calls for reform of the existing dual system have met with resistance. Two major sources of resistance to the REI can be attributed to its roots. First, the REI originated from the field of special education. Calls for reform of the general education system by special educators perceived as outsiders have not been readily welcomed by regular educators, who lack a sense of ownership of the movement. A second source of resistance is the perception of the reform as a top-down approach. While the need for increased collaboration between regular and special educators had been realized in many school districts and school buildings across the country prior to Will's proposal, calls for reform from the federal and state levels served to alienate practitioners at the local level who were already frustrated by a perceived lack of control over programs in their own buildings and classrooms.

Both special and regular educators have raised legitimate concerns in response to the REI, among them:

1. The rights of students with disabilities would be jeopardized if existing categorical labels were changed or eliminated.
2. The rights of students with disabilities to an equal educational opportunity could not be ensured if options for education outside the regular class were eliminated (Kauffman, 1989).
3. Regular educators have not yet fully embraced the idea of mainstreaming. Not all teachers are adequately prepared to meet the special learning needs of all students or willing to assume even more responsibility (Gersten & Woodward, 1990; Kauffman, 1989).
4. Unable to meet the curricular demands of the regular classroom, students with disabilities would exhibit increased frustration levels and behavioral problems and decreased self-esteem.
5. The differences between elementary and secondary schools (e.g., curriculum demands, skill level plateaus at secondary levels, organizational structures) may prevent successful wholesale application of the REI at the secondary level (Schumaker & Deshler, 1988).
6. The placement of students with special learning needs in regular education classrooms may adversely affect other students, as teachers must devote more of their time to the students with disabilities.
7. The combining of general and special education budgets would result in a decrease in special education services available to students with disabilities who need special services (Kauffman, 1989).
8. Special educators would be relegated to advisory roles, and their specialized skills and training would constitute a wasted resource.

Effecting Needed Changes

As with any proposal for radical reform of institutional practices and policies, if changes in the educational system are to occur, compromise will be necessary. Regular educators, special educators, and administrators from the local, state and federal levels must recognize that an "all-or-nothing" approach is not feasible or realistic, given the current educational climate and available resources. Caution must be exercised to ensure that changes in policy and practice are based on defensible research and that such changes uphold the rights of all students to an equal educational opportunity.

Several basic strategies for effecting change can be applied to the REI. Foremost among these is the need to share a common goal. If significant changes are to occur, both regular and special educators from the local level to the district and state administrative levels must assume ownership of the issue. Other necessary strategies include: (a) The realization that significant changes do not occur overnight—that change is an ongoing process; (b) The identification of workable models for an integrated system of service delivery; (c) The development of a shared language between special and regular educators; (d) Cooperative professional development at the preservice and in-service levels; (e) The assumption of a more active role by teachers in staff development; and (f) The empowerment of the building principal as the instructional leader and coordinator of the change process (Loucks-Horsley & Roody, 1990; Schumacher & Deshler, 1988).

Finally, if change is to be effective, professionals involved in the process must be willing to modify some of their own views and practices. Of primary importance is the willingness of all educators to accept the shared responsibility of mainstreaming, assuming responsibility for the educational outcomes of all students and not just those in their own classrooms or programs. Some educators may need to shift their own pedagogy away from a teacher-centered stance to one that is more student-centered. As changes take place, ongoing role clarification most certainly will be needed. This will require both teachers and administrators to relinquish certain aspects of their traditional roles and add new components. Additionally, educators will need to be open to learning new skills and approaches that may differ significantly from those acquired in their preservice training and throughout their teaching careers. Most importantly, educators must not lose sight of the fact that the student is and must remain the focus of the change process. The result of maintaining this focus will be improved educational opportunities and outcomes for all students.

SUMMARY

The movement to mainstream is a reality for all children. Laws have been passed almost continuously over the past 20 years to pave the way for an appropriate education for all children. The at-risk population joined the list of those in need of special help. Special children found individualization first in special placements and now in the mainstream, where it all began—the regular classes.

Chapter 2 presents the prereferral-to-placement process for students who are at risk and may need special education services.

CHAPTER TWO
Assessing Students

Terry Overton

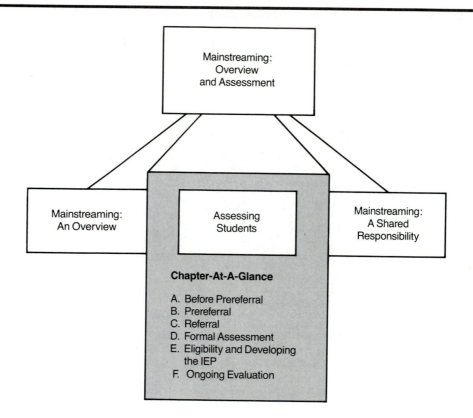

Mainstreaming:
Overview
and Assessment

Mainstreaming:
An Overview

Assessing
Students

Mainstreaming:
A Shared
Responsibility

Chapter-At-A-Glance

A. Before Prereferral
B. Prereferral
C. Referral
D. Formal Assessment
E. Eligibility and Developing
   the IEP
F. Ongoing Evaluation

Educators too often envision assessment narrowly only in terms of state or locally mandated standardized achievement tests or comprehensive assessment for placement of students into special education programs. More broadly defined, assessment is the collection of information to identify problems and make educational decisions (Salvia & Ysseldyke, 1988). Assessment is, therefore, an ongoing and continuous process. As illustrated in Figure 1.1 (p. 18), classroom assessment is a part of instructional intervention in the regular classroom. In practice, teachers assess students in their classrooms on a daily basis. This practice is called *informal assessment* and provides teachers with information to make educational decisions according to student progress. Standardized group and individual test instruments are used for *formal assessment*. Salvia and Hughes (1990) summarized the various methods of obtaining information, which are shown in Table 2.1.

The purpose of assessment varies with the individual student's needs. Informal assessment is used to monitor student progress in the regular classroom. Formal assessment methods are used to measure academic achievement, such as group achievement testing, or determine eligibility for special services (Figure 2.1, p. 38).

Informal assessment includes the information gathered through student work samples, error analyses of student written and oral responses, behavioral observations, responses to teacher-made tests, and daily probes for mastery of skills. Informal assessment occurs in every classroom and is probably the most common type of assessment.

Many of the techniques used to assess students informally involve the use of content taken from curriculum materials that are used in the classroom. This type of assessment is known as *curriculum-based assessment*.

Curriculum-based assessment is thought to be a more sensitive measure of progress made by students than standardized achievement tests because the actual content to which the student has been exposed is used to develop the test instrument (Shapiro, 1989). Standardized achievement instruments may contain items measuring content or skills, which are presented at different grade levels in various curricula. As a result, students' scores may reflect exposure to content or skills as well as actual achievement. It is important that a variety of assessment methods are used for all students to gain an accurate measure of their performance.

STEP 1: BEFORE PREREFERRAL

The regular classroom teacher uses many methods of informal assessment for instructional intervention. These methods are used with all students in the class. These methods include tests that are a part of a curriculum series, teacher-made tests using curriculum content, student work samples, homework, and systematic classroom observation. These methods aid the teacher in classroom planning and adaptation of instruction. The teacher may determine, for example, that the pace of instruction is too rapid or too slow for a particular group of

Table 2.1
Common Distinctions Among Sources of Information

Observations

- Systematic observations are observations of predetermined behavior. These observations are conducted according to a strict set of procedures for defining the times of observation, the conditions of observation, and the target behaviors.

- Critical incident observations are observations of a restricted number of events deemed particularly important by the observer. Unlike systematic observations, the particular behavior that is observed is not specified in advance. Often, the antecedents and consequences of the behavior are also noted.

- Anecdotal records are quite similar to observations of critical incidents. Anecdotal records differ in that there are no restrictions on the number of observations.

- Evaluations of permanent products are assessments made about the outcomes of behavior. Permanent products include anything that can be inspected after it was produced. Written tests and video- or audiotapes of behavior also can be considered permanent products; however, permanent products more often refer to worksheets, essays, drawings, and so on.

Tests

- Norm-referenced tests are tests that compare the performance of the student with the performances of similar students (e.g., students of the same age or grade).

- Criterion-referenced tests are tests that compare the student's performance to an absolute standard (e.g., the student correctly adds 3 + 4).

- Group-administered tests are tests that can be given to more than one student at a time. Students mark their own responses, and the tester may or may not read the questions to the students. Student performance is usually reported as the number (or percent) correct or, if the test is norm-referenced, in terms of relative standing (e.g., percentile rank).

- Individually administered tests are tests that are given to only one student at a time. Usually, the examiner reads the questions and records the student's responses. Student performance is usually reported as a number or in terms of relative standing.

- Objective-referenced tests are norm-referenced tests that have instructional objectives written for individual test items.

- Probes are timed, brief (usually 3 minutes or less) tests that are sensitive to small changes in what a student knows and that can be administered frequently. Student performance is usually reported as a rate.

- Survey tests are tests that contain a sufficient number of test items only to make accurate discriminations among test takers. Survey tests may assess several domains—e.g., reading, math, spelling—or several skills within a domain—e.g., addition without regrouping, addition with regrouping.

- Diagnostic tests are tests that have a sufficient number of test items to allow correct inferences about the type of errors a pupil makes or about a pupil's mastery of particular skills or concepts. Because they contain many more items than survey tests, diagnostic tests usually assess only one domain.

Table 2.1
continued

Impressions

- Rating scales are devices that ask parents, teachers, or others to make judgments about a student's performance or social behavior based upon the rater's experience with the student.
- Interviews are similar to but less structured than rating scales. In interviews, the person being interviewed is asked to make judgments about the subject of the interview. However, unlike rating scales, the interviewer often seeks to ascertain the accuracy of the judgments by requesting additional information. In some instances the interviewer simply records the judgment of the person being interviewed.
- Clinical impressions are professional judgments about an individual. These judgments are often working hypotheses of the professional as opposed to firm diagnoses.

Note. From *Curriculum-based Assessment: Testing What is Taught* (p. 4–5) by J. Salvia & C. Hughes, 1990, New York: Macmillan. Copyright 1990 by Macmillan. Adapted by permission.

students. The teacher may need to check the curriculum materials for readability levels or for the use of complex vocabulary terms. Information gathered on these types of learning problems may be used to modify instruction for all students in the class (Figure 2.2).

An environmental assessment of the classroom will provide insight for the teacher to use in planning instruction. The physical variables of the classroom setting may be evaluated by using an instrument like the Transition Checklist shown in Appendix A. A student may have difficulties in the classroom that are attributed to external variables. The classroom teacher can modify many of these variables and therefore improve the student's academic success.

The regular classroom teacher should also assess teaching methods to determine if the strategies are most appropriate for the students. Teaching strategies that provide structure, guidance, and reinforcement of skills or content are best for all students and are particularly suitable for students who may be at risk for academic failure.

STEP 2: PREREFERRAL

If a student continues to have difficulty after all variables of the classroom setting, instructional methods, behavioral management, and curriculum have been assessed, the classroom teacher may need to take a closer look at the student's ability to master the curriculum. For example, a student may have difficulty with the appropriate grade level math curriculum. The same student may not complete class assignments or math homework. If the student continues to perform poorly on teacher-made math tests, there may be a need for further assessment to determine which skills have not been mastered. The teacher may

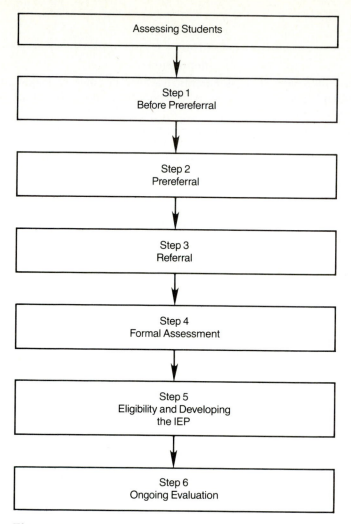

Figure 2.1
Assessing Students

analyze the student's errors to locate specific difficulties in the mathematics operations. Once the target errors are identified, the teacher can prepare additional probes to test the specific errors. The student may provide insight by explaining the process or steps used to solve the math problem. The teacher may observe the student trying to work the problem to identify process errors. These methods of informal assessment may be used with all students in the regular classroom to aid in instructional planning and intervention (Figure 2.3).

When a student appears to have difficulty mastering content or skills at the appropriate grade level, the teacher may use curriculum-based assessment to

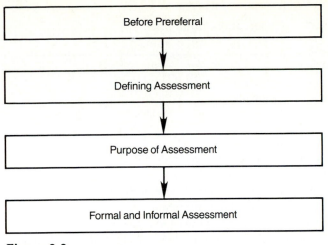

Figure 2.2
Step 1: Before Prereferral

pinpoint the area of difficulty. An error analysis may provide information necessary to make educational interventions. The interventions may include adapting instruction according to the individual student's learning style or organizing the classroom or the lesson presentation in a different format. General

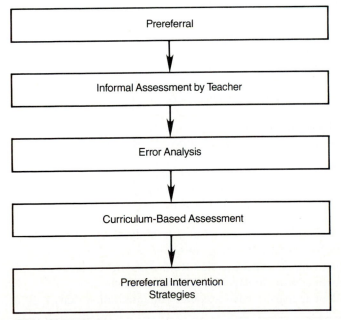

Figure 2.3
Step 2: Prereferral

Table 2.2
Classroom Teacher Observation Guidelines

Name of Student _____

Concerned Teacher _____

Briefly describe area of difficulty:

1. Curriculum evaluation
   _____ Material is appropriate for age/grade level
   _____ Instructions are presented clearly
   _____ Expected method of response is within the student's capability
   _____ Readability of material is appropriate
   _____ Prerequisite skills have been mastered
   _____ Format of materials is easily understood by students of same age/grade level
   _____ Frequent and various methods of evaluation are employed
   _____ Tasks are appropriate in length
   _____ Pace of material is appropriate for age/grade levels

2. Learning environment
   _____ Methods of presentation are appropriate for age/grade levels
   _____ Tasks are presented in appropriate sequence
   _____ Expected level of response is appropriate for age/grade level
   _____ Physical facilities are conducive to learning

3. Social environment
   _____ Student does not experience noticeable conflicts with peers
   _____ Student appears to have adequate relationships with peers
   _____ Parent conference reveals no current conflicts or concerns within the home
   _____ Social development appears average for age expectancy

4. Student's physical condition
   _____ Student's height and weight appear to be within the average range of expectancy for age/grade level
   _____ Student has no signs of visual or hearing difficulties, such as asking teacher to repeat instructions, squinting, holding papers close to face to read
   _____ Student has had vision and hearing checked by school nurse or other health official
   _____ Student has not experienced long-term illness or serious injury
   _____ School attendance is average or better
   _____ Student appears attentive/alert during instruction
   _____ Student appears to have adequate motor skills
   _____ Student appears to have adequate communication skills

Note. From *Assessment in Special Education: An Applied Approach* (p. 10) by T. Overton, 1992, Columbus, OH: Macmillan. Copyright 1992 by Macmillan. Adapted by permission.

Table 2.3
Classroom Teacher's Role in Assessment Process

Steps in the Assessment Process	Regular Classroom Teacher's Role
Prior to Referral	Use informal assessment methods to monitor daily progress, curriculum-based assessment, and behavioral observations, consult with team members, implement educational interventions Consult with parents
Identification of Disabled Student	Recognize behaviors and characteristics of students with disabilities so that these students can be identified, evaluated, and served if appropriate Recognize behaviors and characteristics that are indicative of cultural or linguistic differences and do not warrant special education services
Referral to Placement Process	Document through data collection of student work samples, behavioral observations, teacher-made tests, and other informal measures to identify educational strengths and weaknesses Consult with team members Consult with parents, determine level of understanding of referral and assessment process, provide answers to questions and any materials requested Complete necessary referral documents Attend child study committee meeting and present appropriate data collected on student progress and behaviors Participate during development and implementation of IEP for students in regular class setting
Uses of Test Data	Use IQ and other norm-referenced tests appropriately Respect parents' rights and confidentiality of all test/identification materials Be aware of specific tests and what they do and do not measure Carefully read test interpretations and question how results can help plan educational interventions

guidelines such as the adapted Classroom Teacher Observation Guidelines (Overton, 1992) shown in Table 2.2 may help the classroom teacher with the prereferral process.

The classroom teacher consults with the members of a prereferral committee. The role of the teacher during the referral/assessment process is illustrated in Table 2.3. Some members of the prereferral team may be the same professionals who make up the multidisciplinary assessment team, such as the school psychologist and the school social worker. Other prereferral team members may be professionals who are not active members of the multidisciplinary assessment team. For example, the prereferral committee, sometimes called a child study committee, may include additional regular classroom teachers of the same grade or various grades, the school principal, special education teachers, school counselors, or members of the school curriculum committee. These members may observe the student in different environments, analyze student-teacher interactions, or review the curriculum used to locate possible instructional interventions. A prereferral intervention plan is designed with suggestions for the classroom teacher. The prereferral committee members may suggest changes in the classroom arrangement, behavior management strategies, or curriculum and teaching methods as instructional interventions. The teacher should attempt a variety of instructional interventions and document the changes in the student's behavior or learning that occur as a result of these changes.

The use of prereferral intervention strategies has been found to increase consultation services with the regular classroom teacher and members of the multidisciplinary team, while decreasing the number of students tested and placed in special education (Graden, Casey, & Bonstrom, 1985). When prereferral intervention strategies seem inadequate, the teacher's documentation of which strategies were tried and the results of each may be beneficial to the team members in both diagnosis and educational planning.

After multiple educational interventions have been implemented and the student continues to struggle educationally, the regular classroom teacher may wish to consult with the multidisciplinary special education team for advice. This team may suggest further prereferral intervention strategies or may want to observe the student in the academic setting. If the student continues to have difficulty making progress, the team may suggest that the student be referred for a comprehensive educational assessment. This process begins with completion of a formal referral form and notification of the student's parents.

STEP 3: REFERRAL

The regular classroom teacher will have the documentation necessary for a formal referral if the prereferral plan was in place (Figure 2.4). The classroom teacher may use the observations and documentation of changes in behavior or learning, or the lack of significant changes, as a basis for the referral. All referrals should be written in an objective format, addressing specific academic or behavioral concerns. These concerns should be further supported by quantitative data whenever possible. For example, following a prereferral plan to decrease both the number and level of math problems for homework, supporting data may be used to state that the student was able to complete only 30% of the assignments correctly.

Referrals for behavioral problems should be stated objectively as well. A student who seems to bother other students and does not complete tasks may

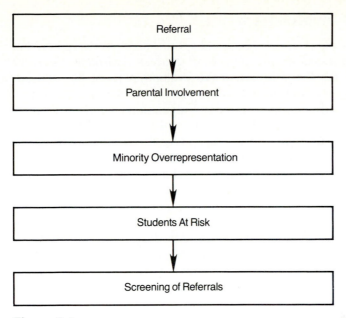

Figure 2.4
Step 3: Referral

be referred using observational data that reveals that she is out-of-seat 75% of the class period, initiates inappropriate conversation during 50% of her peer interactions, and completes a maximum of 20% of her assignments. The following examples illustrate appropriate and inappropriate referral statements written for a fifth-grade student.

Inappropriate	**Appropriate**
John has been a terror in the fifth grade. He seems to enjoy making trouble, and I can't remember the last time he turned in homework. He needs to be in a different class.	Prereferral strategies used include small group instruction, new seating arrangement, and slower-pace adapted curriculum. Talking out of turn: 60% of classroom interactions Completed assignments: 35% Completed homework: 0% Identified areas of difficulty: math, reading, spelling—all below grade level

During the prereferral and referral periods, the parents will become involved in the process. Members of the prereferral and assessment team as well as the classroom teacher should contact the parents from time to time.

Parental Involvement

If referral is necessary, P.L. 94–142 specifically includes parents at many levels of the referral/assessment/placement process (*Federal Register*, 1977). Parental permission for the comprehensive evaluation must be secured prior to the administration of any tests that are used to determine eligibility. This parental consent is further defined in federal regulations as *informed consent* and means that parents are to be informed as to which tests will be used and what these tests are designed to measure. The regular classroom teacher may act as a liaison between the parents and the multidisciplinary team members. In this role, the teacher can help the parents understand the assessment process and assist them in formulating questions to ask of team members.

Federal regulations also provide for parental participation during the formulation of the IEP. It is especially important that the special education teacher and the regular classroom teacher work with the parents during the writing of the IEP. Although the regulations state that parents are to be active participants, research indicates that parents generally remain passive during the process (Barnett, Zins, & Wise, 1984; Brantlinger, 1987; Goldstein, Strickland, Turnbull, & Curry, 1980; Goldstein & Turnbull, 1982; Vaughn, Bos, Harrell, & Lasky, 1988; Weber & Stoneman, 1986). Parents who are passive in the process may not participate in assessment, contribute to the eligibility decision, or share in the development of the IEP. Parental insight into a student's home and cultural background may be one method of decreasing the possibility that students from different cultures are overrepresented in special education.

Minority Overrepresentation

Minority overrepresentation in special education classes has been documented in the literature (Reschly, 1988, Tucker, 1980). Minority overrepresentation occurs when the percentage of a minority population in the special education setting is greater than the percentage represented naturally in the geographic region. For example, if a geographic school district includes a Hispanic population of 12% and the special education classes in that district include a population of 35% Hispanic students, that particular group is overrepresented in special education. It is extremely important that regular education teachers do not misinterpret behaviors that only represent cultural or linguistic differences as indicative of learning problems. The teacher who is not certain of cultural or linguistic differences should consult with the prereferral committee or the parents.

Students At Risk

Many students referred for special educational services are at risk for academic failure but may not have a specific disability. Ysseldyke, Algozzine, and Epps (1983) reported the findings of a study that 85% of average classroom students could be found eligible for services for learning disabled students according to the various operational definitions of this category. Although these students were average, they displayed behaviors that could be considered indicative of learning disabilities.

Students considered to be at risk may be helped through the various prereferral intervention strategies. Shapiro (1988) calls for more administrative support for prevention of academic failure rather than relying only on remediation of existing learning difficulties. A student who seems to be making some progress following the implementation of prereferral strategies should not be referred for assessment. The student's progress should be monitored carefully. A formal referral for a comprehensive assessment should be viewed by all educators as a last resort when all other strategies have failed. This is especially true for students who are from culturally or linguistically different backgrounds. (For further discussion of at-risk populations, see Chapter 1).

Screening of Referrals

The screening committee may be made up of the same professionals as the child study committee or prereferral committee. These educators review the child's educational history and prereferral intervention plan. They discuss the formal referral and consider it thoroughly. The committee members may suggest alternatives prior to submitting the case to the multidisciplinary team. For example, the committee members may consider placement in a different classroom of the same or lower level. Sometimes the at-risk student may be placed in a classroom one grade lower for difficult subjects. A third-grade student may be placed in a second-grade class for reading, but remain in the regular class for other subjects.

When prereferral instructional strategies are not effective in changing the student's learning or behavioral difficulties, the committee may believe that a student needs to be assessed to determine if a specific disability exists that may require special services. In compliance with the federal regulations of P.L. 94–142, the parents are consulted for permission, and the process begins.

STEP 4: FORMAL ASSESSMENT

When the child study committee determines that a student needs a comprehensive evaluation, parental permission must be secured. Federal regulations require that parents grant informed consent prior to the assessment process; however, the regulations also state that parents may revoke their consent at anytime. Parents are to be informed of their rights and the procedural safeguards, in their native language or mode of communication, (e.g., manual communication system). Many states have parents' rights information presented in a booklet format. This booklet is usually given to the parents at the beginning of the evaluation process, and the parents are asked to sign a form indicating that they have been informed of their rights. Parents may request to see a copy of parents' rights, or the regular classroom teacher may help the parents secure a copy from special education personnel.

The regular classroom teacher, acting as a liaison or parent advocate, should be certain that parents are clearly informed and understand their rights. A disadvantage of informing the parents of their rights through written format is that the readability level of the materials may be questionable. In a national study, Roit and Pfohl (1984) found that the readability levels of parental materials distributed during this process ranged from the fifth- to the eighth-grade level, with the average level at about the sixth grade. In addition to readability levels, these materials may contain highly complex legal vocabulary. Parents' rights information that is presented in a different language may become confusing in the translation. The special education teacher and the regular classroom teacher, perhaps with an interpreter, can help the parents understand complex concepts.

Once parental permission has been obtained, the comprehensive assessment process begins (Figure 2.5). P.L. 94–142 stipulates that the comprehensive evaluation include assessment of all areas of suspected disability. This may include academic, intellectual, emotional, perceptual, motor, visual, auditory, language, and physical abilities. This assessment involves a professional team who will assess in their specific area of expertise. Team members design an assessment plan for each student who is to receive a comprehensive assessment. The responsibilities of the team members are listed in Table 2.4.

A safeguard intended to prevent misdiagnosis and promote nondiscriminatory assessment is the provision that students are to be tested by more than one method or instrument. This encourages the use of both formal and informal assessment techniques. Informal assessment information may be collected by the regular classroom teacher, a special education teacher, the school psychologist or educational diagnostician, or the speech-language therapist. The intent is to gather enough information to provide a true picture of the whole child, rather than to base educational decisions upon a single score, such as an IQ score.

Another safeguard for nondiscriminatory assessment is the regulation requiring that all assessment be conducted in the child's native language or mode of communication unless it is clearly not feasible to do so. The regular classroom teacher can provide assistance in the assessment process by informing the diagnostic team about the child's native language.

Identification

Overton (1992) summarized the various disabling conditions that are defined in P.L. 94–142, as listed in Table 2.5. Some of these disabling conditions, such as deaf-blind, are low-incidence disabilities and are not found in many schools. Individual student needs may be so involved that the students may be served in special day schools or in residential facilities. Other conditions such as learning disabilities or emotional disturbances are more common, and students with these conditions are likely to be found in most schools.

The regular classroom teacher may have students with many of the milder learning problems in the regular classroom to receive all or part of their instruction. For example, a teacher may have a student with a language impairment for the entire day, another student who has specific learning

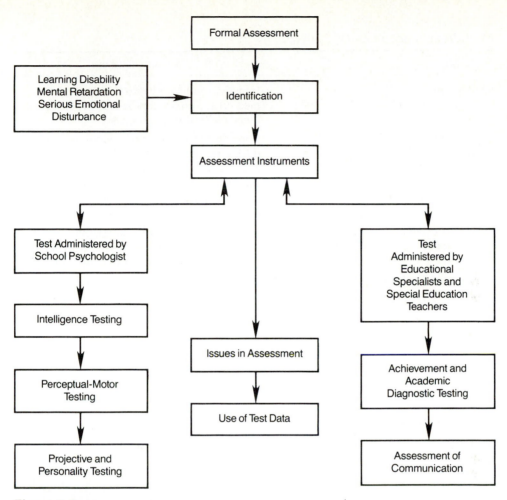

Figure 2.5
Step 4: Formal Assessment

disabilities in reading for most of the day, and a third student with mild mental retardation for art and physical education only. Because the greatest number of students receiving special education are those who have been found to have mild learning problems, the chances are greatest that the regular classroom teacher will have such students in the regular classroom. Knowing the characteristics of mildly handicapped students will help the teacher implement educational interventions that may prove successful for the student receiving instruction in the regular classroom.

Learning Disabilities
Students with learning disabilities may have behaviors or characteristics that signal problems that may vary with age according to expected educational gains.

Table 2.4
Multidisciplinary Team Who's Who

Team Member	Responsibilities
School Nurse	Initial vision/hearing screening, checks medical records, refers health problems to other medical professionals
Special Education Teacher	Consultant to regular classroom teacher during prereferral process, administers educational tests, observes in other classrooms, helps with screening and recommends IEP goals, writes objectives, suggests educational interventions
Special Education Supervisor	May advise all activities of special education teacher, may provide direct services, guides placement decisions, recommends services
Educational Diagnostician	Administers norm-referenced and criterion-referenced tests, observes student in educational setting, makes suggestions for IEP goals and objectives
School Psychologist	Administers individual intelligence tests, observes student in classroom, administers projective instruments and personality inventories, may be under supervision of a PhD-level psychologist
Occupational Therapist	Evaluates fine motor and self-help skills, recommends therapies, may provide direct services or consultant services, may help obtain equipment for student needs
Physical Therapist	Evaluates gross motor functioning and self-help skills, living skills, job-related skills necessary for optimum achievement of student, may provide direct services or consultant services
Behavioral Consultant	Specialist in behavior management and crisis intervention, may provide direct services or consultant services
School Counselor	May serve as objective observer in prereferral stage, may provide direct counseling services, group or individual counseling, schedule students, help with planning of student schedules
Speech-Language Clinician	Evaluates speech-language development, may refer for hearing problems, may provide direct therapy or consultant services for classroom teachers

Table 2.4
continued

Team Member	Responsibilities
Audiologist	Evaluates hearing for possible impairments, may refer students for medical problems, may help obtain hearing aids
Physician's Assistant	Evaluates physical condition of student and may provide physical exams for students from a local school system, refers medical problems to physicians or appropriate therapists
Home-School Coordinator, School Social Worker, or Visiting Teacher	Works directly with family, may hold conferences, conduct interviews and/or administer adaptive behavior scales based upon parental interview, may serve as case manager
Regular Education Teacher	Works with special education team, student, and parents to develop environment that is appropriate and as much like that of nondisabled students as possible, implements prereferral intervention strategies
Parents	Active members of special education team, provide input for IEP, work with home/school academic and behavioral programs

Note. From *Assessment in Special Education: An Applied Approach* (p. 36–37) by T. Overton, 1992, Columbus, OH: Macmillan. Copyright 1992 by Macmillan. Adapted by permission.

Mercer (1987) noted that preschool children with learning disabilities may have difficulty with receptive and expressive language, auditory perception, short attention span, and/or hyperactivity. To compound their problems, preschool educators tend to look for mastery of preacademics and school readiness behaviors, such as attending to tasks and sitting for short periods of time. In addition to these problem areas, Mercer adds that children in kindergarten and first grade may have problems with academic readiness skills, gross and fine motor skills, and social skills. In grades 2 through 6, problems are more academically based, and reading, arithmetic, and written expression problems are added to the list of signals or characteristics of learning disabilities (Mercer). In the secondary school years, study skills and social-emotional problems are added to the already long list of problem areas for the learning-disabled student (Mercer). Specific characteristics may include the following:

1. Average to above-average intelligence
2. Discrepancy between aptitude and achievement

Table 2.5
Definitions of Disabilities in P.L. 94–142*

Deaf	A hearing impairment that is so severe that the child is impaired in processing linguistic information through hearing, with or without amplification, which adversely affects educational performance
Deaf-blind	Concomitant hearing and visual impairments, the combination of which causes such severe communication and other developmental and educational problems that they cannot be accommodated in special programs solely for deaf or blind children
Hard of hearing	A hearing impairment, whether permanent or fluctuating, that adversely affects a child's educational performance but is not included in the definition of *deaf*
Mentally retarded	Significantly subaverage general intellectual functioning existing concurrently with deficits in adaptive behavior manifested during the developmental period, which adversely affects the child's educational performance
Multidisabled	Concomitant impairments, such as mentally retarded-blind, mentally retarded-orthopedically impaired, the combination of which causes such severe educational problems that they cannot be accommodated in special education programs solely for one of the impairments; the term does not include deaf-blind children
Orthopedically impaired	Severe orthopedic impairment that adversely affects a child's educational performance; the term includes impairments caused by congenital anomaly (e.g., clubfoot, absence of some member), disease (e.g., poliomyelitis, bone tuberculosis), and other causes (e.g., cerebral palsy, amputations, fractures or burns that cause contractures)
Other health-impaired	Limited strength, vitality, or alertness due to chronic or acute health problems, such as a heart condition, tuberculosis, rheumatic fever, nephritis, asthma, sickle cell anemia, hemophilia, epilepsy, lead poisoning, leukemia, or diabetes, which adversely affects a child's educational performance

Table 2.5
continued

Seriously emotionally disturbed	A condition exhibiting one or more of the following characteristics over a long period of time and to a marked degree, which can adversely affect a child's educational performance: • An inability to learn that cannot be explained by intellectual, sensory, or other health factors • An inability to build or maintain satisfactory interpersonal relationships with peers and teachers • Inappropriate types of behavior or feelings under normal circumstances • A general pervasive mood of unhappiness or depression • A tendency to develop physical symptoms or fears associated with personal or school problems
Specific Learning Disability	A disorder in one or more of the basic psychological processes involved in understanding or using language, spoken or written, that manifests itself in the imperfect ability to listen, speak, read, write, spell, or do mathematical calculations; the term includes such conditions as perceptual handicaps, brain injury, minimal brain dysfunction, dyslexia, and developmental aphasia; the term does not include children who have learning problems that are primarily the result of visual, hearing, or motor handicaps, of mental retardation, or of environmental, cultural, or economic disadvantage
Speech-impaired	A communication disorder, such as stuttering, impaired articulation, a language impairment, or a voice impairment that adversely affects a child's educational performance
Visually impaired	A visual impairment that, even with correction, adversely affects a child's educational performance; the term includes both partially seeing and blind children

* The terms *traumatic brain injury* and *autism* were added as a result of the passage of the Education of the Handicapped Act Amendments of 1990 and regulations are being drafted at this writing.
Note. From *Assessment in Special Education: An Applied Approach* (p. 16–17) by T. Overton, 1992, Columbus, OH: Macmillan. Copyright 1992 by Macmillan. Adapted by permission.

3. Hyperactivity
4. Distractibility
5. Inability/difficulty processing visual information
   a. Difficulty interpreting written directions
   b. Difficulty transferring information from blackboard to notebook
   c. Inability to separate figure from background
   d. Difficulty remembering what has been seen or read
   e. Difficulty relating parts to the whole
6. Inability/difficulty processing auditory information
   a. Difficulty following verbal directions
   b. Difficulty remembering the order of items presented orally
   c. Difficulty discriminating between similar sounds
7. Difficulty concentrating for long periods of time
8. Lethargy, apathy, indifference
9. Poor organizational abilities
10. Difficulty with the concept of time
11. Difficulty with the concept of direction, such as left/right, up/down, and over/under
12. Inconsistency in performance
13. Poor motor coordination, such as lack of rhythm or problems with balance
14. Tendency to become easily frustrated
15. Tendency to perseverate
16. Limited vocabulary
17. Tendency to lose place while reading and use a finger to follow along
18. Tendency to reverse letters and/or words when reading and/or writing
19. Difficulty associating letter or syllable sounds with printed letter or syllable
20. Difficulty with writing mechanics such as spacing, staying on the line, and size distortions
21. Difficulty with basic number facts such as addition, subtraction, multiplication, and division
22. Difficulty with language expression

Students with learning disabilities may have a few or many of the characteristics or behaviors listed. Many of these students do have the potential to achieve academically and continue their education following secondary school by attending college or vocational training. Early identification and appropriate intervention maximize the chances for successful educational achievement.

Students who appear to have characteristics like those of learning-disabled students who continue to have academic difficulty should be referred for assessment if they are not currently receiving services. Regular education teachers should be aware that social and emotional problems can increase with continued academic failure. Providing opportunities for success in the regular classroom environment with nondisabled students is a major component of the regular classroom experience for students with mild disabling conditions.

Mental Retardation

This disabling condition may be referred to as *educationally disabled* in some states. This condition is typically thought to be manifested by overall deficits in intellectual functioning. In addition to the assessment of intellectual ability, however, adaptive behavior must also be measured. Measuring adaptive behavior provides the assessment team with valuable information about how well the student functions when compared with society's expectations (Salvia & Ysseldyke, 1988). A student who has academic problems but no difficulty in any other area of functioning would probably not be labeled as mentally retarded.

According to the American Association on Mental Retardation, appropriate adaptive behavior varies with age (Grossman, 1983). Children who are very young are expected to be able to develop sensory-motor skills, begin learning language and self-help skills, and begin early interaction or social skills. School-age and early adolescent children would be expected to develop all of the previously listed skills and also apply basic academic skills in everyday life, such as reading signs or making change, and develop reasoning and social skills appropriate for their age. Older adolescents and adults would be expected to develop vocational and social responsibilities in addition to all previously listed skills (Grossman, 1983).

If a student is suspected of having mental retardation, the regular classroom teacher should document information regarding adaptive behavior. Misdiagnosis of this condition can be avoided when adaptive behavior is considered. This is especially important when the student is from a culturally or linguistically different background, which may cause the student to have difficulty functioning within the classroom but not in the everyday world. Adaptive behavior instruments, such as the Vineland Adaptive Behavior Scales, have been designed to measure adaptive behavior in an interview or observational manner. The regular education teacher may be asked to complete an adaptive behavior interview as part of the comprehensive evaluation.

Serious Emotional Disturbance

Students with emotional problems may be labeled *emotionally disabled* in some states. These students are difficult to identify because often they have emotional problems but continue to make progress in school or they become withdrawn and therefore their problems may be less noticeable to the teacher. Behavioral observations made by the regular classroom teacher may be the key to diagnosis of emotional problems.

The best observations will be made in a systematic and objective fashion. These observations may be as simple as a frequency count or recording of events. For example, the teacher makes a notation every time a student fails to complete an assignment or every time a student exhibits an inappropriate behavior under normal circumstances (e.g., crying, hitting, yelling). At the end of a week or so of observation, the teacher can analyze the data to determine, for example, if only math assignments are incomplete, if crying occurs only during the first hour of school, or if yelling occurs only in the presence of one particular student. The data may be represented numerically, such as 3/10 assignments completed, or a 60% increase in yelling during 4th period. This type of information will help the diagnostic team members if a referral for possible emotional problems is made.

When a student continues to exhibit possible signs of emotional problems, the regular classroom teacher should seek the consultation of the school psychologist, guidance counselor, or behavioral specialist. The consulted team member will visit the classroom setting and make formal observations. At this time, a formal referral for assessment may be made.

The diagnosis of a serious emotional disturbance is a complex matter, which requires gathering of informal and formal assessment data. In addition to educational data, the school psychologist may administer projective assessment instruments to determine how the student is functioning emotionally. These instruments must be administered by highly qualified individuals and should be interpreted with caution due to questionable reliability and validity data on some of the instruments.

Students who are receiving special education services due to emotional problems will have IEPs written reflecting the fact that their educational goals and objectives are based on improving behaviors as well as academic performance. A student who is mainstreamed into the regular classroom may be on a strict behavior management plan that requires the participation of the regular education teacher. The teacher may be asked to document completed assignments or cooperative behaviors. It is important that the student with emotional problems generalizes appropriate behaviors in all settings, especially the regular classroom, prior to complete mainstreaming in regular education.

Assessment Instruments

There are thousands of commercially produced assessment instruments available. The assessment team members are trained to select instruments designed to assess skills or abilities in their specific area. Each student to be tested for the purpose of determining eligibility for special education should already have an individual assessment plan. Team members decide on this plan following careful examination of the student's prereferral and referral information, the student's cumulative records, and any other information the child study team provides. Examples of these informal types of instruments as well as commercially produced instruments are listed in Table 2.6.

Table 2.6
Assessment Instruments

Type of Instrument	Examples
Informal	Teacher-made tests; observations; curriculum-based tests; student work samples; student interviews or self-reports
Criterion-referenced tests	Brigance Diagnostic Inventory of Basic Skills; KeyMath-Revised
Norm-referenced academic screening tests	Wide Range Achievement Test-Revised; Peabody Individual Achievement Test-Revised; Kaufman Test of Educational Achievement: Brief and Comprehensive Forms
Norm-referenced academic achievement tests	Woodcock-Johnson-Revised Tests of Achievement: Standard and Supplemental Tests; Kaufman Test of Educational Achievement: Comprehensive Form
Norm-referenced academic diagnostic tests	KeyMath-Revised; Woodcock Reading Mastery Tests-Revised; Test of Mathematical Abilities; Detroit Test of Learning Abilities
Norm-referenced perceptual motor tests	Motor-Free Test of Visual Perception; Bender Visual-Motor Gestalt Test; Auditory Discrimination Test
Norm-referenced language tests and written expression tests	Peabody Picture Vocabulary Test; Test of Word Finding; Test of Language Development-2; Test of Adolescent Language-2
Norm-referenced intelligence tests	Wechsler Intelligence Scale for Children-Revised; Woodcock-Johnson-Revised Tests of Cognitive Ability; Kaufman Assessment Battery for Children; Stanford-Binet Intelligence Scale

Tests Administered by School Psychologists

Many assessment instruments used for eligibility decisions are complex norm-referenced standardized tests. These tests include intelligence (IQ) tests, perceptual motor tests, behavioral inventories, developmental inventories, and projective personality tests. The administration of these tests is often restricted to personnel with advanced training in assessment, such as school psychologists or educational diagnosticians. Intelligence tests are perhaps the most frequently used types of instruments.

Intelligence Testing

Because testing represents a small sample of behavior observed at a specific time, care should be taken not to overemphasize the importance of the scores obtained on an intelligence quotient (IQ) or cognitive ability test. Analysis of items contained on intelligence tests reveals that many of the questions or tasks measure learned material or achievement rather than innate intellectual ability. Cultural fairness of many of the tests items has also been questioned.

Most intelligence instruments contain several subtests designed to measure traits or skills thought to be indications of intelligence. For example, subtests may measure auditory short-term memory, understanding of language concepts, and perceptual motor speed. School psychologists may interpret the tests in a manner that reflects subtest analysis. These interpretations are useful in educational planning. For one student, the results may indicate a short attention span or a tendency toward being easily distracted. For another, the results may indicate that the student has significantly higher perceptual motor or visual motor skills than verbal comprehension skills. This type of information is much more helpful to a teacher than a single numerical value such as an IQ score.

School psychologists may use the scores obtained on a test measuring cognitive ability or IQ to determine the existence of a specific learning disability. The extreme variance in scores on the test, together with other indicators on other measures, may signal possible processing difficulties. Cognitive processing difficulties may result in learning problems and low achievement in academics.

Intelligence test scores may also be used as an indicator of subaverage functioning. If a student has subaverage intellectual functioning, subaverage adaptive behavior, and low academic functioning, the student may be diagnosed as having mental retardation.

Scores obtained on different measures of intelligence may vary from time to time. The student may perform better on one day than another, or a change in a student's score may represent actual developmental growth, maturity, and achievement. In other words, scores on IQ measures are not permanent and should not be viewed as such.

The Wechsler Intelligence Scales, the Stanford-Binet, and the Woodcock-Johnson-Revised Tests of Cognitive Abilities are some commonly used intelligence test instruments. Each test takes approximately an hour or more to administer and will provide the examiner with a sample of how the student responds to a variety of tasks. Other instruments, such as the Cognitive Levels Test or the Slosson Intelligence Test, are designed for use as a quick screening test. Screening tests are not appropriate for use in eligibility decisions.

Perceptual Motor Testing

Research on the usefulness of sensory motor and perceptual motor assessment has yielded mixed results (Hupp, Able, & Conroy-Gunter, 1984; Kavale & Forness, 1987, Locher, 1988; Locher & Worms, 1981; Mather & Kirk, 1985). In this type of assessment, the examiner wants to determine how the student best perceives and responds to information. These instruments may measure auditory memory, auditory discrimination, visual memory, visual discrimination, visual-motor responses, or fine motor skills.

Although this type of assessment may provide insight for the teacher in program planning, it may not be as useful for the purposes of determining eligibility for special education services. One reason it may not be a significant indicator for eligibility is that few students have perceptual problems of such a severe nature that learning is affected (Mather & Kirk, 1985). Nevertheless, using the results of perceptual motor assessment to plan educational strategies continues to be a common practice.

If the teacher is not certain about a child's best learning modality, informal assessment in the classroom may be conducted. The teacher may ask the student to copy different designs or words from the board or a sheet of paper, repeat a series of word or numbers, or perform simple visual-motor or auditory tasks. The teacher may ask the student questions such as, "Would you rather learn about something new by reading about it in a book or by someone telling you about it?" These types of informal measures may provide the teacher with additional insight as to how the student prefers to learn. Often, the student knows how he or she can be most successful in learning new material. The student may say, "I say it over and over until I remember," or "I draw myself a picture or write down words that help me." In fact, the teacher may find it useful to determine the learning styles of all students in the class, rather than only students referred for or receiving special services.

Projective and Personality Testing
The administration of tests to assess personality disorders is usually restricted to psychologists with advanced training. A projective test may consist of showing a stimulus picture card and asking the student to interpret what is happening in the picture. The psychologist attempts to find a trend or pattern in the verbal responses given by the student. Many school psychologists prefer to use informal classroom observation or systematic observation and clinical interviews as a basis for assessing personality disorders. Classroom teachers may be asked to collect behavioral observation data to assist the school psychologist in determining how frequently certain behaviors occur.

Tests Given by Educational Specialists and Special Education Teachers
Many measures of academic achievement may be given by teachers, educational specialists, and special education teachers. These instruments may be norm-referenced or criterion-referenced tests. Some of these tests may not require much advanced training to administer; however, the examiner should become familiar with the test and test manual prior to administering the instrument. The examiner should practice test administration several times before administering the instrument to a student. If possible, the examiner should consult with someone who has had experience in the administration of the instrument.

Achievement and Academic Diagnostic Testing
The test data obtained from achievement testing and diagnostic academic assessment are probably the most useful to the teacher. The scores represent how the student performed at that particular time when material was presented in a specific standardized format. The presentation of the material as well as

the response mode required of the student may make a difference in the way the student performed. For example, most spelling curricula include testing of spelling on a regular basis, often weekly. This format is as follows: the teacher orally states the word, reads a sentence using the word, and repeats the word; the student writes the word on a piece of lined notebook paper. The spelling subtest presented on the Peabody Individual Achievement Test-Revised is quite different. On this subtest, the examiner says a word, and the child is to select the correct spelling of the word from four choices. As the words increase in difficulty, the discrimination becomes more difficult as well. A student who has poor visual memory or poor visual discrimination may find this subtest a much more confusing measure of spelling, and the obtained score may reflect this. This may make a difference in the way the information obtained from this subtest is used.

Teachers should also be aware that the name of a test or subtest may be deceiving. The reading subtest of the Wide Range Achievement Test-Revised is actually only a measure of word recall, and contains no measure of reading decoding or comprehension. This test should be used for screening only, and not for educational planning.

The better achievement tests are those that provide a variety of items and subtests to measure many types of skills and content. One such test is the Woodcock-Johnson Psycho-Educational Battery-Revised Tests of Achievement. This instrument contains standard and supplementary batteries that measure several areas of academics. It may be used to measure skills from the preacademic ages to college and adult levels. The student will be assessed in topics such as reading comprehension, decoding, word recognition, math computation and concepts, applied math, science, social studies, and humanities.

Assessment of Communication

The speech-language clinician or therapist may administer a variety of assessment instruments. These tests may measure articulation, auditory discrimination, verbal expression, receptive language, language concepts, or word-finding ability. Language assessment may be formal or informal. Many of the language areas can be assessed informally in class. The teacher may collect written documentation of the child's ability to construct sentences. Vocabulary development is a part of the language arts curriculum and can be assessed naturally. The teacher should note students who have a limited vocabulary or do not seem to have a command of language or know how to use complex concepts for communication.

Issues in Assessment

The classroom teacher should keep important issues of assessment in mind during the entire prereferral-to-placement process. These issues have been the basis for legal actions in some states and represent areas of education that may change in the future.

One of the most important issues is overrepresentation of minorities in special education. Through parental involvement and improved nondiscriminatory test practices, hopefully the numbers of misdiagnosed students will decrease. Prereferral intervention strategies are changing the focus of the assessment team from a test-and-place sequence to consultation and prevention sequence. This change may also prevent the overrepresentation of minorities in special education.

Another issue of concern for assessment practice is that of exit criteria. It seems that much of the time spent in assessment is devoted to testing with the goal of placement into special education rather than of placing students back in the mainstream of education and, therefore, society. Classroom teachers may help reverse this tendency by designing objectives for special education students with the ultimate goal of returning those students to the mainstream.

Use of Test Data

The primary purpose of assessment is to obtain information that will be useful in making educational decisions and interventions necessary for optimum educational achievement. The regular classroom teacher should be prepared to ask questions and seek information that will aid in educational planning. Test data obtained on the student's intellectual, perceptual, language, and academic functioning can be useful for educational planning.

Norm-referenced tests of intelligence and academic achievement are used to compare a student with the age or grade norm group. The comparison is made to determine if the student deviates significantly from what is expected of the age or grade level. Scores are expressed in a standard score, such as an IQ or cognitive ability score, which may have an average of 100, percentiles, or grade or age equivalents. Using standard scores based on an average of 100 and a standard deviation of 15, a student may be compared with the expectations of the grade or age level and may be reported as being one or two standard deviations below the norm. A student who is functioning two standard deviations below peers would probably be considered eligible for special education services in the specific academic area. If the scores are reported as percentiles, such a student scoring in the 60th percentile is believed to be functioning better than 60% of the norm group.

Teachers and parents may feel more comfortable with scores that are reported as age or grade equivalents. It is important for the classroom teacher to remember that grade equivalents do not represent a grade level of functioning. These equivalents merely represent the number of items answered correctly by the norm group at each grade level, rather than mastery of content at a particular grade. For example, a student who obtains a score of 4.5 (4th grade, 5th month) may not have mastered the skills required of the mid-4th-grade year, but the score means that the student answered the same number of items correctly as did the norm group of 4th graders. It should not be assumed, therefore, that this student has mastered half of the 4th grade curriculum.

Classroom teachers who feel unsure about the educational implications of test interpretations should consult the person who administered and interpreted the instrument. Because tests represent small samples of behavior at a given time, the classroom teacher needs to understand exactly what the test measured and how it was measured. For example, often a teacher may question the results obtained on a particular instrument because of knowing the child's performance level in areas of academic instruction. The teacher may believe the student is capable of successfully completing fifth-grade level reading assignments, yet the test results indicate a third-grade reading level. By questioning the diagnostician, the classroom teacher may learn that the score was obtained in only one area of reading, such as decoding nonsense words, while the reading comprehension score was significantly higher. Diagnostic testing is presented across many specific areas using many different formats. By understanding what each specific score represents, the teacher can make the necessary academic program or curriculum changes.

The teacher will be able to use the scores obtained from norm-referenced assessment as a basis for further criterion-referenced or curriculum-based assessment. These types of assessment will provide information about the student that will be used to develop the goals and objectives of the IEP.

STEP 5: ELIGIBILITY AND DEVELOPING THE IEP

Assessment data will be used to determine eligibility and placement (Figure 2.6). The decision of eligibility should be a group decision and team members should not reach a decision prior to the meeting. Test reports may include placement recommendations that may be considered; however, the actual decision will be made by all members of the group.

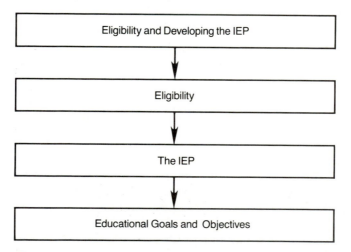

Figure 2.6
Step 5: Eligibility and Developing the IEP

A placement decision should be reached only after considering all possible alternative placements or settings. Maher (1981) advocates a six-step approach to decision-making, which includes: "(a) delineation of program alternatives, (b) determination of program outcomes, (c) assessment of probabilities, (d) assessment of utilities, (e) determination of overall program values, and (f) selection of program to be developed" (p. 341). The result of this decision process should be considered when developing educational goals and objectives.

Eligibility

A decision that a student is eligible for special services does not imply that services will be provided in a special education setting. In compliance with the least restrictive environment regulations of P.L. 94–142, mildly disabled students may be home-based in the regular classroom environment for all or most of the educational day. Services that may be provided while the student remains placed in the regular classroom environment include speech and/or language therapy, resource room support for individual assignments, team teaching with special and regular education teachers in content areas, group or individual counseling sessions, and behavior management programs at home and school.

Eligibility is based on the definition and criteria provided in federal regulations. State definitions may vary somewhat, and teachers should become familiar with their own state definitions and regulations. Generally, eligibility is determined by criteria similar to that in P.L. 94–142 (see Table 2.5).

The IEP

Once the decision has been made for eligibility of services, the multidisciplinary team and the parents discuss the types of services needed and the amount of time the student will receive regular and special education services. As indicated in Chapter 1, the most effective notation for time of services is a specific time period per week, such as two 30-minute sessions each week.

A description of the individualized educational program (IEP) was presented in Chapter 1. A sample of an IEP is shown in Table 2.7. The important components are the amount of special education and/or related services to be provided in the least restrictive environment, a description of the student's present level of performance, and a statement of goals and objectives that may be decided at the eligibility meeting. Because much of the information used in making eligibility decisions is gathered from norm-referenced sources rather than informal assessment, the eligibility meeting is not the most ideal time to write the educational goals and objectives. It is better to write the IEP objectives after the classroom teacher completes further assessment to measure specific skill levels. Therefore, following the determination of eligibility and placement, a second meeting with the student's parents may be arranged after the teacher has completed this assessment. This meeting and the writing of all educational goals and objectives must be completed within 30 days of the determination of eligibility (*Federal Register*, 1977).

Table 2.7
Individualized Education Program

NAME <u>Pam Smith</u>

DATE OF BIRTH <u>8–12–82</u>　　　GRADE <u>5th</u>　　　DATE <u>9–14–92</u>

SUMMARY OF PRESENT LEVELS OF PERFORMANCE:

According to results from the Woodcock-Johnson-Revised Tests of Achievement and teacher reports and work samples, Pam is functioning as expected in all academic areas with the exception of math calculation and applied problems. Pam has difficulty with multiplication concepts and facts. Language arts areas are strengths for Pam, and she enjoys all other subjects.

CONTINUUM OF SERVICES	COMMITTEE MEMBERS
Pam will receive all instruction in the regular 5th-grade classroom. Resource room support for math will be available for independent work. Curriculum will be adjusted by Randy Jones.	Martha White—Principal
	Randy Jones—Special Education Teacher
	Cynthia Murray—5th-grade Teacher
	Tim Brown—Educational Diagnostician
	Linda Smith—Parent
	Martha White
	Randy Jones
	Cynthia Murray
	Tim Brown
	Linda Smith

Educational Goals and Objectives

During the meeting to develop the IEP goals and objectives, the long-term goals of the educational program are discussed by the teachers, special education professionals, and the parents. With the passage of the Education of the Handicapped Act Amendments of 1990, long-range planning has been emphasized with a new focus of the IEP to include transition services, that is, planning for the student's future after public education. These amendments include the requirement that a student's IEP include "a statement of the needed transition services for students beginning no later than age 16 and annually thereafter (and, when determined appropriate for the individual, beginning at age 14 or younger)" (Council for Exceptional Children, 1990, p. 1).

Teachers and parents should discuss the long-range plans of each student. Long-range thinking will aid in the formulation of annual educational goals for the student. For students entering middle school or high school, the guidance

Table 2.7 *continued*
Individualized Education Plan

NAME Pam Smith   DATE 9–17–92

ANNUAL GOALS: Pam will be able to complete 3rd-grade math curriculum materials
and begin 4th-grade materials by May, 1993.

Short-term Objectives	Beginning and Ending Dates	Evaluation Methods and Criteria for Objectives
1. When given multiplication problems for the facts 1–10, Pam will be able to write the correct responses.	9–17–92	Daily probes, teacher-made tests using math curriculum, end of chapter tests. Criteria: 80% accuracy.
2. When given multiplication homework for the facts 1–10, Pam will complete assignments.	9–17–92	Homework assignments will be completed 9 of 10 days.
3. Pam will be able to complete applied math problems from the 3rd-grade math text.	9–17–92	Daily probes, teacher-made tests using applied problems from the 3rd-grade math curriculum. Criteria: 85% accuracy.

counselor may provide insight as to which subjects or courses the student should take to graduate and meet entrance requirements for college or post-secondary training, if that is the long-range goal. If the parents and teachers envision the student entering the world of work following high school, a different curriculum or subject sequence may be followed. In many cases, it is appropriate for the student to be involved in such long-range planning.

With the long-range plans in mind, the special education teacher or another team member will write the annual educational goals. These goals will be targets for the student to move toward during the academic year. The educational objectives will be founded on these goals.

In order for the teacher or special education teacher to write effective short-term objectives, it is necessary to further test the student using criterion-referenced or curriculum-based assessment. Some published curriculum materials provide placement tests that give the teacher a breakdown of skills mastered. These tests may be used to target specific skills for educational objectives. If the curriculum materials do not provide such an analysis, the teacher may need to task-analyze materials or break the skills into very small steps. Next, the teacher will design a test that includes items for each of the small steps in the task. If the teacher uses items from the curriculum material, the test is a form of curriculum-based assessment. For the initial test, several items for each small step should be included. The teacher administers this teacher-made instrument and analyzes mastery of items or errors made by the student. The errors represent skills or content that the student needs to master and will therefore be used as a basis for short-term objectives. The skills mastered may represent areas of strength and should be considered in educational programming. Continued assessment using the curriculum materials will allow for close monitoring of progress.

The teacher must determine the criterion to use in measuring student mastery of an objective. This criterion may be expressed as percentage of accuracy or frequency of correct responses (e.g., 9/10 correct responses). A criterion-referenced test will be designed to measure the attainment of the objective. For example, a teacher may write an objective stating that the student will decode three of five consonant clusters and then design a post-test with the five clusters included. When the student is able to decode three of the five correctly, the criterion has been met. The teacher then changes or adapts the objective.

The short-term educational objectives serve as steps to meet the annual goals. The objectives should be written in observable and measurable terms. Doing so will help the teacher determine when the objectives have been met so that new objectives may be written. The following examples illustrate the difference between behaviorally stated, measurable objectives and unmeasurable objectives.

Measurable	**Unmeasurable**
1. When presented with stories from the fifth-grade reading series, Sue will be able to answer literal comprehension questions orally with 85% accuracy.	1. Sue will understand stories from the fifth-grade reader.
2. When given double-digit addition problems with regrouping, Sue will be able to write 15 of 20 correct responses.	2. Sue will know how to add double digits.

The teacher will know when Sue reaches the two objectives in the first column because a measurable criterion is given for each of the objectives. Close monitoring by using curriculum-based and/or criterion-referenced assessment will provide the teacher with information necessary to write new educational objectives.

STEP 6: ONGOING EVALUATION

Students receiving special education services must have a comprehensive evaluation at least every 3 years (Figure 2.7). This comprehensive assessment is provided as a safeguard for the student who may need an adjustment in educational services or may be ready for full-time regular education with no support services. Teachers or parents who feel a program adjustment is needed during the 3-year period may request that the multidisciplinary team reconvene to examine the student's progress.

Student progress can best be monitored through ongoing evaluation by the classroom and/or special education teacher. Ongoing assessment is composed of many types of informal assessment. The teacher will use classroom observation, teacher-made tests, curriculum-based assessment, criterion-referenced assessment, work samples, student self-reports or interviews, homework assignments, and daily work to monitor student progress.

The importance of close monitoring of student progress through the use of curriculum-based assessment has been studied with promising implications. One study found that special education teachers who employed systematic curriculum-based measurement established more challenging and realistic student goals (Fuchs, Fuchs, & Hamlett, 1989). This study further suggested that special education teachers may need curriculum-based assessment to prompt goal raising for students whose goal might otherwise remain constant even after mastery of the objective.

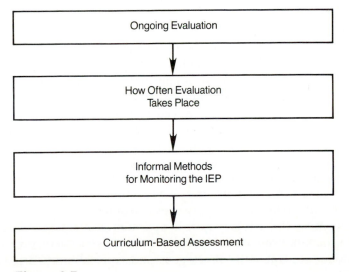

Figure 2.7
Step 6: Ongoing Evaluation

Another study showed evidence that students may gain more awareness of their own goals and actual progress through the use of curriculum-based assessment (Fuchs, Butterworth, & Fuchs, 1989). This study revealed an apparent relationship between student achievement and the student's knowledge of goals and perception of teacher feedback about progress toward those goals. The use of curriculum-based assessment may provide the teacher and the student with clearer expectations and a more realistic understanding of when objectives have been met.

The monitoring of student progress should prompt the teacher to watch closely for the mastery of short-term objectives. The teacher may amend the IEP by updating the short-term objectives. These changes in instruction, not in educational programming, do not warrant an IEP meeting. The short-term objectives should be changed as often as the student masters an objective. In this sense, the IEP is a working document for the teacher. The short-term objectives should be considered daily as the teacher plans for instruction. Student strengths should be used to plan activities of enrichment or reinforcement. With the mastery of each objective, the student moves closer to the attainment of annual goals, and progress is evident.

SUMMARY

Classroom teachers can contribute to the assessment process in many ways. The purpose of assessment is to make educational interventions necessary for academic success. Classroom teachers can aid the multidisciplinary team by making certain that referrals are a last resort rather than a first-choice strategy. Teachers can also monitor student progress and behaviors carefully to ensure that students are referred only for significant academic weaknesses, rather than cultural or linguistic differences.

Classroom teachers can become experienced in collecting data in an objective manner to document academic or behavioral concerns. The teacher should work closely with the parents to make certain that they understand the assessment procedure and contribute useful information.

Assessment data should be employed in making educational decisions. To make the best possible decisions, the teacher should understand what each test measures and how this information can be used in planning. The teacher should become an active and interested member of the multidisciplinary team.

The classroom teacher should keep in mind the issues that concern special educators when working with any at-risk student. The teacher should stay informed and updated on the legal issues surrounding assessment. The teacher should remember the primary goal is optimum academic achievement for all students. Ongoing evaluation through informal assessment provides both the teacher and the student with realistic goals and expectations to promote progress.

CHAPTER THREE

Mainstreaming: A Shared Responsibility

Andrea M. Lazzari

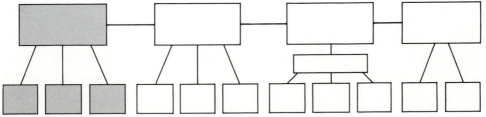

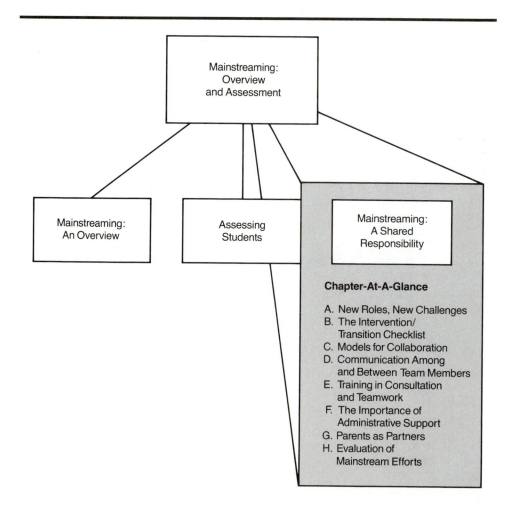

Mainstreaming:
Overview
and Assessment

Mainstreaming:
An Overview

Assessing
Students

Mainstreaming:
A Shared
Responsibility

Chapter-At-A-Glance

A. New Roles, New Challenges
B. The Intervention/
   Transition Checklist
C. Models for Collaboration
D. Communication Among
   and Between Team Members
E. Training in Consultation
   and Teamwork
F. The Importance of
   Administrative Support
G. Parents as Partners
H. Evaluation of
   Mainstream Efforts

One result of the Regular Education Initiative (REI) has been an increased awareness of the need for educators to share responsibility for the educational well-being of all students in their school buildings. No longer can teachers separate students into neat compartments of "mine" and "yours" because the majority of students now fall into the category of "ours." More students have begun to receive services from a variety of teachers and specialists located in their school buildings or visiting on an itinerant basis. Much like students at the secondary level, many elementary students now move from one class to another during the school day to receive instruction from different specialists and take advantage of special curricular offerings. Increasingly, the student with special learning needs who is moving from the regular education home base to receive a special service in another setting is able to blend in with peers as they leave the classroom to participate in a variety of activities.

This chapter examines the implications of the REI and the resulting emphasis on shared responsibility for the educational outcomes of all students from a variety of perspectives: the regular education teacher, the special education teacher, the principal, support staff and ancillary personnel, parents, and the student. A useful checklist is provided to help professionals identify target areas for modification of the classroom environment as well as a question guideline for parents. Teacher training and program evaluation techniques are discussed as they relate to mainstreamed settings.

NEW ROLES, NEW CHALLENGES

The new focus on providing equal educational opportunities for students with disabilities and those at risk has generated a realization that traditional roles and responsibilities must be altered. No longer can regular educators direct their teaching efforts to the middle level of the class using standardized teaching techniques, curriculum, testing procedures, and grading systems. Special educators have realized a need to modify their views of themselves and their roles as separate entities from the rest of the school. A new role is emerging for special educators that involves consultation with regular educators on strategies to use with students with special needs within the context of the regular education classroom (Gersten, Darch, Davis, & George, 1991; Idol, 1988). Building administrators can no longer follow the traditional practices in grouping, placing, and scheduling students, nor can they expect to meet students' needs by the lockstep sequence of the traditional curriculum within the structure of a graded system (Stainback, Stainback, Courtnage, & Jaben, 1985). District administrators must realize that maintaining separate budgets for general and special education is not cost-efficient and therefore not fiscally defensible. Increasingly, parents are realizing that they can no longer leave their children's education in the hands of the experts, for they too are now considered expert members of their children's educational teams. And finally, students with disabilities and those at risk must assume some responsibility for their own educational outcomes, as much as their abilities allow. They must let their teachers and parents know when modifications in the regular environment are needed, which modifications are successful in meeting their individual needs, and which ones are more burdensome than helpful. Perhaps the biggest change that has accompanied the new reality of mainstreaming is that no individual can or should assume full responsibility for a student's success in the mainstream. Teachers, parents, administrators, related services personnel, counselors, students, and the general school community must accept the shared responsibility to provide equal educational opportunities to all students, regardless of their ability levels and individual needs.

Role Definition

Role definition is the first step in any successful team effort, especially if team members are taking on new roles or altered versions of previous roles. A good starting point is to identify all potential team members who will share the responsibility for an individual student's educational program. At first, it may seem obvious that the team consists of the regular and special education teachers, the parents, the principal and, when appropriate, the student. It is also important, however, to consider all members of the school community who may be involved in a student's educational program. Other team members could include paraprofessionals, speech-language, occupational or physical therapists, guidance counselors, administrators other than the principal, specialists (e.g., vision specialist, sign language interpreter, orientation and mobility specialist, adaptive physical education teacher), other school-based staff (e.g., band director, media specialist, coordinator of the talented and gifted program), vocational education coordinators, and community-based employment supervisors.

A common pitfall of team development is to place students in supplementary classes such as music, art, or physical education classes without providing those staff members an opportunity to learn about the student's special needs and participate in problem-solving (Kjerland, Neiss, Franke, Verdon, & Westman, 1988). To avoid this situation, it is important to view each individual in the school building who has contact with the student as a potential team member. Important questions to consider about each potential member are whether the individual is a teacher who would need to make modifications in the curriculum to accommodate the special learning needs of the student or a person whose services and expertise would be needed to help support the student in another teacher's classroom or during certain school activities. These criteria determine whether to identify that individual as a needed team member.

Once team members have been identified, it is helpful to delineate the basic contributions or expectations of each individual, as illustrated in Table 3.1. Since the roles of team members can be expected to change over time as the student's needs change, role definition should be an ongoing process. Team membership also may change as the student progresses and no longer needs the support of certain team members or as the student moves from one grade or level to the next and is faced with new challenges requiring different types of support.

Table 3.1
Sample Roles and Responsibilities of Team Members

Regular Education Teachers
- View the student as a regular member of the class, not as a visitor
- Modify teaching techniques, course content, evaluation and grading procedures to accommodate the student's special learning needs
- Seek and use the expertise of others in making necessary adaptations
- Incorporate IEP goals in typical activities and interactions according to the team's instructional plan

Parents
- Present family values and priorities for the student's educational program
- Provide insight into the student's functioning in a variety of environments
- Provide a vision of the student's future

Paraprofessionals
- Facilitate the student's direct participation with other students and adults
- Provide individual support to student as necessary
- Incorporate IEP goals in activities and interactions as directed

Special Education Teachers
- Provide consultation and collaboration
- Suggest and/or make adaptations in curriculum, materials, or equipment
- Incorporate IEP goals in typical activities and interactions

Paraprofessionals
- Facilitate the child's direct participation with other students and adults
- Provide individual assistance to student when necessary
- Incorporate IEP goals in typical activities and interactions

Administrators
- Draw together regular and special education resources
- Insure staff training and team consultative support
- Assist in problem-solving logistical and programmatic issues

Therapists
- Insure functional approaches to addressing therapy needs in typical activities and interactions (i.e., self-care, getting on bus or swing, using equipment in shop or home economics)

Note. From "Team membership: Who's on first?" by L. Kjerland, J. Neiss, B. Franke, C. Verdon, & E. Westman, 1988, *Impact Newsletter*, Minneapolis: University of Minnesota, Institute on Community Integration. Copyright 1988 by University of Minnesota. Adapted by permission.

Role Expectations and the Special Education Process

Another helpful practice is to identify the role expectations of each team member according to the sequence of the special education process. At different stages of the process, team membership may shift temporarily. As shown in Figure 3.1, the regular education teacher, the parents, and the special education teacher

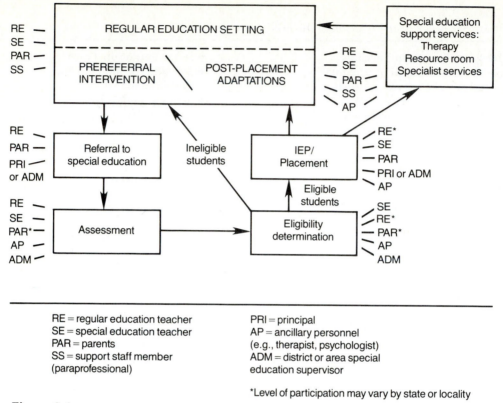

Figure 3.1
Prereferral and the Special Education Process: Team Involvement

play key roles at the prereferral stage, functioning as co-consultants in the development of strategies to meet the needs of students at risk in the regular education setting. A support staff member or paraprofessional also may help at this point by both gathering information about the student and implementing intervention strategies. Ideally, the process would end at this point, as modifications of the regular education setting are successfully implemented and monitored.

If the student continues to have difficulty after a variety of prereferral strategies have been tried, the regular education teacher in consultation with the parents may decide to refer the student to the principal, or another designee, as the first step in the special education process. Depending on district or state policy, an intermediate step may occur between referral and assessment. This step involves presenting the student to a school-based screening committee, which may be known as a child study committee (CSC), pupil personnel team (PPT), or educational management team (EMT). This committee may either recommend alternative strategies to try in the regular classroom or, with informed parental consent, refer the student for assessment.

A variety of multidisciplinary team members must participate in the assessment process, as specified in the P.L. 94–142 regulations. The regular education teacher and the parents are not required to participate as team members, but they can provide valuable information on the student's current performance levels across a variety of settings. In this manner, they fulfill the role of advisors to the multidisciplinary team.

The next step in the special education process is to use the consolidated data obtained during the assessment process to determine if the student is indeed eligible for special education and/or related services. State or local policy or practice may dictate whether the parents or the regular education teacher are directly involved in this step. Ancillary staff, including the school psychologist, the home school counselor or social worker, and one or more therapists will continue to play key roles at this step, as will the special educator.

As illustrated in Figure 3.1, two different outcomes may emerge from eligibility determination. Some students will be found ineligible for special education services at this point and will continue their placement in the regular education classroom. In most cases, these students will continue to need the expertise of the prereferral team in developing additional adaptations to accommodate them in the regular education setting.

The other outcome of eligibility determination is the decision that the student needs special education and/or related services. At this step, it is imperative for the regular educator and the parents to play active roles in developing the student's IEP. While the expertise of the special educator in writing IEPs is essential, the input of the regular education teacher who has an in-depth knowledge of curriculum content is also critical (Rocha, Wiley, & Watson, 1982). The parents' input is essential to identify the placement that can best meet the student's unique educational needs in the least restrictive environment. For many students, the determination will be that the most suitable placement is the regular education classroom. An important difference is that the student now returns to that setting with an IEP to guide the regular and special education teachers and ancillary staff in developing appropriate post-placement adaptations. In addition, the student may now receive needed support services, such as physical therapy, vision specialist services, auditory training with an audiologist, or adaptive physical education, and/or resource room services for a portion of the school day. Specialists who deliver support services must join with the special and regular education teachers to develop and implement adaptations across the student's full range of educational activities and settings.

An important feature of the process shown in Figure 3.1 is that it is a closed-loop system. Students found eligible for special education services, as well as those referred for assessment but found ineligible, continue in their regular education placements both during and after the assessment and eligibility process. This enables students to maintain their home base in regular education as the process unfolds, while continuing to receive the benefit of mainstream adaptations planned and implemented by the collaborative efforts of the regular and special education teachers.

THE INTERVENTION/TRANSITION CHECKLIST

The key to success in any mainstream placement is the appropriate adaptation of the learning environment. A major function of the school-based team guiding the student's learning outcomes is the identification of needed areas of adaptation in the mainstream environment. A helpful and practical method of identifying where adaptations in the learning environment may be needed is the Intervention/Transition Checklist developed by Wood (1991). This simple device enables teachers and other team members to compare characteristics of the regular class setting to the performance levels of the student in that setting (see Appendix A for a copy of the checklist).

The checklist is divided into three sections. In Section 1, three components of a content area classroom are assessed: (a) the Emotional/Social/Behavioral Environments; (b) the Physical Environment; and (c) the Instructional Environment. Identification of possible mismatches between a student's performance and any of these aspects of the learning environment is the first step in developing prereferral or post-placement interventions. For example, if the checklist reveals that a history teacher requires students to copy extensive notes from the board and the student has difficulty copying, then a mismatch has been identified. The regular and special education teachers would then work cooperatively to develop necessary adaptations for that student, for example, by providing a graphic organizer for note-taking. Chapters 4 through 10 provide numerous suggestions for ways to adapt each of these learning environments. Section 2 of the checklist assesses related environments, which include the cafeteria, the physical education class, music/art classes, assemblies/school programs, transition between classes, and the library. Completion of this section helps team members assess the student's performance during the nonacademic portions of the school day. The final section of the checklist addresses interpersonal/social relations within the general school environment.

Figure 3.2 displays a section of the checklist that assesses the skill of note-taking. In this classroom, as indicated by the checkmarks in the column at left marked "Check if it Applies," students are expected to copy notes from the board, copy notes prepared by the teacher, take notes from a lecture, and copy notes from a textbook. Lecture outlines or carbon copies of other students' notes are not available. According to the notations in the columns reflecting the student's present performance level, this student is able to copy notes from the chalkboard and can read teacher-written notes, but is unable to take organized lecture notes, take notes from a textbook without assistance, or take notes using an outline as a guide. Thus, for these skill areas, a mismatch is evident between the mainstreamed environment and the student's present skill level. The special and regular educators and the student can now work together to develop adaptations that will enable the student to be successful in completing assignments that require note-taking.

Beyond the basic identification of needed areas for adaptation, the checklist can be used in several other ways. For students receiving instruction in a variety

Characteristics of Mainstream Setting	Check if it Applies	Student's Present Performance Level	Has Mastered Skills	Is Working on Skills	Is Unable to Perform Skills
IV — MEDIA					
A. Note-taking Technique Used					
1. Copied from board	✓	Can copy notes from chalkboard	✓		
2. Prepared by teacher	✓	Can read teacher-written notes	✓		
3. From lecture	✓	Can take organized lecture notes			✓
4. From textbook		Can take notes from textbook			✓
5. Lecture outline provided by teacher		Takes notes with outline as guide			✓
6. Carbon copy of notes available		Reads notes taken by other student		✓	

Figure 3.2
An Example of a Completed Section of the Intervention/Transition Checklist (Wood, 1991)

of classrooms, the checklist or appropriate subsections can be used to compare the student's performance across educational settings. Each of the student's teachers may complete a copy of the checklist, or the special education teacher consultant may complete copies of the checklist while observing each classroom. This enables team members to compare their observations about the student's learning environments and needs throughout the school day and develop consistent adaptations as needed.

Use of the checklist can also be effective for students making a transition into the regular education setting from a prior self-contained placement. The special education teacher would fill out the Student's Present Performance Level sections and review the checklist with the regular education teacher prior to the student's entry into the regular classroom. This would provide insight into the student's learning characteristics and special needs, enabling the regular education teacher to make accommodations in the learning environment to facilitate a smoother transition for the student. For transitioning students who continue to be identified as special education students, the checklist also can be used to generate objectives for the IEP.

Teachers can also make valuable use of the checklist in conferences with the parents. Too often, teachers present the parents with test scores or grade reports that provide information about the student's achievement or failure, but offer no reasons for that success or failure. Using the checklist as a pre-post comparison of the student's current level of performance (e.g., at the beginning and midpoint of the school year), teachers can provide parents with concrete information about how the student's educational environment may be contributing to performance and which adaptations have proven successful. Parents, in turn, can use this information to help structure an appropriate learning environment for the student at home. This will help prevent the frustration that often results when parents attempt to help students with homework but use inappropriate pacing, methods, or materials.

MODELS FOR COLLABORATION

Collaboration is the cornerstone to successful integration of students at risk and those with disabilities into the regular education environment. In the past, collaboration between special and regular educators has occurred on a limited basis outside of the required team meetings during the steps of the special education identification and placement process. Consultation has most often been linked to existing special education resource programs, whereby the resource room teacher fulfills a limited consultative function to regular education teachers (Kauffman & Pullen, 1989). In many school districts, resource room teachers by definition are allowed to serve only those students with valid IEPs. In practice, consultative services under this model are typically delivered in the resource room as opposed to the regular education classroom. In many instances, resource room teachers are unable to carry out their responsibilities as consultants, with their activities limited to assessment and instruction in the resource room (Wiederholt & Chamberlain, 1990).

Collaborative Consultation

A more responsive approach to collaboration between regular and special educators has emerged over the past decade. This approach of *collaborative consultation* is defined as "an interactive process that enables people with diverse expertise to generate creative solutions to mutually defined problems" (Idol, Paolucci-Whitcomb, & Nevin, 1987, p. 1). West and Idol (1990) identified three major purposes of collaborative consultation: (a) to prevent learning and behavioral problems, (b) to remediate learning and behavioral problems, and (c) to coordinate instructional programs. Using a collaborative approach greatly enhances the likelihood of success because the proposed solutions or strategies are generated from a wider knowledge base than possessed by any individual team member.

The special education teacher consultant model was developed to address the learning difficulties of students with disabilities through support and consultation provided to their regular classroom teachers (Greenburg, 1987). In contrast to traditional consultative services that typically involve calling in an outside expert for a one-time look at a program, classroom, or student, the teacher consultant model is built on the collaboration of school-based staff. In this manner, ongoing consultation is available as staff members pool their resources and expertise to generate solutions to in-house problems and issues.

The role of the special education teacher consultant encompasses several basic functions. A pervasive aspect of the role is to help regular educators understand that students with special needs can successfully participate in mainstreamed settings (Lewis & Doorlag, 1987). Beyond this, the most important component of the teacher consultant's role is to facilitate instructional or curricular decision-making by the regular classroom teacher or among team members regarding an individual student's educational needs. Key to the teacher consultant's success is establishing an atmosphere of mutual exchange of ideas and advice, as opposed to following a more traditional practice of providing advice to those seeking guidance. Figure 3.3 displays goals for the regular and special educator that support the reciprocal nature of the collaborative relationship.

Much of the decision-making carried out by team members will concern adapting the regular classroom environment to accommodate the needs of mainstreamed students. Idol and West (1987) have described a hierarchy of intensity levels for team members to consider when modifying instruction for students with special needs (Table 3.2). Among the main functions of the special education consultant are gathering information, making observations, and facilitating discussion among team members that will result in instructional modification at the appropriate level of the hierarchy for each student.

Other duties of the special education consultant will depend in part on the type of consultation program in effect. Teacher consultative services usually take one of two forms, indirect or direct consultation (Schulte, Osborne, & McKinney, 1990). Each of these models appears to be used with approximately equal frequency (West & Brown, 1987). In the model of *indirect consultation*, the special educator fulfills the role of providing technical assistance to the regular

Figure 3.3
Facilitating Collaborative Consultation: Goals for Special and Regular Educators

The special educator should strive to. . .
- Recognize that the techniques of instructional and behavioral management used by regular educators can be effective means of working with students with special needs.
- Understand that teachers in regular classrooms must respond to the needs of many students in rapid fashion.
- Acknowledge that placing a student with special needs in a regular classroom does not relieve the teacher of any responsibilities to the other students.
- Realize that no classroom teacher can devote the majority of time to any one student for any length of time.
- Recognize that teaching techniques or programs that may be a success in a separate special education class may not be appropriate for the regular classroom environment.

The regular educator should strive to. . .
- Understand that the special education consultant may be responsible for a large number of students in a variety of settings and therefore have a limited amount of time to devote to each student.
- Realize that it is unlikely that a new intervention strategy or instructional approach will have an immediate effect and that a fair trial must be given before a technique is judged ineffective.
- Acknowledge that all students differ in the extent of instructional adaptations they need; many mainstreamed adaptations recommended by the consultant will therefore be extensions of techniques from regular education.
- Maintain a familiarity with each student's IEP, sharing responsibility with the consultant for determining how goals and objectives can be reinforced during the course of regular classroom activities.

Both the special and regular educators should strive to. . .
- Acknowledge that both teachers have specialized knowledge and skills, but that their experiences, values, and knowledge bases may differ.

class teacher. In this role, the consultant helps the regular education teacher assess needs, arrange the physical environment, plan for instruction, and prepare or adapt lesson plans, materials, and student evaluation and grading procedures for the students with disabilities. The consultant does not, however, deliver any direct instruction to students, a role that is maintained by the regular education teacher. The main advantage is that the indirect approach allows the consultant to serve many students in a limited amount of time. A primary disadvantage is that it may be difficult to determine conclusively whether improved student performance is directly related to the intervention efforts of the consultant via the teacher (Heron & Harris, 1987). Another drawback is that the consultant may not have an adequate amount of time to spend addressing any one student's needs.

Table 3.2
Modifying Instruction for Students with Special Needs:
Seven Levels of Intensity of Intervention

Level I	What can the student learn in the regular program of instruction with the same performance standards as nondisabled peers?
Level II	What can the student learn with nondisabled peers, but with adjustments in performance standards according to the student's needs as identified through curriculum-based assessment?
Level III	What can the student learn with adjustments in pacing, method of instruction, and/or special materials or techniques provided with consultant support to the regular classroom teacher?
Level IV	What can the student learn with adjustments in pacing, method of instruction, and/or special materials or techniques provided jointly with regular and support or ancillary staff?
Level V	What can the student learn with adjustments in the content of the classroom curriculum to be taught jointly by regular and special support or ancillary staff?
Level VI	What classroom curriculum content must be modified significantly and taught by special staff?
Level VII	In what situations is some or all of the content of the classroom curriculum inappropriate for this student? What alternative curriculum or program will be used to provide for this student's educational needs?

Note. From "Consultation in Special Education (Part 2): Training and Practice" by L. Idol & J. F. West, 1987, *Journal of Learning Disabilities, 20*, pp. 474–494. Copyright 1987 by Journal of Learning Disabilities. Adapted by permission.

In contrast, in the model of *direct consultation*, the special education teacher consultant carries out some direct instruction with students within the regular classroom setting, in addition to providing the technical assistance functions listed above. The main disadvantage of providing direct consultative services to individual students is the added demand on the consultant's time, a factor that can be directly translated into increased costs (Heron & Harris, 1987). An obvious advantage is that direct service to the student provides more opportunities for one-to-one instruction. The direct model also benefits the regular classroom teacher by freeing more time for other students and the consultant by enabling more direct and consistent monitoring of the effects of the interventions.

Both the direct and indirect consultation approaches enable the students and teachers to realize many benefits. While research that conclusively demonstrates the effectiveness of the consultative model is limited (Schulte, Osborne, &

McKinney, 1990), there is a substantial amount of professional literature that addresses the practical benefits of collaborative consultation. These include:

- Reduced referrals to special education
- Maintenance of regular education placements for students with disabilities, promoting inclusion with peers and reducing stigmatization (Lewis & Doorlag, 1987)
- Ongoing feedback and professional growth opportunities for teachers
- Increase of student-teacher direct contact time (Thousand & Villa, 1990)
- Provision of needed resources that can be used with all students in the classroom (Reynolds, Wang, & Wahlberg, 1987)
- Increased likelihood that instruction of the student will match the general education curriculum
- Potential for increasing teachers' accountability
- Potential for maximizing instructional outcomes
- Professional and personal needs satisfaction for teachers
- Improvement of staff morale (Thousand & Villa, 1990)
- Reduction of feelings of isolation by teachers (Bauwens, Hourcade, & Friend, 1989)
- Consistent availability of the consultant in contrast to use of outside consultants
- Availability of an effective vehicle for instructional decision-making for students with disabilities as well as those without (Idol & West, 1987)

Considering the many advantages of the consultative approach leads one to wonder why its use is not more extensive for all students with special needs in all school districts. There are, however, some perceived disadvantages to this approach that have interfered with its widespread implementation. One commonly cited drawback, especially by those not experienced in its use, is that it may seem to eliminate or reduce a teacher's freedom and autonomy (Thousand & Villa, 1990). Regular education teachers may fear having another educator in their classrooms on a regular basis, assuming it will interfere with their individual teaching styles and they will be expected to modify the tried-and-true instructional approaches they have developed and refined over the course of their professional careers. They may be concerned that having another adult in the classroom will prove disruptive to the students. And, while regular education teachers may welcome assistance for their students with special needs, they may have concerns about the performance and behavior of those students at times when the special education consultant is not physically present to provide individual support and instruction.

Special educators also have concerns about implementing the consultative model. Perhaps their greatest concerns relate to schedule and caseload—whether they will have sufficient time to meet the needs of all students and their teachers or to carry out all the duties of their consultative role (Idol-Maestas & Ritter, 1985). Lack of administrative support is another factor that inhibits success in school consultant programs reported by practitioners (Idol-Maestas & Ritter,

1985; Nelson & Stevens, 1981). Another concern relates to providing feedback to regular educators. The observation of on-the-job teaching performance of colleagues can threaten even close relationships (Rocha, Wiley, & Watson, 1982). This can be an uncomfortable task for the untrained consultant, especially if the regular education teacher is resistant to the consultant's role or does not enthusiastically endorse mainstreaming of children with disabilities. A less obvious concern may be that of the security of the consultant's role. Consultants may believe that successful performance of their roles will threaten the security of their own positions. They may fear that special education consultants will no longer be needed if they do an outstanding job helping regular educators to become skilled in meeting the needs of mainstreamed students.

Cooperative Teaching

Also known as co-teaching, *cooperative teaching* is another model for integrating students with special needs in the regular education classroom. As in direct consultation, the special educator participates in instruction in the regular classroom. In cooperative teaching, however, the special educator has increased responsibility for classroom instruction. In most co-teaching situations, special educators continue to take the lead in activities such as child study, consulting with parents, and offering individual, intense instruction to those students in need (Reynolds, 1989). In contrast to a strict consultation model, co-teaching involves both teachers in sharing responsibility more equally for the educational outcomes of all members of the classroom. A distinct advantage of cooperative teaching is the opportunity for the co-teachers to combine their individual strengths and expertise to address particular student needs (Relic, Cavallaro, Borrelli, & Currie, 1986). In this manner, co-teachers assume equal responsibility for planning, instruction, evaluation, and monitoring for all students in the classroom.

Typically, minimal standards are set for co-taught programs, which limit the number of students in any one class and prescribe an allowable ratio among teachers, general education students, and special education students. For example, a program might designate that there will be two full-time teachers assigned to the class, and no more than one quarter of the class may be comprised of students with IEPs or identified high-risk students. Students also may need to meet certain standards, such as the ability to read content area materials, before being placed in co-taught classes. Co-taught classes offer the obvious advantage of enabling students to receive instruction in the mainstream environment with the necessary support without being singled out as the targets of special instruction (Relic et al., 1986).

Teacher Support Teams

A third school-based approach to meeting the needs of all students in main-streamed settings is that of *teacher support teams*. Several types of team arrangements have proven successful in promoting collaborative consultation between special and regular educators. Perhaps the most broad-based type of support is provided by *teacher coaching teams*. In a generic sense, the purpose of coaching teams is "to build communities of teachers who continuously engage in the study of their craft" (Showers, 1985, p. 63). These teams are often organized during training activities designed to promote the use of a certain instructional strategy or curriculum approach. Teachers then have the support of their peers as they try to implement new strategies in their classrooms subsequent to the training.

Intervention assistance teams and school-based resource teams are similar in that both are formed to address a particular type of problem. *Intervention assistance teams* are formed on an as-needed basis, and their members may come from within or outside of the school building. Each member will have expertise in a particular intervention strategy. As the name denotes, *school-based resource teams* are formed by personnel within the building. A variety of professionals including teachers, administrators, and support staff may serve as members (West & Idol, 1990).

Teacher assistance teams (TAT) are the most strictly defined type of teacher support team. Like the models described above, the TAT model promotes the use of a school-based problem-solving team to generate intervention strategies for individual students or groups. A team is usually comprised of a core of three members representing various grade levels or disciplines, with the classroom teacher who has requested assistance serving as the fourth member. The team may address a wide variety of issues, including intervention strategies for a particular student, modification of the curriculum, or communication with parents. A distinguishing characteristic of a TAT is that it is teacher-oriented as opposed to child-oriented, since the main purpose of the TAT is to provide support to teachers. Another distinctive aspect of the TAT approach is the importance that training plays in the ultimate effectiveness of team members (Chalfant & Pysh, 1989).

COMMUNICATION AMONG AND BETWEEN TEAM MEMBERS

Establishing clear channels of communication among and between team members can address and quite possibly prevent many of the concerns surrounding the collaborative consultation and co-teaching models. This need affects the regular education teachers and the special education consultant, the student and the parents, ancillary and support personnel, and administrators. As discussed previously, there are predetermined occasions in the special education process when team members will have a specific need and opportunity to communicate (e.g., CSC, PPT, or EMT meeting; IEP development). It is the less formal, daily communication that may be of greater concern to educators and parents as they assume a wide variety of duties in a limited amount of time.

Safran and Safran (1985) developed a practical model of communication between regular and special educators that can be effectively used in collaborative consultation. Their flexible strategies model includes both personal meetings and written communication and enables teachers to systematize and streamline communication. One very useful component of this model is a three-way meeting early in the student's placement between the regular education teacher, the special education teacher consultant, and the student to discuss goals, expectations, and scheduling. At this meeting, the teachers and the student may clarify important issues about the role of each teacher, such as who will grade the student's work and assign the final class grade or who will be primarily responsible for communicating with the parents. Another issue is deciding which teacher the student should approach to discuss the ongoing appropriateness of adaptations and identify any unmet needs. Even the youngest students should have the benefit of this type of meeting, for it encourages them at an early age to assume some responsibility for their own educational outcomes.

Group conferences can be an effective means of sharing information among time-limited professionals (Safran & Safran, 1985). Meetings can be arranged for teachers and others who share a particular grade level, subject, or students. For example, teachers of one student could periodically meet as a group with the consultant to discuss the student's common needs across classes and successful adaptations that individual teachers may have tried. This will not only save the consultant time in meeting individually with the teachers but will enable the teachers to draw on one another's expertise. Grade-level meetings may be helpful in an instance where a standardized test will be given to all students. The consultant could meet with all teachers in advance to discuss allowable adaptations in administering the test to students with disabilities. In subject-centered meetings, teachers might confer with the consultant as a group when revising curriculum, developing study guides or selecting texts or materials, to be sure that the materials and techniques are appropriate for special students or can be adapted without too much difficulty.

While special educators may have cornered the market on excessive paperwork, written communication can nonetheless be effective in supplementing face-to-face contact between busy educators. The SOS form displayed in Figure 3.4 is a quick way for regular class teachers to solicit the assistance of the special education consultant.

TRAINING IN CONSULTATION AND TEAMWORK

Another front-line attack strategy in overcoming the perceived disadvantages of collaborative consultation is teacher training. Through systematic, ongoing training efforts, teachers, administrators, and other team members can learn to become both effective providers and consumers of consultative services as well as to be valuable team members. In spite of the national focus over the past decade on the need to end traditional pullout services for students with mild disabilities, most regular classroom teachers have received little training on how to work with these students within a typical classroom setting or how to function as effective team members (Baker & Gottlieb, 1980; Courtnage & Smith-Davis,

Figure 3.4
SOS Form

SOS
(Something Out of Sync)

_____ is having some problems in _____.
(Name)   (Subject Area)

Please: _____ Stop by the classroom to see the student at _____
                                                                                              (time)

_____ Contact me to arrange a meeting. Most convenient time would
be: _____

_____ Other _____

_____
(Regular Class Teacher)

Note. From "Organizing Communication for the LD Teacher" by J. Safran & S. Safran, 1985, _Academic Therapy, 20_, pp. 427–436. Copyright 1985 by PRO-ED, Inc. Adapted by permission.

1987). There is an urgent need for such training to take place, particularly in schools that serve a substantial number of students at risk or that appear to have an excessive rate of referrals of students to special education (Gersten et al., 1991).

A look at the status of training efforts at the preservice level underscores the discrepancy between training and practice. In a national survey to obtain information on the status of preservice team training, Courtnage and Smith-Davis (1987) found that 48 percent of the 360 responding special education preservice training programs did not offer interdisciplinary team training. Courtnage and Healy (1984) were able to locate only eight special education teacher training institutions that offered distinct team training programs outside of the context of other course offerings.

The status of preservice training in consultation appears to be equally limited. The lack of adequately defined and implemented training programs has been cited as a major obstacle in consultant training (Kurpius, 1978). West and Brown (1987) found that the majority of states (23 of 35 respondents) surveyed reported no certification requirements for competency in consultation, indicating that there appears to be little incentive for institutions to develop programs to prepare teacher consultants.

Because of this limited availability of and incentives for developing preservice training programs in team building and consultation, much of the training that does take place occurs at the inservice level through state-, university- or locally sponsored inservice offerings. Inservice training is by nature more limited in scope and sequence than preservice training. Therefore, it is important to identify those skills and knowledge critical to the successful functioning of teams and teacher consultants when developing inservice training or seeking out training opportunities to further develop one's own skills.

One skill area common to training programs in consultation and team building is that of interpersonal communication and interactive skills (Idol & West, 1987; Safran & Safran, 1985). This can take the form of generalized training in human relations or address more specific interaction techniques such as interviewing, conflict resolution, and negotiation (McKenzie, Egner, Knight, Perelman, Schneider, & Garvin, 1970). Aside from their obvious application to group interaction, these skills also help providers and consumers of consultation as they negotiate the ups and downs of shared responsibility for students in the mainstream.

A second objective of many training programs is to develop a strong underlying knowledge base for problem solving. Common targets for training in this area include: (a) techniques for individualization of instruction; (b) characteristics of students with disabilities and awareness of factors that place a student at risk; (c) identification of resource personnel and awareness of their roles; (d) knowledge of adaptive evaluation techniques; (e) knowledge of educational materials and how to adapt them; (f) knowledge of positive behavior intervention techniques; and (g) understanding of the learning process (Courtnage & Smith-Davis, 1987; Idol & West, 1987).

Building on this foundation, the special education teacher consultant also needs to develop an in-depth knowledge of the regular education environment throughout the school building. It is this type of on-the-job training that can make the difference in the teacher consultant's effectiveness and acceptance by other staff members. The teacher consultant should strive to:

1. Acquire a working knowledge of the special subject areas including curriculum content and sequence, materials, and teaching strategies used in the regular classroom (McKenzie et al., 1970; Rocha et al., 1982; Spodek, 1982);
2. Develop and use a shared vocabulary with regular educators (Spodek, 1982);
3. Learn what nonacademic skills are deemed important by mainstreamed teachers (Salend & Salend, 1986) and what social skills are needed for the student to be accepted by peers in the regular education setting;
4. Learn a variety of monitoring techniques to ensure that instruction is effective (Rocha et al., 1982);
5. Recognize and reinforce strategies of regular educators that are effective with *all* learners and acknowledge the relevancy of regular classroom activities to the student with special needs (Spodek, 1982).

The teacher consultant who has acquired these skills and knowledge and continues to update them will more likely be perceived as one of the regular grade- or subject-level staff members as opposed to an outsider straying from special education to offer advice to regular educators on "their" students. Teacher consultants may periodically assess their own performance using the self-evaluation questions shown in Figure 3.5.

Regular educators also must strive to develop certain competencies that will enable them to be better consumers of consultative services and, in many

Figure 3.5
Self-evaluation Questions for the Special Education Teacher Consultant

1. Are the approaches I have recommended feasible for use in the regular education environment, or are they more appropriate for use in a separate special education class?
2. Do the adaptations enable the student to participate in cooperative learning activities with peers, or do they serve to isolate the student with a disability within the classroom?
3. If I have recommended an adaptation requiring new materials or supplies, have I helped the regular education teacher obtain them?
4. Am I recommending adaptations for the regular educator to carry out that I would be able to implement under similar conditions without undue stress?
5. Do I continually update my understanding of what occurs in regular classes and what regular educators realistically can and cannot accomplish within the confines of a typical school day?
6. If there are unresolved issues or questions regarding any aspect of the consultative relationship, do I share them with the regular education teacher before discussing them with other teachers or administrators?

instances, function in a co-consultant capacity. A key role the regular educator plays in the consultative relationship is that of asking the right questions and relaying critical information to the special education teacher consultant, especially if the consultant has a limited amount of time to spend in the classroom. Figure 3.6 displays some self-evaluation questions that may be used periodically by regular education teachers to assess their contributions to the consultative relationship.

THE IMPORTANCE OF ADMINISTRATIVE SUPPORT

Administrators are in a unique position to promote successful collaboration between special and regular educators. Because of their dual roles of instructional leader and building administrator, principals are central to the implementation and maintenance of effective collaborative arrangements among and between staff members. Not only can they effect the necessary administrative procedures to accommodate students with special needs in mainstreamed settings, but they also can provide access to the necessary training opportunities for staff members who are implementing classroom adaptations. District-level administrators, who play more central roles in allocation of resources and development of district-wide policies, also can have a direct influence on the implementation of integrated programming at the building level.

Student-Related Administrative Issues

Careful scheduling may enhance a student's chance of success in the mainstream environment (see Chapter 6). A basic concern of administrators should be to

Figure 3.6
Self-evaluation Questions for the Regular Educator

1. Do I give the suggested adaptations a fair trial before concluding that they are inappropriate or ineffective?
2. In the consultant's absence, do I keep a running log of questions, observations, and comments regarding mainstreamed students to share with the consultant at a later time?
3. If a recommended approach is not feasible for use in my classroom or conflicts with my professional values, do I clearly make the consultant aware of this instead of carrying it out inconsistently or not at all?
4. Do I make a conscientious effort not to treat the students with disabilities as too "special," particularly during activities when adaptations are not necessary?
5. Do I and other staff members under my supervision maintain confidentiality pertaining to the identification of and issues related to the individual needs of mainstreamed students in our classroom?
6. If there are unresolved issues or questions regarding any aspect of the consultative relationship, do I share them with the special education teacher consultant before discussing them with other teachers or administrators?

schedule students with special learning needs in the classes of teachers who have received training in techniques for integration or who demonstrate a willingness to accommodate the needs of individual learners. Building administrators usually maintain a good awareness of individual teacher's strengths and preferences and should be able to make a good match for most students and teachers. Ideally, as training opportunities in collaboration and teaming are made available all teachers, choice of teacher will no longer be a prime consideration when scheduling students with disabilities or those at risk.

A second student-related issue is that of grade-level expectations. In the past, some administrators have held to rigid, standardized grade-level expectations when determining placement, tracking or grouping, promotion, and graduation of students. As the student body changes to include more students at risk and the number of students with disabilities who are educated in the mainstream increases, such rigid standards must be abandoned in favor of more practical and student-oriented procedures (Stainback et al., 1985). In some instances, building-level administrators may have to negotiate with district-level administrators for permission to deviate from district-mandated procedures. Chapters 11 and 12 provide many alternatives to the lockstep sequence of the standard curriculum as applied to evaluation, grading, promotion, and graduation of students.

Faculty-Related Administrative Issues

One of the most critical factors in the continued success of any collaborative model is the availability of adequate support systems to assist the general educator in developing and implementing alternate instructional strategies (Greenburg, 1987). While staff training is the key to instituting a collaborative approach, access to ongoing support by the regular education teachers is necessary for its continuation. In addition to making funds available for teachers and other school-based staff to receive initial training to accommodate students with special needs in regular education environments, administrators also need to be aware of the need for continued training to keep staff abreast of current developments in assessment, curriculum, adaptive approaches, and application of technology.

An additional need of teachers in collaborative settings that administrators must address is that of building time into teachers' schedules to allow for collaborative problem solving, team meetings, peer coaching sessions, documentation of student progress, and development and adaptation of materials (Idol & West, 1987; Spodek, 1982). Administrators also can work to balance the teacher's share of the responsibility for mainstreaming by making adjustments in their schedules. For example, administrators can adjust the schedules of regular classroom teachers who have several students with disabilities mainstreamed in their classrooms without the support of a direct teacher consultant by decreasing class size. If this is not possible, a paraprofessional can be made available to decrease the student:teacher ratio for at least part of the day. Care should be exercised that an overload in the teacher's schedule does not, by default, leave too much responsibility for adapting curriculum and delivering individualized instruction to paraprofessionals, unless they have received special training (Kjerland et al., 1988).

Another caution for administrators trying to foster collaboration among faculty members is to avoid placing the special education teacher consultant in a supervisory role to those regular education teachers with mainstreamed students. Doing so jeopardizes the give-and-take nature of the collaborative relationship and can have negative consequences for the students if problems arise.

A final consideration for administrators is the allocation of resources. If district- and building-level administrators continue to allocate funds separately for special and regular education, a clear message is sent to personnel that collaboration is not required or even supported. By pooling resources, duplicative spending can be reduced while providing visible evidence of administrative support for collaborative activities (Greenburg, 1987).

PARENTS AS PARTNERS
Parental Involvement During Prereferral

While some parents may be reluctant to become members of a team comprised mainly of professionals, all parents possess a wealth of information that can be extremely helpful in promoting the success of their children in mainstreamed classrooms. As discussed in Chapter 1, parents can observe their children across a variety of settings and have the unique advantage of being able to assess their children's performance over time. For this reason, parents may be the first ones to notice that a child is having difficulty in the regular classroom environment. This may be especially true for children with mild disabilities or those at risk, whose problems in the classroom initially may be manifested as emotional or behavioral difficulties at home. In these instances, parents may choose to initiate a conference with the teacher to discuss proactive classroom adaptations. At this point, parents can be very helpful in providing information on the child's learning style and on how past educational experiences may be influencing the child's present level of performance. The Question Guidelines for Parents presented in Figure 3.7 suggests some key questions that parents may want to ask their child's classroom teacher prior to the time a referral is initiated.

Parental Involvement During Assessment and Placement

As illustrated in the earlier discussion of roles in the special education process, parents are notified of key steps in the special education placement process, such as giving permission for initial assessment or writing the IEP, and encouraged to participate. In addition to providing consent, parents may contribute particularly valuable information to the assessment process. Parental involvement and consent must be obtained before a student transfers from special education services to receiving full-time regular education without benefit of an IEP. Requirements for participation in other phases of the process, such as the school-based screening committee or eligibility determination, will vary from one state to another and may vary among school districts within states. In most instances, however, schools are agreeable to a parent's request to participate in all phases of the process (Anderson, Chitwood, & Hayden, 1990).

Parental Involvement During Post-Placement

The Question Guidelines for Parents also can be effective in helping the parent obtain information about post-placement adaptations to the regular education curriculum that have been made or that may need to be developed. Some of the necessary adaptations may be apparent when the IEP is written, but the need for others may not become obvious until the student has spent time in the regular education environment. For this reason, parents as well as other team members must maintain a continual awareness of the student's status in the mainstream setting. They should keep in mind that the IEP is not meant to be a static document. Instead, they should view the IEP as a document that may be changed as often as necessary to represent the student's current educational status and needs.

Parental Support Needs

It is unlikely that the effects of a child's disability or at-risk condition will be noticeable only at school. Parents usually will be the first to suspect that their child has special learning needs or notice that their child is frustrated, discouraged, and unhappy in the regular class environment. As their child's levels of frustration and anxiety grow, so do the parents'. For parents of children

Figure 3.7
Question Guidelines for Parents

Academic—Classroom

In which subject is my child having particular difficulty?

Is my child having difficulty in all or most subject areas or only in certain subjects?

Are there any medical concerns (e.g., seizures, hearing loss, visual impairments) that should be looked into as a possible cause for my child's difficulties?

Does my child's performance vary significantly between the morning and afternoon or on certain days of the week?

What is my child's current level of performance in this skill area in comparison to the performance of others at this age level and in the class?

What modifications in course content, pacing, and materials have been tried with my child? Which ones have proven successful? Which of these modifications should I carry out at home?

How will I know when homework has been assigned? Is my child aware of the penalty for late or incomplete work?

What appear to be my child's favorite subjects in school?

Nonacademic—Classroom

Does my child stay in his/her seat?

Does my child raise his/her hand and wait to be acknowledged?

Does my child walk quietly in line and follow other school rules in the cafeteria, library, gym, etc.?

Is my child's behavior significantly different from that of other children in the class? If so, exactly what does my child do or not do that is considered inappropriate?

What do you (the teacher) do when my child behaves inappropriately?

Does my child understand the classroom rules? Are they posted in a place where students can refer to them as needed?

Does my child's behavior vary significantly between the morning and afternoon or on certain days of the week?

What can I do to provide a consistent approach to behavior management between school and home?

How many times a day is my child leaving the classroom for support services? Does he/she have difficulty reorienting to the classroom upon return?

Is my child able to keep track of his/her belongings? Is there a system in place in the classroom for storing belongings?

What types of leadership responsibilities is my child given? Are they carried out successfully?

Nonacademic—Social

Does my child have friends in the classroom?

Does my child initiate contact with other students? Does he/she respond appropriately when others initiate contact?

Does my child interact appropriately with other students on the playground, in the cafeteria, on the bus, and during other free times?

Is my child being teased or ridiculed by other students? If so, are there any adjustments we can encourage in behavior, appearance, or manner to improve this situation?

What are my child's favorite activities during the school day?

Does my child appear to be happy at school most of the time?

---

at risk and others at the prereferral stage, each school week may bring a roller coaster of good and bad days, with no apparent pattern to or explanation for their child's successes and failures. Parents may try techniques for support and encouragement that were successful with their other children, but feel helpless or inadequate when these same approaches meet with limited success with their child with special needs. As their children enter the formal referral and assessment process, parents may feel ambivalent. Typically, they hope their child will not be identified as having a disability, yet they hope to find a reasonable explanation for their child's difficulties and gain some relief in the form of effective intervention.

Once children have been referred for an evaluation, their parents can be put in touch with a parent resource center or parent-to-parent program, if such resources exist in their state or locality. In doing so, parents can become informed of the special education process and of their rights and responsibilities and also contact other parents of children with similar disabilities and resulting needs. Such resources are not usually available during the prereferral process, however, when the child's regular education teacher may be the parents' main source of information and support. For this reason, an important responsibility of the special education consultant or resource teacher is to make all team members, particularly those regular educators who have primary contact with parents during prereferral, aware of sources of support within both the school system and the community.

Like all parents at one time or another, parents of children with special needs may benefit from reminders of helpful suggestions to use in their interactions with their children, as well as from receiving positive feedback on those techniques that are successful. Figure 3.8 provides helpful hints for parents to try during the prereferral stage and thereafter.

Levels of Parental Involvement

Parental awareness of their child's educational program and the level of coordination between home and school can make an important difference for many students in the mainstream (Lewis & Doorlag, 1987). However, an important consideration for professionals to keep in mind when interacting with parents is that of the different levels of involvement in their children's educational programs and the variety of roles that parents may or may not choose to assume. Some parents may elect to be involved in each step of the process, while others may choose or be able to participate only in those events they view as critical, such as IEP development. The level of parent involvement will vary not only from one student to another, but also between two parents of the same child and for an individual parent over time.

Differences also will exist in parents' preference for the level of integration into the mainstream that they feel is appropriate for their children. Some parents will want their children to receive services only in regular education settings without the stigma of special labels or services. The collaborative consultation or co-teaching models may be particularly appealing to these parents, as they

Figure 3.8
Helpful Hints for Parents of Children with Special Needs

As a parent, try:

- to show that you love and respect your child.
- to accept your child as is. Become knowledgeable about the child's strengths and weaknesses.
- to be consistent with discipline, demands, and expectations. All children need to know their restrictions as well as the consequences for certain behaviors and actions.
- to ask for details, such as who, what, when, and where, when your child is trying to tell you something, but is confused.
- to keep your child's decision-making as simple as possible.
- to set a schedule or routine for things such as bedtime, homework, meals, chores. All children, especially those with special needs, need the security of definite routines, schedules, and expectations.
- to keep a chart of job tasks and times that the tasks are to be done, and have your child record the time of completing a chore.
- to avoid putting your child under a time pressure.
- not to assume that your child has heard something you said. After giving directions, have your child repeat them to you. This will help avoid misunderstandings.
- to make eye contact and call your child by name.
- to simplify complicated tasks by breaking directions into steps.
- to set up situations in which your child can succeed as frequently as possible. This will help to build the child's self-image.
- to keep your child's room organized, letting the child be responsible. Organization is one of the biggest problems that most children with learning problems face. Help bring more and more organization to your child's life—the child's room is a good place to start.
- to encourage open communication with your child. Discuss the child's strengths and weaknesses and explain why certain teaching methods will not work with the child. Show your child that learning in a different way is similar to wearing glasses to help with weak eyes. It is definitely nothing to be ashamed of or embarrassed about.
- not to compare your child with others at home or in the classroom. All people have the right to be their own person.
- not to pester your child about school. If your child has a good day, you'll soon know about it; if not, your child most likely won't want to talk about it anyway.
- to offer reminders that your child is not alone in having learning problems. Famous people with disabilities have contributed greatly to the advancement of the human race.
- to work with your child's teacher. Consistency between home and school is a great asset.

Note. Condensed from an unpublished list by Shirlene Allen, Teacher of Students with Learning Disabilities, Chesterfield County Public Schools, Virginia.

enable the student to be educated alongside peers without being labeled or singled out for special services. Other parents may prefer a self-contained or separate setting, believing that their child can receive a more appropriate and individualized education in a special program. In any case, parents' preferences and the personal values, experiences, and beliefs that support their decisions must be respected. As Turnbull and Turnbull (1986) advised, "Professionals should be particularly sensitive and tactful when they discuss special educational placement with parents, remembering that values, competing interests, and service availability are three important components of parental decisions." (p. 185)

Although parents' preference for their child's placement may be an integrated setting, they may continue to have mixed feelings about the benefits gained from having their child in a mainstreamed setting. On one hand, parents may feel that an integrated setting has many advantages to offer their child, including the reduction of the stigma of a *handicapped* label and the positive academic and social influence of peers in the regular education setting (Heron & Harris, 1987). In addition, parents may view the regular education setting as one that can more adequately prepare their child for the demands of the regular work environment and the mainstream of adult life after leaving school.

In contrast, parents may have qualms that the students in the regular education setting will not accept their child as an equal and may not make the mainstreamed student feel welcome. If their child has been in a self-contained setting, parents may worry that their child has not acquired the appropriate social skills to be readily accepted in the mainstream and, therefore, may be the target of teasing or ridicule. Of greater concern to some parents is the increased student:teacher ratio in mainstreamed settings, which they fear may prevent their child from receiving the necessary individualization of instruction or special programming that their child needs. They may be unsure of their child's ability to conform to certain teacher expectations and perform successfully in the competitive climate of many regular education classrooms (Heron & Harris, 1987).

EVALUATION OF MAINSTREAM EFFORTS
Evaluation of Individual Student Outcomes

Once students with special needs have been placed in a regular education setting, they must be monitored constantly and closely to ensure that the instruction is effective and continues to meet their needs (Rocha et al., 1982). Such monitoring is needed for students who have been found eligible for special services as well as for those students who were found ineligible or whose needs were addressed by prereferral strategies.

Responsibility for student evaluation should be shared among all team members, with the regular educator and the special education teacher consultant taking the primary responsibility for the task. Student evaluation data should be gathered by direct observation of the student in the mainstream setting as

Figure 3.9

Sample Evaluation Questions for Nonacademic Student Outcomes

1. Is the student involved whenever feasible as a decision-maker regarding the educational program?
2. Does the student's schedule permit grouping with same-grade peers across a range of academic and nonacademic subjects?
3. Do the instructional adaptations tend to draw undue attention to the student in the classroom? If so, how can they be made less obtrusive?
4. Is adequate support provided for the student when re-entering the classroom after receiving a support service in another setting?
5. Does participation in support services or resource room activities cause the student to miss nonacademic activities such as assemblies, free time, enrichment classes?

well as by review of the student's work and tests (see Chapters 11 and 12 for suggestions on adapting tests and grading procedures). The overall goal of student evaluation should be to determine whether instructional adaptations are working or a reevaluation is needed so that further adaptations can be made. While the collaborating professionals should be able to adequately answer questions concerning the effectiveness of educational methods or content, they also need to address other less technical yet equally important questions regarding the student's functioning in the mainstream environment. Figure 3.9 displays some sample evaluation questions related to nonacademic areas of a student's mainstreamed program. Similar questions reflecting each student's individual needs and educational environment should be presented periodically to team members, parents, and the student to evaluate the continued appropriateness of the nonacademic aspects of the student's program.

Evaluation of General Program Outcomes

In addition to the evaluation of an individual student's program, the adequacy of the total mainstreaming effort should be evaluated periodically to determine the positive effects of the program and identify needed areas for program modification. Ferrara (1984) targeted four areas of focus for evaluation of mainstreaming efforts:

1. Determine the impact of implementation of mainstreaming efforts on the achievement and social adjustment of students with mild disabilities and on teachers and other students. How have teachers modified instruction, materials, and assessment procedures, and how have these modifications been implemented and supported and by whom?
2. Examine the number, types, and nature of contact between special and regular educators. Are the contacts student-related? Do they address all mainstreamed students? Do most of the contacts concern discipline or instruction or both?

3. Examine inservice training provided to team members on the topic of mainstreaming. How many teachers participated in the training, did they find it valuable, and was the information specific enough to be of use?
4. Determine the degree and appropriateness of mainstreaming practices. Do students attend all periods in which a course is taught, are they mainstreamed with same-age or same-grade students, and are some students attending only nonacademic classes?

In addition to these areas of focus, mainstream program evaluation efforts also should address team effectiveness and participation. Questions could address the composition of the team, the coequal nature of the team relationships, the frequency and length of team meetings, and the directness of the relationship of team activities to student outcomes.

When planning evaluation of a school's mainstreaming program, evaluators should keep in mind that the most useful evaluation techniques are responsive to the persons who receive or benefit from the services being offered (Idol, Paolucci-Whitcomb, & Nevin, 1987). A responsive evaluation must address the interests of *stakeholders*, or those individuals whose lives are affected by the program or whose decisions will influence the program's future (Bryk, 1983). Stakeholders in mainstreamed intervention programs include teachers, support and ancillary staff members, administrators, parents, and the students. Since each of these individuals holds a slightly different perspective on the mainstream efforts and outcomes, solicitation of their input through either formal or informal evaluation techniques will result in evaluation data that can have a noticeable impact on the school's mainstreaming program and promote the success of every student in the regular education environment.

SUMMARY

While collaborative consultation may not provide an easy answer to every issue or problem that has surfaced in response to the Regular Education Initiative, effective consultative services to students with mild disabilities, students at risk, and their regular education teachers can make a difference in the educational outcomes for individual students in the mainstream as well as for the success of general mainstreaming efforts in a school building. Regular educators, special educators, support and ancillary staff, administrators, and parents will continue to be faced with the challenge of working collaboratively to extend the benefits of mainstreaming efforts to all students in the school building and the school community, as the line of demarcation between special and regular education becomes less rigid and eventually is erased.

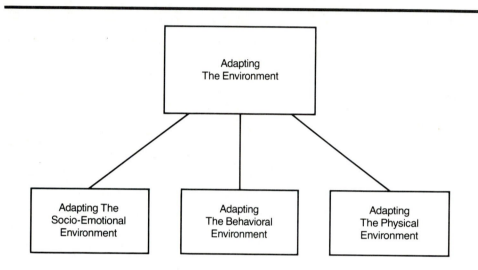

PART TWO
Adapting the Environment

Part 2 of the text includes three chapters: "Adapting the Socio-Emotional Environment," "Adapting the Behavioral Environment," and "Adapting the Physical Environment." This section of the text begins the building of an appropriate environment in which to teach students. The socio-emotional aspect of a class considers teachers' attitudes, how children feel about themselves, and focuses on school-related social skills. The behavioral environment aspect considers ways of managing student behaviors when necessary, and the physical environment aspect looks at making necessary adaptations within physical aspects of the school. Each of these environments must be in place before instruction begins. Each chapter is designed to give specific information for doing so.

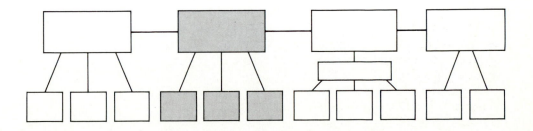

CHAPTER FOUR
Adapting the Socio-Emotional Environment

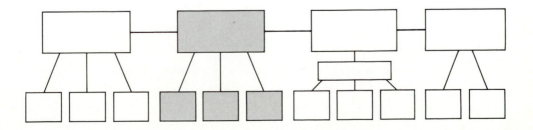

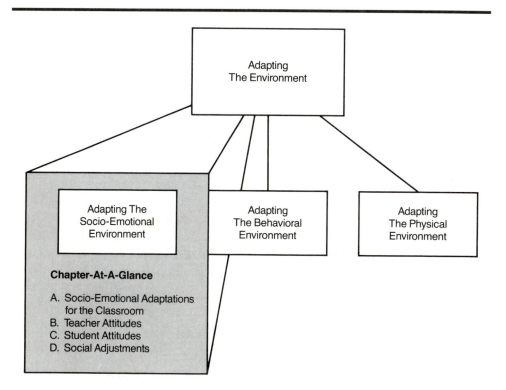

Adapting
The Environment

Adapting The
Socio-Emotional
Environment

Adapting
The Behavioral
Environment

Adapting
The Physical
Environment

Chapter-At-A-Glance

A. Socio-Emotional Adaptations
for the Classroom
B. Teacher Attitudes
C. Student Attitudes
D. Social Adjustments

The socio-emotional climate of a classroom has a significant effect on a student's success or failure. The *socio-emotional environment*, or the affective climate and social interactions that occur in the classroom setting, is the foundation to an effective classroom. Before instruction begins, the stage is prepared for a successful learner. Many times when a student is experiencing difficulty within a school setting, we immediately focus on what the learner cannot do instructionally. Perhaps the true mismatch lies in the socio-emotional aspects of the school or class. In this chapter we will focus on possible areas where mismatches can occur within the learning environment that relate directly to socio-emotional environments.

SOCIO-EMOTIONAL ADAPTATIONS FOR THE CLASSROOM

In a warm, positive environment, all children feel more comfortable and learning has an opportunity to grow. Educators should strive to develop a *risk-free environment*, one which is relaxed and nonthreatening to students. There are many components to establishing this risk-free environment. These include the teacher's attitude, the students' attitudes, and the social preparation of students.

TEACHER ATTITUDES

The classroom teacher plays an important role in the success of a mainstreamed child. Establishing a warm socio-emotional climate helps teachers to maximize student achievement (Rosenthal, 1974). The teacher's attitude toward students is the major catalyst that affects interaction and achievement.

According to current research, teachers' attitudes about mainstreaming are becoming more positive (Wood, 1989). When mainstreaming first became a reality, teachers generally expressed reservations about accepting special education students into the regular classroom setting. The primary concerns of classroom teachers were that they were unprepared to work with the special population and that these students would demand too much of their time (Flynn, Gack, & Sundean, 1978; Johnson & Cartwright, 1977; Middleton, Morsink, & Cohen, 1977). Teachers were also concerned about increased paperwork, possible conflict with special education teachers (Ryor, 1978), and appeal procedures for incorrect placements (Morsink, 1984). Additionally, regular educators tended to underestimate special students' abilities (Final, 1967; Macmillan, Meyers, & Yoshida, 1978), exhibit a lower tolerance for inappropriate classroom behaviors than special education teachers (Doris & Brown, 1980), and believe that special students would be more appropriately educated in special classrooms (Barngrover, 1975).

More recent studies suggest that elementary school teachers' attitudes toward mainstreaming are more positive than in the past (Marston & Leslie, 1983; Reynolds, Martin-Reynolds, & Mark, 1982; Schmelkin, 1981). Among secondary teachers, positive attitudes are developing, but at a slower rate than at the elementary level (Post & Roy, 1985; Powers, 1979; Young & Shepherd, 1983). Donaldson (1980) suggested that negative attitudes of both regular teachers and students can be moved in a positive direction by providing (a) interaction with individuals with disabilities, and (b) structured activities where information about individuals with disabilities is presented and discussed.

Teacher Expectations and At-Risk Students

According to Good (1987), the issue of teacher expectations drew wide attention when Rosenthal and Jacobson (1968) released their research on the self-fulfilling prophecies within the class. In brief, the studies focused on giving false data to teachers regarding student achievement. Student learning outcomes increased when the teacher *expected* them to achieve. Even though the work received wide acclaim, yet also has been attacked by professionals, it is agreed that teacher expectations do affect learning outcomes.

> Studies show that a teacher's expectations are often an accurate assessment of student ability. Hence, teacher expectations for student behavior are not necessarily inappropriate. The problem of teacher expectations may not be one of simple identification or labeling of students (i.e., recognition that one student is relatively less able than another) but rather of *inappropriate knowledge* of how to respond to students who have difficulty learning (Good, 1987, p. 33).

Drawing on research by Good and Brophy (1987), Good (1987) provides a list of 17 behaviors teachers exhibit that illustrate the differential teacher treatment in communicating expectations. Teachers display a difference in their behaviors toward low achievers by:

1. Waiting less time for "lows" to answer.
2. Giving low achievers answers or calling on someone else rather than trying to improve their responses by giving clues or repeating or rephrasing questions.
3. Rewarding inappropriate behavior or incorrect answers by low achievers.
4. Criticizing low achievers more often for failure.
5. Praising low achievers less frequently than highs for success.
6. Failing to give feedback to the public responses of low achievers.
7. Paying less attention to low achievers or interacting with them less frequently.
8. Calling on low achievers less often to respond to questions.
9. Seating low achievers farther away from the teacher.
10. Demanding less from low achievers.
11. Interacting with low achievers more privately than publicly, and monitoring and structuring their activities more closely.
12. Grading tests or assignments in a differential manner, in which high achievers but not low achievers are given the benefit of the doubt in borderline cases.

13. Having less friendly interaction with low achievers, including less smiling and fewer other nonverbal indicators of support and less warm or more anxious voice tones.
14. Providing briefer and less informative feedback to the questions of low achievers.
15. Providing less eye contact and other nonverbal communication of attention and responsiveness in interaction with low achievers.
16. Evidencing less use of effective but time-consuming instructional methods with low achievers when time is limited.
17. Evidencing less acceptance and use of low achievers' ideas. (pp. 34–35)

Preparation of Teachers

Teachers' attitudes toward mainstreamed and at-risk learners play an important role in the success or failure of mainstream placements. Preparing teachers for the changes that will occur when a student is mainstreamed improves attitudes and greatly enhances the chances for a successful match occurring between the mainstreamed student and the classroom setting. Donaldson (1980) concluded that the negative attitudes of regular teachers and students can be made more positive by providing interactions with persons with disabilities and by providing structured instructional activities in which accurate information is presented and discussed. The inservice training of regular education teachers should include experiences whereby teachers get to know persons with disabilities. Leyser and Lesser (1985) concluded that first, preservice and inservice training should provide opportunities to work with information for teaching students with disabilities. Second, it is important for educators to obtain knowledge about specific disabilities and special students' capabilities. Third, educators should be aware of the roles of professional team members and the availability of resources to help them provide appropriate instruction. Fourth, teachers need to be aware of material adaptations and instructional methodologies for use with special students. Frequently, the specifics for preparing teachers to work with mainstreamed and at-risk youth are neglected in their training programs. Educators receive limited preparation in how to work with students with special needs.

Limited Preparation and Training Of Regular Educators

Ysseldyke and Algozzine (1990) report that 70% of students with disabilities "spend a substantial part of the school day in a regular classroom" (p. 258). However, teachers frequently do not possess the knowledge and skills to meet the needs of these special students due to the absence of training in specific intervention strategies during their own preservice coursework (Wood, 1989). Attitudes are more positive when educators know how to teach the special student.

The educational reform movement has spotlighted the need to improve teacher training at the preservice level, charging institutions of higher education with training educators in specific strategies for teaching students with disabilities, including "how to work with students with disabilities within the context of the regular education curriculum, how to assist students with disabilities in becoming involved in the school's social network, and the development of effective pedagogy" (National Council on Disability, 1989, p. 57).

According to a survey conducted in 1989 by the National Association of the State Directors of Teacher Education and Certification, only 12 of the 50 states reported a requirement of a specific course or sequence of courses in special education as part of their minimum requirements for the secondary teaching certificate (National Council on Disability, 1989). The results of a 1989 Lou Harris survey, *A Report Card on Special Education*, found a weakness in the training of regular educators in pedagogical techniques for use with students with disabilities. As reported by the National Council on Disability (1989), the survey revealed that while regular education teachers have an average of three to four students with disabilities in their classes for at least part of the day, only 49% have had training in special education.

A 1988–89 research study conducted by Phi Delta Kappa (PDK) among 808 PDK member delegates revealed discrepancies between professionals' practices and beliefs that have direct implications for training in working with at-risk students. While 91% of the regular education teachers reported that individualizing instruction was effective, only 71% said they did so regularly. Although 85% of the teachers said they believe special teachers were effective with at-risk students, only 67% reported using special teachers regularly. Special textbooks were also considered effective with at-risk students by 71% of the teachers, but only 48% reported using them regularly. And, while 69% of the teachers reported that flexible scheduling was effective, only 48% said they used it. Reasons cited for these discrepancies were that professionals may not know how to use these special techniques or that they may be unable to obtain help in using them (Frymier, 1989).

Special Education Teacher's Role in Preparing the Regular Class Teacher

Special educators are in a unique position to promote positive mainstreaming experiences as well as to offer support and expertise to their regular education peers. Special personnel and regular teachers of special students need to work together to plan and implement mainstreaming. The special education teacher may employ several methods of providing support for regular teachers who serve special education students in their classrooms. According to Dardig (1981), the special educator may:

1. Reassure colleagues that their fears are unfounded and that mainstreaming can be a beneficial experience.
2. Help the regular teacher identify regular classrooms that appear to be appropriate for the student with a disability.
3. Arrange for selected special students to visit the regular classroom prior to placement to become acquainted with the teacher and classmates.

4. Seek inservice training on characteristics of various disabling conditions and methods of working with these children.
5. Provide instructional materials and resources. Regular teachers may reciprocate and share materials that might be useful in the special classroom.
6. Arrange for support services as needed for consultation or delivery of services (e.g., school psychology, physical therapy).
7. Provide special skills by modeling or demonstration to help the teacher learn to help the child function well.
8. Explain the benefits of mainstreaming for all children.

Communication

Communication, the exchange of ideas, information, and suggestions, is crucial to establishing a good working relationship between the special and regular education teachers. Because the regular educator faces the task of adapting instruction in the mainstreamed classroom, the special educator bears more, though not all, of the responsibility for making the communication process easier. To communicate better, special education teachers must understand themselves, realize that others see and respond to them as they project themselves, be able to listen, demonstrate an understanding of others' concerns by acting in positive ways, respect the problems and concerns of their colleagues, and respond quickly to the needs of others.

Understanding the self leads to good communication. Also, knowing and internalizing the role of special educator and then projecting that role in a positive way provides others with guidelines by which to communicate. Others see us as we project ourselves. If special educators project confidence in their abilities, others trust that competence. However, the reverse is also true. If special educators project a lack of confidence in their abilities, others may view them as incompetent. Thus, projecting one's positive qualities facilitates good communication among colleagues, which in turn opens instructional doors for children with disabilities.

Listening is the basis of any communication. Many times we listen to what is being said without actually hearing what is being communicated. Special educators must not only listen, but also hear the concerns of regular educators. They show evidence of hearing those concerns by reacting to their colleague's needs in a positive manner. For example, special education teachers who quickly provide the appropriate instructional material, suggest an alternative teaching technique, or assist in designing a behavior management plan for a mainstreamed student show that the problems of others are major concerns of theirs. Once regular educators believe the door of communication is open, effective mainstreaming becomes a reality. Special educators cannot always respond immediately, but collaboration among teachers can generate many instructional alternatives. (See Chapter 3 for information on collaborative consultation models).

Thus, the development of a positive working relationship between regular and special educators has a significant effect on the child with special needs. For mainstreaming to succeed, the special and regular class teachers must communicate. To promote effective communication, special and regular educators should:

1. Establish a communication system;
2. Discuss each placement together;
3. Assist each other in individualizing instruction;
4. Work together to adapt subject matter;
5. Share materials;
6. Assist each other in adapting evaluation procedures;
7. Exhibit characteristics of flexibility, dedication, reliability, organization, imagination, energy, initiative, and enthusiasm;
8. Involve others by sharing plans and ideas;
9. Seek support and suggestions from others;
10. Set realistic goals;
11. Work to improve interpersonal relations;
12. Be happy and proud about working with students with special needs; and
13. Remember that presenting a positive attitude will change attitudes about mainstreaming both inside and outside the school.

STUDENT ATTITUDES

Just as adults, students develop a set of attitudes about themselves and about their peers. Students who have been found eligible for special education services or are at risk for school success usually have experienced learning difficulty for a long period. Many times, educators wonder why students have low self-esteem or why they are unmotivated. Failure is a cumulative process. It does not occur overnight, and the damage it causes cannot be repaired overnight. Students with disabilities traditionally have held lower positions of status than their nondisabled peers, and this pattern of rejection holds true whether in a regular or special class (Simpson, 1980).

Simpson (1980) noted four factors that are crucial in understanding the attitudes of regular students toward students with disabilities. First, patterns of discriminatory behavior may actually be relatively normal patterns. This is to say that discrimination may be a type of subtle characteristic. Infants discriminate among people based on differences in voice sound or physical characteristics. Attitudes can be modified, but they may be a natural response to developmental or perceptual characteristics.

Second, attitudes toward students with disabilities may exist with or without labels. Some students with disabilities are discriminated against because of their social skills or lack thereof. Even though a label identifies a student as obviously different, the actual identification probably occurred prior to the label.

Third, the attitudes of students toward disabilities are significantly influenced by others with whom they relate. Our attitudes in general are greatly influenced by people with whom we associate. This factor places great importance in the positive attitudes of the teacher and significant others in children's lives.

Fourth, the attitudes of students toward persons with disabilities are greatly influenced by numerous social, physical, and experiential factors.

Simpson (1980) identified four patterns of positive attitudes toward students with disabilities. They are: (a) "Nonexceptional individuals with the most positive social adjustments have the most accepting attitudes toward disabled persons (Lazar, Houghton, & Orpet, 1977)"; (b) "Females generally seem to be more accepting of disabled persons than are their male counterparts (Goodman, Gottlieb, & Harrison, 1972; Newman, 1978)"; (c) "Persons with previous positive experiences with disabled persons tend to have more favorable attitudes toward them than do those lacking prior experiences (Jaffee, 1966; Bateman, 1962)"; and (d) "Younger children have more accepting attitudes of the disabled than do older children (Billings, 1963; Newman, 1978)" (p. 3).

Preparation for the Mainstream

Even though we consider the regular classroom as the home base for the mainstreamed student, there are several areas in which preparations should be made to provide a smooth transition for all concerned. Some special students may spend a large portion of their day receiving services in alternative settings. Students with mild disabilities will spend most of their day within the regular classroom. In either case, students, as well as teachers, need support.

Preparing Regular Education Students

Wood and Reeves (1989) provide three suggestions for preparing regular students for mainstreaming. These include (a) understanding the nature of disabling conditions; (b) instructional units; and (c) simulation activities.

Helping students *understand the nature of disabling conditions* is crucial to peer acceptance. When we understand that everyone has strengths and weaknesses, it becomes okay to be different. A student once wrote, "If everyone in the world were just alike, we wouldn't miss anyone when they died" (Scott F. Wood, personal communication). This student was expressing his belief that to be different is really to be special. A simple activity for teachers to use in helping students understand their similarities and differences is to have them sit in a group and list ways in which they are alike and ways in which they are different. When the group discusses their responses, the teacher can help them see that being different is really being special. From the list, their interests and strengths will surface. Let the students share these interests and strengths and decide how they can use their strengths to help others in the class. For example, a student who is good in math can volunteer to be a math tutor. Another student who excels on the playground can offer to assist others with games. Find areas for each student to share with the class.

Teachers may also utilize *instructional units* to help regular education students develop more positive attitudes toward students with disabilities. These units may be either infused into the curriculum or taught by separate programming. Infusion involves teaching within the daily topic. For example, a teacher may be teaching a civics unit on citizen rights and, along with this topic, may also address the rights of persons with disabilities. Separate programming refers to teaching as a separate unit. A unit on the rights of persons with disabilities could be taught as a single subject. Other suggestions would include researching persons with disabilities; a class discussion on barrier-free environments; learning the causes of various disabilities; in science, surveying students regarding attitudes toward persons with disabilities; and learning of the many outstanding contributions of persons with disabilities.

Simulation activities are also helpful in teaching students about disabilities. Simulations should not be used as introductory activities; rather, they can be applied successfully after students are instructed in the use of coping skills as responses to various disabilities. One idea that has proven helpful for younger students prior to the entry of a student in class who has an obvious disability is to let the students make hand puppets and decorate the puppets to look like themselves. The teacher also has a hand puppet that portrays the disability of the new student. A student's puppet may ask the teacher's puppet questions that are puzzling: "How did you get this way?" "How can I help you?" "Can you play with the rest of the class?" This activity allows students to ask questions in an open environment and helps them to have a better understanding of persons with disabilities.

Preparing Students With Special Needs

There are many skills that special students need to function within the regular class environment. Whether a student is new to the regular class or has previously spent a large portion of time in the regular class, there are skills that need to be taught to help make the transition smoother.

The structure of the class, or the rules and routines, can present major problems for students with special needs. They must be taught class rules and routines. Simply posting and reviewing rules may not mean that the students truly understand them. After reviewing the rules and routines of the class, teachers should encourage special students to discuss the rules and ask questions when a rule is unclear. For older students, this could be done after school or during a study break. Always be careful not to embarrass the student in front of peers. In most classes, rules encompass the seating arrangement, proper behavior, or teacher-expected behavior for entering and leaving the class, the required format for heading papers, the proper procedure for turning in completed work, grading policy, how to request a drink of water or permission to go to the restroom, the proper procedure for sharpening pencils and requesting supplies, what to do when tardy to class, class policy for making up work, penalty for late work, testing schedule, structure of class procedures, and procedures for class participation. Figure 4.1 presents a checklist that a teacher may complete and give to the student. The student may keep this quick reference

Figure 4.1
Checklist for Rules and Routines

Class _____ Teacher _____
Period _____
  1. Seating Arrangement:
     _____ Open seating
     _____ Assigned seating
  2. Behavior for Entering the Class:
     _____ Visiting with friends allowed
     _____ Visiting with friends *not* allowed
     _____ Place personal belongings in desk, locker, bookshelf
     _____ Place class materials on desk
     _____ Copy class work from board
     _____ Copy homework assignment from board
     _____ Other _____
          _____

  3. Behavior When Leaving the Class:
     _____ Leave when the bell is sounded
     _____ Leave only when dismissed by the teacher
  4. Format For Heading Papers:
     _____ Model of format

                              _____
                              _____
                              _____

     _____ Location On Paper

  5. Procedure for Turning In Completed Work:
     _____ Will be discussed with each assignment
     _____ At beginning of each class
     _____ At end of each class
     _____ Only when requested by teacher
  6. How To Request a Drink of Water:
     _____
     _____
     _____

  7. Procedures For Going to the Restroom:
     _____
     _____
     _____

Figure 4.1 *continued*

8. Procedures For Going to the Nurse:
_____
_____
_____

9. Procedures For Sharpening Pencils and Requesting Supplies:
_____
_____
_____

10. What To Do When Tardy To Class:
_____
_____
_____

11. Class Policy For Making Up Work:
_____
_____
_____

12. Penalty For Late Work:
_____
_____
_____

13. Grading Policy:
_____
_____
_____

14. Testing Schedule:
_____
_____
_____

15. Structure of Class Procedures:
_____
_____
_____

16. Where To Put Trash:
_____
_____
_____

17. Policy On Chewing Gum or Having Snacks:
_____
_____
_____

Figure 4.1 *continued*

18. Procedures For Class Participation:
    How to ask for assistance:

    _____
    _____
    _____

    When talking is allowed:

    _____
    _____
    _____

    How to properly ask questions:

    _____
    _____
    _____

    How to properly respond with answers to questions:

    _____
    _____
    _____

    What to do if you are unsure about asking a question in front of peers:

    _____
    _____
    _____

in a notebook and refer to it when in doubt of a certain expected classroom behavior.

SOCIAL ADJUSTMENTS

In addition to specific rules and class outlines, the special student often displays a mismatch in the area of social skill development. Frequently, a student may fall behind academically, and the teacher will become concerned. When the student's social behavior is inappropriate, the concern increases. School-related social skills can and should be taught to students. Many special needs and at-risk children do not have a repertoire of appropriate skills to respond to school-related events, and they need to be taught such skills. Table 4.1 presents selected school-related social skills with accompanying teaching suggestions. For older students, the teacher may wish to discuss these areas, add any that are appropriate to Figure 4.1, and use it as a student handout. For educators working with younger students, the activities provided in this section may be used as class activities.

Table 4.1
School-Related Social Skills

Skill	Vocabulary To Introduce	Activities For Teaching Skill
Understanding Student/ Teacher Roles	• Student • Teacher • Responsibility • Authority	1. Discuss responsibilities of the teacher and the student. *Teacher* • Takes roll • Writes lesson plans • Keeps things in order *Student* • Listens carefully • Follows directions • Cooperates 2. Have class add rules to each list in number one. 3. Role-play the following situations: *Adult as Authority* • "Get in line" • "Be quiet in the hall" • "Put equipment away" • "Clean-up Time" *Student as Authority* • "Close the door" • "Work quietly" • "Collect papers" 4. Have class add rules to each list in number three.
	• Inappropriate • Responsibility	5. Write the following list on the board. Let the students put an "S" next to things that are the student's responsibilities and a "T" next to those that belong to the teacher. • Plan lessons • Develop tests • Grade papers • Do homework • Give homework assignments • Take lunch count/ money • Write assignments on board • Complete all assignments • Play during recess • Pass out papers • Write notes to parents • Correct inappropriate behavior • Work quietly • Follow directions • Make sure everyone does homework • Give out report cards • Go on errands • Raise hand to ask for help • Stay in seat unless told

Table 4.1
continued

Skill	Vocabulary To Introduce	Activities For Teaching Skill
		6. Make a list of classroom situations and allow students to take turns role-playing. • Taking roll/lunch count • Clean-up time • Time to go to P.E. • Test time • Dismissal • Giving a lesson
Respecting Others' Space	• Space • Invade • Touch • Grab • Share • Cooperate • Nervous • Threatened	1. Have a discussion on *space* and what space belongs to the students. • Desk • Bedroom • Chairs • Work stations • Closet • Lockers/cubbies 2. Discuss what it means to respect each other's space. 3. Discuss the importance of maintaining appropriate personal distance in a conversation. Let students demonstrate comfortable and uncomfortable distances. 4. Play "What If." Provide a list of experiences or situations for students to discuss. • When someone sits too close • When someone "tugs" at your clothes • When someone takes something off your desk
Ignoring Distractions	• Distraction • Ignore • Interrupt • Disturb • Space • Signal	1. Have the students make a list of distractions in the classroom that slow them down or prevent them from completing their work. 2. Brainstorm ways for coping with the distractions listed in number one. 3. Develop a signal to use when the student becomes distracted.
Listening	• Listening • Attending • Hear • Look • Eye contact • Listen	1. Have a class discussion on the importance of being a good listener. 2. List situations at home when one must listen. 3. List situations at school when one must listen. 4. Role-play the situations in groups of two and three.

Table 4.1 *continued*

Skill	Vocabulary To Introduce	Activities For Teaching Skill
		5. Develop a *listening cue* for the class. This could be a big ear for younger children and a hand signal for older students.
		6. When there is a problem with listening, have the student repeat the directions or instructions.
		7. Develop a listening checklist for older students.
		8. Play "Simon Says" and let students carefully listen to directions.
		9. Teach students to maintain eye contact while listening.
		10. Discuss the importance of careful listening for specific information.

Following Directions	• Directions
	• Listen
	• Follow
	• Understand
		1. Have a class discussion on the importance of following directions.
		
		2. Review behaviors necessary for following directions:
		  • Look at speaker
		  • Listen
		  • Repeat directions to yourself
		  • Ask for clarification if needed
		  • Perform directions
		
		3. Develop simple worksheets with pictures of trees, stars, balls. Give the student directions to follow: Draw a circle around the tree, connect the stars to the balls with a red color.

Requesting Permission	• Permission
	• Polite
	• Information
	• Emergency
	• Asking
		1. Conduct a class discussion on reasons for requesting permission in different settings:
		  • At home • At school
		  • With friends • On the bus
		
		2. For each situation listed under the four settings, have students answer these questions:
		  • *What* types of things would you request permission for?
		  • *Whom* would you request the permission from?
		  • *How* do you request the permission?
		  • *When* would you request the permission?
		
		3. Discuss the steps for requesting permission in each setting in number one.

Table 4.1 *continued*

Skill	Vocabulary To Introduce	Activities For Teaching Skill
Requesting Assistance	● Help ● Ask ● Assistance ● Thank you ● Please ● Procedures	1. Discuss the correct procedures for asking assistance. ● Have you clearly thought through the problem? ● How will you make the request? ● How will you indicate to another that you need assistance? ● Did you wait for your turn to be assisted? ● Did you thank the person assisting you? 2. Make a list of times a student would need assistance at home. ● When doing homework ● When doing chores ● When they do not understand a request 3. List persons at home whom you may request assistance from: ● Mother ● Sister ● Brother ● Aunts/uncles ● Grandparents ● Babysitter ● Father 4. Model the appropriate way to make a request at home. 5. List situations when students may need assistance at school: ● When they do not understand directions ● When they cannot find materials ● When they have made a mistake ● When they do not understand a lesson 6. List school personnel whom you may request assistance from: ● Teacher ● Aide ● Clinic aide ● Librarian ● Principal ● Secretary ● Custodian ● Cafeteria worker 7. Model the appropriate way to request assistance at school. 8. Role-play the request for assistance for home and for school.

Table 4.1 *continued*

Skill	Vocabulary To Introduce	Activities For Teaching Skill

Requesting Clarification	• Clarify
	• Information
	• Directions
	• Understand
		1. Discuss the necessity for asking for clarification so that we can follow directions or act on information.
		2. Discuss the consequence of not requesting clarification.
		3. Make a list of situations where clarification might be needed.
		4. Discuss the steps one takes when requesting clarification.
		  • Think carefully about what was said
		  • Think about your request
		  • Raise your hand
		  • Look at the person and speak clearly
		  • Ask for more specific information if you do not understand
		  • If still confused, ask the person to meet with you later
		  • Thank the person for assisting you
		5. Practice requesting clarification for the situations listed in number three.

Participating in Class	• Participate
	• Volunteer
	• Join
	• Cooperation
	• Appropriate
		1. Discuss what *participation* means and the importance of voluntary participation.
		2. Establish guidelines for class participation.
		  • Be a good listener
		  • Ask appropriate questions
		  • Volunteer answers
		  • Don't interrupt
		3. List situations when you would participate in a class discussion:
		  • When the teacher asks for a response
		  • Volunteering a response
		4. Role-play the situations listed in number three.
		5. Discuss road blocks and keys to participating in class.
		  • *Road blocks* (lack of interest, fear of looking foolish, not understanding, not knowing the answer, fear of giving the wrong response)
		  • *Keys* (listen to activity, look at speaker, realize that many students are afraid of looking foolish)

Table 4.1 *continued*

Skill	Vocabulary To Introduce	Activities For Teaching Skill
		6. List on the board ways in which students can participate in class or in groups. • Giving ideas • Offering and accepting help • Agreeing or disagreeing • Listening to others • Following directions • Following rules • Encouraging others
Solving Problems	• Problem • Solution • Choose • Options • Cooperation • Situation	1. Discuss a problem-solving or choice-making process. • Identify the problem or options • Consider all possible solutions • Discuss the pros and cons of each listed solution • Develop a plan of action • Put the plan into action • Evaluate the success of the plan
		2. Have students make a list of problems they have encountered.
		3. Role-play solving the problems listed in number two using the procedures in number one.
		4. Help the student understand choice-making and its prerequisite role in solving problems
		5. Provide situations where choices must be made. Let the student select a choice in each situation.
		6. Discuss what the ramifications of each choice would be.
		7. Present the class with a problem scenario and have them solve each problem using the steps provided in number one. • A fight begins in the hall and no teacher is present • Someone pushes you in the hall • A member of the class is "acting up" and the whole class is going to lose a privilege if the student does not stop • Someone teases you at school • You are told to do tomorrow's homework for reading and you need to do today's math homework

Table 4.1 *continued*

Skill	Vocabulary To Introduce	Activities For Teaching Skill

Accepting Responsibility	• Responsibility
	• Accept
	• Fulfill
	• Contribute
	• "In charge of"
		1. Discuss the concept of *accepting responsibility*.
		2. Review the responsibilities you have as the teacher.
		  • Arrive at school on time
		  • Prepare lesson plans in advance
		  • Grade papers
		  • Take care of students in your class
		3. List on the board the responsibilities for the student at school.
		  • Be on time to class
		  • Prepare homework on time
		  • Study for class
		  • Exhibit appropriate conduct
		  • Respect others' space and property
		4. List on the board the responsibilities for the student at home.
		  • Be on time for meals
		  • Do chores
		  • Take care of possessions
		  • Watch over younger brothers/sisters

Transitioning Activities	• Transition
	• Change
	• Order
	• Quiet
	• Smooth
		1. Make a list on the board of school-related transition times.
		  • From home to bus/ride
		  • From bus/ride to school
		  • From school to classroom
		  • Changing activities
		  • Changing periods/classes
		  • From classroom to bus/ride
		2. Discuss ways for making transitions smoother.
		  • Stop what you are doing
		  • Look at the teacher/driver/aide
		  • Listen to any directions or explanations
		  • Remain quiet
		  • Ask questions if you do not understand
		  • Discuss any problems with a teacher/driver/aide
		3. Role-play transitioning for various situations.
		  • Snack time
		  • Lunch time
		  • Change in activities
		  • Going to bus
		  • Change in classrooms
		  • End-of-day activities
		  • Recess/physical education

Table 4.1 *continued*

Skill	Vocabulary To Introduce	Activities For Teaching Skill

Using Free Time Wisely	• Free time
	• Choose
	• Busy
	• Productive
	• Wise
	• Play
	• Break
		1. Lead a class discussion on the meaning of *free time*.
		2. Make a list of free-time situations at home.
		3. Make a list of free-time situations at school.
		4. List positive consequences of the wise use of free time.
		    • Finishing homework
		    • Getting extra help
		    • Extra after-school time
		5. Set up a free-time center in the classroom. Provide a selection of activities to do for the wise use of free time.
		6. Have students keep a list of how they use their free time.

Working Cooperatively In a Group	• Cooperate
	• Give and take
	• Work together
	• Compromise
	• Negotiate
	• Bossy
	• Know-it-all
	• Flexible
		1. Ask students to help make a list on the board of situations where cooperation is needed.
		2. Make a list of ways to cooperate in a group.
		    • Sharing materials
		    • Sharing responsibilities
		    • Compromising/negotiating
		    • Participating
		    • Dividing up tasks
		    • Exchanging information
		    • Asking for information
		    • Helping other group members
		3. Role-play situations listed in number two.
		4. Make a list of consequences when we do not cooperate.
		5. Decide on a project for the class to do to practice their skills. Let the students evaluate their efforts.

Following Rules	• Rules	1. Discuss why rules are important.
		2. Make a list of various situations and the rules necessary for each.
		School Bus Rules:
		    • Sit in seat
		    • Talk quietly
		    • Listen to the bus driver
		    • Follow directions
		    • Enter and exit bus safely
		    • Keep hands inside the bus
		    • Use safety belts

Table 4.1 *continued*

Skill	Vocabulary To Introduce	Activities For Teaching Skill
		Hall Rules:
		• Keep hands and body to self
		• Be quiet
		• Walk instead of running
		Library Rules:
		• Speak quietly
		• Look at books on shelf
		• Select one to three books from shelf
		• Sit with books at table
		• Select one book to check out
		Cafeteria Rules:
		• Wait your turn in the lunch line
		• Take appropriate utensils, napkin, dishes
		• Make choices for food items and drink
		• Pay cafeteria clerk
		• Seek place to sit (look for friend to sit near)
		• Stay in seat
		• Use good manners
		• Throw away trash
		• Talk quietly
		• Return tray
		• Wait to be dismissed and leave quietly
		Playground Rules:
		• Play within designated areas
		• Play alone or with friends
		• Share playground equipment and take turns
		• Cooperate with others' ideas
		• Stop playing immediately when called
		• Tell teacher if ball goes over fence
		Assembly Rules:
		• Enter quietly and be seated
		• Listen for other instructions
		• Speak softly if you must speak at all
		• Keep hands to self
		• Watch performance by keeping eyes on performer
		• Clap after the performance
		• Wait to be dismissed
		• Leave quietly

Table 4.1 *continued*

Skill	Vocabulary To Introduce	Activities For Teaching Skill
		Office Rules: • Look to see if the person is busy before speaking • Use nonverbal messages to signal if you need help • Use polite language • Close door quietly 5. Ask students to make a list of coping skills needed when they are told that they have broken a rule and they do not understand. • Be polite • Keep calm • Ask for the rule to be stated • Ask for the rule to be clarified • Repeat the rule back to another person • Ask for another opportunity to show that you know the rule

Note. From "Social Competency Curriculum: Communication School-related," by Department of Special Services & Special Education, Fairfax County Schools, 1990, 3. Copyright 1990 by Department of Special Services & Special Education, Fairfax County Schools. Adapted by permission.

SUMMARY

The stage must be set for an environment that is risk-free for students to maximize learning. Students need a class setting built on trust, respect, and good will. Teachers who reflect positive attitudes toward *all* students, help students begin to build stronger self-esteem, and assist students in developing school-related social skills necessary to function within a regular class setting will help build a solid foundation for learning. The next step in adapting the environment is to establish an organized behavioral environment.

CHAPTER FIVE

Adapting the Behavioral Environment

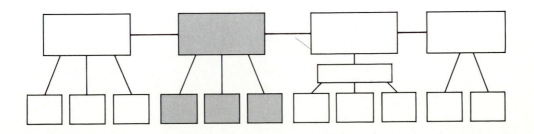

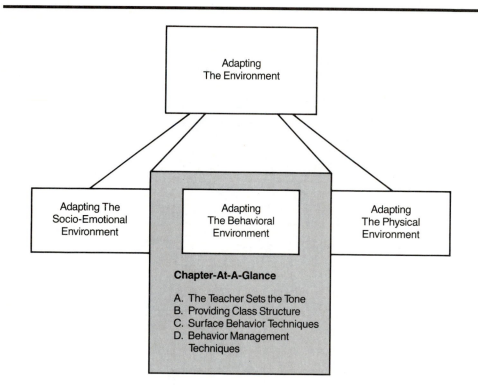

Adapting
The Environment

Adapting The
Socio-Emotional
Environment

Adapting
The Behavioral
Environment

Adapting
The Physical
Environment

Chapter-At-A-Glance

A. The Teacher Sets the Tone
B. Providing Class Structure
C. Surface Behavior Techniques
D. Behavior Management
   Techniques

Managing student behaviors is an ongoing process that occurs simultaneously with teaching. When teachers have assessed their students properly, when they have carefully adapted the socio-emotional environment, and when they have appropriately planned instruction to fit students' needs, most management problems will disappear. But no system is foolproof; sometimes problem behaviors distract from the positive instructional atmospheres teachers have so carefully built.

This chapter addresses the importance of teacher behavior, providing structure, surface behavior techniques, and behavior management techniques.

THE TEACHER SETS THE TONE

The teacher, the key controlling classroom variables, sets the tone in the classroom. The teacher adjusts the lighting, controls the temperature, arranges the seating, decides on the method of lesson presentation, elects when to give a test, and chooses what type of test to administer. The teacher sets the affective atmosphere of the classroom and the stage for learning. According to Purkey (1978), the teacher alone has the power to invite or not invite each student to learn. The teacher's attentiveness, expectations, encouragement, attitudes, and evaluations strongly influence students' perceptions of themselves as learners. An impetus to learning as well as a controlling factor in the classroom management process, the teacher's behavior influences the students' behavior. To assess their potential influence on student behavior, teachers can ask themselves the following questions:

- Do I leave my personal problems at home?
- Am I in good physical as well as emotional health?
- Am I happy with my role in life?
- Does my voice convey confidence?
- Does my walk convey confidence?
- Do I have a positive self-concept?
- What is my attitude toward my peer group?
- What is my attitude toward children?
- Do I accept the responsibility of mainstreaming students?
- Do I feel comfortable admitting a mistake?
- Will I change my opinion when a valid reason for doing so is presented?
- Do I have a sense of humor?
- Can I laugh at myself?
- Am I an attentive listener?
- Do I teach subjects or children?

Weber (1977) lists teacher behaviors that contribute to effective teaching.[1] From this list, teachers can select and develop the behaviors that will help them

[1]From "Classroom Management" by Wilford A. Weber, in *Classroom Teaching Skills: A Workbook* (pp. 237–239) James M. Cooper, Gen. Ed. 1977, Lexington, MA: D.C. Heath. Copyright 1977 by D.C. Heath. Reprinted by permission.

manage their own particular classroom situations more appropriately. According to Weber:

1. The teacher encourages students to communicate openly.
2. The teacher addresses the situation rather than the character or personality of a student when handling a problem.
3. The teacher expresses true feelings and attitudes to students.
4. The teacher makes expectations clear and explicit to students.
5. The teacher reinforces appropriate student behaviors.
6. The teacher trains students to perform leadership functions and shares leadership with them.
7. The teacher listens attentively to students.
8. The teacher accepts students as persons of worth.
9. The teacher does not behave in a punitive or threatening manner.
10. The teacher displays an awareness of what is going on in the classroom.
11. The teacher praises the accomplishments of the group.
12. The teacher uses expressions indicating that the students constitute a group of which the teacher is a member.
13. The teacher elicits and accepts student expressions of feelings.
14. The teacher clearly communicates appropriate standards for student behavior.
15. The teacher clarifies the norms of the group.
16. The teacher provides students with opportunities to work cooperatively.
17. The teacher ignores inappropriate student behavior to the extent possible.
18. The teacher encourages the establishment of productive group norms.
19. The teacher does not ridicule or belittle students.
20. The teacher does not encourage student competition.
21. The teacher communicates an awareness of how students feel.
22. The teacher respects the rights of students.
23. The teacher accepts all student contributions.
24. The teacher guides students in practicing productive group norms.
25. The teacher encourages and supports individual and group problem-solving.
26. The teacher provides students with opportunities to succeed.
27. The teacher removes students from rewarding situations or removes rewards from students in the event of misbehavior under certain circumstances.
28. The teacher initiates, sustains, and terminates classroom activities with smoothness.
29. The teacher directs attention toward the group rather than toward the individual during general classroom activities.
30. The teacher allows students to experience the logical consequences of their behavior when physically safe to do so.

31. The teacher praises the accomplishments of students rather than the students themselves.
32. The teacher accepts students and encourages them to be accepting of one another.
33. The teacher promotes group morale by helping students engage in total-class activities.
34. The teacher makes use of "time out" to extinguish inappropriate student behavior.
35. The teacher uses nonverbal communication that supports and is congruent with verbal communication.
36. The teacher promotes group unity.
37. The teacher encourages students to use time wisely.
38. The teacher trains students to behave appropriately in the teacher's absence.
39. The teacher displays the ability to attend to more than one issue at a time.
40. The teacher discusses issues with students rather than arguing with them.
41. The teacher accepts a productive level of noise in the classroom.
42. The teacher is nonjudgmental in discussing problem situations.
43. The teacher anticipates certain types of problems and works to prevent them.
44. The teacher respects student privacy.
45. The teacher treats students as persons capable of dealing with their own problems.

Table 5.1 presents a checklist for teacher behavior that is helpful for teachers to evaluate whether they are contributing to misbehaviors.

When trouble occurs in the classroom, teachers should first assess the environment and then themselves. Often, teachers can manage the classroom more effectively by changing their own behavior. When teachers have evaluated both the environment and themselves but still have difficulty managing student behaviors, they should look at class structure.

PROVIDING CLASS STRUCTURE

Frequently, mild misbehaviors will disappear when the student is provided structure within the class environment. Providing boundaries for students facilitates a *risk-free environment* and allows students the freedom to relax within the class, knowing what is and is not expected. Not knowing how to behave or being unclear about the teacher's expectations presents a confusing situation to many students.

By effectively introducing structured rules, teachers can control the environment of the class and prevent inappropriate behaviors. For example, the teacher

Table 5.1
Possible Contributions to Misbehavior: A Checklist of Teacher Behavior

Am I consistent in responding to children's behavior? If your response to children's conduct—good or bad—is unpredictable, children will have difficulty learning how they are to behave. Your students should know what the consequences of appropriate behavior and misbehavior will be. Give clear directions, hold firm to your expectations, and be consistent in following through with rewards and punishment.

Am I rewarding the right behavior? Children who present difficult management problems often are ignored when they are behaving appropriately. Often, about the only time they receive attention is when they are criticized or reprimanded for misbehavior. Sometimes teachers make the mistake of praising them for something else or making physical contact with them in attempts to offer loving correction when they misbehave. Make sure that children are receiving your attention primarily when they are behaving appropriately. Make certain that desirable conduct receives a hefty amount of recognition and that misbehavior does not.

Are my expectations and demands appropriate for children's abilities? When expectations are too high, children feel too much pressure and experience too much failure. When expectations are too low, children become bored and may feel resentful. Make certain that your expectations fit each child's ability level so that the children are challenged while their progress is obvious.

Am I tolerant enough of children's individuality? Children have as much right as adults to express their individuality. Many children rebel against teachers who demand strict uniformity and regimentation or are unwilling to encourage appropriate individuality. Make certain that your rules and expectations allow sufficient room for harmless preferences and idiosyncracies.

Am I providing instruction that is useful to children? People do not learn quickly or happily when they see no point in what they are doing. First, make sure that you have chosen the most important things to teach. Then, if children do not see the importance of what you are teaching, point out the value of what they are learning. If they still do not understand, find a way to make the material interesting or worth their while, perhaps by offering meaningful rewards of privileges for learning.

Are children seeing desirable models? Children are great imitators of their teachers and their high status peers. Make certain that if children are imitating you, they are behaving appropriately. Monitor your own behavior, and change it if necessary. Call attention to the desirable conduct of children's peers. Point out the kind of behavior you want to see.

Do I avoid being generally irritable and overreliant on punishment as a control technique? Teachers set a tone in their classrooms by their general attitudes toward persons and events. A teacher who is easily upset, frequently short-tempered, quick to punish minor misbehavior, and hesitant in expressing approval is virtually certain to foster irritability and defiance in students. General irritability and a focus on punishment suggest depression, and a teacher's depression may contribute to children's depressive behavior.

Table 5.1
continued

Am I willing to try a different tack on the problem or to seek the help of colleagues or consultants? A teacher who resists the suggestions of others, who insists on "going it alone," or who discards any different approach as useless or doomed to failure is not likely to be successful for long. Teaching presents complex behavior management problems for which even the most competent teacher needs consultation. An attitude of openness and a willingness to look outside oneself are essential to success.

Note. From "Classroom Management: Teacher-Child-Peer Relationships" by J. M. Kauffman, P. L. Pullen, & E. Akers, 1986, *Focus on Exceptional Children, 19,* p. 3. Copyright 1986 by Focus on Exceptional Children. Adapted by permission.

should let all students, and especially those with special needs, know what behaviors are permitted. Inappropriate behavior will often disappear when students know their limits. For teachers, setting rules for behavior establishes a structure for managing the classroom environment, and for students, working within the boundaries of the rules establishes a structure for being responsible. Teachers may use the following guidelines when setting rules:

1. Involve students in formulating the rules.
2. Keep the list of rules short.
3. Keep the rules themselves short and to the point.
4. Phrase the rules in a positive form.
5. Rather than mention the rules only when someone misbehaves, remind students about them at other times.
6. Post rules in a conspicuous place and review them regularly.
7. Record the number of times rules are reviewed with the class.
8. Make different sets of rules for different activities.
9. Let students know when those different rules apply.
10. Be careful to make rules that can be enforced.
11. When a student breaks a rule the first time, review the rule on a one-to-one basis. Explain that the student should now be familiar with the rule since it has just been reviewed and that the next infraction of the same rule will result in a consequence. Make clear exactly what that consequence will be.

Setting boundaries by clearly establishing defined, understood rules provides an environment that is conducive to learning.

SURFACE BEHAVIOR TECHNIQUES

When problems occur with students with mild disabilities, teachers often anticipate and fear long and involved management strategies, which can be both time-consuming during the instructional period and last over a period of months. However, not all behavior problems are that serious. Long and Newman (1980) have developed techniques for what they call *surface behaviors*—behaviors that merit attention but do not demand total management programs. Teachers should think of surface behaviors as minor infractions—those disruptive behaviors that occur but do not demand serious disciplinary measures. In fact, many teachers already have the techniques developed by Long and Newman in their repertoires and merely need to remember a few tricks for coping with certain minor behavior problems. Before considering intervention, however, teachers should realize that some behaviors deviating from the norm should simply be tolerated.

Tolerating Behaviors

Long and Newman (1980) identified three situations in which teachers should tolerate some behaviors that they would otherwise not tolerate. These include learner's leeway, behavior symptomatic of a disability, and behavior reflecting a developmental stage.

Learner's leeway refers to the times when a student tries to master a new academic skill or learn or practice a new social skill. Teachers cannot expect perfection the first, second, or even third time the student attempts to master the new skill or idea. At this stage, teachers tolerate mistakes and students understand that mistakes are normal and permitted.

Providing such leeway often eliminates the frustration felt by the mainstreamed student. Students with mild disabilities typically need many trials before they acquire skills. Teachers can relax the learning climate for students by acknowledging that errors will occur and will be permitted while learning progresses. In addition, teachers need to understand that social skills often require learner's leeway just as academic skills do. Often students with mild disabilities simply do not pick up on social cues and, as a result, do not behave acceptably. For example, when a teacher corrects a student for interrupting, other students may learn not to interrupt from that example. But the student with a mild disability may or may not learn through this indirect and incidental experience, and thus may continue to interrupt.

To tolerate *behaviors symptomatic of a disability*, teachers must become aware of what such behaviors are. Many teachers do not tolerate specific behaviors because they lack knowledge about disabilities. Thus, school systems need to provide ongoing training for teachers to recognize and identify disabilities and the behaviors associated with them. Some such behaviors are obvious, for example, a student with asthma certainly would be exempt from strenuous physical exercise during days when the asthma was active. However, children with learning disabilities may behave impulsively, have the teacher misread their behavior as disruptive, and suffer unwarranted consequences. Also, children with emotional problems often display behaviors symptomatic of their disabilities, but these behaviors are considered inappropriate within the regular class environment. Although these behaviors must at times be tolerated, they should not be overlooked. The special class teacher, in conjunction with the regular class teacher, should address these overt behaviors within the objectives of the student's IEP.

Behavior reflecting a developmental stage refers to behavior typical of a certain developmental or age level. For example, all teachers expect second-grade students to behave impulsively at times; however, they may become upset when sixth-graders act the same way. Knowing what behaviors are usual for a certain development level helps teachers overlook them. In addition, teachers need to know that some students with disabilities develop at a slower rate than nondisabled students and that developmental norms may vary among students with disabilities. For example, a student with mild retardation will develop mentally at one half to three fourths the rate of a student with normal intellectual capabilities. Developmentally, the student with retardation at age 10 would not function in the same ways as an average student at the same age. A nondisabled child usually will pass through the impulsive developmental level by Grade 5, but the student with a disability at Grade 6 may not have left it behind. Once teachers understand developmental differences, they can more easily tolerate a variety of behaviors.

Interventions for Misbehaviors

In other situations, the teacher cannot permit or overlook certain behaviors in the classroom. At these times, the teacher needs a systematic plan for intervening with the inappropriate behavior. Long and Newman (1980) discuss techniques they found to be successful in interventions with surface behaviors. These techniques can be used on a daily basis. The trick is to match the correct technique with the surface behavior and employ it immediately when the behavior occurs.

Planned Ignoring
A simple technique that requires little training but a great deal of patience is planned ignoring (Figure 5.1). Research psychologists refer to this technique as extinction, that is, eliminating a behavior by ignoring it. Planned ignoring means the teacher immediately rewards students when they act appropriately, and totally ignores students as long as they behave inappropriately. But the teacher must be patient. When a behavior that was previously rewarded with attention is suddenly ignored, the inappropriate behavior usually increases before it decreases. This occurs because the student cannot understand why the teacher is not paying attention to a behavior that has always elicited a response, albeit a negative one. Teachers should keep calm, grit their teeth if necessary, and wait for the appropriate behavior. An example of this technique is a teacher ignoring a student pulling on the teacher's clothing for attention. Ignoring the behavior will cause the student to stop.

Signal Interference
In signal interference, teachers use a nonverbal signal to let a student know that they see the inappropriate behavior occurring or about to occur (Figure 5.2). For examples, a teacher may use hand gestures to say, "Be quiet," "Sit

Figure 5.1
Planned Ignoring

Figure 5.2
Signal Interference

down," "Come here," or "Give it to me." Teachers may also snap their fingers, use eye gestures, flick the light switch, or turn their backs to the group. Frequently, by using the technique of signal interference, teachers can stop the inappropriate behavior, or better yet, never let it start.

Proximity Control

Teachers can use proximity control—and never interrupt the lesson—merely by moving close to the student exhibiting inappropriate behavior (Figure 5.3). Often a teacher need only stand near the student or place a hand on the student's shoulder. This technique has a calming effect on some students and helps maintain control without interrupting the current activity.

Defusing Tension Through Humor

This technique employs humor to defuse a potentially explosive situation. For example, one teacher could have used humor during story time on Halloween.

Figure 5.3
Proximity Control

Figure 5.4
Defusing Tension Through Humor

The teacher was reading a book about witches to a class of kindergarten students (Figure 5.4). One bright young boy looked up at the teacher and said, "You are a witch, aren't you?" The teacher immediately slammed the book down and had all the students return to their seats and put their heads on the desk for 15 minutes. Instead, if the teacher had laughed and replied, "And you should see how fast I can ride my broom!" she would have eliminated the problem, and the story time would have gone uninterrupted.

Support for Routine

A simple but effective technique for young children and students with mild disabilities involves providing support for the student's routine (Figure 5.5). Displaying a chart in a special place on the board to show the week's or day's schedule provides security for the student. Then, the teacher can announce in advance whenever schedules need to change and what the new schedules will be. Such preparation gives the student consistency and avoids problems like the following. The school nurse appears at the door of a first-grade class and tells all the children to line up. A little boy begins to cry and nothing can calm him. At last the nurse says, "I'm only going to check your eyes." The young lad replies, "But I thought you were going to give me a shot!" Advance preparation for the change in the routine can prevent anxiety and save the teacher as well as the class from disruption.

Figure 5.5
Support for Routine

Interest Boosting

This technique involves taking an interest in the student who may be off-task or on the verge of acting-out. Walk up to the student and mention one of the student's hobbies or interests. After a brief conversation, walk away. Often the student will go back to work and the inappropriate behavior will not recur. Sometimes a student may become interested in only one aspect of a lesson or a topic unrelated to the lesson. The teacher can use interest boosting to channel the student's interest and get the student back to work. For example, a fourth-grade class was studying prehistoric animals when one young student, becoming fascinated with dinosaurs, would not attend to any other class assignments. The teacher, realizing the problem, suddenly became greatly interested in dinosaurs and decided to do a unit on dinosaurs, placing the fascinated student in charge of the unit. The student could work on the dinosaur topic only during a selected period of the day and after other work was completed. Thus, interest boosting encouraged the distracted student to learn more, but allowed the teacher to maintain the day's structure (Figure 5.6).

Figure 5.6
Interest Boosting

Removing Distracting Objects

Many a well-planned and well-intentioned lesson has gone astray because the teacher failed to remove distracting objects from the classroom (Figure 5.7). When using this technique, simply walk up to the student and remove the object from the desk or the student's hand. Or, begin the lesson by saying, "I see some very tempting objects on some desks. I don't want to be tempted to stop our lesson to play with them, so please remove the objects when I count to three." The time teachers invest in removing such objects takes away instructional time.

Antiseptic Bouncing

Antiseptic bouncing requires that the teacher remove the student from the class for a limited amount of time or until the inappropriate behavior diminishes (Figure 5.8). A teacher may ask the student with uncontrollable giggles, for example, to run an errand or get a drink of water. Once the student completes the task, the inappropriate behavior usually will stop.

BEHAVIOR MANAGEMENT TECHNIQUES

When the mainstreamed student is the source of a classroom management problem, the teacher tries to prevent disruptive behavior through planning.

Figure 5.7
Removing Distracting Objects

Teachers need to understand surface behaviors and simple ways to deal with them. Sometimes, however, teachers need to know about more complex behavior management processes. According to Sulzer-Azaroff & Mayer (1977), teachers should implement a behavior management process when the student makes several independent requests for assistance, the student behaves differently from the comparison group, or the student's behavior dramatically changes. If any of these conditions exist, the teacher should first identify the target behavior.

Identifying Target Behaviors

Teachers identify target behaviors as those clearly needing change, but such behaviors must be explicitly defined, observed, and measured so that individuals administering the program agree that the behaviors are detrimental to the student's social or academic development. When defining a target behavior, the teacher must refer to observable, unambiguous characteristics. For example, to state that Bobby misbehaves in class or that Joy is not doing well in science

Figure 5.8
Antiseptic Bouncing

neither provides measurable data nor defines a specific behavior. However, by stating that Bobby hits the other students in class, grabs their paper and pencils, and throws spitballs across the room, the teacher identifies and lets everyone know exactly what behavior needs modifying. Similarly, by saying that Joy is failing science, has difficulty grasping fifth-grade concepts, cannot take class notes, and cannot focus on the important points of the lesson, the teacher pinpoints Joy's specific behavior weakness.

After clearly defining the target behavior, the teacher must record or count how often the behavior occurs. Recording target behaviors is necessary initially to determine the extent to which the target behavior occurs and later to evaluate the effectiveness of the technique used to change the target behavior. Once teachers establish that a student's behavior needs to be changed or modified, they can implement a behavior management program.

The teacher should become familiar with several behavior management techniques and select one best suited for the student. Many articles in the education field describe various behavior management techniques. A few of the more common techniques are positive reinforcement, token economy, contingency contracting, and free time.

Positive Reinforcement

Most people feel good when someone says, "Gee, you look nice today" or when they get paid or when they overhear a compliment. Educators call such examples *positive reinforcement*. Positive reinforcement means giving a reward to increase or maintain a behavior. In the classroom, for example, a teacher smiles at the student who has satisfactorily completed an assignment or compliments a student on sharing nicely with a neighbor. When using positive reinforcement, teachers must be sure they have chosen the appropriate reinforcer, because what reinforces one student may not reinforce another. One way to find out what reinforces a student is to ask. In fact, some teachers develop a reinforcement menu for every student in their class. The teacher has a card indicating all the items each student finds reinforcing. When it becomes obvious that a student has tired of a specific reinforcer, the teacher replaces it with another one. Students can even complete an interest inventory (Table 5.2) so that the teacher knows what reinforces the student. Teachers can also observe students closely to find out what to use. Regardless of the selection method, teachers must learn what type of reinforcer works the best for each student.

Reinforcers fall into three major categories: social reinforcers, tangible reinforcers, and activity reinforcers. Teachers should use tangible or activity reinforcers initially with a student and ultimately strive to transfer to a social reinforcer. Since society basically functions on social reinforcement, such as praise for a job well done or a smile of acknowledgement, students need to learn to perform tasks related to their jobs or behave in a socially acceptable manner without tangible or activity reinforcements. However, teachers should use tangible or activity rewards when beginning a behavior management program. Examples

Table 5.2
Student Interest Inventory

These are the things I like:

My favorite school subject is _____

The best reward anyone could give me is _____

Three of my favorite things are:

    1. _____

    2. _____

    3. _____

My favorite TV show is _____

I do not like to do _____

Three things I would like to have are:

    1. _____

    2. _____

    3. _____

Three places I would to go to are:

    1. _____

    2. _____

    3. _____

Tangible Reinforcement: "Pencil Mate"

Materials: pencil
5-inch pompom made from yarn or purchased felt
(for hands, feet, nose, and mouth)
glue
movable eyes
scissors

Instructions:
1. Make a hole through center of pompom.
2. Cut felt to make hands, feet, nose, and mouth.
3. Glue appendages to the pompom.
4. On back of pompom, attach a note about student.
5. Mount figure on the pencil.

Use of Reinforcement: Tell students they will receive a "Pencil Mate" after
they complete a specific assignment. If their progress
continues, they may take the pompom home to show
their family.

Figure 5.9

of the three groups of reinforcers and suggestions for rewards in each group
follow:

- **Social**—Verbal, physical, or gestured stimulus with purpose of increasing
  or maintaining behavior:
    Getting praise from the teacher, getting a smile, getting personal time
    with the teacher, playing with a classmate of own choice, getting a
    pat on the back, sitting next to the teacher at lunch
- **Tangible or Token**—Tangible item given for performance of specified
  target behavior:
    Checkmarks, points, happy faces, stars, stickers, rubber stamp marks,
    balloons, award buttons, award slips, magazines

Tangible Reinforcement:	"My Pencil Warmer"
Materials:	Styrofoam cone (3-inch diameter) felt (for arms, feet, buttons, and hat) cardboard pompom made from yarn, or purchased scissors glue tinfoil two-sided tape hole puncher thread and needle
Instructions:	1. Press a pencil into cone to form pencil holder. 2. Fit a piece of tinfoil into hole to secure. 3. Cover entire cone with felt. 4. Cut feet, arms, and buttons out of remaining felt. 5. Attach pompom to cone with needle and thread. 6. Make hat out of cardboard. 7. Cover hat with felt. 8. Glue arms, feet, buttons, and hat to cone.
Use of Reinforcement:	This pencil warmer is attached to a child's pencil at the beginning of the day. It may be taken away for a short period of time for inappropriate behavior.

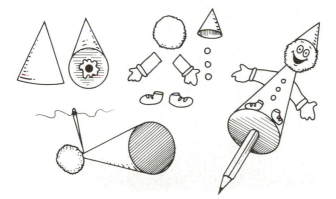

Figure 5.10

- **Activity**—Activities earned for appropriate behavior:
    Dot-to-dot pictures, word games, crossword puzzles, coloring books, getting free time, bingo, art activities, field trips, frisbees, reading with a friend, watching a film, watching TV, time in the library, playing teacher, extra time to complete homework

Figures 5.9 through 5.20 (pp. 140–150) provide samples of art for children that may be used as tangible reinforcers.

Tangible Reinforcement: "The Key to Success"

Materials: poster board of different colors
yarn or string
markers

Instructions:
1. Draw various sizes and shapes of keys on the poster board.
2. Write each child's name on a key. On other keys, write phrases such as " _____ minutes of free time," "this can be traded for _____ ," or "you are the owner of _____ ."
3. Give each child a key.
4. From yarn or string, let them make key rings.

Use of Reinforcement: During the day children can earn keys for appropriate academic/social behavior. They may collect their free time at the end of each day by turning in their keys.

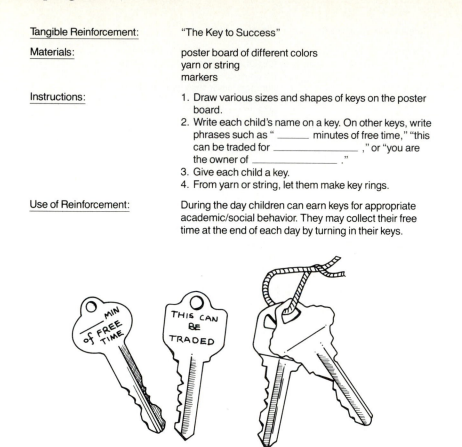

Figure 5.11

After target behaviors have been identified and measured, and the appropriate type of reinforcer selected, the implementation of a positive program should follow these guidelines: select appropriate reinforcements for the student; reinforce only those behaviors that need changing, modifying, or increasing; reinforce the appropriate behavior *immediately*; reinforce the desired behavior each time it occurs; once the student has learned, changed, or modified a behavior, reinforce only *intermittently* (i.e., on an alternating basis); if using a tangible or activity reinforcement, apply a social reinforcer simultaneously; and withdraw the tangible or activity reward slowly and keep reinforcing the student's behavior with social rewards. It is important to use immediate, continuous, and consistent reinforcement when a behavior is being learned.

Tangible Reinforcement: "Leader of the Pack" Bookmark

Materials: poster board paper
scissors
glitter, sequins, etc.

Instructions: Design different bookmarks for the students to use
or keep.

Use of Reinforcement: Give a bookmark to a student reading when not required
to do so. Use it for a student who returns a library book
and can answer questions about the book.

Figure 5.12

<u>Tangible Reinforcement:</u>	"Finger Puppet"
<u>Materials:</u>	heavy felt
	scissors
	needle and thread or yarn
	movable eyes
<u>Instructions:</u>	1. Cut two pieces of felt in the shape of a finger (about 3 inches by 1½ inches).
	2. Stitch together with thread of the same color.
	3. Glue on two eyes and draw a face with a permanent marker. Add hair made of yarn, if you wish.
<u>Use of Reinforcement:</u>	Each child gets a puppet in the morning. A student may lose the puppet for 5 minutes for inappropriate or disruptive behavior.

Figure 5.13

Tangible Reinforcement: "Shining Star"

Materials: poster board
bright, colored felt
glitter

Instructions:
1. Cut out stars from poster board (3 or 4 inches wide).
2. Cut felt using the poster board for a pattern.
3. Glue together.
4. If desired, put glue around edges and sprinkle with glitter.

Use of Reinforcement: The stars can be given or pinned to those children exhibiting behaviors such as "Star Pupil," "Top Dog," "Excellent Work." These can be taken home or worn as a necklace.

Figure 5.14

Tangible Reinforcement:	"Squiggly"
Materials:	yarn movable eyes
Instructions:	1. Crochet or chain stitch a small circle and a long chain stitch for a tail. 2. Glue eyes on.
Use of Reinforcement:	"Squiggly" can keep children company at their desks if they are in their seats when needed. It can be tied to a pencil or put around a wrist and then taken home at the end of the week.

Figure 5.15

Tangible Reinforcement:	"Everybody Loves a Clown"
Materials:	Popsicle sticks white construction paper Magic Markers
Instructions:	1. Cut out patterns of clown on construction paper and decorate. 2. Glue to Popsicle stick with child's name or behavior written on it.
Use of Reinforcement:	Display the clown in the room and let children take it home at the end of the day to share with the family.

Figure 5.16

146

Figure 5.17

Figure 5.18

Figure 5.19

Figure 5.20

Token Economy

A token is a tangible item given to the student for performing a specified target behavior. It has no intrinsic value, but acquires value when exchanged for a material reinforcer or reinforcing event. For example, a paycheck has no intrinsic value until a person cashes it in for money. And after the cash is received it is often exchanged for material items or reinforcing events.

Figure 5.21 shows the eight steps necessary to implement a *token economy* system within the classroom. As in any behavior management program, the first step involves identifying the target behavior. Once the behavior is identified, the student must understand what behavior must be exhibited to receive the tokens. Additionally, the teacher must clearly explain the tokens and what they may be exchanged for. The student should be capable of performing the desired behavior; otherwise, the token system will be marked for failure before it is initiated. The teacher can record the desired behavior on a wall chart or on a small chart on the student's desk. For younger students, draw pictures of the desired behavior on the charts. For secondary level students, who may resent having behaviors recorded on a wall chart, the teacher can respect their privacy by listing behaviors in a small reward book.

The teacher must then select the back-up reinforcers for which the tokens will be exchanged. Back-up reinforcers may be small toys, candy, privileges, special activities. The reinforcer must appeal to the student. Teacher and student may choose an appropriate back-up reinforcer together. When the token system involves more than one student, the teacher should have a variety of back-up reinforcers. The student needs to clearly understand what a token is, how many tokens have to be earned before receiving the back-up reinforcer, when the reinforcer will be received, and how the number of tokens will be recorded. The teacher should explain the rules of the system and ask the students to explain them to ensure their understanding.

A well-designed token system will allow the teacher to gradually withdraw material reinforcers and replace them with social reinforcement. An effective token system should be implemented simply, function well, and not distract from the instructional process. The teacher should evaluate the token system's effectiveness and, as with any technique, change it when it loses its effectiveness.

Contingency Contracts

With a *contingency contract*, a student and teacher agree to accomplish a specific objective. Contracts formally apply "Grandma's Law": "You get to do what you want to do after you do what I want you to do." To set up a contract, the teacher and student should choose the behavior, task, or skill to work on; agree on how many times the behavior should occur or how long the student should spend on the task; determine how long the contract should be in effect; decide what the reinforcer should be if the student successfully completes the task;

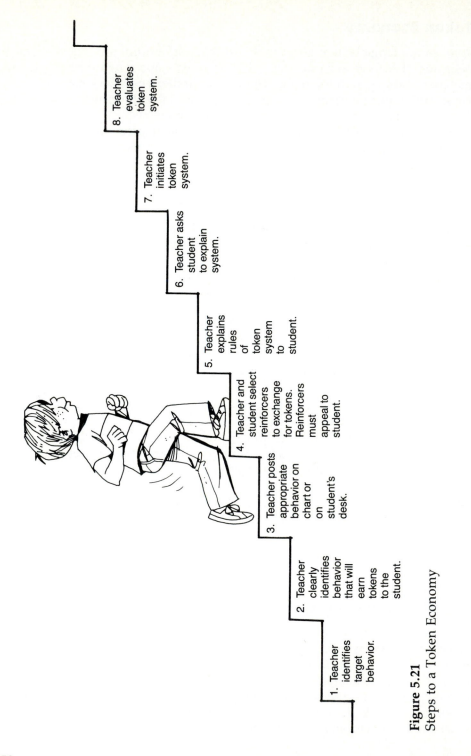

Figure 5.21
Steps to a Token Economy

1. Teacher identifies target behavior.

2. Teacher clearly identifies behavior that will earn tokens to the student.

3. Teacher posts appropriate behavior on chart or on student's desk.

4. Teacher and student select reinforcers to exchange for tokens. Reinforcers must appeal to student.

5. Teacher explains rules of token system to student.

6. Teacher asks student to explain system.

7. Teacher initiates token system.

8. Teacher evaluates token system.

and sign the contract. Consequences of the contract should be realistic and understood—students should know what to expect if they meet the criteria of the contract and what to expect if they do not. Whether or not students meet the contract's criteria, they and the teacher should eventually evaluate the contract and decide if a new one is needed.

Contracts are fun to develop and design, and students should assist the teacher in designing and developing them. Contracting works well in mainstreamed classes because contracts provide students with mild disabilities with structure—they know what is expected of them socially and academically. Also, the contract provides a visual and ongoing progress report for the mainstreamed student. Most important, the regular and special education teachers can develop the contract together, providing a bridge between two classrooms for the mainstreamed student.

Free Time

Free time is the time given to students as a reward for successfully completing their assignments or for doing something special. The student may use the free time to work on an art project, listen to a record, go to the library, or simply sit at the desk and choose an activity. The key phrase in the definition is "for successfully completing their assignments." Students must earn free time. Teachers using free time should designate special areas in the room for it; place varied activities on different instructional levels in the free-time areas; remember that activities too difficult for students are not rewards; and explain how the students can earn the free-time privileges. Teachers may also want to try the following ideas for free time: use movable screens to divide the areas, making special places for the students; place an old-fashioned bathtub filled with pillows, books, and magazines in the back of the classroom; take the door off a closet and place a large bean bag in it for free-time reading; use pieces of carpet for magic rides to free time; have areas for boys only and for girls only; provide free-time art areas; provide popular free-time game areas; select one of the student's friends to share the free-time area; provide free-time library passes; and allow 10 minutes at the end of each period for free-time winners.

SUMMARY

By being aware that the teacher sets the tone for a positive behavioral environment and using simple surface management techniques, teachers continue to establish an environment that is *risk-free* for students. By looking at classroom management as a total process, not just as handling students' behavioral problems, teachers can cope with any problems that do occur. The last component within this section is the physical environment.

CHAPTER SIX

Adapting the Physical Environment

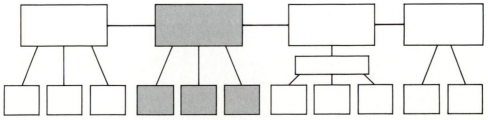

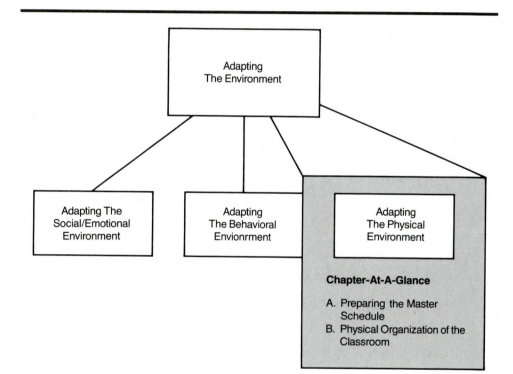

Teachers instruct students within the tightly woven framework of the school day. For harmonious and structured management, schools design the school day around the various types of schedules and physical arrangements. This framework affects students and teachers because it affects types of subjects, class sizes, resources, students' choice of subjects, and the educational program's philosophy. Schedules and physical environments vary in different schools, districts, and states. Regardless of the framework used, however, educators want to be able to adapt it to make instruction easier and more productive.

After teachers assess the needs of students with mild disabilities and those at risk for school success, they prepare to teach. As discussed in Chapters 4 and 5, teachers must first prepare the socio-emotional and behavioral environments for successful learning to take place. In addition, they must properly prepare the physical environment. This chapter presents ideas and strategies for doing so. Although not inclusive, the ideas presented here emphasize the importance of preparing the physical environment before teaching. The components of this chapter include scheduling of educators and suggestions for the physical organization of the classroom.

PREPARING THE MASTER SCHEDULE

Schools organize the parts of a school day according to a master schedule. The soundness of this schedule determines the effectiveness of administrative detail, plant facilities, instruction, and overall school organization.

Both special and regular educators need a working knowledge of the school's master schedule. Special teachers need to understand the administrative framework of the school's schedule to place the mainstreamed student appropriately; regular classroom teachers need input into selecting the types and degrees of disabilities they will need to prepare for; and both can suggest minor changes that will prevent major mainstreaming problems.

Because elementary schools have self-contained grade units, with only occasional class changes for specific academic subjects such as reading or math, their master schedules are less complex than those of secondary schools. Many elementary schools function with heterogeneous grouping within each class, while some use the homogeneous grouping methods, such as having classes within one grade level grouped around students of similar ability and achievement. Elementary schools usually schedule art, music, and other such subjects on a weekly revolving basis.

Many elementary schools schedule the language arts and math blocks in the morning. Allowing students with mild disabilities to float in and out of the block provides appropriate instruction and allows more time for other subjects. For example, a language arts block running for $2\frac{1}{2}$ hours may contain reading, spelling, and grammar skills sections. In such a case, the special student should be able to attend the spelling and grammar skills sections in the regular classroom and attend reading in the resource room. Planning these blocks of time with the resource teacher before designing the elementary master schedule helps keep the daily schedule running smoothly.

At the secondary level, planning the master schedule becomes more difficult and, as a result, placing students with mild disabilities appropriately presents greater problems. The principal usually has the ultimate responsibility of preparing the master schedule; however, the guidance counselor or other individuals may do much of the actual planning. Whoever schedules special students should consult the special education teacher and the mainstreaming regular teacher before the master schedule is finished.

Basic Types of Master Schedules

Master schedules can be classified into two basic types, conventional or traditional and flexible. Most American secondary schools use the conventional approach to master schedule planning. This type of schedule arranges the school day into five to seven instructional periods, each lasting from 40 to 55 minutes, with allotments for lunch period and special arrangements for assemblies. The flexible approach to scheduling is slowly replacing this traditional schedule. Philosophically, the flexible approach permits the educator to exercise more control over the day's events. The flexible schedule moves away from five to seven straight blocks of time and provides more creative ways of using the school day, such as having extended first periods, rotating class days, or making a schedule change each week.

Methods of Scheduling Within the Master Schedule

Once a school decides on a master schedule, it must place students within it. Schools usually use one of three types: computer scheduling, self-scheduling, or hand scheduling. No matter what kind of schedule administrators choose, the special and regular mainstreaming educators should provide input into class selection for the student with disabilities. According to Wood (1989), hand scheduling is the most common method used; and 81% of regular educators and 93% of special education teachers report that they assist in the scheduling process for special students.

Computer Scheduling

Because a computer can carry the work load of many staff members, numerous schools have changed to computerized master scheduling. With the ability to store a large number of parameters in the computer's memory, this method assists administrators with processing and by rapid printing of individual students' schedules.

Even though computerized scheduling handles large school populations efficiently, most programs currently available present problems in scheduling mainstreamed students. For example, computerized scheduling prohibits the school from selecting particular regular teachers to work with mainstreamed students. It also makes grouping students with mild disabilities into particular resource classes or regular classes virtually impossible. In addition, the computer makes it especially difficult to meet the individual needs of special students. For example, it may not be flexible enough to schedule the student into morning rather than afternoon sections, alternate required courses with electives, or provide resource for academic relief.

Self-scheduling

A number of schools let students self-schedule all classes within the master schedule. Even though numerous schools succeed using the self-scheduling method, problems do occur. Kelly (1979) surveyed approximately 700 students to determine which variables most influenced them during scheduling. The students named parents, friends, counselors, teachers, and written information as variables, ranking parents as the most influential variable in self-scheduling. Kelly recommended that schools change pre-registration advising to coincide with parental and peer advice; change written materials; make self-scheduling procedures more rigid; and consider self-scheduling for juniors and computer scheduling for freshmen and sophomores.

Kelly failed, however, to identify other problems inherent in self-scheduling, such as class overcrowding, popularity differences among teachers, and the percentage of students selecting inappropriate classes. Most important, Kelly omitted the self-scheduling of the special student from his survey. If a school uses self-scheduling, teachers must consider the placement of the student with mild disabilities carefully and use the following suggestions to make the process go more smoothly. First, a resource teacher should be familiar with the overall master plan and the scheduling of all classes. In addition, each student with mild disabilities should be assigned to a resource teacher during the self-scheduling process. The school might impose some limitations on special students. For example, the school might designate the resource period or choose specific regular teachers to teach such students, leaving the students with only the option of period selection. Finally, the school should give students with mild disabilities a checklist of required courses before registration.

Hand Scheduling

Many of America's schools design the master schedule by having an administrator place the components of the school's day into the master plan by hand. Even though hand scheduling is a frustrating, tedious, and time-consuming job, it is the most efficient way to schedule the mainstreamed student. Whatever scheduling method a school uses, it should hand schedule all special needs students into the master plan.

Students with disabilities need a great deal of individual attention, much of which is mandated by the IEP. Selecting appropriate classes for the student with mild disabilities requires much attention. Whoever schedules the special student must consider the personality of the student, the personality of the teacher, and existing conflicts between students. Potential problems can be avoided through hand scheduling.

Hand scheduling also allows administrators to select one or two teachers to serve as the home base for the special needs student. Such an arrangement allows the regular and special class teachers more time together to prepare instruction. If a school has selected a team teaching model, hand scheduling also allows for closer grouping of students for whom special education teachers need to provide consultation or teaming with regular teachers. At the same time, hand scheduling allows the scheduler to select teachers who understand that students learn through different modes, at different rates, and with different strategies. On the other hand, hand scheduling allows regular classroom teachers to say which types of special students they feel more adequate teaching. By carefully selecting a common core of teachers to serve all mainstreamed students, the scheduler reduces the number of teachers with whom a resource teacher has to communicate. Also, when a common core of regular teachers serves one grade level of mainstreamed students, the scheduler can plan common off-periods to allow for greater collaboration among teachers. Finally, hand scheduling can also reduce the number of resource teachers with whom the regular teacher must communicate and thus reduce the regular teacher's paperwork.

Some disadvantages exist with the use of hand scheduling for mainstreamed students even though they are outweighed by the advantages. For example, hand scheduling costs more time, money, and staff effort. The students' schedules and class rolls for the teachers must be typed, and both the scheduling and the typing must be done in the summer. Also, staff members should complete the hand scheduling of mainstreamed students before they schedule regular students.

Specific Considerations in Scheduling

After a school decides which type of master schedule to use for adapting the mainstreamed student's learning environment, it must try to avoid specific scheduling problems. Table 6.1 provides a checklist for avoiding such problems. Teachers and administrators should note that most planning problems can be avoided if all groups keep the lines of communication open.

The following suggestions, although not appropriate for every school's situation, give schools and teachers specific guidelines that will improve the outcome of preparing the master schedule.

1. Maintain manageable class size in resource class.
2. Place resource students taking the same course with the same mainstream teachers.
3. Group students in each resource class by grade or ability levels. For example, four students who read poorly and need extra help, but are scattered among three 8th-grade classes, should be in the same resource class.
4. Include special education teachers in the preparation of the school's master schedule so that they can prevent scheduling problems and represent special students' needs.
5. Schedule off-periods for special education teachers around the resource schedules of special students.

Table 6.1
Checklist: Avoiding Problems in Planning Master Schedule For Students With Mild Disabilities

	Yes	No
1. Include resource classes on the master schedule as a regular class offering.	___	___
2. Obtain input from resource teacher about:		
• Student groupings desired (ability and personality);	___	___
• Selection of regular teachers, especially teachers to be avoided; and	___	___
• Other individual needs of mildly disabled students.	___	___
3. Obtain input from regular teachers about categories of students desired.	___	___
4. Obtain input from counselors or teachers about peers to be separated from one another because of discipline problems.	___	___
5. Obtain input from counselors or teachers about peers to be scheduled together for purpose of tutoring or assistance.	___	___
6. Obtain input from resource teacher about possible conflicts between student's request and IEP.	___	___

6. Schedule one-period elective offerings concurrently.
7. Select effective regular education teachers who are successful in working with special needs and at-risk children to serve as home-base teachers.
8. Notify regular education teachers when schedules are complete so that they have time to select materials and prepare individual assignments.
9. Balance sections throughout the day. (If courses are taught on different levels, sections should be available in the morning as well as the afternoon.)
10. Plan morning sections for vocational students, co-op students, and athletes.
11. Alternate academic courses with basic and college preparatory sections.
12. Match student's learning style and teacher's teaching style.
13. Schedule common planning periods for regular education teachers and resource teachers.
14. Provide a balance in class size in home-base classes.
15. Provide basic instruction to primary level students in the morning.
16. Use hand scheduling for resource students.
17. Allow all teachers who will serve as home-base teachers or special education teachers to help plan the schedule collectively to encourage their feeling of ownership.

In the process of preparing a master schedule, planners should consider the needs of regular education teachers. If possible, schools should offer teachers incentives for their willingness to serve special needs students and those at risk.

Administrators, curriculum supervisors, and directors of special education should first identify the potentially good regular teachers by their ability, positive attitude toward the special student, enthusiasm, and concern for the self-concepts of students. To give needed praise and reinforcement, they should include those teachers on committees to develop future changes and make them a part of the decision-making process; lighten their class loads and exempt them from other duty assignments; select them to attend conferences or workshops at the expense of the school district; and ask them to serve as ongoing inservice trainers to assist other teachers in deciding what help to give special needs students.

No matter what type of master schedule a school chooses, it must build some flexibility into that schedule for the benefit of students with mild disabilities and the teachers who work with them.

Problems and Suggested Solutions In Scheduling

Over one half of educators feel that problems are created when students with disabilities move back and forth between the regular class setting and the resource setting (Wood, 1989). These problems occur in three areas: (a) transition concerns after the initial identification of a disabling condition; (b) transition concerns as students move back and forth between the resource class and the regular class (home base); and (c) instructional or class-transitional problems related to transition within the regular education class. The physical environment for a student can be disrupted if a smooth transition is not a reality. Tables 6.2 through 6.4 (pp. 161–163) present examples of problems with suggested solutions for each of these areas of concern.

Scheduling Within the Resource Setting

Although the regular class setting is the placement choice for most students with mild disabilities, numerous special students must, for instructional purposes, go to the resource setting. The resource room has become a viable alternative to self-contained placements for educating the student with mild disabilities in the least restrictive environment. Presently, schools use numerous variations on the resource room model. D'Alonzo, D'Alonzo, and Mauser (1979) describe the five basic types of resource rooms typically found in schools:

1. The *categorical* resource room, which focuses on one primary type of disability.
2. The *cross-categorical* resource room, where clusters of two or more categories of children are grouped.
3. The *noncategorical* resource room, where students with mild or severe learning and behavior disabilities are serviced with the possible inclusion of nondisabled students.

Table 6.2
Transition Concerns After Initial Identification of Disabling Condition

Problem	Suggested Solutions
Student does not want to go to a resource setting.	• Talk with the student concerning focus, questions, needs. • Explain *why* the student is going to the resource class. • Slowly phase the student into the new setting. • Assign a "special student" peer to answer questions. • Review concerns after first visit. • If the student does not respond positively, evaluate the situation and consider consultation services.
Student does not want to leave a self-contained or partial resource setting to go to the regular class setting.	• Talk with the student concerning fears, questions, needs. • Explain the "reality" of the new classroom prior to placement. • Explain *why* the student is going to the regular class. • Slowly phase the student into the new setting. • Complete the checklist for rules and routines with the student (Figure 4.1, pp. 109–111). • Stay in close contact with the student after placement. • Assign a regular class "buddy."
Initial transition from resource to regular setting is difficult	• Talk with the student to develop a clearer understanding of the problem. • Talk to the teacher to obtain a different or second view of problem. • Go over the checklist (Figure 4.1) with the student. • Assign a "buddy."
Student feels lack of support during the initial change.	• Always have a scheduled time to visit with the student. • Provide a "bonding" teacher for the student. • Regular and special teachers should work closely together to discuss progress or problems. • Develop a mainstreaming checklist to be used periodically.

Note. From Wood, J. W. 1991. *Project SHARE* Richmond, VA: Author.

Table 6.3
Transition Concerns As Students Move Back and Forth Between Resource
Class and Regular Education Class (Home Base)

Problem	Suggested Solutions
Student takes too much time traveling to room assignments.	• Check to see if sufficient time is allotted. • Provide a core of teachers in one area of building to cut traveling to a minimum. • Assign resource teacher to a certain number of grades and locate the resource class within that grade cluster. • Talk to students to see if they have an answer to the problem. • Assign a "buddy" if the student approves.
Student is always late to resource/regular class.	• Check to see if the student is embarrassed about going *into* the special class. • Provide an alternate plan that alleviates the embarrassment. • Allow the student to return to the locker with a pass after checking into the class.
Student cannot cope with activity in the hallways.	• Allow the student to travel between bells/periods. • Allow the student to go to next class a minute or so before the bell.
The special and regular classes are too far apart.	• Do not isolate special education classes. • Allow extra time for the student to reduce the stress of rushing.
Movement of children during classes is disruptive to the regular class.	• Movement should be made between periods/bells. • Have the student collect materials for the move prior to beginning of class. • Prior to movement, seat the special student close to class door.
Teachers cannot keep track of individual students.	• Provide a seating chart of class. • Write into the lesson plan who will leave and when they will leave.

Note. From Wood, J. W. 1991. *Project SHARE*. Richmond, VA: Author.

4. The *specific skills* resource room, where a specific curriculum area or deficit (e.g., reading, mathematics) is targeted.
5. The *itinerant* resource room, which is a mobile nonstationary resource environment that travels to the geographic area when and where the specialized education services are needed (pp. 91–92).

Table 6.4

Instructional/Class Transitional Problems Related to Transition Within Regular Education Class (Home base)

Problem	Suggested Solutions
Student is unable to cope with changes when entering the room after returning from resource class.	• Have an assigned seat so the student will know immediately where to go. • Have an assignment on the desk for the student. • Assign a "buddy" to work with the student. • Move close to the student to signal reassurance. • Have a specific schedule for the student.
Teacher has difficulty integrating students back into the curriculum when they reenter the room.	• As soon as the student enters the class, review for the whole class what you are doing and where you are—a checkpoint for the lesson. • If taking notes, provide a carbon copy for the student. • Use a lecture outline to orientate the student. • Use a "buddy." • Have a constant class structure.
Student forgets to bring the proper textbooks, homework, materials to class.	• Provide folders for each student in which to keep papers that are often lost. • Provide a checklist for the student for materials needed. • Place this checklist on the locker door or in front of the text notebook.
Special needs student has difficulty functioning in groups.	• Assign a peer "buddy." • Keep groups small. • Assign a specific task that is appropriate academically and socially for the student. • Provide a checklist of activities or expectations.
Student needs to be excused from certain class projects, assignments.	• Be clear with the regular teacher about what the student should be excused from. For example, do not count off for spelling for a student who has difficulty with or a disability in spelling. • Provide alternative or more appropriate assignments for the student.
Lack of communication between regular and special teachers or lack of time for communication.	• Use a mainstreaming checklist to communicate student progress. • Keep lines of communication open. • Resource teachers should touch base with one another on a regular basis. • Schedule common planning periods.

Table 6.4 *continued*

Problem	Suggested Solutions
Students become frustrated by the regular class subject matter.	• Check as to the appropriateness of the subject matter. • Explain to the teacher that the student may not be on grade level. • Work closely to provide appropriate instructional adaptations. • Be sure that student experiences success.
Regular teacher expresses concern over a different standard and expectation for the special student.	• Realize that all students should have individualized expectations. • Help teachers to see that expectations that are too high do not best serve the student. • Provide support for the teacher in helping them with the ''how-to's'' of working with the special student.
Special students cannot complete assigned work in the time allotted.	• Check to see if the work is appropriate for the student's functional level. • Provide additional time. • Reduce the *amount* of work. • Realize that all students cannot do the same amount of work.
Different teacher expectations pose a problem to the special student.	• Make a list of each period with each teacher's expectations for the student. Figure 4.1 may be helpful. • Help students understand expectations. • Help teachers coordinate expectations. • Check to see that expectations are reasonable.
Student has difficulty in performing on grade level.	• Realize that in reality many students do not perform on the grade level where they are placed. • Individualize for each student. • Provide appropriate adaptations for each student.
Regular class teacher feels overworked with the range of functional levels within the class.	• Provide the teacher with adaptations for group instruction, such as graphic organizers. • Team teach or co-teach with the regular teacher. • Help develop adaptations for the teacher.
Special student is unable to get along with regular students.	• Develop school-related social skills for the student. • Evaluate the problem to see the true source. • Work with the regular student if necessary. • Teach coping skills to the special student. • Work out a coping plan.

Table 6.4 *continued*

Problem	Suggested Solutions
Groups/class lesson is already in session when the special student arrives.	• Have a constant class structure so student upon reentry will know what to expect. • Do a "lesson checkup" and review what you have covered and where you are. • Use a lecture outline and refer to the outline to orientate the student. • Provide a "buddy."
Student misses work from the regular class when attending the resource class.	• Do not hold the student accountable for work missed, especially if it is for a whole period, such as a science class. • Provide a set of class notes. • Tape-record the section that was missed. • Remember that the student identified for special help cannot function as the average student. Consequently, the student will have great difficulty with the classwork when present, and even more difficulty when not present. • Try not to doubly punish the student for having special learning needs.
Student/teacher has difficulty remembering when it is time to go to resource class.	• Never embarrass the student in front of peers by announcing it is time to go to "special education." • Remember that the secondary level student is extremely sensitive about going to a resource setting. • Write on your lesson plan book and on the seating chart the day and time when a student should go to a resource class. • If you realize that it is time for a resource class, quietly remind the student. • Respect a student's need for confidentiality, as this is a concern for the student. • Remember that this may seem so small to an adult and so large to a child.
Special student is embarrassed when entering the regular education class.	• Try to have entry times between bells/periods. • Have a specific task or assignment for the student. • Do not call attention to the student entering the class. • Provide a seat assignment that allows the student to enter the classroom discreetly.

Table 6.4 *continued*

Problem	Suggested Solutions
Regular education teachers display negative attitudes regarding special needs students.	• Try to schedule students into classes where they are wanted. • Provide strong support for the teacher. • Remember that when you see anger, the hidden emotion is fear. • Remember the fear may indicate a feeling of not knowing what to do.
The class pace is too fast for the special needs student.	• Check the class level to see if it is appropriate. • Develop adaptations for the student. • Above all else, work to help the student not be frustrated. • Remember that setting up a student for failure serves no one.
Special student feels unwelcome in regular education class.	• Talk to students about their feelings. • Develop an action plan with the teacher, child, and parent. • Assign a peer "buddy."
Proliferation of specialists serving the student resulting in splintered services and greater scheduling difficulties.	• Carefully plan schedules with children in mind. • Assign specialists by age groups and/or IEP objectives. • Closely monitor the number of times a student is removed. • Refer to the IEP committee if the success of the student is in jeopardy because of our zealousness to serve the child.
Taking special students out of subjects they enjoy or where they experience success, such as art, music, physical education, assembly, to go to resource class.	• Allow special students to attend special subject areas. • Remember that these areas are frequently stress-free and offer opportunities for success. • Arrange resource for a different period on days when special subjects are offered. • Remember that the student who is pulled from a special subject or class is being "punished" for needing special services. • Develop the student's schedule for student's convenience, not the teacher's.

Note. From Wood, J. W. 1991. *Project SHARE.* Richmond, VA: Author.

Resource rooms provide the student with mild disabilities with distinct advantages. Assuming that the teachers have a positive attitude toward mainstreamed students, resource rooms will enhance each student's sense of self-worth. Resource rooms also make it possible for mainstreamed students to build and maintain relationships with nondisabled peers and have nondisabled role and age models. The resource room gives mainstreamed students more opportunities for intentional learning, more provisions for incidental learning (e.g., media, field trips, guest speakers, and group interaction), and more occasions for the resource teacher to reinforce their regular class work. In fact, the resource room model is designed around constant and positive reinforcement and feedback. The resource room also provides the mainstreamed student with additional time for completing class work, homework, or tests; an environment free of anxiety; alternative materials, learning stations, and equipment not available in the regular classroom; and an environment more easily adaptable to special behaviors such as short attention spans and hyperactivity.

According to Hart (1981), scheduling within the resource room, or intraresource scheduling, requires close attention to structure. Children who have limited attention spans, perseverate in their activities, or have difficulty transferring learning from one activity to another can all benefit from a carefully developed schedule. Hart lists three major factors for teachers to consider when developing the resource room schedule.

First, the teacher should present the most difficult subject early in the day while students are fresh. For example, elementary schools commonly schedule reading and language arts during the first time blocks of the day. Secondary schools should also consider placing subjects requiring the most concentration during the morning periods. Second, teachers need to make schedules for resource students consistent so the students can become familiar with the day's events. Teachers should discuss schedule changes, such as a field trip or a guest speaker, with the students before they occur. Third, after students become thoroughly comfortable with the schedule, teachers should deliberately alter the schedule once in a while. In this way, teachers can help their students become more comfortable with change (Hart, 1981, pp. 130–31).

These considerations apply primarily to students who spend a large percentage of the school day in the resource room. But structure in the resource room is also important for those who attend class in a resource setting only occasionally and spend the remainder of their day in the regular academic setting. Such students also need an established routine. For example, a teacher might require students to check their assignment box for the day's activities when they enter the classroom rather than wait for the resource teacher to tell them what to do. Also, students need to keep materials and books in a definite place and maintain separate notebooks for each subject. In addition, they should follow set procedures when completing homework, studying for tests, and taking tests within the resource room. Following a daily routine helps the student, who often feels anxious and frustrated, to develop good work habits and a sense of

Figure 6.1
Examples of Students with Mild Disabilities Scheduled Intraresource

	Student A—Second-Period Resource
9:00–9:10:	Teacher reviews spelling words.
9:10–9:20:	Student studies words.
9:20–9:30:	Teacher calls out words.
9:30–9:50:	Student defines words and writes sentence with each word.
9:50–9:55:	Teacher reviews assignments for next period and homework assignments with student.
	Student B—Third-Period Resource
10:00–10:15:	Teacher explains English homework.
10:15–10:40:	Student works in group with other students on English homework and assignment.
10:40–10:55:	Student works independently at computer station on English exercise.

stability and security. Figure 6.1 offers two examples of mildly disabled students' schedules within the resource room setting.

Scheduling Within the Mainstream

As resource students move into regular classes, teachers must make numerous adjustments in their teaching, and they must adapt the learning environment for those students. A little preparation with the following guidelines will make scheduling within the mainstream flow smoothly.

1. Before beginning a new task, give the mainstreamed student a warning; simply announce to the class or to the mainstreamed student in private that, in 5 minutes, the old assignment will end and a new task will begin.
2. Give instructions in short, direct sentences.
3. List the instructions sequentially on the board.
4. Give a short handout to students so that they will know the expectations for the period.
5. Hand out written assignments, with the expected date of completion noted, at the end of the period.
6. Be sure that the student understands all assignments.
7. Give a copy of the day's schedule and assignments to the resource teacher so that they may be reinforced.

Once teachers have adapted the learning environment through appropriate scheduling, they can turn their attention to the physical organization of their classroom. Slowly, teachers can accommodate the entire instructional process to the mainstreamed student's needs.

PHYSICAL ORGANIZATION OF THE CLASSROOM

When a school system has completed the master schedule, placed all students into the appropriate classes, and carefully looked at any problems resulting from the scheduling process, teachers can then design the physical organization of the classroom in preparation for the instructional process: grouping students, designing the classroom, setting up learning stations, and presenting bulletin boards for incidental and intentional learning.

Grouping for Instruction

Grouping procedures vary from school to school and from teacher to teacher. Many teachers feel that grouping within the classroom creates an even heavier work load. However, children do learn at different rates and, therefore, do not always learn best in one large group. According to Affleck, Lowenbraun, and Archer (1980), because of "the diversity of academic skills found within any regular classroom, small-group instruction is more appropriate than whole-group instruction for basic academic subjects" (p. 152). Suydam (1985) found that in the teaching of mathematics, achievement of students is significantly higher in students who were taught in the individual and team modes as compared to the achievement of students given whole-group instruction. Key variables for the difference were the ability to self- or partner-check and frequent mastery checks.

The issue of class size is much discussed within education today. According to the National Association of Elementary School Principals, a teacher should be assigned no more than 15 students per class up to the third grade for good learning environments. The U.S. Department of Education reports the average teaching load to be approximately 21:1 or 26:1, factoring in all professional staff positions. The State of California reports a 33:1 ratio and in some cases 38:1 to 40:1 (Kelly, 1990). The increases in class size within our schools usually dictate whole-group instruction. However, whole-group instruction does not provide the best benefits to students academically—questions go unattended, easily distracted students remain off-task, and students become lost in the masses. Instruction continues to move along, leaving special needs and at-risk students lost and confused, frequently resulting in their dropping out of school.

The following section describes a variety of ways in which to group students that will assist in individualizing within whole-group situations. The section is divided into general methods of grouping and cooperative learning groups.

Creative Grouping

When teachers group students, labeling occurs. This can present a problem, because no matter what the teacher calls the group, all children know which ones are bright, average, and slow. Because creative grouping allows for a

Figure 6.2
Creative Groups

	Jason	Anna K.	Scott	Valerie	Eddie
Identifies penny, nickel, and dime by name					
Identifies penny, nickel, and dime by value					
Identifies quarter, half-dollar, and dollar by name					
Identifies quarter, half-dollar, and dollar by value					

diversity of academic skills, it eliminates labels and gives students the freedom to move among groups.

Creative grouping may be used at the secondary or elementary level. Teachers set up the groups by academic subjects and then break the subjects into specific objectives or skills. Teachers assign a student to a creative group based on the specific skill that the student needs to work on. No one is locked into a group, because each student moves into another group after mastering the skill. Figure 6.2 presents a creative group in which a student completes a skill, keeps a personal record, and then moves on.

Creative grouping may include at least three variations, all working simultaneously: a learning station, a seat work station, and a small-group instructional station. When class begins, the teacher color codes or numbers the stations and gives each student a direction card or uses a list on the board to indicate the station the student should use first. Remember, a student who masters a given skill can enter a new creative group.

Interest Grouping

Interest grouping is a method of grouping students based on their specific interests. For example, in reading, students may select the same types of books to read. In social studies, students may be interested in the same period of history. These students may be grouped by interest and develop a series of questions, review a specific book, or research a certain period.

Research Grouping

Research groups can be established by giving each group a specific problem to research. Each group then reports back to the class with the results of the research. A checklist may be provided which lists specific research questions to be answered with possible sources to investigate.

Cooperative Learning Groups

Cooperative learning, a worthwhile grouping strategy for heterogeneous student populations, is a method of structuring the class where students work together to achieve a shared academic goal (Schniedewind & Salend, 1987). Students become accountable for their own academic behaviors as well as those of their peers. Although structured procedures for implementing cooperative learning within a class are reported in the literature, teachers may choose to develop the type of structure that best suits their teaching styles and the group's learning style.

Teacher's Role in Cooperative Learning. The teacher's role in developing a cooperative learning environment includes four major areas: decisions, monitoring and intervening, setting tasks and positive interdependence, and evaluating and processing. (Johnson, Johnson, & Holubec, 1987)

First, teachers decide what size of group will be most appropriate for the class and which students will be assigned to each group. The room must be arranged to facilitate group interactions, and all material must be organized and developed. The roles for each group member must be assigned. These roles include a summarizer, who restates the major conclusions or answers at which the group has arrived; a checker, who ensures that all members can explain an answer or conclusion; an accuracy coach, who corrects any mistakes in another member's explanations or summaries; and an elaboration seeker, who asks other members to relate material they previously learned (Johnson & Johnson, 1986, p. 558).

Second, teachers monitor and intervene during the cooperative learning lesson. During this stage, teachers monitor the students' behavior, observing each group member to see what problems are developing. Teachers also provide task assistance, clarify instruction, review important aspects of the lesson, and answer questions. Intervention may become necessary if a teacher sees that a student does not have the collaborative skills needed for working in a group. The teacher also provides closure to the lesson, summarizing major points covered (Johnson & Johnson, 1986).

The third responsibility of the teacher is setting tasks and positive interdependence. Teachers should clearly explain the academic task at hand and the lesson's objectives. Teachers then structure positive goal interdependence, explaining the group goal and the importance of working collaboratively. The accountability of each individual must be structured, maximizing the learning of each group member. The intergroup cooperation for each group must be structured. The criteria for success must be clearly stated and the desired behavior for each group member clearly defined (Johnson & Johnson, 1986).

Fourth, teachers evaluate the learning outcomes for each student as well as how the group functioned as a whole (Johnson & Johnson, 1986). Teachers must be clear about individual and group expectations at the beginning of the activity so that each student will know the desired behavior to try to obtain.

Tips for Starting Up Cooperative Learning Groups. Cooperative learning is a carefully planned process. Prior to starting up a cooperative learning effort within the class, teachers may wish to observe a few tips about the process, as presented in Table 6.5.

Three Basic Formats for Implementing Cooperative Learning. The beginning teacher can use three basic formats to implement cooperative learning (Salend & Schniedewind, 1987). These include peer teaching, group projects, and the "jigsaw."

Teachers should not overlook one of a school's most valuable resources—its students. Within class groups, teachers can assign *peer tutors* to assist students having difficulty with the content of a lesson. Peer tutors may be glad to record assignments for the student with mild disabilities to listen to for extra reinforcement. Peers also work well one-on-one using a flannel board, manipulating real or paper money, or assisting a special student in a brief instructional period at the computer. At the secondary level, peer tutors often succeed when they help small groups of students with disabilities look up their study questions at the end of chapters, work on classwork or homework assignments, and participate in study or review sessions. A peer can also call

Table 6.5
Tips About Cooperative Start-Up

Some Ways to Ensure Positive Interdependence
  1. Give only one pencil, paper, or book to a group.
  2. Assign one paper to be written by the group.
  3. Divide task into jobs; it can't be finished unless all help.
  4. Pass one paper around the group, each member must do a part.
  5. Jigsaw materials; each person learns a part and then teaches it to the group.
  6. Give a reward (like bonus points) if everyone in the group succeeds.

Some Ways to Ensure Individual Accountability
  1. Tell students to do the work first, then bring it to the group.
  2. Pick one student at random to orally answer questions studied by the group.
  3. Have everyone write, then certify correctness of all papers; you pick one to grade.
  4. Listen and watch as students take turns orally rehearsing information.
  5. Assign jobs or roles to each student.
  6. Give students bonus points if all group members do well individually.

Some Expected Behaviors to Tell Students
  (Pick four or five that fit)
  1. Everyone contributes and helps.
  2. Everyone listens to others with care.
  3. Encourage everyone in your group to participate.
  4. Praise helpful actions or good ideas.
  5. Ask for help if you need it.
  6. Check to make sure everyone understands.
  7. Stay with your group.
  8. Use quiet voices.

Table 6.5 *continued*

Some Things to Do When Monitoring
1. Give immediate feedback and reinforcement for learning.
2. Encourage oral elaboration and explanation.
3. Reteach or add to teaching.
4. Determine what group skills students have mastered.
5. Encourage and praise use of good group skills.
6. Determine what group skills to teach students next.
7. Find out interesting things about your students.

Some Ways to Process Group Interactions
Small Groups
1. What did your group do well in working together today?
2. What could your group do even better tomorrow?

Whole Class
1. What skills did we do well in working together today?
2. What skills could we do even better tomorrow?

Individual (Self)
1. What did you do well in helping your group today?
2. What could you do even better tomorrow?

Individual (Other)
1. Name one thing a group member did that helped your group.
2. Tell your group members that you appreciated their help.

Note. From *Structuring Cooperative Learning: Lesson Plans for Teachers* (p. 55–56) by R. T. Johnson, D. W. Johnson, & E. J. Holubec (Eds.), 1987, Edina, MN: Interaction Book Company. Copyright 1987 by Interaction Book Company. Reprinted by permission.

out words to students during group or individual spelling tests. In addition, students with disabilities often need to have their words called out more slowly, and using peers and grouping for spelling tests makes such an adaptation possible.

Peer tutoring has numerous advantages that include facilitating the interaction between nondisabled students and students with disabilities; making use of the insights children often have about how to teach recently learned or newly presented content to another student; making learning more cooperative and less competitive; and providing experiences of living in a democracy, caring, and being cared for (Cartwright, Cartwright, Wood, & Willoughby-Herb, 1981).

Within a *project group* format, "students pool their knowledge and skills to create a project or complete an assignment" (Schniedewind & Salend, 1987, p. 22). All students are included in the process, and motivation is heightened. All students contribute to the group project based on their skill level. If not structured, however, the group project could place the burden of task completion on one or a few students. Providing structure to the group project would produce a similar cooperative format, *jigsaw*.

In a *jigsaw* format, "each group member is assigned a task that must be completed for the group to reach its goal" (Schniedewind & Salend, 1987, p. 22). In this format, the teacher has more specific task input, and more individual accountability is established. Steps for structuring a *jigsaw* lesson include:

1. Distribute a set of materials to each group. The set needs to be divisible into the number of members of the group (2, 3, or 4 parts). Give each member one part of the set of materials.
2. Assign students the individualistic tasks of (a) learning and becoming an expert on their material and (b) planning how to teach the material to the other members of the group.
3. Assign each student the cooperative task of meeting and sharing ideas about how best to teach the material with someone who is a member of another learning group and has learned the same material. This is known as an "expert pair" or "expert group."
4. Assign students the cooperative tasks of (a) teaching their area of expertise to the other group members and (b) learning the material being taught by the other members.
5. Assess students' degree of mastery of all the material. Reward the groups whose members all reach the present criteria of excellence (Johnson, Johnson, & Holubec, 1987, p. 57).

Classroom Designs

The physical environment of a classroom should stimulate students if effective learning is to occur. Prior to developing a classroom design, teachers may use the checklist in Table 6.6 to evaluate the effectiveness of the classroom's physical environment. The physical environment includes all physical aspects of the room: wall areas, lighting, floors, and room area. Being aware of the classroom's physical organization can help teachers prevent classroom problems.

Class designs should be developed around the type of grouping strategies selected by the teachers. Whether at the secondary or elementary level, classroom designs are important because they dictate whether a teacher uses small-group instruction, one-on-one group instruction (one student per group), or total group instruction. Once teachers decide which type of instructional design to use during a lesson, they can alter room arrangements to meet instructional needs. No one design works best for every student. Teachers need to change from time to time. Students can often help to choose a viable design for the day's lesson.

Designing Learning Centers

A *learning station* or *learning center* is a selected space in the classroom where students may go to work on a new assignment or on a skill or concept previously taught. The learning-station approach to teaching or reinforcing skills saves the classroom teacher's time and energy. At the same time, the learning station allows the mainstreamed student freedom of choice in activities, successful

Table 6.6
Checklist for Effective Classroom Environment

	Yes	No
Wall Areas		
Walls clean to prevent distractions	____	____
Bulletin boards neatly designed and seasonally up-to-date	____	____
Bulletin boards available for students' use and display	____	____
Windows clean or neatly covered	____	____
Blackboards in view of all students, clean and undamaged	____	____
Lighting		
Proper window lighting	____	____
Ceiling lighting sufficient	____	____
Floors		
Clean	____	____
Obstructive objects removed	____	____
Barrier-free, for example, for wheelchairs	____	____
Room Area		
Appropriate chair sizes for age level	____	____
Arrangements for left- as well as right-handed students	____	____
Areas provided for small-group instruction	____	____
Areas provided for independent instruction	____	____
Areas in room designated for specific behaviors, such as quiet time, reading in twos, game areas, motor areas, art areas	____	____
Learning centers provided	____	____
Study carrels provided	____	____
Areas designated for listening to tapes, such as recording of lessons or chapters in books	____	____

completion of tasks, and immediate feedback for correct or incorrect responses. The learning station also gives the teacher a way to individualize instruction and work with specific educational objectives. Commonplace in elementary schools, learning stations are used infrequently in secondary classrooms; yet, learning stations also can provide the secondary teacher with a desirable instructional alternative.

Setting Up the Learning Station

For a teacher who has never used the learning station approach to learning or has used only commercial learning stations, a review of the criteria for establishing a good station may be helpful. Voight (1973) lists six criteria to consider in establishing such centers:

1. Each learning center should contribute to the achievement of the individual's purposes. Each child should confront basic skills, facts, concepts, and large ideas.

2. The learning center should deal with a significant area of study that the student finds interesting. It should be open-ended to foster individual creativity. It should provide opportunities to develop problem solving, critical thinking, and creative thinking. It should challenge an individual to strive toward higher levels of learning.
3. Learning experiences at the center should be related to past personal experiences and should lead to broader and deeper new experiences.
4. Learning center activities should have practical time limits related to the child's developmental level so that the child can complete tasks.
5. Directions at each learning center should help students quickly gain an overview of the task. Directions need to be clearly stated so that students understand where to begin each task and when they have completed a task successfully.
6. The design of a learning center should depend on the subject matter presented to the student. (pp. 2–3)

With the criteria for learning stations established, the teacher must decide what subject to emphasize within a station. There are many different types of stations: reading stations, math stations, just-for-fun stations, social studies stations, vocational interest stations, and things-to-make stations. The creative teacher can think of many more possibilities. Kaplan, Kaplan, Madsen, and Taylor (1973) suggest that teachers seriously consider the reasons for student and teacher use. They say that the learning station can serve the student as a self-selected activity for independent study; a follow-up of a lesson; an activity in place of a regular assignment; or an enrichment activity. For the teacher, the learning station can become a place for the follow-up of lessons; a place for small-group instruction; and an excellent resource for individualized activities (p. 21). But a learning station should never be a place for busy work or for getting students out of the way for a few minutes.

After teachers establish standards for the learning center and decide on subject areas, they must locate resources. Piechowiak and Cook (1976) suggest teachers begin by going through the enrichment materials that have probably been stored away. Also, teachers should notify other teachers about items needed in the center. Supplies will multiply rapidly. Other suggestions from Piechowiak and Cook include:

1. Break language arts material into short lessons and write them on individual task cards.
2. Group math sheets into skill areas, and combine them in a box with plastic overlays and grease pencils, thus making programmed learning kits.
3. Gather good art projects, divide them into step-by-step procedures, and write the directions on cards for independent use at the make-it table.
4. Cross-index the basal science and social studies texts. Make them available for student research.

5. Accumulate odds and ends of everything to use as valuable materials for the art center, the make-it table, or experimentation.
6. Record some of your favorite children's stories for the listening center. Devise follow-up activities to check comprehension.
7. Make some blank books for creative writing. Gather pictures for writing and thinking exercises.
8. Use old basal readers and workbooks; they may supply a wealth of material for activity cards. Cut them apart and make books of individual stories. Rip up pages to use for word study activities. Cut pictures to use for phonic task cards or sequential development exercises.
9. Do the same thing with old math texts. Turn the supplemental exercises in the back into math games.
10. Spend allotted school funds for a variety of materials. Instead of buying 30 copies of the same reading text, buy five different series in groups of six. When teachers use learning stations, they no longer need to place large group orders for texts.
11. Collect tables, chairs, boards, and other items that other teachers discard—they may be just the thing you need later.
12. Haunt the media center. Most directors are delighted to have someone show interest in audiovisual aids. When they know the type of material teachers are looking for, they will do all they can to locate it.
13. Rediscover the school building. Some valuable resources may be hiding in the back of a storage closet. (Piechowiak & Cook, 1976, pp. 20–21)

Designing Learning Stations Based on General Principles of Learning

If teaching is the interaction between teacher and learner, effective teaching is planning that interaction based on learning principles. Teachers should use three general principles of learning—acquisition, retention, and transfer—when designing learning stations. Table 6.7 lists these three general principles of learning with definitions and corresponding strategies for teaching each principle.

As teachers construct learning stations, they should divide their material into the three different teaching strategies. They can even set up three different kinds of stations: the acquisition station, the retention station, and the transfer station. At each station, base the activities offered on particular strategies for teaching.

Learning Stations for Acquisition

Acquisition means the learning of a new skill, or original learning. The teacher may or may not build within the learning station all 10 teaching strategies for acquisition, but each can help the teacher teach a new skill.

Instruction and Intent. To teach a student a new skill, the teacher must first focus the student's attention on the task. Making the acquisition station colorful and attractive gets the student's attention, and then the teacher can give instructions. For example, a teacher can provide step-by-step directions, one

Table 6.7
General Principles of Learning and Strategies for Teaching Each Principle

Principle of Learning	Definition	Strategies for Teaching
Acquisition	Original learning; the learning of a new skill	• Instruction and intent • Whole and parts methods • Distribution of practice • Amount of material • Recitation • Knowledge of results • Amount of practice • Oral and visual presentations • Orientation and attention • Structure
Retention	Remembering over an extended period of time	• Overlearning • Type of retention measure • Instructions to recall • Reminiscence
Transfer	Taking what is learned in one situation and using in a second situation	• Intertask similarity • Instructions to transfer • Overlearning

Note. From *Program Development in Special Education* (pp. 77–101) by P. Wehman & P. J. McLaughlin, 1981, New York: McGraw-Hill. Copyright 1981 by McGraw-Hill. Adapted by permission.

step per 3-by-5 inch index card, for each task. Younger children's directions can be in picture form. Teachers can also use tape recorders to give directions. So that students can move efficiently from step to step without omissions, teachers should hand out checklists or tape them to the learning station. Wall charts with picture and word clues are excellent instructional tools. Since students themselves can effectively present information, why not assign student assistants to each learning station on a rotating basis to give verbal directions and demonstrations?

Whole and Parts Methods. *Whole methods* present a task as a whole, while *parts methods* present a task in parts. Some children learn better using the whole method: the teacher presents the whole, for example, the word *dog*, then breaks the word down into parts or sounds.

Other children learn better by using the parts method. The teacher must break the skill down into the steps required to complete or learn it and place the steps in sequential order so that the child can work from the simplest step to the most difficult. This technique, called *shaping*, means teaching each step in a sequence before moving to the next. In an acquisition center, the teacher can put each step on a separate sheet of paper or checklist. If the student completes a step correctly, the teacher checks it off and tells the student to go to the next step. For older students who learn best by the parts method, the teacher can select a literary work, for example, and record it on tape so that students can listen to it in sections. Periodically, the tape pauses and requires the students to complete a short exercise. This activity makes the student write statements about the story in sequential order.

Distribution of Practice. The amount of distribution of practice depends on the attention span of the student. On the back of an activity card, the teacher can list the student's name and type of practice needed. Students with short attention spans should practice for a given period of time, such as 10, 15, or 20 minutes, and then move to a different activity. Students with longer attention spans, on the other hand, should practice until they achieve a set number of correct responses.

Amount of Material. Material amount refers to the size of the task and the number of items in the task. This amount should vary. For example, though several worksheets in math may have the same content, the teacher should make sure each sheet has a different number of items. The teacher should then number the sheets and assign them to students according to their needs at the time.

Recitation. Recitation means practicing a new task after the teacher has removed the original lesson. For example, after reviewing a new list of vocabulary words, the student uses the words without having the list. The teacher might introduce the new word *car*, have the student find as many pictures of cars as possible, and then ask the student to use the word *car* in three simple sentences. Or, the teacher might use a tape recorder to present new words orally, and then have the student repeat sentences into the recorder.

Knowledge of Results. Instant feedback is necessary for students to know whether their responses are correct or incorrect. Computers can give immediate feedback, and self-correcting materials also provide students with a quick response to answers. Teachers may want to adapt the following suggestions for their own learning stations:

1. Provide a math problem in puzzle format so that only the correct answer completes the puzzle.
2. Put the correct response on the reverse side of activity cards.
3. Develop overlays for tests, such as fill-in-the-blank, multiple choice, or true-false.
4. Develop overlays for activities so that correct answers appear either beside the answer given by the student or on top of the student's answer.

Amount of Practice. "Amount of practice is the total number of practice sessions (the time) students spend to learn a task" (Wehman & McLaughlin, 1981, p. 85). The teacher should vary materials and practice by providing a variety of activities based on the teaching of the same concept. For example, in a math acquisition station, provide many different types of activities to teach the same multiplication concept.

Oral and Visual Presentations. Teachers should present materials both orally and visually so that students grasp concepts better. Visual presentations include bulletin boards, transparencies, flashcards, TV, filmstrips, games, and pictures. Oral presentations include tape recorders, TV, radio, and recorders with earphones.

Orientation and Attention. "Orientation means surveying information and getting ready to respond to it. Attention is the selective scanning of information to focus on particular instances" (Wehman & McLaughlin, 1981, p. 85). Within the acquisition station, the teacher can use these principles by outlining stories, color coding important events, or underlining particular concepts or facts.

Structure. Teachers should organize material so that the student understands the task at hand. Before sending the student to the acquisition station to select a task, outline the activities to be used. For example, the teacher could prepare a brief flow chart for each activity, showing how to begin, what to do, and what to do when finished.

Learning Stations for Retention

Retention is remembering over an extended period of time what has been previously taught. There are four basic strategies for teaching retention: over-learning, type of retention measure, instructions to recall, and reminiscence.

Overlearning. Overlearning means practicing beyond the point of learning a new skill, beyond acquisition. The teacher should stock the learning station for retention with numerous activities designed to reinforce the newly acquired skill.

Type of Retention Measure. A teacher can use different retention measures to help a student remember material. According to Blake (1974), these measures are:

> *Recognition* is the selection of previously learned items from unlearned or false items, for example, a multiple-choice test.
> *Structured recall* is supplying items within a specific context, for example, essay tests or fill-in-the-blank test items.
> *Relearning* is the time or effort required to relearn previously learned material. (p. 254)

Teachers should design retention stations, then, with a specific type of retention in mind. For example, a teacher who plans to give a multiple-choice test on activities studied in the station should direct the student to recognize items and facts for an objective test.

Instructions to Recall. "Instructions to recall refers to directing the student to learn with the specific idea of recalling the material at a later time" (Wehman & McLaughlin, 1981, p. 91). Within the station, the teacher should specifically label activities and color code or underline important information that the student will need to know at a later date.

Reminiscence. After a long practice session and rest, the student should have an increase in performance. To plan for reminiscence, the teacher can design short check-up tests for the student to complete after rest and extended practice.

Learning Stations for Transfer

Transferring means that the student takes what is learned in one situation and uses it in a second situation. Strategies for teaching transfer include intertask similarity, instructions to transfer, and overlearning.

Intertask Similarity. This strategy shows the student the similarity between two different tasks. For example, a teacher could show a student who is working on manuscript writing how to move to cursive writing. The teacher might show the student that multiplication is an extension of addition.

Instructions to Transfer. Here, the teacher shows the student how learning in one situation will be useful in another. For example, learning basic math facts will help the student keep a checkbook; learning certain words will transfer into pattern reading; and filling out forms directly relates to applying for a job, a driver's license, or a social security card.

Overlearning. Overlearning means practice beyond the point of mastery. The teacher must take care to present the same concepts using different activities or techniques. Boredom does not aid overlearning.

Advantages of Learning Stations for the Mainstreamed Student

Learning stations serve multiple purposes in instructing students. For one thing, the teacher saves time during the day because a group or an individual can work alone at the station. In addition, learning stations in mainstream classrooms have the following specific advantages:

- Many students prefer to work alone, and the learning station gives them this option;
- Self-correcting learning stations provide immediate feedback on correct or incorrect responses without embarrassment;
- Mainstreamed students can work at their own pace without pressure;
- With a variety of activities presented, students can select the most appropriate;
- Because students in the mainstream may work below the level of other students in the regular classroom, learning stations provide them with appropriate activities at their levels;
- Activities at the learning station can reinforce the objectives specified on the mainstreamed student's IEP;
- Learning centers reinforce the mode of learning best suited to the mildly disabled student. For example, if the student learns better visually, the teacher can present more activities in a visual manner, but if the student learns better auditorially, the teacher can put activities on tape recorders.

Designing Bulletin Boards for Incidental and Intentional Learning

Most classrooms have at least one bulletin board. Teachers usually design bulletin boards as seasonal decoration or as special places to display work, but bulletin boards can also reflect a specific learning purpose. Bulletin boards designed for incidental learning are simply placed around the room in hope that students will pick up a little extra learning. For example, in one school, the halls are painted to look like highways, street signs hang over classroom doors, and the ABCs run around the walls. It is even hard to get a drink of water without learning a little multiplication. As children line the halls, incidental learning takes place in every direction they look. Many books have ideas that teachers can use to design bulletin boards.

On the other hand, intentional learning is planned learning. Teachers can design bulletin boards based on a lesson or current events. One school has a "good morning news" bulletin board for the class. The teacher broadcasts the news and each student brings an item for the bulletin board or announcements. This method uses intentional learning in a first-class form.

Types of Bulletin Boards

Table 6.8 presents different types of bulletin boards with a brief description of each. Teachers may adapt the format of content of the different types to match the individual needs of students.

Bulletin Board Planning

Greer, Friedman, and Laycock (1978) list the following eight steps to use in planning for bulletin boards.

1. Decide early on a theme or key idea to be expressed by the bulletin board. Seek a new, fresh approach to content. Think of putting the title in an eye-catching location; consider the expected size and location of the audience; plan for lettering and arrangement that can be seen at the normal viewing distance.
2. Start early to determine exactly what the display should communicate and have students participate. Determine specific student goals, which may include, for example, giving at least eight students responsibility for planning and making a bulletin board display and providing the opportunity for them to develop headings, captions, and other written materials.
3. Plan the display on paper well ahead of time.
4. Keep in mind persons who will see the bulletin board or display.
5. Consider where the bulletin board could best be exhibited to achieve instructional purposes. Placing it in the classroom is not always necessary; it might best be seen in a corridor, in a special display, or other location.
6. Think of attention-getting devices. Use push buttons, strings to be pulled, items to be touched, or any technique to invite viewers to react to or study the display. Give viewers choices, ask them to make decisions, challenge them to avoid making mistakes in responding.

Table 6.8
Types of Bulletin Boards

Language Involvement Bulletin Board	• This type of bulletin board is designed with round rotating disks that are used interchangeably for any subject or content.
Slide-Study Bulletin Board	• This type of bulletin board can be used for any subject area. Slides are taken on the desired subject matter and stored in compartments attached to the bulletin board.
Auditory-Action Bulletin Board	• The auditory-action bulletin board contains an activity mounted beneath the display on the bulletin board. A cassette is prepared by the teacher, which guides the students through the required lessons.
Lift Panel Bulletin Board	• Lift panel bulletin boards are made with pieces of construction paper folded in half. The outer flap of the panel contains a question or idea. The inner flap is secured to the bulletin board and contains the answer or solution.
Sentence Strips Bulletin Board	• Strips are attached to the bulletin board and may convey printed relevant information or questions. They may be changed frequently to maintain interest.

Note. From "Instructional games." (pp. 267–293) by J. G. Greer, I. Friedman, and V. Laycock. In R. M. Anderson, J. G. Greer, and S. Odle (Eds.), *Individualizing Educational Materials for Special Children in the Mainstream*, 1978, Baltimore: University Park Press. Copyright 1978 by PRO-ED., Inc. Adapted by permission.

7. Use color. Tastefully used, color can contribute to attractiveness. Color can make important content stand out.
8. Incorporate audiovisual devices. Many slide projectors have an automatic slide-changing feature; have students develop photographic or hand-drawn slides or titles. (pp. 267–293)

Teachers must adapt the learning environment before adapting instruction. But once they have prepared the master schedule, planned scheduling for resource with the best interest of the child in mind, and designed the actual physical environment of the room, they can take a close look at how to teach.

SUMMARY

This chapter focused on adapting the physical environment for students with mild disabilities. Preparing the physical environment for special needs and at-risk learners as for all students helps build a framework for learning. When the master schedule has been carefully planned, when scheduling or transitional concerns have been addressed and when grouping techniques have been established, the teacher can begin the instructional process. Part 3 will develop a model for adapting the instructional environment.

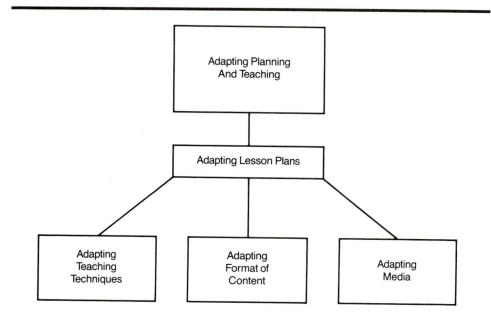

PART THREE
Adapting Planning and Teaching

Part Three of the text includes four chapters: "Adapting Lesson Plans," "Adapting Teaching Techniques," "Adapting Format of Content," "Adapting Media." In these chapters, you will begin to learn how to impose structure on students' learning. Many practical ideas to use with students are presented.

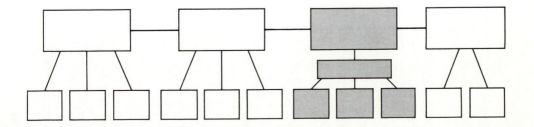

CHAPTER SEVEN

Adapting Lesson Plans

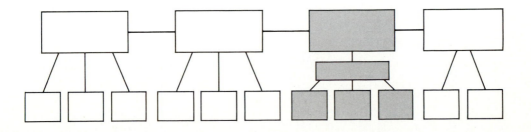

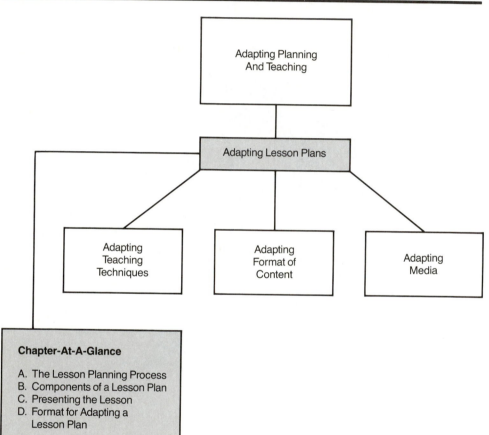

Adapting Planning And Teaching

Adapting Lesson Plans

Adapting Teaching Techniques

Adapting Format of Content

Adapting Media

Chapter-At-A-Glance

A. The Lesson Planning Process
B. Components of a Lesson Plan
C. Presenting the Lesson
D. Format for Adapting a Lesson Plan

Lesson plans are blueprints of the day's events that dictate student-teacher interactions and instructional outcomes. Effective teaching usually springs from a well-planned, well-organized, and well-presented lesson plan. According to Hoover and Hollingsworth (1975), a good lesson plan has many educational benefits: it provides teacher guidelines, allows time for teachers to motivate students and prepare for individual differences, and allows teachers to evaluate their activities and improve their teaching skills.

In a special education class, "a lesson plan focuses directly on the teaching objectives that should derive from the student's goals and objectives on his/her IEP" (Payne, Polloway, Smith, & Payne, 1981, p. 119). The IEP is a linking system between the student's needs and the appropriate education that is to be delivered; however, the IEP does not indicate the specific planning process to be followed in developing lessons (Hudson & Graham, 1978). In a regular classroom setting, the lesson plan focuses on the teaching objective not only for a special student but also for the total group. The regular educator uses the same lesson plan for many students. However, the special student or the student at risk often cannot follow the activities as presented in the lesson plan and may fall behind.

This chapter presents suggestions to help the regular and special education teachers adapt the regular class lesson plan to meet the specific needs of students who are having difficulty within the class. The chapter will (a) present the process of lesson planning and collaboration during the process; (b) develop the components of a lesson plan and provide specific suggestions for teacher intervention for each segment; (c) provide techniques for delivering the lesson; and (d) present a format for adapting the lesson plan in collaborative planning.

THE LESSON PLANNING PROCESS

The planning process begins many months prior to the time when an educator formally sits down to develop weekly lesson plans. The process actually begins when the school system selects the curriculum to be implemented within its schools. At this point, texts are adapted to teach skill scope and sequence. Frequently, state departments of education dictate the skill scope and sequence for their school systems, which must then be translated into curriculum components and lesson plans at the local level. When teachers plan, (a) several stages of planning occur; (b) collaboration is necessary; and (c) benefits are derived from a careful planning process.

Stages of Planning

Research suggests that *subject matter*—the selection of content for instructional tasks—plays a larger role in teachers' planning considerations than students' abilities or needs. The grade level studied may be a factor in this finding, however, since the vast majority of planning studies have been conducted at the elementary school level. By contrast, Taylor (1970), in one of the few planning studies focusing on secondary teachers, suggests that teachers' ideas about students' needs, abilities, and interests are the major concerns in planning. In any event, it seems that when students are considered in planning decisions, they are thought of in different ways at different points in the school year. The beginning of the school year is clearly the most important period in teacher planning and the period in which student ability levels play the greatest role in teachers' planning decisions. As the school year progresses, different levels of attention may be devoted to considerations of students in planning (Morine-Dershimer, 1978–79).

What teachers think about or take into account in planning thus may vary according to the time of year and also vary across the different levels of planning in which teachers engage. Teachers formulate tested or embedded plans focused on different units of time. Yinger (1980), for example, identified five levels in an elementary school teacher's planning: yearly, term or semester, unit, weekly, and daily. What was planned and the kinds of information used in planning varied from one level to another.

> In *yearly* planning, the teacher focused on establishing the general content of the course, working out the basic curriculum sequence, and organizing materials. The only data on students used in this level were the number of students and whether there were any returning students.
>
> In *term* planning, the teacher detailed the content to be covered in the next 3 months and established a weekly schedule for the term. The student data used for this level came from the teacher's direct contact with students.
>
> In *unit* planning, the teacher developed a sequence of tasks for presenting content. In this level of planning, the teacher focused on students' abilities, interests, and other factors.
>
> In *weekly* planning, the teacher sketched out the week's activities, adjusting them for any schedule interruptions to maintain continuity and regularity. In making planning decisions at this level, the teacher used information based on students' performance in the preceding days.
>
> Finally, *daily* planning involved "setting and arranging classroom, specifying activity components not yet decided upon; fitting daily schedule to last-minute intrusions, preparing students for day's activities." In this level of planning, the teacher relied upon an assessment of the class's "disposition" at start of day, and their continued interest, involvement, and enthusiasm throughout the course of the day. (Yinger, 1980, p. 114)

Collaboration in Lesson Planning

Most often, the special education teacher becomes actively involved in the lesson planning process only when the mainstream teacher is in the last stage of planning and developing the daily lesson plan. However, it is more beneficial to the special needs student if the special education teacher becomes involved in the first phase of planning. A year's worth of learning outcomes as set forth in daily plans might be attainable for nondisabled students, but difficult for a student with disabilities to master. Trying to maintain a special student in a regular class where skills are taught that are instructionally too advanced for the student becomes a losing battle. A balance must be maintained between skills taught and those that are reasonably attainable by the special needs student. However, many special needs and at-risk students can achieve success during the regular lesson plan activities when intervention points are identified and appropriate adaptations or modifications are provided. This process depends on careful, well-planned collaboration between the regular and special education teachers.

As the regular and special education teachers work together in the planning process, there are several guidelines to consider:

1. Realize that modifications to the regular class lesson plan may be necessary.
2. Be specific in listing what will occur in each component of the lesson plan: objective, strategies, materials or resources, and evaluation.
3. Allow time for both teachers to review the lesson plan and develop appropriate modifications.
4. Be flexible when an adaptation or modification does not work.
5. Be prepared to develop an alternative modification.
6. Realize that when a modification is made to the lesson plan, the plan is still valid and not watered down.
7. Be as flexible in modifying the student assignment or evaluation section as you are in modifying the objective and strategies sections.
8. Realize that you are always modifying the lesson plan for student success and attainment of objectives.

Benefits of Lesson Planning

Formats of lesson plans and ways of presenting lessons vary from teacher to teacher. But effective teaching usually springs from a well-developed lesson plan. Hoover and Hollingsworth (1975) suggest that lesson planning has several benefits. For example, plans can serve as "useful guidelines or blueprints" for the teacher. They must, however, remain flexible enough to allow the teacher to adapt to whatever situation may arise. In fact, if the prepared teacher has set up "general goals, some definite activities, and some specific sources of materials," then students can play a part in planning. Planning also allows the teacher to direct attention to the "important problems of motivation and individual differences." Indeed, planning often increases the teacher's understanding of the problems students have with learning. Planning lessons can help a teacher both focus and balance "goals, subject matter, activities, and evaluation." The teacher can even use the lesson plan as a "reference to important statistics, illustration, difficult words, special procedures." Teachers who make notes on their plans after lessons are finished can use their plans to see patterns in successful approaches and outcomes to improve their teaching in later years. Finally, since every teacher plans lessons in a different way, planning allows a teacher to put a personal stamp on the lesson and the classroom (pp. 159–160).

During the planning process, educators are working toward the goal of developing an appropriate lesson plan for all students. The next section will look more carefully at the traditional components of a lesson plan and possible intervention points with suggested modifications for each component.

COMPONENTS OF A LESSON PLAN

All lesson plans have several essential parts, although various authors may name these parts differently. Jarolimek and Foster (1981), for example, provide a simple and useful description of four major lesson plan parts. The *purpose* states instructional objectives, including what students should learn from the lesson. The *learning process* lists learning materials or media needed to teach the lesson. The *sequence of lesson* describes the work-study activities that will occur during the lesson. And, finally, the *evaluation* describes the activities designed to close the lesson (p. 190).

Certain components such as objectives, procedures or strategies, materials, and evaluation always appear in a well-constructed lesson plan, no matter what names or formats are used. These components, generic to all lesson planning, will be used in the following sections. Ways in which educators can adapt or modify the plan after the point of intervention have been identified for each component.

Figure 7.1 graphically depicts the four components of the lesson plan and the subcomponents necessary for intervention planning.

Objective

The objective of the lesson is a statement of specific learner outcomes that should result from the lesson. Objectives should be clearly stated, express the intended outcome behavior, and identify how the outcome behavior will be measured and focused on the student. Objectives should be carefully written in the domain level appropriate for the student. These levels include knowledge, comprehension, application, analysis, synthesis, and evaluation. A description of these levels and verbs appropriate for each level may be found in Chapter 8. Objectives should be shared with learners so that they will be aware of the purpose of the lesson at all times. For younger students, the teacher may need to paraphrase the objective or provide a visual representation of the desired outcome to help them understand the objective. It may be helpful to graphically show the learner how the day's objective continues yesterday's objective and will tie into tomorrow's objectives. This provides a connection for students who may not readily see the logical sequence of the skills being taught.

After an objective is selected and found appropriate, other steps include (a) making a list of all sub-objectives, or breakdowns of the class objective; (b) task-analyzing the sub-objectives, or putting them in sequential order from simple

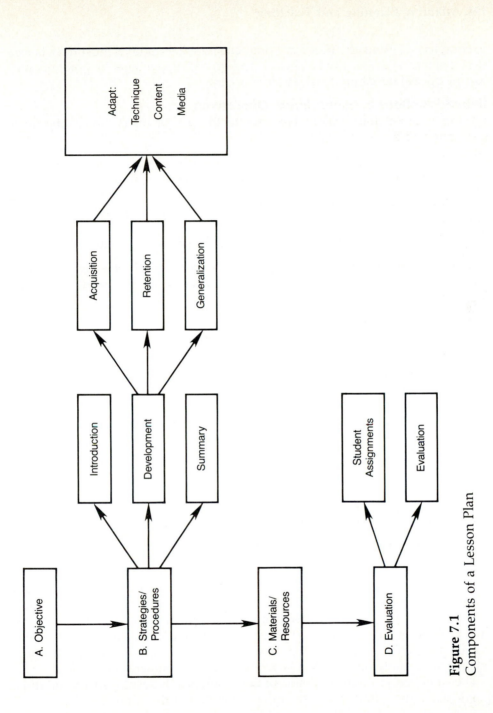

Figure 7.1
Components of a Lesson Plan

193

to complex; (c) listing the necessary prerequisite skills students must have before they can master the selected objective; and (d) deciding where the point of entry for the special needs or at-risk student occurs.

Useful Functions of Instructional Objectives

Educators report four major objections to the use of instructional objectives (Tenbrink, 1977):

1. Writing good instructional objectives requires a lot of work and expertise.
2. Using instructional objectives hampers the process of individualizing and humanizing education.
3. The use of instructional objectives curtails spontaneity and decreases the teacher's flexibility.
4. Using instructional objectives leads to trivial learning outcomes (p. 77).

Although these points may be valid, the benefits of objective planning and writing far outweigh such objections. Among many useful functions, instructional objectives are useful in:

1. Lesson planning;
2. The selection of learning aids such as textbooks and films;
3. Determining appropriate assignments for individual students;
4. Selecting and constructing classroom tests;
5. Determining when to gather evaluation data;
6. Summarizing and reporting evaluation results; and
7. Helping learners determine where they are and where they need to go as they strive toward becoming independent learners (Tenbrink, 1977, p. 79).

Table 7.1 presents a summary of suggestions for adapting the objective component of lesson plans. After the objectives have carefully been selected, written, displayed, and explained, the educator begins the second phase of lesson planning—developing strategies/procedures.

Strategies/Procedures

In this major section of the lesson plan, the teacher must determine the instructional makeup of the lesson as well as the sequence the lesson should follow. During the development of this section, the teacher should be mindful of the stated objectives in the first component of the plan and develop strategies and procedures carefully around those objectives. It is not uncommon to find excellent objectives and excellent procedures that do not match. This instructional mismatch certainly can result in lack of objective attainment for a student.

The strategies/procedures section of the lesson plan is developed around three major parts: the introduction, the development, and the summary.

Lesson Introduction

In the lesson plan introduction, it is suggested that the teacher state and/or demonstrate what students should learn; use a provocative question, artifact,

Table 7.1
Lesson Plan Objective

Lesson Plan Component	Definition	Suggested Adaptations/ Modifications
Objective	A statement of specific learner outcomes that should result from the lesson.	Clearly state the objective to reflect the behavior outcome and how the behavior will be measured.
		Check to see that the objective is student-oriented.
		Select instructional objectives for the lesson that are in the appropriate domain level for the learner.
		Graphically show the learner how today's objective fits into yesterday's lesson and will tie into tomorrow's lesson.
		Make a list of all possible sub-objectives for the main objective.
		Put all sub-objectives in the logical sequential order for teaching.
		Make a list of all prerequisite skills needed before the student can master the stated objective.
		Be prepared to alter any objective if it is not meeting the needs of the learner.

or hands-on-activity to stimulate student interest in the lesson; or link the present lesson to past lessons or student experiences.[1]

Five essential steps to planning should be included within the lesson's introduction. First, the teacher reviews what is to be learned. During the introduction to the written lesson plan, the teacher reviews the major instructional objective and lists of all sub-objectives. The teacher thinks in terms of preparing the student for the lesson itself and must make sure that instructional objectives are on the student's level and in sequential order. Additionally, the teacher should include an assessment of the students' prerequisite skills in the plan's introduction. Second, the teacher demonstrates what the student should

[1] The Division of Teacher Education and Special Education uses this lesson plan guide for all instructional programs in the School of Education at Virginia Commonwealth University. The following discussion is adapted from: *Student Teaching Handbook*, pp. 21–22. Copyright 1982 by the Division of Teacher Education, School of Education, Virginia Commonwealth University. Adapted by permission.

learn. This might include a whole-part-whole method using a lecture outline and providing sequential, written directions. Third, the teacher will use a mind-capturer or activator such as a manipulative or hands-on-activity to boost interest. Fourth, the teacher provides a link to past lessons or the students' current or past experiences. The lesson is more meaningful when a student can relate it to past experiences or current activities. Fifth, the teacher relates the lesson to a future event. Lessons also become more meaningful when students can see purpose in learning a lesson as it relates to their functional future. See Table 7.2 for a breakdown of the introduction to a lesson.

Lesson Development

In the development section, the teacher selects activities to achieve the lesson's purpose, describes these activities, and chooses an instructional model around which to organize the lesson. As shown in Figure 7.1, the development stage of lesson planning should be built around three aspects of a learning model: acquisition, retention, and generalization. For each of the model's parts, the educator should plan on the appropriate adaptation or modification if needed. Frequently, by the time of developing a lesson, the educator may be aware of intervention points for specific students. For other students, however, the need for identifying an intervention point may emerge as the lesson progresses. The Intervention/Transition Checklist in Appendix A and described in Chapter 3 is a useful tool for intervention point identification. As the lesson develops, there are several major considerations for the teacher to keep in mind:

1. Select strategies for teaching for acquisition, retention, and transfer.
2. Select the appropriate activities for teaching for each part of the mode.
3. Be sure that all activities are based on the appropriate objective level.
4. Sequence all activities.
5. Identify any necessary intervention points during the lesson for students experiencing difficulty.
6. Identify the areas that need modification or adaptation: technique, content, and/or media.
7. Develop the appropriate modification for the areas identified in item 6. (Suggestions for adapting teaching techniques, the format of content, and media are discussed in Chapters 8, 9, and 10, respectively.)
8. Plan for an adapted learning environment.

Table 7.3 presents these eight considerations in lesson plan development with suggested adaptations or modifications for each.

Lesson Summary

In the lesson summary part of the procedures, the major points of the lesson are summarized and the lesson's events are tied together. The teacher may choose to have students describe what they have learned by performing one of several activities, such as question/discussion, demonstration, or presentation of a project. Table 7.4 presents the components of the lesson summary with considerations for the teacher in adapting or modifying this section of the plan.

Table 7.2
Lesson Plan Procedures/Strategies

Component	Definition	Suggested Adaptations/ Modifications
Introduction	Setting the stage for the work-study activities that will occur during the lesson.	
Review what is to be learned.		Review the instructional objective before developing the lesson's activities.
		Modify the objective if necessary for student success.
		Reassess the students' prerequisite skill level.
		Explain to students how today's lesson is related to yesterday's lesson.
Demonstrate what student should learn.		Provide a model of completed assignment on task to be completed.
		Using whole-part-whole method, review the assignment/task.
		Provide directions that are sequential, written, and reviewed orally.
Use mind-capturer or activator.		Use manipulative or hands-on activity to boost interest.
		Note whether or not students have prerequisite skills for mastering objective.
Provide link to past lessons or students' experiences.		Ask questions on students' taxonomy levels about past lessons.
		Provide example from own experience and relate to lesson (modeling technique).
		Ask students to share similar experiences; relate student comments to present lesson.
Relate lesson to a future life event or purpose for learning the lesson.		Show students how today's lesson will have meaning in their future.
		Let students provide examples of how or what they learn today will be helpful tomorrow.

Table 7.3
Lesson Plan Procedures/Strategies

Component	Definition	Suggested Adaptations/ Modifications
Development	The sequence of work-study activities that will occur during the lesson.	
Select strategies for teaching for acquisition, retention, and transfer.		*Acquisition:* The learning of a new skill
		Get the student's attention and explain the intent of the lesson.
		Use whole-part-whole activities. (e.g., provide a lecture outline)
		Plan for practice and distribute the practice throughout the lesson.
		Cover only small segments of material if the lesson is long.
		Provide students with immediate feedback on their progress.
		Use multisensory approaches while teaching the activities.
		Point out specific details that you want the student to learn.
		Plan for appropriate note-taking procedures.
		Plan for adaptation for note-taking if needed.
		Provide structure during the lesson by explaining how the activities relate and how the lesson will be evaluated.
		Retention: Remembering over an extended period of time
		Provide for overlearning by developing extended activities which teach the lesson.
		Help students see that how you teach relates to how you will test.
		Teach students the different types of retention measures. (Chapter 10)
		Point out specific information you will want students to recall at a later date.

Table 7.3
continued

Component	Definition	Suggested Adaptations/ Modifications
		After a short rest from the material, check for recall and retention.
		Reteach if the student has not retained the skills.
		Generalization: Transferring what is learned in one situation and using the information in another situation
		Point out the similarities between the tasks learned.
		Show how the information learned will be useful in another situation.
		Assist in overlearning by letting students participate in independent practice. Overlearning does not mean boredom.
Select the appropriate activities for teaching each part of the model.		Carefully select appropriate activities for teaching for acquisition, retention, and generalization.
		Remember that each part of the three-part model must be mastered before the student begins the next step.
Be sure that all activities are based on the appropriate objective level.		Check each activity to be sure that you are teaching the objective and that you are teaching on the appropriate instructional level.
Sequence all activities.		Organize all activities from lowest to highest level of difficulty.
		Sequence the activities within each segment of the model.
Identify any necessary intervention points during the lesson for students experiencing difficulty.		Using the Intervention Checklist (Appendix A), identify any intervention point within the lesson for a student who is experiencing difficulty.
		Remember that to continue with the lesson when a student is lost defeats the lesson's purpose.

Table 7.3 *continued*

Component	Definition	Suggested Adaptations/ Modifications
Identify the necessary areas of modification or adaptation: technique, content, media.		Identify the necessary areas of mismatch for the student (teaching technique, content, media). Chapters 8, 9, and 10 develop these sections in detail.
Develop the appropriate modification for the areas identified above.		Select the appropriate adaptation or modification for the identified area.
Plan for an adapted learning environment.		Assign peer tutors to students with disabilities, if needed.
		Organize creative groups for instruction.
		Select grouping arrangements.

Materials/Resources

In the *materials/resources* section of the lesson plan, the teacher identifies any materials and media to use to achieve the lesson's purpose. Such resources may include pages or chapters in a pamphlet, text, or workbook, filmstrips or films, guest experts, field experience, special settings, art supplies, cooking supplies, or audiovisual equipment. Assessing the instructional level of materials, matching perceptual learning styles to media, using a variety of materials and/or media, and adapting the learning environment are all part of developing resources. Table 7.5 presents considerations for teachers for material/resource selection.

Student Evaluation/Assignment

Evaluation, the final component of the lesson plan, is designed to measure student outcomes, identify a teacher's need for reorganizing lesson plans, and target areas for reteaching. Evaluation may occur as the last component within the lesson plan format; however, it should be an ongoing process.

During the evaluation, the teacher notes ways to assess student learning and/or the success of the lesson. Teachers can assess students by checking behavioral objectives, using informal questions, or administering formal pre- and posttests. Instead, a teacher may choose to have students check their own work by providing them with feedback, a model of a completed activity, or an illustration of the lesson's concept or process. Another method teachers may want to use is to have students assess one another's work. To determine the lesson's degree

Table 7.4
Lesson Plan Procedures/Strategies

Component	Definition	Suggested Adaptations/ Modifications
Summary	Tying together the lesson's events.	
Conclude lesson.		Select closing activities on an instructional level of mainstreamed students.
		Assess students' mastery of concepts.
Students describe what they have learned.		Assist mainstreamed students in selecting what to share.
		Ask students to tell about what they have learned.
		Have students draw pictures of what they have learned.
		Invite students to present projects.

Table 7.5
Lesson Plan Materials/Resources

Component	Definition	Suggested Adaptations
Materials/Resources	A list of the learning materials and media needed to teach the lesson.	
Compile all materials to be used in presenting the lesson.		Assess materials as to instructional level.
		Select a variety of materials that address different perceptual learning styles (e.g., visual, auditory).
Select appropriate media to be used with the lesson.		Adapt media.
		Select a variety of media and uses for lesson plan implementation.
		Match media to perceptual learning styles of student.
Prepare resources for adapting the learning environment.		Select bulletin boards for incidental and intentional learning.
		Design learning centers to enhance the instructional activities.

of success, a teacher may analyze students' reactions during the lesson, the value of the lesson as a learning experience, or the teacher's own teaching performance.

Student assignments are also a major evaluation component of the lesson plan. Assignments are part of the evaluation process as well as an extension of the content mastery. Assignments provide the teacher with an opportunity to see if the student has mastered the skill taught and if reteaching will be necessary. Table 7.6 provides suggestions for student evaluation and assignments. A detailed discussion is presented in Chapter 11.

Table 7.6
Lesson Plan Student Evaluation/Assignment

Component	Definition	Suggested Adaptations/ Modifications
Evaluation	Checking for mastery, need to reorganize lesson plans, and areas for reteaching.	
Teacher assesses student learning.		Check to see that the way you test reflects the way you taught for retention during the strategies/procedures component of the lesson plan.
		Provide the student with information regarding test type prior to test.
		Teach the student how to study for the test based on test type.
		Use model in Chapter 11 to adapt regular classroom test for mildly disabled students.
		Assess effectiveness of instructional objective.
		Assess instructional level of activities.
		Assess activities not mastered and consider further adaptations of plan.
Student assesses self.		Give student self-correcting materials for immediate reinforcement.
		Provide models to which students can compare their work.
Students assess each other.		Provide one-on-one peer tutor to give feedback.
		Oversee student assessment of peers—peer's criticism can harm self-concepts.

PRESENTING THE LESSON

While planning lessons, teachers should also think about how they will present those lessons to students. Cooper et al. (1977) suggest five stimulus variation techniques that teachers can use to more effectively deliver the lesson: the kinesic variation, focusing, shifting interaction, pausing, and shifting the senses.

The *kinesic variation* refers to changes in the teacher's position in the classroom. It contrasts with the practice of the teacher sitting behind the desk for an entire lesson and assumes that a teacher will move from place to place within the

Table 7.6 *continued*

Component	Definition	Suggested Adaptations/ Modifications
Teacher assesses self.		Were all students included in lesson plan's activities?
		Did each student experience success?
		Was I aware of the instructional level of each student?
		Did each student reach expected learning outcome?
		Did I effectively manage student behaviors?
		Was the learning environment adapted to meet students' learning needs?
		What changes should I make the next time I present the lesson?
Student Assignments.		Be sure that assignments are on the appropriate instructional level for students.
		Do not overwhelm students with too much of an assignment.
		Design assignments so that students will experience success.
		Relate all assignments to the lesson.
		Give assignments for a specific reason, not just to give an assignment.
		Inform students of the purpose of the assignment.
		(Chapter 9 develops assignments in detail).

room to improve communication. The movements should be smooth and natural, not distracting from the lesson or to the student. The kinesic variation includes one or a combination of the following: moving freely from right to left and then from left to right in front of the classroom; moving freely from front to back and then from back to front; and moving freely among and/or behind students (Cooper et al., 1977, p. 124). This technique also enables the teacher to use proximity control to intervene with problem behaviors (see Chapter 5).

Focusing is the "teacher's way of intentionally controlling the direction of student attention" (Cooper et al., 1977, p. 136). Focusing can be verbal or behavioral or both. Teachers can focus students' attention verbally by asking specific questions or using accent words such as "for example," "look", "how", or "find." Behavioral focusing may involve teachers using body language, for example, facial expressions, eye contact, or pointing or other hand gestures, to attract or direct attention.

Shifting interaction refers to the teacher's use of any one of these interaction styles: teacher-group, teacher-student, student-student. The teacher-group interaction puts the teacher in control, lecturing and directing discussion as needed. The teacher-student interaction style is also teacher-directed, but the teacher becomes more of a facilitator, asking questions to clarify a story or answering questions raised by students after completion of a lab assignment. The student-student interaction style centers around students, with the teacher "redirecting student questions to other students for comment or clarification" (Cooper et al., 1977, p. 138). When planning a lesson, teachers should strive to include a variety of interaction styles, both during and throughout the day's lessons.

Teachers can also use *pauses* or moments of silence effectively during a lesson. For example, a teacher can completely regain students' attention by becoming silent. Cooper et al. (1977) list 10 effective uses of pausing:

1. It can break informational segments into smaller pieces for better understanding. Reading oral problems or dictating material for transcription requires careful attention to the effective use of pausing.
2. It can capture attention by contrasting sound with silence (alternating two distinctly different stimuli). Remember that attention is maintained at a high level when stimuli are varied, not when one increases the intensity of a single stimulus.
3. It can be a signal for students to prepare for the next teacher action.
4. It can be used to emphasize or underscore an important point.
5. It can provide time for thinking about a question or formulating an answer.
6. It can prevent teachers from unconsciously dominating discussion.
7. It encourages teachers to listen to individual student responses. People do not listen well when they are talking.
8. It can create suspense or expectation. For all types of literature, the effective reader uses the pause to stir emotion and heighten anticipation in the listener.

9. It can help provide a model of listening behavior for other students.
10. It can be used to show disapproval of undesired student behavior (p. 139).

Shifting the senses means presenting information through more than one of the five senses—seeing, touching, hearing, smelling, and tasting. The importance of the teacher's shifting senses for mainstreamed students cannot be overemphasized because assimilating information through various perceptual modalities helps those students learn the information in as many ways as possible.

Teachers who use these stimulus variation techniques enhance their teaching. When teachers plan the lesson carefully, adapt it when necessary for mainstreamed students, and include techniques for adding variety to the presentation, they increase their chances of stimulating all students to learn.

FORMAT FOR ADAPTING A LESSON PLAN

Developing and adapting the lesson plan is a shared responsibility for regular and special education teachers. There are numerous ways in which this process can be completed. For educators working side-by-side within the regular class, the task of adapting for a specific child is easy. For regular educators who do not have a special education teacher within the room or who have numerous at-risk students within the class, the lesson plan format developed in Figure 7.2 becomes a helpful tool. This form can be (a) completed by the regular education teacher for each day's lesson, with adaptations made by the special education teacher for a specific student; or (b) completed in total by the regular education teacher. Suggestions from an intervention plan will be helpful in completing the form.

Figure 7.2 presents a five-column format for one day's lesson plans. In the first column, a blank space is provided for the date. Under the date, the teacher indicates the taxonomy level of the objective. This checklist helps the regular education teacher to be aware of the taxonomy level and be consistent in following through with the level across the objective, strategies, and evaluation sections and provides a reminder to the special education teacher of the objective level. If the level is inappropriate, the special education teacher can make a note on the plan for the regular class teacher. In the second column, the teacher lists the lesson objective. In the third column, the teacher records the strategies used; in the fourth column, the lesson's materials and resources; and in the fifth, plans for evaluation. The lower section of each column provides space for the special education teacher to note adaptations. Under adaptations, in the first column, the special education teacher may list specific names of students who will use the adaptation and make note if they will be working at a different taxonomy level. In the second column, space is provided for notes regarding the objective. The third column is divided into three sections: teaching techniques, format of content, media. The special education teacher can provide specific suggestions for each area as they relate to the strategies in the lesson.

OBJECTIVE	STRATEGIES/ PROCEDURES	MATERIALS/ RESOURCES	EVALUATION/ ASSIGNMENT
Date: _____ Taxonomy Level ___ Knowledge ___ Comprehension ___ Application ___ Analysis ___ Synthesis ___ Evaluation			
Adaptations:	Teaching Techniques: Format of Content: Media:	Adapted Media:	Evaluation Test: Student Assignment:

Figure 7.2
Format for an Adapted Lesson Plan

In the fourth column, space is provided for material/resource suggestions. In the fifth column, space is provided for the special education teacher to comment on the lesson evaluation and student assignment sections of the regular class plan. This simple format encourages ongoing suggestions for the teacher during the lesson process. Examples of completed forms can be found in Chapters 8, 9, 10, and 11.

SUMMARY

As teachers prepare lesson plans, they should take a moment to provide adaptations as needed for mainstreamed and at-risk students. By working collaboratively in the development and implementation of the lesson plan, the regular and special education teachers can provide appropriate instruction for all students. Teachers will discover that when they adapt their lesson plans to the specific needs of at-risk and mainstreamed learners, those students *can* learn the lessons.

Lesson plans are the starting point for planning and teaching. The remaining chapters in this section will assist educators in adapting lesson plans with a focus on adapting teaching techniques (Chapter 8), adapting the format of content (Chapter 9), and adapting media (Chapter 10).

CHAPTER EIGHT
Adapting Teaching Techniques

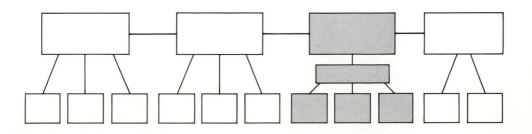

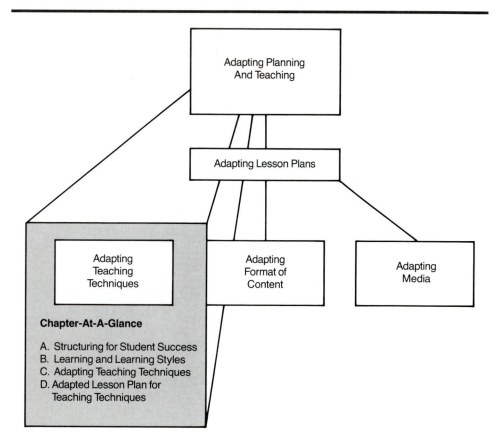

Adapting Planning
And Teaching

Adapting Lesson Plans

Adapting
Teaching
Techniques

Adapting
Format of
Content

Adapting
Media

Chapter-At-A-Glance

A. Structuring for Student Success
B. Learning and Learning Styles
C. Adapting Teaching Techniques
D. Adapted Lesson Plan for
Teaching Techniques

The teacher's major responsibility to the children, the school, and the total community lies in instruction. Good instructional planning paves the way for an organized school day and for the smooth delivery of information vital to the academic development of children. Instead of defining instruction as only the imparting of specific content, however, teachers should think of instruction as an ongoing process: the teacher delivers information to children who receive and assimilate it. Teachers who adapt instruction to meet the needs of all children, especially students with mild disabilities, discover that they deliver information more effectively and students learn it more easily. Instruction becomes a continuous process of presenting information, adapting information, re-presenting information, and testing for concept mastery. Making adapting a natural component of this continuum of instruction helps students to succeed.

This chapter, the second of four in the planning and teaching process, presents information for teachers to use in adapting teaching techniques. During the instructional process a teacher delivers the information or content via a specific teaching technique. The teaching technique is the delivery system which transmits content to students. If the technique is not appropriate for a student, then chances are the content will never be delivered. This chapter introduces the teaching components of our model. It covers (a) the importance of structure in student's lives, (b) learning styles, and (c) teaching and adaptations for specific modes of teaching.

STRUCTURING FOR STUDENT SUCCESS

According to Carbo and Hodges (1988), "many at-risk youngsters thrive in well-structured learning situations" (p. 57). A structured environment provides for predictability, and predictability reduces anxiety. Students who have difficulty imposing structure on the learning process benefit greatly from the efforts of educators who incorporate *structure* within the instructional process. Students who naturally do well in school appear to have the ability to reduce the chaos of disorganized information and impose self-structure on material presented and to be learned. However, there is a natural tendency within our system not to impose structure for the random learner under the cloak of a belief that "no one will do this when the student leaves school and moves into adult life." If we do assist disorganized learners in learning to impose structure, they will begin to transfer the skills learned into adult life.

Lessons in which the pattern of organization reflects structure are effective for all learners for the following reasons:

1. Structure provides a pathway for organizing information;
2. The work effort is reduced for learners because they do not have to process the information first and then establish order or a connection to proceed to an understanding of the information; and

3. The patterns of thought in a structured lesson or class can be generalized into other learning situations.*

Providing structure instructionally is imperative for many learners. We cannot wait for learners to figure out how to structure or organize information to be learned. Structuring must become a natural part of instruction.

This and the next three chapters, "Adapting Content," "Adapting Media," and "Adapting Evaluation," will weave the thread of structure throughout the teaching process.

George Frowert, a successful young adult, defines structure as "the ability to organize oneself efficiently enough in order for one to remain self-sufficient." Perhaps through imposing instructional structure we can assist children and young adults such as George with this process.

LEARNING AND LEARNING STYLES

Students ultimately want to learn to acquire knowledge or skills. Designing and implementing effective instruction so that students learn to their fullest capacity challenges us all. If learning means the acquisition of knowledge or skills and the teacher wants to help the students with that acquisition, then the teacher needs to understand the process of learning in general. The following sections on learning styles, conditions affecting learning styles, and learning domains will better acquaint teachers with that process.

Learning Styles

Learning styles are students' individual approaches to learning. Knowledge of the different ways that students may approach a learning situation and awareness of the influences on these approaches pave the way for successful teaching. Charles (1980) suggests that students generally approach learning situations in one of three distinct ways: as adventurers, ponderers, or drifters. Adventurers respond quickly, are impulsive, show little concern with the way parts fit together to make a whole, and do not worry excessively about doing things the correct way or producing incorrect answers. Ponderers are more reflective and analytic in nature and have the ability to synthesize information. A ponderer can work on a task for a long time without getting bored, but wants reassurance from authority sources about correct responses. The drifter is "more mechanical, plodding, and hesitant" (p. 68) and depends on others for motivation and initiative. Drifters work better in small groups and in one-on-one situations and require reinforcement to keep working on a task.

Some students with mild disabilities may use one learning style or another, but many may reflect a composite of the different styles, showing that children learn in many different ways.

*A special thanks to Greg Stults, Knoxville, Iowa, for his input and thoughts on the section on structure.

In addition to having a distinctive approach to a learning situation, the student has a cognitive style. According to Fuhrmann (1980), "the cognitive components create learning. . . Each of us develops a typical approach in our use of our cognitive characteristics to perceive, to think, and to remember. This approach constitutes our cognitive learning style" (p. 2).

Keefe (1979) places the many cognitive styles into two major categories: reception styles, which involve perceiving and analyzing functions, and concept formation and retention styles, which pertain to generating hypotheses, solving problems, and remembering. According to Fuhrmann, these two cognitive categories "can be described by a series of continua, with an individual style being found at any point" (p. 2). See Table 8.1 for individual differences in reception and in concept formation and retention styles.

Conditions Affecting Learning Styles

In addition to an awareness of these learning styles, teachers should understand the many other conditions affecting the way children learn. The relation between teaching and learning styles, students' perceptual styles, time, sound, seating arrangements and place, class procedures, group size, and students' attention spans—all these factors influence the learning process.

Interaction Between Teaching and Learning Styles

How students respond, how well they respond, or why they do not respond at all often depends on the interaction between teaching and learning styles. Johnson (1976) describes two student learning styles—the *dependent-prone* and the *independent-prone*. The Fuhrmann-Jacobs model of social interaction (Fuhrmann, 1980) adds a third, the *collaborative-prone*. A student may be learning in all three styles but prefer a certain style in a certain situation. Thus, if some students prefer the dependent style for learning new information, but the teacher presents the material in the independent style, they may not learn as quickly or as well as they could otherwise. Teachers should try to match their teaching styles to their students' learning styles as often as possible or vary their teaching styles so that, in any given situation, different students can use the learning style they prefer. See Table 8.2 for a description of the three learning styles and the learner needs, teacher roles, and teacher behaviors that correspond to each.

Students in a mainstreamed classroom usually prefer the dependent learner style. But when mainstreamed students have some information about the subject, they tend to use the collaborative style. Teachers can use the table to match their teaching styles to the learning styles of their students, thus improving the students' chances of learning.

Perceptual Styles

A student's perceptual style refers to the sense through which the student best receives information: visual (sight); auditory (hearing); or kinesthetic (touching). Most children tend to use one perceptual style more than others. For example, 80 to 85 percent of all people are visual learners and so learn best when they can see the information presented, such as with lessons on the chalkboard,

Table 8.1
Continua of Styles

Reception

Field dependent <----------------------------------> Field independent

Witkin, Goodenough, and Oltman (1977) have conducted extensive study into the degree of influence the surrounding environment has on an individual's perception. Field dependent persons are heavily influenced by the background or context in which an item is embedded. Field independent persons perceive items discretely, without being influenced by the background.

Acceptance of incongruity <------------------> Preference for conventional
or unreality   ideas and reality

Lein et al. (1962) studied readiness to accept perceptions that differ from the conventional. People tolerant of incongruity more willingly accept the unusual, while those less tolerant resist acceptance until they have extensive data.

Receptive <--> Perceptive

McKenney and Keen (1974) label as receptive those who tend to take in raw data as it is, while perceptives assimilate data into preformed concepts.

Systematic < --> Intuitive

McKenney and Keen (1974) also differentiate the tendency to develop ordered plans (systematic) from the tendency to develop spontaneous ideas and understandings (intuitive).

Concept Formation and Retention

Impulsive <--- > Reflective

Kagan (1966) labels quick responders impulsive and slow responders reflective. Reflective thinkers tend to accomplish less than impulsives, but they are more accurate in their responses.

Focusing <---> Scanning

Schlesinger (1954) describes the different ways people attend to detail in their attempts to solve problems. Focusers approach problems by narrowing their perception to intensify a solution, while scanners approach problems by broadening their perception to get a broad view. Scanners see the forest; focusers see the trees.

Broad Categorizing <--------------------------> Narrow Categorizing

Brunner and Tajfel (1961) differentiate people by their preference for either including many items in a category to insure not leaving something out (broad) or including few items to insure excluding irrelevant items (narrow).

Abstract <--> Concrete

Cognitive <---> Cognitive Simplicity

Individual preference for complexity and abstraction vs. simplicity and concreteness has been studied by Harvey, Hunt, and Schroder (1961) and Kelly (1955). The abstractor

Table 8.1
continued

effectively processes highly divergent, even conflicting information, while the concretizer prefers constant information.

Leveling <————————————————————————————————> Sharpening

Gardner (1959) studied memory processing. Leveling is roughly equivalent to generalizing, the process of merging new concepts with previously assimilated ideas. Sharpening is roughly equivalent to discrimination, in which the differences of new information from old are emphasized.

Note. From ''Models and Methods of Assessing Learning Styles'' by B. S. Fuhrmann, 1980, paper prepared for the Virginia Educational Research Association. Copyright 1980 by B. S. Fuhrmann. Reprinted by permission.

overhead projectors, or filmstrips. Auditory learners, however, learn best when they can hear the information presented. Thus, a classroom teacher using the lecture method can help the visual learner by recording the lecture for the student to play back later. Kinesthetic learning means learning through touch. Some students need kinesthetic feedback to learn; for example, the teacher can provide sandboxes so that students draw or trace the letters of the alphabet in the sand and get kinesthetic feedback. Teachers need to plan instruction so that it addresses the student's dominant perceptual mode. Table 8.3 presents techniques for each mode.

Seating Arrangements

When students first come into class, where do they sit? Do they return to the same places the next day? Teachers attending a class or meeting prefer certain places—by the window, next to the door, in the front row, in the back of the room—and children also have such seating preferences. Teachers should try to provide students with a seating arrangement flexible enough for variety but structured enough for consistency. Some students lose interest in assigned tasks when they sit in the same seats day after day. Some possible variations are having students sit on small mats on the floor, taking students to the library for class, or going outside for the lecture. One secondary school, for example, provides learning stations under the trees and uses logs for seating. Teachers then register for outside stations at the times they want.

When adapting classroom seating arrangements for students with mild disabilities, the teacher must consider any special needs the children may have. Also, many students with disabilities are easily distracted and need to be placed close to the teacher.

Class Procedures

Class procedures are more effective when based on the teacher's awareness of students' various learning styles. It is important to match assignments to learning styles, such as assigning students to projects, library work, reports,

Table 8.2
Learner and Teacher Descriptors

Learner Style	Learner Needs	Teacher Role	Teacher Behavior
Dependent style may occur in introductory courses, languages, some sciences when learners have little or no information upon entering course.	Structure Direction External reinforcement Encouragement Esteem from authority	Expert Authority	Lecturing Demonstrating Assigning Checking Encouragement Testing Reinforcing content Transmitter Grader Materials designer
Independent style may occur when learners have much more knowledge or skill upon entering the course and want to continue to search on own. May feel instructor cannot offer as much as they would like.	Internal awareness Experimentation Time Nonjudgmental support	Facilitator	Allowing Providing requested feedback Consultant Listener Negotiator Evaluator
Collaborative style may occur when learners have knowledge, information, ideas and would like to share them or try them out.	Interaction Practice Probe self and others Observation Participation Peer challenge Peer esteem Experimentation	Co-learner Environment setter	Interacting Question Providing resources Modeling to share Providing feedback Coordinating Evaluator Manager Process observer Grader

Note. From *A Practical Handbook for College Teachers* (p. 115) by B. S. Fuhrmann and A. F. Grasha, 1983, Boston: Little, Brown. Copyright 1980 by B. S. Fuhrmann and B. Jacobs. Slight modifications under Teacher Behavior. Adapted by permission.

Table 8.3
Learning Processes in the Perpetual Modes

Pupil Strengths	Pupil Weaknesses	Teacher Formal Assessment Techniques	Teacher Informal Assessment Techniques	Instructional Techniques
		Auditory Modality		
Follow oral instructions very easily.	Lose place in visual activities.	Present statement verbally; ask pupil to repeat.	Observe pupil reading with the use of finger or pencil as a marker.	Reading: Stress phonetic analysis; avoid emphasis on sight vocabulary or fast reading. Allow pupils to use fingers, pencils to keep places.
Do well in tasks requiring phonetic analysis. Appear brighter than tests show. Sequence speech sounds with facility. Perform well verbally.	Read word by word. Reverse words when reading. Make visual discrimination errors. Have difficulty with copying from the chalkboard.	Tap auditory pattern beyond pupil's point of vision. Ask pupil to repeat pattern. Provide pupil with several words in a rhyming family. Ask pupil to add more. Present pupil with sounds produced out of field of vision. Ask if they are same or different.	Observe whether pupil whispers or barely produces sounds to correspond to reading task. Observe pupil who has difficulty following purely visual directions.	Arithmetic: Provide audio tapes of story problems. Verbally explain as well as demonstrate arithmetic processes. Spelling: Build on syllabication skills, use sound clues. Generally: Use worksheets with large unhampered areas. Use lined, wide-spaced paper. Allow for verbal rather than written response.

Table 8.3 *continued*

Pupil Strengths	Pupil Weaknesses	Teacher Formal Assessment Techniques	Teacher Informal Assessment Techniques	Instructional Techniques
		Visual Modality		
Possesses good sight vocabulary.	Have difficulty with oral directions.	Give lists of words that sound alike. Ask pupil to indicate if they are the same or different.	Observe pupil in task requiring sound discrimination, i.e., rhyming, sound blending.	Reading: Avoid phonetic emphasis; stress sight vocabulary, configuration clues, context clues.
Demonstrate rapid reading skills.	Ask, "What are we supposed to do?" immediately after oral instructions are given.	Ask pupil to follow specific instructions. Begin with one direction and continue with multiple instructions.	Observe pupil's sight vocabulary skills. Pupil should exhibit good sight vocabulary skills.	Arithmetic: Show examples of arithmetic function.
Skim reading material.				
Read well from picture clues.	Appear confused with great deal of auditory stimuli.	Show visually similar pictures. Ask pupil to indicate whether they are the same or different.	Observe to determine if pupil performs better when able to see stimulus.	Spelling: Avoid phonetic analysis; stress structural clues, configuration clues.
Follow visual diagrams and other visual instructions well.	Have difficulty discriminating between words with similar sounds.			
Score well on group tests.				Generally: Allow a pupil with strong auditory skills to act as visual child's partner. Allow for written rather than verbal response.
Perform nonverbal tasks well.		Show pupil a visual pattern, such as block design or pegboard design. Ask pupil to duplicate.		
		Tactile/kinesthetic Modality		
Exhibit good fine and gross motor balance	Since tactile/kinesthetic is usually a secondary mo-	Ask pupil to walk balance beam or along a painted line.	Observe pupil in athletic tasks.	Reading: Stress the shape and structure of a

Table 8.3 *continued*

Pupil Strengths	Pupil Weaknesses	Teacher Formal Assessment Techniques	Teacher Informal Assessment Techniques	Instructional Techniques
Exhibit good rhythmic movements. Demonstrate neat handwriting skills. Demonstrate good cutting skills. Manipulate puzzles and other materials well. Identify and match objects easily.	dality, pupil depends on the guiding or preferred modality. Weakness may be in either the visual or auditory mode.	Set up obstacle course involving gross motor manipulation. Have pupil cut along straight, angled, and curved lines. Ask child to color fine areas.	Observe pupil maneuvering in classroom space. Observe pupil's spacing of written work on a paper. Observe pupil's selection of activities during free play—does pupil select puzzles or blocks rather than records or picture books?	word; use configuration clues, sandpaper letters, and/or words. Arithmetic: Use objects in performing the arithmetic functions, provide buttons, packages of sticks, etc. Spelling: Have pupil write word in large movements, in air, on chalkboard, on newsprint; use manipulative letters to spell the word. Call pupil's attention to the feel of the word. Have pupil write word in cursive to get the feel of the word by flowing motion.

Note. From *Teaching Children with Special Needs: Elementary Level,* Owings Mills, MD: Maryland State Department of Education, Division of Instructional Television. Reprinted by permission of Maryland State Department of Education, Division of Instructional Television.

seat work, or learning centers, especially since the average class assignment is usually too difficult for the student with mild disabilities. The teacher can divide the same assignment into several short segments and use a variety of techniques for presenting the information. Class evaluation procedures also should vary according to learning styles. For example, a teacher can evaluate the work of a student with mild disabilities by simply observing, collecting work samples, or using formative evaluation procedures. Matching the evaluation procedure to the student's learning style helps the teacher evaluate instructional objectives as well as appropriately evaluate the student.

Class procedures must also take into account the emotional aspects of learning styles. Fuhrmann (1980) eloquently summarizes the work of Dunn, Dunn, and Price (1979) on these emotional elements: motivation, persistence, responsibility, and structure.

A teacher need only give requirements and resources to highly motivated students, but poorly motivated students require special attention to bring out their interest and desire to learn. For example, a student who is poorly motivated by a traditional lecture class may be highly motivated by a programmed text or small discussion group.

The same length and type of assignment is probably not appropriate for all students, because both attention span and persistence vary greatly. Furthermore, persistence is related to motivation; the greater the motivation to achieve in a particular learning experience, the more persistent a student is likely to be in completing the task. Sequenced learning tasks, with clearly defined steps and a final goal, offer the teacher some flexibility in meeting the needs of students with differing degrees of persistence.

Like motivated students, responsible students require only clear assignments and resources to succeed. Irresponsible students, however, often experience failure and discouragement in such an environment. Usually, students lacking responsibility have historically failed to achieve in school and therefore lack the confidence to assume responsibility. Teachers must attend first to their lack of confidence by offering opportunities for them to experience small successes. Individualizing assignments, breaking objectives into smaller components, trying experimental assignments, and using all types of learning aids and resources may encourage such students.

Students also differ in their response to structure, to the specific rules and directions they must follow to achieve certain objectives. More creative students often like a wide variety of options from which to choose, while those who are less creative may respond better to a single, well-defined method. Again, the emotional elements are related to one another, since the more motivated, persistent, and responsible students require less structure than do the less motivated, less persistent, and less responsible (Fuhrmann, 1980, p. 17).

Teachers, therefore, should make assignments, instruct, evaluate students, and carry out various other class procedures on the basis of what they can determine about their students' learning styles and the emotional factors contributing to those styles.

Group Size

The group size most effective for instruction varies according to the different learning styles of students and the content and purpose of the instruction. Some students learn better in small groups, some in large groups, whereas others learn best on a one-to-one basis. Careful analysis of student performance helps the teacher select the most appropriate method. Most students with disabilities do not function well in large groups; instead, very small groups and one-to-one instruction are usually more effective.

Attention Span

Although each student has a different attention span, many students with mild disabilities have short ones. Thus, teachers in the mainstream should vary teaching techniques and activities accordingly. In fact, teachers who match task to attention span find that students master tasks at a faster rate.

For example, a teacher can divide a math lesson for a student with a short attention span into working problems at the desk, completing additional problems at the board, and going to the learning center to continue with the same math skill but in a different setting. Teachers should first evaluate tasks according to the type of attention span required to complete them. Then they should adapt both their method of delivery and the tasks themselves to the variations of attention spans within the classroom.

Domains of Learning

After teachers understand students' various learning styles and how certain conditions affect those styles, they need to know about the three domains or taxonomies of learning: cognitive, affective, and psychomotor. Instruction falls into one of these three domains and then into one of several levels within each domain. Teachers, to know their instructional domain and level, should consult Table 8.4, which presents the major levels of the three taxonomies as constructed by Bloom (1956), Krathwohl, Bloom, and Masia (1964), and Dave (1970).

A teacher's instructional objectives fall into a specific level of one of the taxonomy structures. Usually, teachers teach in the cognitive domain. Teachers should determine the student's present level within the cognitive domain and begin teaching at that level. For example, if an English teacher is presenting a unit on sentence writing (synthesis) and has a student with mild disabilities in the class who is learning the parts of speech (knowledge), the teacher must switch to the knowledge level for that student. The student's present level determines where the teacher should begin teaching. Table 8.5 presents the levels of the cognitive domain and explains how each level relates to students with mild disabilities.

Learning Styles and Instruction

After assessing the learning styles of thousands of at-risk students, Carbo and Hodges (1988) concluded that:

The majority of these youngsters learn best in an informal, highly structured environment that contains soft light and has headsets available for those who learn best with quiet or music—such environments that seldom are provided in our schools.

Compared to achievers, at-risk youngsters also tend to be significantly less visual and auditory and have higher preferences for tactile/kinesthetic stimuli and greater needs for mobility and intake (food or drink). They tend to be unmotivated or strongly adult-motivated, can concentrate and learn best with an adult or with peers, are most alert during the late morning or early afternoon hours, and most important, they are global learners. (p. 55)

Table 8.4

Major Levels of Cognitive, Affective, and Psychomotor Domains

Level	Objective	Description
	Cognitive	
Basic (low)	Knowledge	The learner can recall information (i.e., bring to mind the appropriate material).
	Comprehension	The learner understands what is being communicated by making use of the communication.
	Application	The learner uses abstractions (e.g., ideas) in particular and concrete situations.
	Analysis	The learner can break down a communication into its constituent elements or parts.
	Synthesis	The learner puts together elements or parts to form a whole.
Advanced (high)	Evaluation	The learner makes judgments about the value of material or methods for a given purpose.
	Affective	
Basic (low)	Receiving (or attending)	The learner is sensitized to the existence of certain phenomena or stimuli.
	Responding	The learner does something with or about the phenomenon beyond merely perceiving it.
	Valuing	The learner believes that a thing, behavior, or phenomenon has worth.
	Organization	The learner arranges internalized values into a system of priorities.
Advanced (high)	Characterization (or Value Complex)	The learner organizes the value hierarchy into an internally consistent system.

Table 8.4 *continued*

Level	Objective	Description
	Psychomotor	
Basic (low)	Imitation	The learner begins to make an imitation (i.e., copy) when exposed to a behavior.
	Manipulation	The learner performs an act according to instructions.
	Precision	The learner performs an act independent of a model or instructions.
	Articulation	The learner coordinates a series of acts by establishing appropriate sequences and harmony.
Advanced (high)	Naturalization	The learner acts automatically and spontaneously with the least amount of energy.

Note. From *Disturbed Students: Characteristics and Educational Strategies* (pp.229–230) by H. C. Rich, 1982, Baltimore: University Park Press. Copyright 1982 by PRO-ED, Inc. Reprinted by permission. Original material adapted from *Taxonomy of Educational Objectives: The Classification of Educational Goals, Handbook I: Cognitive Domain* edited by B.S. Bloom et al., 1956, New York: Longman. Copyright 1956 by Longman. *Taxonomy of Educational Objectives: The Classification of Educational Goals, Handbook II: Affective Domain* edited by D.R. Krathwohl et al., 1964, New York: Longman. Copyright 1964 by Longman. *Taxonomy of Educational Objectives: Psychomotor Domain* by R.H. Dave, 1970, New Delhi, India: National Institute of Education. Copyright 1970 by the National Institute of Education. Adapted by permission of the publishers.

Table 8.6 presents information on analytical and global student characteristics.

Carbo and Hodges (1988) present successful strategies used by teachers for at-risk students.

1. Identify and match student's learning style strengths, especially perceptual and global/analytic abilities.
2. Share information about learning styles with students.
3. De-emphasize skill work requiring a strong analytic learning style.
4. Begin lessons globally.
5. Use a variety of methods in reading.
6. Provide appropriate amounts of structure.
7. Allow youngsters to work with a peer, friend, teacher, or alone depending on their sociological preferences.
8. Establish quiet working sections sufficiently distant from noisy areas.
9. Create at least one special work area in the classroom by placing file cabinets or bookcases perpendicular to a wall.
10. Experiment with scheduling the most difficult subjects during the late morning and early afternoon hours. (pp. 56–57)

Table 8.5
Cognitive Domain and the Student with Mild Disabilities

Level	Consideration for the Student with Mild Disabilities
Knowledge	If the teacher uses a variety of teaching methods and adapts content, students with mild disabilities can succeed at this level. Long-term retention may be difficult.
Comprehension	Most students with mild disabilities can comprehend information. Repetition may be necessary. Concrete rather than abstract information is easier to comprehend. Children with comprehension problems need special assistance.
Application	Applying concrete rather than abstract information is easier for students. Hands-on teaching and functional uses of information make application easier for students.
Analysis	Use whole-part-whole teaching method. Make analysis concrete by letting students with mild disabilities see or touch the division of whole into parts.
Synthesis	Use whole-part-whole teaching method. Make synthesis concrete by letting students with mild disabilities see or touch the combining of parts into a whole.
Evaluation	Most difficult level for many students with mild disabilities. Evaluation in life situations is a natural teaching approach here.

ADAPTING TEACHING TECHNIQUES

A teaching technique or strategy is a method of imparting knowledge, skills, or concepts to a learner. Historically, colleges and universities have recommended various teaching techniques to educators, who in turn have used those techniques in public and private schools. How teachers teach and what types of strategies they employ depend greatly on previous training, models observed, areas of interest, value judgments, and common sense. According to Jarolimek and Foster (1981), "There is a great deal of disagreement, even among well-informed persons, about what constitutes good teaching and how teaching should take place" (p. 109). The following section, then, does not try to teach teachers how to teach, but simply presents a variety of teaching techniques that teachers can use in different situations. Teachers will find that they can modify

Table 8.6
Analytical and Global Student Characteristics

Analytic Students Often:	Global Students Often:
1. Process information sequentially and logically.	1. Concentrate and learn when information is presented as a gestalt or whole.
2. Solve problems systematically.	2. Respond to emotional appeals.
3. Concentrate and learn when information is presented in small logical steps.	3. Tend to like fantasy and humor.
4. Enjoy doing puzzles (e.g., crossword, jigsaw).	4. Get "wrapped up" in a story and do not concentrate on the facts.
5. Like to follow step-by-step directions.	5. Process information subjectively and in patterns.
6. Can understand a rule without examples.	6. Need to know the essence of a story before reading/hearing it.
7. Enjoy learning facts such as dates and names.	7. Need examples of a rule to understand the rule itself.
8. Enjoy learning rules and using them.	8. Understand concrete examples better than those that are abstract.
9. Enjoy learning phonics.	9. Easily can identify the main ideas in a story.
10. Understand and apply phonic rules.	10. Are unconcerned about dates, names, or specifics.
11. Recall letter names and sounds easily.	11. Recall information easily when it is presented in the form of an anecdote.
12. Can decode words out of context.	12. Will concentrate and pay attention better if the goal of the lesson is clearly stated at the beginning.
13. Recall low-interest words (e.g., *what*, *fan*) almost as easily as high-interest words (e.g., *elephant*, *monster*).	13. Need to learn with high-interest, meaningful materials.
14. Are critical and analytic when reading.	14. Do not enjoy doing isolated skill exercises.
15. Can identify the details in a story.	15. Are able to learn a reading skill if the lesson is DRAWN from a story already read.
16. Recall many facts after listening to and/or reading a story.	16. Understand better if a story is enhanced by visuals (drawings, cartoons, photographs).
17. Easily list story events in logical, sequential order.	17. Recall high-interest words (*elephant*, *circus*, *dinosaur*) much more easily than low-interest words (e.g., *met*, *bet*).
18. Like to do reading skill exercises.	18. Use story context to figure out unknown words.

Adapted from *Reading style inventory*, by M. Carbo, 1982, Roslyn Heights, NY: Learning Research Associates. Copyright 1982 by M. Carbo. Reprinted by permission.

many of these techniques for the students. More specifically, this section covers adapting instruction within three major teaching techniques: mastery learning, teaching modes, and Bloom's taxonomy.

Mastery Learning

Mastery learning, a term first used by Bloom (1968), provides the learner with immediate feedback from the teacher and a process for making corrections when necessary. According to Guskey (1981), the mandates of P.L. 94–142 emphasize individualizing instruction for students with disabilities. The move to individualize, however, can increase managerial problems within the classroom. The diversity of students' abilities, demands placed on teachers for learner outcomes, increased class sizes due to economic constraints, and demands for new instructional skills are all pressures that can be eased by using one instructional strategy—mastery learning.

Bloom says that the teaching and evaluation process needs "some sort of 'feedback and corrective' procedure," a way of monitoring student progress so that teachers can "certify competent learners," "diagnose individual learning difficulties (feedback)," and "prescribe specific remediation procedures (correctives). . . When the student does not understand a concept or makes an error, the ideal tutor first identifies the error, then reexplains the concept from a different perspective or in a different manner, and finally checks the student again before moving on" (Guskey, 1981, p. 12).

According to Guskey, mastery learning has three major steps. First, the teacher divides the material for a year or a semester into small segments or units. Pacing of the units is left up to the teacher. Second, instruction begins and an evaluation is conducted. Third, test questions are carefully designed to test only the units taught. A student who answers any questions incorrectly consults the key. Alternative sources for further instruction and finding the correct answer accompany each test question.

Through this systematic correction of missed questions, students master more of the material. Mastery learning works well with students who have mild disabilities because it allows the teacher to individualize instruction within the group setting of the regular classroom. Table 8.7 presents the three steps of mastery learning and suggests ways to adapt or apply each step in the mainstreamed classroom.

Adapting Teaching Techniques Correlated with Specific Modes

Jarolimek and Foster (1981) identified four major teaching modes: the expository mode, the inquiry mode, the demonstration mode, and the activity mode (Table 8.8). Each mode has specific teaching techniques common to it, and teachers can adapt or modify all these techniques for their mainstreamed students.

Table 8.7
Adapting Mastery Learning for the Mainstream

Steps in Mastery Leaning	Possible Adaptions for the Regular Classroom Teacher
Step 1. Divide material into units or objectives for teaching.	Select teaching objectives on instructional level of student. Select units on student's interest level. Consult with special education teacher about units or objectives the student with disabilities may be unable to complete.
Step 2. Begin instruction. Conduct evaluation.	Determine prerequisite skills needed before teaching objective. Use task analysis to break down objectives. Note student's learning style. Assign tutors to assist student in learning objectives. Use alternative grouping procedures. (See Chapter 3) Adapt evaluation process. (See Chapter 11)
Step 3. Students check test questions missed and go to key to find additional resources for relearning missed items.	Be sure students were able to answer test questions. Could they read the test? Did they understand the directions? Did the test questions need modification? Assist students in finding supplementary resources for missed test questions. Before student begins remedial work, assess material. Is it on student's instructional level? Be sure student understands what to do. Assign peer tutor to mainstreamed student for reading material, answering questions.

Table 8.8
Specific Techniques Used in Various Teaching Modes

Expository Mode	Inquiry Mode	Demonstration Mode	Activity Mode
Lecture	Asking questions	Experiments	Role-playing
Telling	Stating	Exhibits	Constructing
Sound filmstrip	hypotheses	Simulations	Preparing exhibits
Explanation	Coming to	Games	Dramatizing
Panels	conclusions	Modeling	Processing
Recitation	Interpreting	Field trips	Group work
Audio recording	Classifying		
Motion pictures	Self-directed		
Discussion	study		
	Testing		
	hypotheses		
	Observing		
	Synthesizing		

Note. Adapted from "Specific Methods Associated with Various Modes of Teaching" pp. 131–132 in *Teaching and Learning in the Elementary School* (2nd ed.) by J. Jarolimek and C. D. Foster, 1981, New York: Macmillan. Copyright 1981 by Macmillan. Reprinted by permission.

Expository Mode

Teaching in the expository mode centers around the "concept exposition, which means most simply to provide an explanation" (Jarolimek & Foster, 1981, p. 110). This mode, probably the most popular among educators, requires extensive directive teaching. The class focuses on the teacher, who explains or disseminates the information, and students are involved only minimally. Regular education teachers report using this mode 53% of the time during instruction, while special education teachers use the expository mode only 24% of the time (Wood, 1989). Table 8.9 presents the specific teaching techniques used in the expository mode with suggested adaptations for each. Four of these techniques—lecture, telling, explanation, and discussion—focus on the teacher orally delivering information. These four techniques account for 93% of the time that regular education teachers teach in the expository mode and 87% for special education teachers (Wood, 1989).

A Model for Presentation for Lectures, Explanation, Discussion, and Telling. Presenting new skills or concepts orally (lecturing, explaining, discussing, telling) can make learning extremely difficult for the student who cannot impose structure to learning. Educators can utilize the following suggestions for adapting these types of techniques.

Multisensory Input. Visual aid materials that address a variety of learning styles should be an important instructional consideration. Because students

Table 8.9
Alternative Teaching Techniques for Expository Mode

Teaching Techniques	Alterations or Modifications for Mainstreamed Students
Lecture	• Provide lecture outlines • Provide copy of lecture notes • Use transparencies to provide visual presentation simultaneously with lecture
Telling	• Be specific in information given • Be sure you have attention of students • For students with short attention spans, give information in small segments
Sound Filmstrip	• Provide visuals when possible • Give earphones to students easily distracted by sounds
Explanation	• Keep simple and direct • Give in simple declarative sentences • Provide outline of explanation
Audio Recording	• Present with visuals • Give earphones to students easily distracted by sounds
Motion Pictures	• Orient students to movie before showing • Be sure length is appropriate • Place students with auditory problems close to sound • Review main points of film • Provide brief outline of main points
Discussion	• Ask questions you know students can answer • Keep discussion short • As points are made, list on board or transparency • Divide class into groups for brief discussions

learn through many sensory systems, educators need to use numerous modes to enhance oral presentations and to provide multisensory input for students. Students need to be taught in the different perceptual styles—visually, auditorially, and tactually. Using the overhead projector to present main points or underline or circle main ideas is an excellent technique for orientation to material. Videotapes provide instant playback of information for reinforcement. Students who miss a portion of the class will also benefit from a videotape. Audio tape recorders are excellent audiovisual aids for reinforcement of oral materials. Graphic materials such as globes and maps reinforce visually as well as tactually the material to be learned. Bulletin boards assist the teacher in presenting new information or providing reinforcement. Presenting information for multisensory input not only enhances classroom instruction but also provides for and addresses the perceptual learning styles of students.

Acquisition Outlines. Acquisition outlines present students with a graphic whole-part-whole method of learning. This method of adapting assists the students in seeing the *whole* of the presentation and then hearing a discussion of the *parts*. The acquisition outline serves as a formative study guide. The teacher should provide an acquisition outline when presenting new information, concepts, or skills to be learned. Prior to the test, a summative study guide (Chapter 9) will be provided, which sets the stage for studying. The teacher can place the acquisition outline on the overhead projector or provide each student with a copy to be completed. When introducing the outline, the teacher should follow these steps:

1. Introduce the topic.
2. Explain how the topic for today continues yesterday's lesson and will extend into tomorrow's lesson.
3. Introduce each of the major topics (I, II, III).
4. Point out that related topics are listed beneath each major point.
5. Return to Point I.
6. Review the topics listed under Point I.
7. Begin the discussion of Point I.
8. When lesson is over, return to the whole outline and review the topics.
9. Have the student file the outline in the appropriate notebook section.
10. Save a copy for the teacher's note-taking file.

Acquisition outlines keep students from guessing what will be coming next, assist the student in perceiving the organization of the presentation, and serve as a formative study guide for test review. Examples of acquisition outlines are shown in Figures 8.1 and 8.2.

General tips for using acquisition outlines include:

1. The acquisition outline can be developed into one of three formats: blank, partial, or completed. The more difficulty a student has in organizing and absorbing orally presented information, the more information should be provided on the outline.
2. When covering a point that is further explained within a text or handout, tell the students to write the page number from the text or the name of the handout in the left margin.
3. If some points on the outline require extensive note-taking, the teacher may provide a handout to promote accurate reception of information and save instructional time.

Structured Organizers. A structured organizer is a visual aid used to graphically present the major and minor topics of a presentation. As with acquisition outlines, structured organizers may be developed into transparencies or hand-

Figure 8.1
Acquisition Outline: Blank Format

Subject: World Geography   Class Date: _____
Topic: The Midwest   Student Name: _____

   I. Size of the Midwest
      A. Boundaries
      B. States

  II. Hills and Plains
      A. Formation During the Ice Age
      B. Till or Boulder Clay

 III. The Great Lakes
      A. Lake Superior
      B. Lake Michigan
      C. Lake Huron
      D. Lake Erie
      E. Lake Ontario

  IV. The Rivers
      A. Mississippi River
      B. Missouri River
      C. Ohio River

   V. Climate

Figure 8.2
Acquisition Outline: Partial Format

Subject: Health   Class Date: _____
Topic: Muscles   Student Name: _____

   I. Definition
      Muscles are _____ which move body parts.

  II. Numbers
      About _____ muscles are in the human body.
      About _____% of male weight.
      About _____% of female weight.

 III. Types of Muscles
      Two types of muscles include _____ and _____.
      _____ muscles can be controlled.
      _____ muscles cannot be controlled.

outs or displayed on a flip chart or chalkboard. The organizers may be blank, partial, or complete.

Lovitt (1989) reports six benefits of structured organizers.

1. Students are better able to follow the teacher's presentation, helping to keep them actively involved.
2. New information can be related to previous learning, allowing teachers to build in cumulative review.
3. Charts, tables, and graphs can stimulate student interest, making lessons more appealing.
4. Teachers are more systematic and thorough in their presentations. By preparing graphic organizers ahead of time, teachers are more likely to present material in a step-by-step manner.
5. Students learn organizational skills through example and use. They may generalize and transfer these skills to other areas, which in turn increases student achievement.
6. Graphic organizers can be used to promote higher-level thinking skills. (p. 1)

Figures 8.3 through 8.8 (pages 232–238) present different types of structured organizers.

Audio-taping Presentations. Frequently, students are unable to write down all the important information provided. The student who is a strong visual

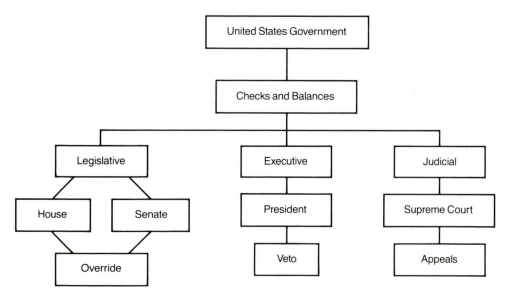

Figure 8.3
Structured Organizer: Top-Down-Bottom-Up Format

Note: A special thanks to Tom Lovitt for the general concepts presented in Figures 8.3–8.6.

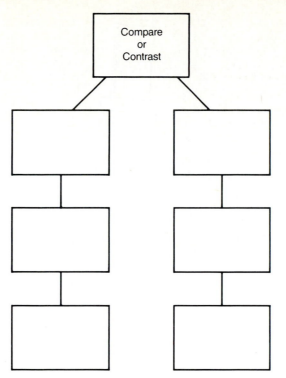

Figure 8.4
Structured Organizer: Compare-and-
Contrast Format

learner may miss important facts. Letting students tape-record the presentations
provides for additional reinforcement at a later time.

Inquiry Mode

The *inquiry mode* involves "asking questions, seeking information, and carrying
on an investigation" (Jarolimek & Foster, 1981, p. 116). The inquiry mode of

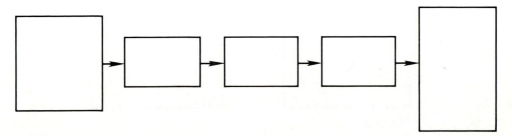

Figure 8.5
Structured Organizer: Sequential Format

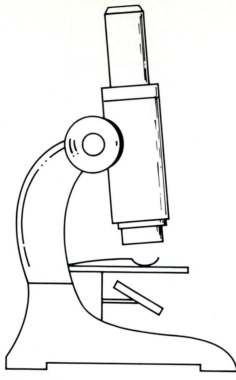

Figure 8.6
Structured Organizer: Design Format

teaching follows five basic steps: "(a) defining a problem, (b) proposing hypotheses, (c) collecting data, (d) evaluating evidence, and (e) making a conclusion" (p. 116). The teacher's guidance is still important, but the inquiry mode allows for more teacher-pupil interaction and encourages a team approach to teaching. For many students, however, the teacher often needs to provide some additional structure. The inquiry mode is used 23% of the time by regular

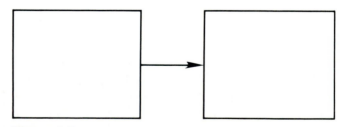

Figure 8.7
Structured Organizer: Cause-Effect Format
Note. A special thanks to Penny Shockley for this concept.

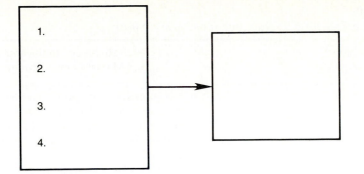

Figure 8.8
Structured Organizer: Conclusion Format
Note. A special thanks to Penny Shockley for this concept.

educators and 35% by special educators. Of the techniques listed for the inquiry mode (Table 8.10), regular education teachers report asking questions 66% of the time, while special education teachers use this technique 59% of the time (Wood, 1989).

The technique of *asking questions* of students with disabilities and those at risk for school success may be used to accomplish many things within the class lesson. Questions should accomplish at least four major objectives (Davies, 1981). Questions assist in motivating students by getting their attention or gaining their interests; encourage students to think; involve more than one student in the instructional process; and provide feedback to the teacher on the students' progress.

Question Types. Raphael (1982) suggests four types of questions that can be placed into either of two categories, "in-the-book" questions and "in-the-head" questions. Assisting students to understand question types or marking the question type for them helps when they are attempting to answer questions orally or look in a text to find answers to written questions. Table 8.11 presents these four types of questions with characteristics.

Bloom's Taxonomies of Learning and Questioning. As teachers teach, they deliver information, require students to learn the information, and ask questions from one of the six levels of Bloom's cognitive taxonomy to see if students have retained the information. Asking questions is a natural part of instruction. Teachers ask questions to assess student attention and comprehension, but they need to realize that questions also reflect taxonomy levels. Adapting instruction for students in the mainstream involves knowing the level of one's questions and changing that level if necessary. Questions directed at mainstreamed students should relate to their specific levels of learning. Table 8.12 presents the six levels of Bloom's taxonomy for the cognitive domain with definitions and typical stem words. The table is also divided into convergent and divergent

Table 8.10
Alternative Teaching Techniques for Inquiry Mode

Teaching Techniques	Alterations or Modifications for Mainstreamed Students
Asking questions	• Ask questions on appropriate level of taxonomy scale; vary questions to meet different taxonomy levels of students • Call students' names before directing a question to them • Do not embarrass students by asking questions they cannot answer
Stating hypotheses	• Have students choose from two or three hypotheses instead of having to formulate their own
Coming to conclusions	• Present alternative conclusions
Interpreting	• Assign peer tutors to help • Present alternative interpretations
Classifying	• Use concrete instead of abstract concepts
Self-directed study	• Give specific directions about what to do • Make directions short, simple, and few • Collect and place resources for study in one area
Testing hypotheses	• Assign peer tutors to help
Observing	• Give explicit directions about how to and what to observe • Provide sequential checklist of what will happen so students see steps • Have students check off each step observed
Synthesizing	• Assign peer tutors to help • Provide model of whole

question types. Students work from the lower-order to the higher-order levels. Asking a question within a level where a student cannot respond eliminates the possibility of class participation for that student.

General Suggestions for Asking Questions. The following general suggestions will help teachers in determining how to ask questions of students with disabilities and those at risk for success.

1. Ask questions with a taxonomy level where the student is functioning.
2. Provide "wait time" for responses to questions. Extra time is necessary for responses to divergent questions (Kindsvatter, Wilen & Ishler, 1988).

Table 8.11
Question Types and Characteristics

Broad Categories	Question Type	Characteristic
"In-the-Book" Questions	1. Right-there questions	• Literal questions • Detailed in nature • Found *right* in text • Example: "What color are the girl's eyes?"
	2. Think-and-search questions	• Answer is in text, but not in one place • Example: "Put these events into sequence."
"In-the-Head" Questions	3. Author-and-you questions	• Inferences or conclusions required • Involve learner's prior knowledge • Example: "Why did the man decide to wear black?"
	4. On-your-own questions	• Cannot be answered from the text • Learner must use own experience • Questions asked prior to reading • Extensive questions • Example: "How are modern cars and the cars of the '20s different?"

Note. From "Teaching Question and Answer Relationships" by T. E. Raphael, 1986, *The Reading Teacher*, *39*, pp. 516–523. Copyright 1986. Reprinted with permission of Taffy E. Raphael and the International Reading Association..

Research shows that teachers usually allow about 1 second for a response, but students typically need about 3 to 5 seconds (Rowe, 1974).

3. Allow "wait time" for all students to think about an answer given by one student before proceeding to the next question.

4. Ask questions in a planned and patterned order or sequence. Factors that influence the choice of sequence include the lesson's objective, student's ability level, and student's understanding of the content covered (Kindsvatter et al., 1988).

5. Remember that some sequencing begins with lower-level questions and progresses to higher-level thinking. Some students will start with higher-level questions and remain there (Kindsvatter et al. 1988).

Table 8.12
Categories of Questioning Based on Bloom's Structure

Questioning Category	Definition of Questioning Category[3]	Bloom's Category[1]	Definition of Bloom's Category	Student Activity[2]	Typical Stem Words
LOWER ORDER CONVERGENT	Requires students to think reproductively. Teachers have students recall or recognize information. Emphasis is on memorization and observation.	Knowledge	Requires students to use memory only, repeating information exactly as memorized.	Remembering facts, items, definitions, concepts, principles.	Define, recall, recognize, remember, who, what, where, when, list, name, define, describe
HIGHER ORDER CONVERGENT	Requires students to begin to engage in first levels of productive thinking. Students go beyond recall and demonstrate an understanding of information by organizing material mentally. Students apply information learned.	Comprehension	Requires students to rephrase, reword, compare information.	Understanding the meaning of material	Describe, compare, contrast, rephrase, put in your own words, explain the main idea, interpret, summarize, give examples, predict, translate
		Application	Requires students to apply knowledge to determine a single, correct answer.	Selecting a concept or skill and using it to solve a problem	Apply, solve, classify, choose, employ, write an example, which, what is, complete, modify, contrast

Level	Category	Require students to...	Definition	Requires students to...	Examples
HIGHER ORDER DIVERGENT	Analysis	Require students to think critically. Students analyze information to discover reasons or causes, draw conclusions or generalizations, find evidence in support of opinions.	Breaking material down into its parts and explaining the hierarchical relations	Requires students to identify motives or causes, draw conclusions, determine evidence.	Support, analyze, conclude, why, how does . . . . apply, why does . . . . work, how does . . . . relate to . . . . , what distinctions can be made about . . . . and . . . . .
HIGHER ORDER EVALUATIVE	Synthesis	Require students to perform original and evaluation thinking. Students make predictions, solve life-like problems, produce original communications, judge ideas and information.	Producing something original after breaking material down into its component parts	Requires students to make predictions, produce original communications, solve problems.	Predict, produce, write, design, develop, synthesize, contrast, how can we improve, what happens if, how can we solve, can you devise, can you predict
	Evaluation		Making judgment based on a preestablished set of criteria	Requires students to make judgments, offer opinions.	Judge, validate, decide, evaluate, assess, give your opinion, which is better, do you agree

[1] From "Review of the Taxonomy" in *Classroom Teaching Skills: A Workbook* (p. 118) by J.M. Cooper, J. Hansen, P. H. Martorella, G. Morine-Derhimer, D. Sadker, M. Sadker, S. Sokolve, R. Shostak, T. Ten Brink, and W.A. Weber, 1977, Lexington, MA: D.C. Heath. Copyright 1977 by D.C. Heath. Reprinted by permission. Original material adapted from *Taxonomy of Educational Objectives; The Classification of Educational Goals, Handbook 1: Cognitive Domain* edited by B.S. Bloom et al., 1956, New York: Longman, Copyright © 1956 by Longman. Reprinted by permission.

[2] S.S. Goudwin, G.W. Sharp, E.F. Cloutier, and W. A. Diamond. *Effective classroom questioning* (p. 5) 1981, University of Illinois at Urbana-Champaign. Adapted by permission.

[3] *Dynamics of effective teaching* by R.R. Kindsvatter, W. Wilen, and M. Ishler 1988, New York: Longman. p. 111. Adapted by permission.

6. Since responses to lower-level questions determine student understanding of content, use those responses as an indication of starting points for reteaching.
7. Allow student to formulate questions to ensure active participation in the questioning process (Kindsvatter et al., 1988).
8. State questions clearly and specifically.
9. When asking a question, state the question, call the student's name, and repeat the question.
10. Encourage all students to participate in the questioning process by responding in a positive way to all student responses.
11. Avoid sarcasm, reprimand, personal attack, accusation, or no response at all as teacher responses to student answers (West, 1975).

Demonstration Mode

Essential components of the demonstration mode are "showing, doing, and telling" (Jarolimek & Foster, p. 120). Like the expository mode, the demonstration mode depends on directive teaching. Because it presents information in a concrete way, this method is essential for teachers to use in instructing students with disabilities. The demonstration mode is used only 3% of the time by regular educators and 6% by special educators (Wood, 1989). Table 8.13 presents the techniques used in the demonstration mode with suggested alterations for mainstreamed students. Of the techniques listed, regular educators use experiments 34% of the time, while special educators use modeling 36% of the time (Wood, 1989).

Modeling is an excellent technique to use for students who are having difficulty understanding the information presented. Models may be visual, such as a map, chart, or globe, or verbal, such as a language mode. Models may also be participatory, where the teacher demonstrates a skill and the students become actively involved. Suggestions for modeling include:

1. Exaggerate the modeling presentation.
2. If the steps in the model are lengthy or difficult, utilize several short time spans rather than one long demonstration.
3. Videotape the modeling demonstration for students to replay and replicate.
4. When repeating the steps in a model, do so in the same sequence used in the original presentation.
5. Provide a checklist of the steps in the model for students to follow as the teacher demonstrates.
6. Provide auditory clues along with visual cues.
7. When a student is implementing a model, reward the student's behavior.
8. Use modeling for social, technical, or academic skills.
9. As a student models a desired skill, use the situation to point out the behavior to other students.

Table 8.13
Alternative Teaching Techniques for Demonstration Mode

Teaching Techniques	Alterations or Modifications for Mainstreamed Students
Experiments	• Provide sequential directions • Have students check off each completed step • If teacher demonstrates, let students assist • Be sure students fully understand purpose, procedures, and expected outcome of experiment • Set up incidental learning experiences
Exhibits	• Assign projects according to students' instructional level • Have students select project topic from a short list • Provide directions and list of materials needed • Be sure project does not require skills students lack • Have students display their exhibits
Simulations	• Do not embarrass students by requiring them to do something they cannot do • Make sure students understand directions, terms used, and expected outcome
Games	• Design games in which acquisition of skills, not winning, is the priority • Make directions simple • Highlight important directions with color codes • With peer tutors, let students prepare own game • Design games, emphasize skills needed by students
Modeling	• Model only one step at a time • Use task analysis on steps • Use visual models when possible
Field Trips	• Prepare students by explaining destination, purpose, expected behavior, and schedule

Activity Mode

The activity mode of teaching is "a set of strategies that involve pupils in learning by doing things that are, for the pupils, meaningfully related to the topic under study" (Jarolimek & Foster, 1981, p. 127). This method of teaching is best described by an old Native American proverb, "I hear and I forget, I see and I remember, I do and I understand." By using the activity mode, teachers provide students with actual experience and thus a clearer understanding of concepts. This mode is used 21% of the time by regular educators and 35% by special educators. Within this mode, the technique of group work is used 66% of the time by regular educators and 72% by special educators (Wood, 1989). Ideas for group work were discussed in detail in Chapter 6. Table 8.14 presents ideas for the techniques used in the activity mode.

OBJECTIVE	STRATEGIES/ PROCEDURES	MATERIALS/ RESOURCES	EVALUATION/ ASSIGNMENT
Date: _____ Taxonomy Level	Lecture on the parts of the ear and how sound travels.	Display of ear Filmstrip Chapter in text Handout of parts of ear	Fill-in-blank Test and listing
The student will be able to list and define the parts of the ear and the steps for the travel of sound in the ear.	Teaching Techniques: — Use acquisition outline. — Use structured organizer to show relationship of parts of ear. — Use visual of ear with lecture. Format of Content:	Adapted Media:	Evaluation Test: Student Assignment:

Date: _____
Taxonomy Level
X Knowledge
X Comprehension
___ Application
___ Analysis
___ Synthesis
___ Evaluation

Adaptations:

Figure 8.9
Format For an Adapted Lesson Plan: Teaching Techniques

Table 8.14
Alternative Teaching Techniques for Activity Mode

Teaching Techniques	Alterations or Modifications for Mainstreamed Students
Role-playing	• Be sure student understands role • Short lines or no lines at all may be best • Respect privacy of students who do not want roles • Let such students assist other role-players
Constructing	• Select project for students or have them select from a short list • Try to use projects that include special education objectives • Provide sequential checklist
Preparing exhibits	• Assign peer tutors to help • Use same alterations suggested for Constructing technique
Dramatizing	• Respect privacy of those who do not want parts • Let such students help others prepare sets
Processing	• Clearly state steps • Make steps sequential and short
Group work	• Assign peer tutors to help • Select activity student can succeed in • Use variety of grouping procedures

ADAPTED LESSON PLAN FOR TEACHING TECHNIQUES

Figure 8.9 extends the adapted lesson format presented in Chapter 7. The regular class objective, strategies, materials, and evaluation are completed for a lesson on sound and the ear. In Figure 8.9 the strategies section of the lesson plan has suggested adaptations to be used by the teacher. These adaptations will better provide structure to the lesson's delivery.

SUMMARY

Providing structure by organizing information to be learned for the student as you present new skills or concepts helps all learners, especially the random learner who has difficulty imposing structure. Providing structure, understanding learning and learning styles, and incorporating alternative modes of instructional delivery help students receive information in an organized manner. Learning takes place more quickly because structure is imposed prior to the processing of information. The next step within our model is "Adapting Format of Content."

CHAPTER NINE

Adapting Format of Content

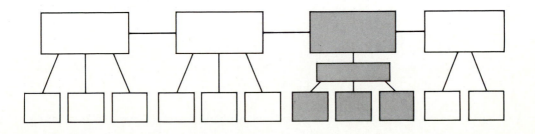

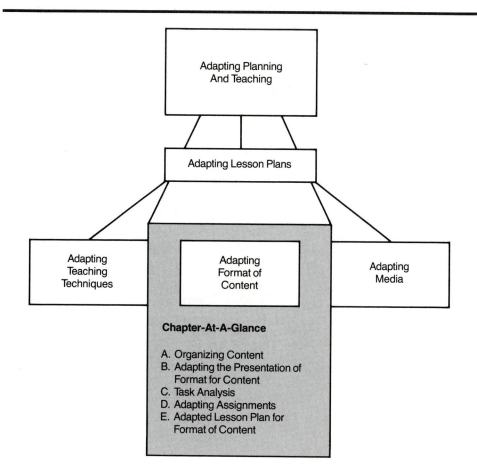

Adapting Planning And Teaching

Adapting Lesson Plans

Adapting Teaching Techniques

Adapting Format of Content

Adapting Media

Chapter-At-A-Glance

A. Organizing Content
B. Adapting the Presentation of Format for Content
C. Task Analysis
D. Adapting Assignments
E. Adapted Lesson Plan for Format of Content

After teachers select the appropriate teaching technique to deliver the lesson, they may have to consider alternative ways of presenting the academic content. For example, teachers usually teach the subject of reading from a basal textbook and math using exercises and examples in a textbook. Assignments may be given at the end of a class to prepare for tomorrow's class. Worksheets traditionally are used in classrooms across the country. What happens to the student who simply cannot be successful with the content being taught? Many times, the technique may have been adapted, but the student still may not understand the material being taught. Thus, the regular class teacher should ask the following questions about the student experiencing difficulty:

1. Does the student have the skills to complete the required task?
2. If not, does the student have the prerequisite skills for beginning the required task?
3. Does instruction begin at the student's functioning level?
4. Was the teaching technique appropriate for delivering the instruction to the student?

After answering these questions, the teacher may see a need to modify the presentation of the format of the content.

This chapter discusses four aspects of modifying content: (a) organizing the content; (b) adapting the presentation of the format of content; (c) task analysis; and (d) adapting assignments. At each of these intervention points, adjustments can be made that will continue our model in adapting the planning and teaching process.

ORGANIZING CONTENT

As teachers continue to provide structure for students unable to do so themselves, note-taking, notebooks, and study guides are logical places to continue *structuring* within the area of content. Remember, when educators provide structure, students will eventually learn to impose their own structure. *Structuring* then becomes a natural component for the child.

Note-taking

Note-taking is a skill that requires instruction, structure, and practice but is often assumed to be an easy task. Many mainstreamed and at-risk students have difficulty taking notes because of an inability to organize ideas or concepts, distinguish main points or ideas presented, or transfer information from a written format or from information presented orally, or because of a deficit in processing and/or motor skills.

A point often overlooked is that the successful completion of a test relies heavily on the completeness of the student's notes. Many students fail tests because of incomplete notes, not because they do not know the material. One must have the material to study in order to learn. Having a complete set of class notes is crucial for students. The point of intervention could be the lack of note-taking abilities. The following section discusses the needs which note-taking can meet and adaptations teachers may employ for note-taking.

Needs Met Through Note-taking

Several needs of students are met through note-taking. First, and most important, students must have the correct information in a format for study if we expect them to learn class information and pass class tests. The note-taking process serves as a study process for many students, especially if the class is organized and/or systematic. Learning how to take notes in difficult situations is a skill that may be carried not only into other classes but into adult life as well. Learning how to take notes, learning the method of adaptation which is required, and getting a complete set of notes provides instructional security for students. Students have reduced anxiety when they know that they have the proper information from which to organize their study.

Note-taking Adaptations

Prior to providing adaptations to the note-taking process, educators need to consider the sources from which the notes will be given. Will the information be orally presented, using lectures, movies, videotapes, or filmstrips, or will it be in written format, using the chalkboard, an overhead projector, a textbook, newspapers, or magazines? Students should also develop an awareness of the source of the notes and specific adaptations they need for each source. Second, teachers should tell students the type of test, such as multiple-choice, essay, or short-answer, to expect from the notes. This helps the student focus on how the material will be presented in the testing situation.

Notes Taken from Information Presented Orally

One of the most common situations whereby a student takes notes from oral information is the lecture. Mainstreamed students have difficulty taking notes from a lecture for a number of reasons. These include (a) inability to impose structure; (b) visual processing problems; (c) deficient motor skills; and (d) auditory processing problems. Structure must be imposed upon the information being heard. Many students are unable to listen to the teacher, extrapolate the major and minor concepts, and put this information on their paper. Students at-risk for school success have difficulty imposing structure. Everything that the teacher says appears equal. Second, students with visual processing deficits may not be able to move their eyes from one focus point, the teacher, to a new focus point, the paper, smoothly enough to take notes quickly. Deficient fine motor control may cause handwriting problems so that students cannot read their own notes. Finally, auditory processing problems may cause students to be unable to hear the lecture clearly and accurately, resulting in incomplete or incorrect notes.

One suggestion for adapting the note-taking process for the lecture is providing a *lecture outline*. An outline gives the student the major and minor parts of the lecture to be discussed, either on a single page or on one or more pages with space allotted for filling in notes. The different types of lecture outlines were presented in Chapter 8. Prior to beginning the lecture, the teacher should follow these steps:

1. Present the topic or objective of the material to be covered.
2. Relate the material to the sequence of material taught yesterday and to the total course sequence.
3. Introduce the lecture outline by pointing out the major points (I, II, III).
4. Remind students that minor or supporting information will be listed under each major topic.
5. Give the page numbers where students can find the information in the text.
6. Begin the lecture and indicate important or "noteworthy" information.
7. Throughout the lecture or discussion, refer to the outline number to keep students on track.
8. If paper shortage is a concern, present the outline on the chalkboard or overhead projector.
9. At the conclusion of the lecture, briefly summarize the information covered.

Students can also be given structured overviews for taking notes. These are discussed in detail in Chapter 8.

Use tape recorders for recording lectures and/or class discussions. The students may bring their own recorders or the teacher can record the lecture and allow students to check out tapes at a later date.

As a class lecture progresses, use the chalkboard to help organize the information. Develop a chart format with headings. During the lecture, fill in key information for students to copy. When the class is completed, students will have a set of notes organized by categories to make studying and review easier.

Good listening is essential for taking notes from lectures, class discussions, reviews, or other oral presentations. Students should be trained to listen. Teachers should remember that, after a while, everything begins to sound the same. Therefore, it is important that to take an occasional "listening break." Pause for a stretch break, tell a story that is related to the topic, insert a joke. Breaking the constant flow of the lecture helps the listener attend to "noteworthy" information.

Give signals to let students know what is important to write down. Students who have difficulty with structure may also have difficulty distinguishing major and minor details. When you come to a part of the lecture that you know students must remember for a test or other reason, give a clue, for example, "this is noteworthy." Be sure that students know what the clue words are. Tell students they should either underline the "noteworthy" information or put a star in the margin. By giving clues, you are (a) keeping the students on track; (b) helping students attend to the important information; and (c) teaching the difference in major and minor information.

Other note-taking adaptations may be found in the General Tips Section at the end of this section.

Notes Taken from Written Material

Taking notes from the chalkboard relies heavily on good skills in visual tracking, handwriting, and organization. If the skills are not fully developed, the mainstreamed student may have great difficulty getting the notes. The arrangement of the seating is essential. The teacher should be sure that students are seated so they can see the chalkboard easily as well as avoid distractions. If you are going to provide a complete set of notes for students who are unable to copy from the board, you may have them copy only certain sections. This will keep students working with the class, but take away the stress of trying to get all of the notes. Students can then focus on the discussion, knowing that a complete set of notes will follow.

When giving notes from the overhead projector, you may make the same adaptations described for the chalkboard. In addition, keep covered any information you have not yet discussed, so students cannot see it until you are ready to present it. When you are ready to discuss the information, allow time for students to copy it before you begin. If you are talking as the students write, many will miss your discussion.

Many times, you may ask students to take notes from preprinted material such as textbooks, magazines, and newspapers. If the notes are being written for future study and review, the students may wish to use the format presented in Figure 9.1. If the student is copying material on a note card, similar information may be placed on the card. Be sure to put the page number of the material on the card and number the cards when finished.

Figure 9.1
Format For Taking Notes From Printed Matter

Topic:_____	Class: _____
Source of Material:_____	Period: _____
Page Numbers:_____	Date: _____

As you develop the outline, put important facts, vocabulary, dates in this column. The specific page number may also be listed.	Outline material in this section
	I. A.
	B.
	C.
	II. A.
	B.
	C.
	III. A.
	B.
	C.

General Note-taking Tips

The information in this section applies to note-taking from any material, whether presented orally or in written form. The information is divided into three categories: note-taking ideas (Table 9.1), formatting the paper (Table 9.2), and when the note-taking process is over (Table 9.3).

Providing adaptations for notes is a crucial support for students. If students are unable to get a complete set of notes, how can we expect them to be successful on tests? Perhaps when we test, we are evaluating the students' ability to take complete notes, and not their knowledge of content. The ideas presented in Tables 9.1 through 9.3 help bridge the gap between notes and students.

Notebooks

At the beginning of each school year, teachers announce in classes across America, "In this class, you will keep a notebook. . ." Some teachers provide the format for the notebooks, while others leave the format open. The following are suggestions for helping students organize and keep notes, notebook checkups, and test review from notes.

Organizing the Notebook

Prior to organizing the notebook, the teacher should examine the structure of the class. For example, how does the class structure relate to the types of tests given? Does the class follow a certain structure each day? An example is provided in Table 9.4 for a class in geography. The class structure is provided in column A, and the format for the notebook in column B. Column C shows the reorganized notebook format to match the class structure in column A. Column D lists the type of test item to be used for each class section. By reorganizing the class notebook, making students aware of the match between the class structure and the notebook format, and providing the test item type for each section, teachers help students impose structure on the class, allowing them to think of the class from beginning to end. Other tips for organizing notebooks include using dividers for each subject and section and keeping separate notebooks in a looseleaf binder for each subject.

Keeping the Notebook

This can become a major problem for many students. During the first day or two of class, work with students as they "build" their notebooks. Explain the overall format, provide an example of a completed notebook, show students the relationship of the class, notebook, and tests (Table 9.4), and have each student compile the notebook in class. Review the final product. This may seem like wasted time, but you will find that it is time well spent. Remember, the student who will never get a notebook together alone is the one who will benefit most from notebook building in class. For many students, the directions are not sufficient because they cannot follow through with the structure without support. For the first two or three weeks, continue to work with the class each day on keeping the notebook in order. Eventually, you can fade the prompts.

Table 9.1
General Tips for Note-taking: Notes from Oral/Written Materials

Suggestions	Examples/Notes
1. Save a set of notes from another class to give to the student.	
2. Give the student a copy of the teacher's notes.	
3. Let students copy their own notes to give to others who have difficulty taking notes.	A special carbonless paper that makes up to five copies at one writing and a notebook designed to hold the paper can be purchased from: Campus Connections Rochester Institute of Technology 1 Lomb Memorial Drive P.O. Box 9887 Rochester, New York 14623 (716) 475–2504 $5.95 for a package of 200 sheets of paper $3.95 for the notebook
4. Use an organizer for taking notes on poems.	

Title	Author	Type	Poetic Devices Used

Summary of Poem:

What I learned from the discussion:

_____

_____

Class Discussion:

Questions I have about the poem:

_____

_____

5. Seat the student to avoid auditory or visual distractions.	
6. Provide structured organizers for the student for note-taking.	The types of organizers presented in Chapter 8 may be used here.

Table 9.1
continued

Suggestions	Examples/Notes

7. Provide a lecture outline for note-taking.	**The Circulatory System**
	I. The Heart
	    A. Location
	    B. Chambers of the heart
	II. Blood Vessels
	    A. Arteries
	    B. Veins
	    C. Capillaries
	III. Circulation of the Heart
	    A. Right atrium
	    B. Superior vena cava
	    C. Inferior vena cava
	    D. Right ventricle
	    E. Left ventricle
	    F. Arteries
	    G. Veins
	    H. Aorta

8. Develop a *who, what, when, where, how,* and *why* outline for note-taking.

Who – – – – – – – – –

What – – – – – – – –

When – – – – – – – –

Where – – – – – – – –

How – – – – – – – –

Why – – – – – – – –

Table 9.1 *continued*

Suggestions	Examples/Notes

or

Who	What	When	Where	How	Why

Notebook Checkup

A checkup is an easy way to help students continue to keep their notebooks organized. Inform the class that you will have a notebook quiz from time to time. The quiz will consist of asking questions from different sections of the notebook by date of notes. This type of quiz will be an easy way to get an A. On the first quiz, record only the As and remind the rest of the class that simple organization guarantees an A. The second quiz will count for all students.

The notebook is also used for test review. Prior to a test, distribute a study guide and review it for the test. The notes become a vital part of the study process. Tie together the study guide and the notes taken during this study period. Help students see that studying and reviewing notes will improve their test scores significantly. Teach students to distribute their studying over shorter periods of time.

Study Guides

A *study guide* assists students in developing a focus plan for study and review. As teachers teach, study guides become instruments for improving structure both as the lesson develops and when the lesson is over and test review begins. Study guides benefit students in numerous ways:

1. Study guides provide organization of information for study purposes.
2. Study guides help students develop a whole-part-whole concept for the material being presented.

Table 9.2
General Tips for Note-taking: Formatting the Paper

Suggestions	Examples/Notes
1. Teach students to use only two thirds of their paper for note-taking, leaving one-third blank for later study and review.	<table><tr><td>Space for study and review</td><td>Take notes here</td></tr></table>
2. Use these ideas to assist students with note-taking: <ul><li>Have students take notes in the right column.</li><li>As you give the notes, point out important dates, facts, vocabulary for the student to put in the left column.</li><li>When you have completed a section of notes, stop and ask the class to review their notes and list possible test questions in the left column.</li><li>Review the questions presented and have the class complete missing information.</li></ul>	
3. After note-taking, students can work with a "buddy" to study and review notes (see table 9.3).	
4. Have students develop a format for their note papers. This will help them to organize, file, and retrieve for later review (see Figure 9.1).	
5. For easier filing, use looseleaf paper for note-taking.	
6. Purchase commercial notebooks if you prefer to have students keep the notes in a spiral book.	Source: Law Notebook AMPAD Corporation Holyoke, MA 01040 <ul><li>College-ruled</li><li>Wide law margin</li><li>80 sheets per notebook</li><li>Perforated for easy removal to looseleaf notebook</li></ul>

Table 9.3
General Tips for Note-Taking: After the Note-Taking Process

Suggestions	Examples/Notes
1. Teach students how to use the notes for study and review.	Many students stuff the notes into backpacks, never to be seen again. Take time to teach how to use the notes.
2. Assign "buddies" or study-and-review" teams to work together using the notes.	
3. Have "buddies" color-code notes. Use three colors: one each for vocabulary, facts to remember, and concepts to study.	
4. Have "buddies" check one set of notes with another and write missing information in the left column.	
5. Teach students to file their notes in an organized manner. This process should be done with the class for an extended period until the students have developed the structure.	The next section on notebooks suggests ways to file notes.
6. Prior to a test, refer to notes by dates or topics that should be reviewed. Tell the student the test type for specific notes.	When students are studying notes to look for a short answer or listing, they will have a different focus than when they are studying for a multiple-choice test.
7. It is good practice to keep an extra set of class notes on file. Students who are absent or have missed sections of notes can refer to this set for assistance. File the notes by class date for easy retrieval.	

3. Study guides present information in a sequential, logical manner.
4. Study guides tie together the information from yesterday to today and for tomorrow.
5. Study guides impose structure on information to be learned.
6. Study guides impose a point of focus for the teacher.
7. Study guides help facilitate collaboration between special and regular education teachers.
8. Study guides are helpful for parents to assist their children in study and review.
9. Study guides aid students in preparing for specific test types.
10. Study guides help students to impose structure in other classes without guides.

Table 9.4
Organizing Notebooks

A Class Structure	B Notebook Format	C Reorganized Notebook Format	D Test Item
Class Opening			
Atlas questions from the overhead projector	Class notes Maps	Atlas notes/maps	Listing questions
Study questions from homework	Quizzes	Study questions/notes	Short-answer
Class lecture	Exams	Lecture outline/notes	Multiple-choice True or false
Tomorrow's assignment		Quizzes	
Class closing		Exams	

Types of Study Guides

Two types of study guides are formative and summative study guides. Each of these types serves a specific function for imposing structure and organizing material.

A *formative study guide* organizes information in short, distributive segments. The guide focuses on specific details of the information covered. An example is the acquisition outline or lesson frame presented in Chapter 8. As a new concept or section of information is presented, students follow the class discussion and record important details in an organized manner. As discussed in Chapter 8, this outline or frame may be on one page or on several pages, and it should have space provided for notes. The teacher may provide an incomplete outline for students to complete or an outline that has the details already completed. The second option is helpful to the student who has difficulty taking notes. Each outline or frame should list the page numbers for the specific information, the title or objective for the lesson, and the lesson date. After the class, students should be instructed to place the outline in the appropriate notebook section.

As an aid to students preparing for a quiz or test on information learned, the teacher may present the *summative study guide*. Summative study guides are designed to provide general information on the notes to be quizzed, which lays the foundation for the organization of the study effort. The teacher may direct the student to put all formative study guides in sequential order by date and place the summative study guide first. The summative study guide will provide structure for the student's study effort. Figure 9.2 presents a sample summative study guide. The summative study guide can be completed by the teacher or with the class.

Figure 9.2
Summative Study Guide

Student: _____   Date of Test: _____

Subject: _____   Date Guide
                                            Issued: _____
Teacher: _____

STUDY GUIDE

1. Lesson/test objective:
2. Textbook/workbook/manual pages to be covered:
3. Handouts/lecture/films/speakers/demonstrations/labs/maps/charts to be covered:
4. Key words/vocabulary to be learned. location:
5. Review questions for organizing study:
6. Type of test to be given:

Test Type	Number of Items	Point Value
_____Multiple-Choice	_____	_____
_____Matching	_____	_____
_____True-False	_____	_____
_____Fill-in-the-Blank	_____	_____
Word bank included:		
_____Yes _____No		
_____Short-Answer	_____	_____
_____Essay	_____	_____
_____Diagrams/Charts	_____	_____
_____Maps	_____	_____
Word bank for map:		
_____Yes _____No		
List of maps to review:		
Math Items:		
_____Computation/	_____	_____
Equations		
_____Word Problems	_____	_____
_____Formulas	_____	_____
_____Graphing	_____	_____
_____Proofs	_____	_____
_____Other, please describe:		

7. Other suggestions for study and review:

Thank you for your help!

Student signature: _____
Parent signature: _____

Students are directed to the guide to review the lesson or test objective, the textbook, workbook, or handouts to be covered, and key words or vocabulary to be learned. If the test includes short-answer or essay test items, review questions are a must. These questions will help provide focus for the student for organizing study and reviewing essay questions. The type of test and number of items and point value are also a necessity. The type of test reflects the type of retention measure the teacher used while teaching the lesson. This is to say, if the lesson focus was on specific dates, people, and facts, then the test would become a recognition measure. If the lesson focused on general concepts, such as, "How did the invention of irrigation affect the lives of the people?" then the test would become a subjective measure.

Organizing for Study

After the student has completed the formative and summative study guides, organizing for study becomes the next focus. Many students still need the guided practice of planning for the study process. Using the monthly organization chart and the subject time organization chart facilitates this process. The teacher may provide a chart form for students to complete by themselves or with the class.

The *monthly organization chart* can be placed at the beginning of the notebook and completed daily. As tests, quizzes, projects, and papers are assigned, the student records each in the appropriate daily box for the month. A sample monthly organization chart may be found in Table 9.5.

Table 9.5
Monthly Organization Chart

	MONDAY	TUESDAY	WEDNESDAY	THURSDAY	FRIDAY
Week of May 1–5	Math Quiz		Science project due	Map quiz	English vocabulary test
Week of May 8–12		Social Studies report: Mexico		Test over short story unit	
Week of May 15–19		Social Studies test Chapters 5–7	Science lab due		
Week of May 22–26		Math quiz	English paper due	P.E. test Tennis	
Week of May 29– June 2		Oral report P.E.			Math test

The *subject time organization chart* is designed to provide structure for organizing the study time needed for each subject on a weekly basis. In planning the subject time organization chart, the student refers to the monthly organization chart to be sure to include any important study items. These charts can be kept in the notebook or some other convenient place. Table 9.6 presents a sample subject time organizer.

General Study Tips

General study tips include keeping notes and guides organized, planning study time for each task, nightly review of all class notes, developing flash cards for recognition of information, planning a specific time and place for study, developing a plan for reinforcement of study, and helping students to see the value of planned, organized study.

Table 9.6
Subject Time Organization Chart

Subject	MON	TUE	WED	THU	FRI	SAT	SUN
Time			1st period				
Social Studies							
Task			Report on routes due				
Time		2nd period			2nd period		
Science							
Task		Read Chapter 5			Test on Chapter 5		
Time							
Language Arts (English)							
Task							
Time			4th period				
Math							
Task			Complete exercise 4, p. 6				
Time							
P.E./ Health							
Task							

ADAPTING THE PRESENTATION OF FORMAT FOR CONTENT

Student success may depend on the teacher's ability or willingness to adapt the presentation of content. The following examples of activities are designed to provide a starting point for developing one's own ideas. Many creative educators use inventive adaptations in the class. These represent only a small number.

ACTIVITY: Understanding rules and laws

ADAPTATION: Often students do not understand the meaning and purpose of rules and laws. They cannot always equate a crime with the appropriate consequence. Students can role-play selected rules or law-breaking vignettes, then discuss what consequences would be suitable for certain crimes. This is a good opportunity to discuss why certain rules and laws exist and look at their positive aspects.

ACTIVITY: Understanding different cultures

ADAPTATION: Students with disabilities often have trouble visualizing life in other countries. When studying different cultures, allow students to "live" in that culture. Encourage students to dress, act, speak, eat, work, and play in that culture. Class periods could be devoted to such experiences as cooking and eating authentic meals, making costumes, or learning the languages. Discuss what is important to the culture and how it would feel to be a person from that setting.

ACTIVITY: Using maps

ADAPTATION: Begin with something familiar to the students. Make a map of the school and have students label specific points, then have them map out their neighborhoods. Eventually progress to states, sections of a country, and finally whole countries.

ACTIVITY: Reviewing maps

ADAPTATION: Make an overhead transparency of a blank map. Project the map on the chalkboard and have students write in specific information being reviewed, such as states, capitals, rivers. The student can erase and repeat until learned.[1]

---

[1] A special thanks to Jim Eads from Iowa.

ACTIVITY: Understanding graphs and charts
ADAPTATION: Use high-interest information to begin graph and
              chart reading. Favorite TV shows, foods, and sports
              are topics that would hold students' interests as they
              interpret graph information.

FAVORITE FOODS

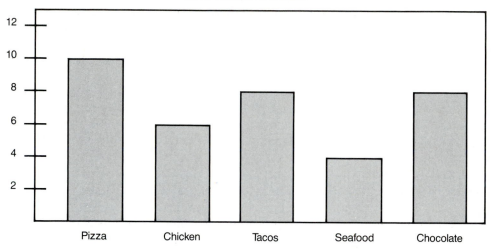

ACTIVITY: Understanding sequence of events on a time-line
ADAPTATION: Before beginning work on time-lines, have students
              list important events in their lives and approximately
              when each occurred. Provide a time-line and have stu-
              dents transfer the information onto it.

EXAMPLE:

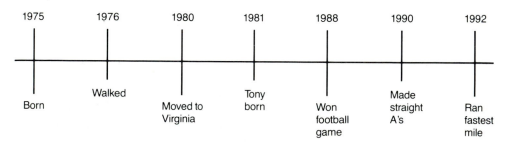

ACTIVITY: Studying products made in different sections of U.S.
ADAPTATION: On the bulletin board, draw an outline of the U.S. De-
              velop a series of transparencies with shading for dif-

ferent areas of the country. Pose a question, such as "What are the major corn-producing states?" A student selects the correctly shaded transparency to project on the U.S. outline on the bulletin board.[2]

ACTIVITY: Sentence writing

ADAPTATION: Prepare substitution tables (Anderson, Greer, & Odle, 1978) for teaching sentence structure. Begin with a simple sentence substitution table using the subject-predicate pattern.[3]

1	2
Girls	play.
Boys	run.
Children	sing.

This activity can be extended from teaching simple agreement between subjects and predicates to more complicated sentences.

1	2	3
I'm		to White Heaven.
You're		home.
He's		to school.
She's	going	to Frayser.
It's		to Dixiemart.
We're		to the grocery.
You're		downtown.
They're		to the post office.

ACTIVITY: Punctuation

ADAPTATION 1:   Record sentences on a tape recorder. Provide a worksheet that has the same sentences with punctuation marks omitted. As students listen to each sentence, they follow along on the worksheet and add the correct punctuation. The teacher may want to include two or three choices of punctuation marks at the end

[2] A special thanks to Doreen Howell, Texas.

[3] From *Individualizing Educational Materials for Special Children in the Mainstream* (p. 177) edited by R.M. Anderson, J.G. Greer, and S.J. Odle, 1978, Baltimore: University Park Press. Copyright 1978 by PRO-ED, Inc. Reprinted by permission.

of each sentence so students can circle correct responses.

Example: Is your house on fire (. ! ?)

ADAPTATION 2: Use cartoon characters and put sentences to be punctuated in speech bubbles. Again, providing a selection of punctuation marks may be helpful.

ADAPTATION 3: Give students a punctuation key to use when punctuating sentences. The key consists of four cards, each containing a punctuation mark and sample key words or sentences.

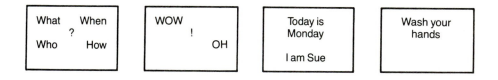

ADAPTATION 4: In preparing worksheets or listing sentences on the board, group sentences by punctuation types. For example, list all sentences requiring question marks or periods together. After students have acquired the skill, begin to mix the sentences, first using only two types of punctuation marks and then adding a third.

ACTIVITY: Compound words

ADAPTATION: Give students a work list with three columns. Tell students to select the first word from Columns 1 and 2 and place in Column 3. After students have learned the concept, mix the words in Column 1 and 2, have students select the appropriate word from Column 1 and match with a word from Column 2 to make a compound word in Column 3.

Column 1	Column 2	Column 3
After	Noon	Afternoon
Some	One	Someone
With	Out	Without
Any	Body	Anybody

ACTIVITY: Spelling

ADAPTATION 1: Divide the spelling list into halves or fourths, if necessary, for students with mild disabilities. Many times, the mainstreamed students can learn how to spell the words, but not as quickly.

ADAPTATION 2: Provide "structure spellers" for students who have trouble remembering all of the words on the spelling list.

Examples: interesting i _ t _ _ e _ _ _ _ g

America _ m e _ i _ _.

ACTIVITY: Reading math signs

ADAPTATION: Students learning math skills will often answer incorrectly because they do not attend to signs. Color-code the signs, circle the signs in bold colors to call attention to them, or arrange math problems on the page by signs. For example, arrange all addition problems in the first two rows, subtraction in the next two rows. Mixing math signs on the page makes solving problems too difficult for students who have problems concentrating or reading signs.

ACTIVITY: Pluralization (irregulars)

ADAPTATION: Develop a format for making plurals on transparencies. Students can use the format over for each new word.

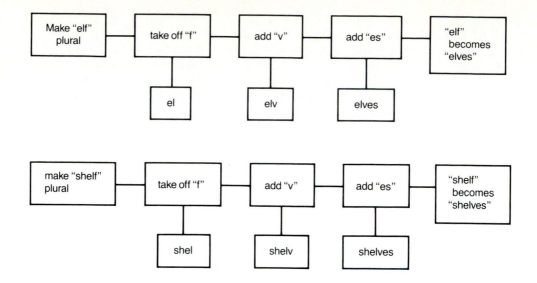

ACTIVITY:	Money
ADAPTATION:	Make the concept of money meaningful to students with mild disabilities by using paper money. Begin by using several paper one-dollar bills. To show that two half-dollars constitute one dollar, cut one paper dollar in half. Then place the two halves on the whole paper dollar and ask the student to put the cut paper dollar together. This activity functions just like putting parts of a puzzle together. The activity may be extended to other fractions of a dollar such as fourths or tenths.

ACTIVITY:	Addition and subtraction
ADAPTATION:	Mainstreamed students often find it difficult to keep math aligned as they perform computations. Block off each column of numbers so that students don't get distracted visually.

$$\begin{array}{c|c} 7 & 2 \\ +\ 3 & 4 \\ \hline 1\ |\ 0\ |\ 6 \end{array} \qquad \begin{array}{c|c|c} & & \\ 4 & 8 & 6 \\ +\ 3 & 5 & 1 \\ \hline 8\ |\ 3\ |\ 7 \end{array} \qquad \begin{array}{c|c} 3 & 6 \\ -\ 1 & 5 \\ \hline 2\ |\ 1 \end{array}$$

ACTIVITY:	Division
ADAPTATION:	Use a model to teach division. Fade parts of the model as students begin to understand where each number belongs.

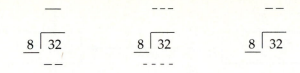

$$\overline{} \quad\quad \overline{\text{-- --}} \quad\quad \overline{\text{-- --}}$$

$$8\overline{\smash{\big)}\,32} \qquad 8\overline{\smash{\big)}\,32} \qquad 8\overline{\smash{\big)}\,32}$$

ACTIVITY:	Solving word problems	
ADAPTATION 1:	Develop a structured organizer	
Word Problems	Dr. Jones bought a dress on sale for 20% off. The original price of the dress was $80.00. She had a coupon for $5.00 off any purchase. After paying with a $100.00 bill, how much change would she get?	

Find out 20% discount

$$\frac{20}{100} = \frac{x}{80}$$

$$100x = 1600$$

$$x = 16$$

Subtract discount from original price

$$\begin{array}{r} 80 \\ -16 \\ \hline 64 \end{array}$$

Subtract $5.00 for coupon

$$\begin{array}{r} 64 \\ -5 \\ \hline 59 \end{array}$$

Subtract final price of dress from $100 bill

$$\begin{array}{r} 100 \\ -59 \\ \hline 41 \end{array}$$

ADAPTATION 2: Develop a structured organizer[4]

STEPS   EXAMPLE

1. Read the problem → Judy had 10 puppies and 4 of them were sold. How many puppies were left?

2. Write down equation lines → ___ 0 ___ = _____

3. Look for clues → "left"

4. Decide which operation → subtraction

5. Fill in equation with numbers and sign → $\underline{10} - \underline{4} = \underline{n}$

[4] A special thanks to Diane Damback, Wilmington, Delaware.

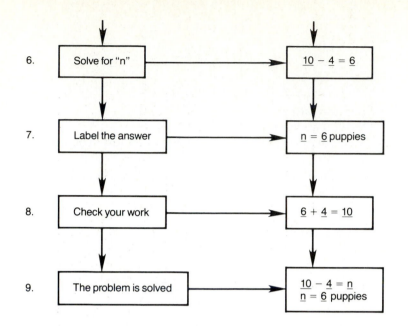

6. | Solve for "n" | → | $\underline{10} - \underline{4} = \underline{6}$ |

7. | Label the answer | → | $\underline{n} = \underline{6}$ puppies |

8. | Check your work | → | $\underline{6} + \underline{4} = \underline{10}$ |

9. | The problem is solved | → | $\underline{10} - \underline{4} = \underline{n}$
$\underline{n} = \underline{6}$ puppies |

ACTIVITY: Lab assignments

ADAPTATION: A major assignment in science classes is the lab. Many schools ask students to complete part of a lab assignment sheet before the teacher's demonstration, and upon completion of the demonstration, to finish the remainder of the lab assignment sheet. Table A presents a standard lab assignment sheet and how to adapt the assignment for the mainstreamed student.

When thinking of ways to adapt the presentation of format of content, do not overlook teacher manuals. Many resources are provided for teachers to use that are excellent for the student.

After the teacher has adapted the content, a further step for adaptation within any specific format can be utilized: task analysis.

TASK ANALYSIS

Task analysis is the breakdown of skills within a task into sequential steps. When teaching specific content and realizing that a student still does not grasp the concept, check to see if the skill could be broken down into smaller steps and teach each step separately.

Task analysis can be used for the entire course, dividing all content into specific skills to be taught. As Anderson, Greer, and Odle (1978) point out, "At any point in the learning process, the child may have failed to acquire mastery of any skill or concept necessary for success at subsequent levels" (p. 168). Such

Table A
Adaptation of Lab Assignment

Lab Assignment Outline	Standard Student Response	Adaptations for Mainstreamed Student
Title of Lab	Student completes.	Fill in for student.
Materials	Student completes from observing teacher or reading text.	Complete for student or let peer tutor assist.
Purpose of Lab	Student completes from text or lecture.	Complete for student.
Lab Procedures	As teacher demonstrates, student records the procedure.	List procedures on the board so student can follow each step. Provide a check sheet and have student check off each step.
Observations	Student records the observed experiment.	Let student record the observed demonstration into a tape recorder.
Conclusion	Student records.	This step requires evaluation level of Bloom's taxonomy, so the teacher may choose to omit it for mainstreamed student.
Analysis/Questions	Student responds.	Provide answers for mainstreamed student.

gaps in acquiring a skill then make it difficult for students to go beyond a certain point in an assignment. Anderson, Greer, and Odle suggest that teachers can help prevent such gaps from occurring by using task analysis on textbooks, dividing the text into smaller sections and rearranging those sections in sequential order. The teacher needs to assess the text, break it down into skills, and reorganize those skills for easier teaching and learning. Anderson, Greer, and Odle suggest three steps for teachers to follow in rearranging textbooks. First, the teacher should study the table of contents and identify the skills covered by the book. Second, the teacher divides those skills into major tasks and subtasks and arranges subtasks sequentially in order of planned instruction. Third, the teacher tabulates page numbers for examples of all the subtasks. The teacher can then use these examples in class as exercises, practice assignments, or test examples or questions. See Table 9.7 for an example of using task analysis to reorganize the content of a mathematics textbook.

Using task analysis to break down textbooks for mainstreamed students offers them more opportunities for success. They can acquire major skills more easily when the instructional material is organized for quick access to specific and smaller skills.

Teachers can also reorganize language arts texts so that they can sequentially teach the skills required at a specific level. Many times, the major subjects in a basal language arts text, as listed in the table of contents, are not in sequential order. For example, the table of contents may list these areas: writing sentences, writing letters, learning parts of speech, writing paragraphs, and using correct punctuation. But learning the parts of speech is a prerequisite skill for writing sentences, just as knowing how to write a paragraph is necessary before one can write letters correctly. To reorganize the table of contents, the teacher must first determine the prerequisite skills for each major area. Table 9.8 presents excerpts from a basal language arts text and a sequential reorganization of the table of contents. The teacher does not deviate from the basic topics to be taught, but simply redesigns the order of the material. By rearranging texts into small, sequential skills, the teacher makes it possible for mainstreamed students to complete assignments.

Breaking down skills into specific parts provides the learner with smaller increments to learn. According to Wehman and McLaughlin (1981), task analysis "provides an instructional sequence and allows for the presentation of materials in small chunks" (p. 60). Educators break a concept or skill down into small steps and place the steps in sequential order. In applying the task analysis model, the regular classroom teacher uses the same principle underlying Bloom's domain of cognitive learning, identifying the specific skill being taught and breaking the skill down into steps, proceeding from the easiest to the most difficult. Table 9.9 shows how a task analysis works: Learning how to use the dictionary has been broken down into 14 steps.

In the example, students with no dictionary skills would have difficulty beginning with step 10 in the task analysis sequence, but because the task has been broken down into such small steps, the teacher can begin where the student presently functions, whether it be step 1 or a higher level. When teaching a concept or skill in a specific academic area, the teacher needs to analyze the skill and decide whether or not the student has the prerequisite skills for learning it. A teacher who thinks a student is ready to learn the new skill should then examine the skill further to see if it can be organized into sequential steps. Breaking a new task into small, sequential steps makes learning easier for the student who may have learning difficulties.

Table 9.7
Task Analysis of Mathematics Textbook's Content

Major Tasks and Subtasks	Instructional Examples on Page:	Text Examples on Page:
Addition		
Addition combinations	5–7	9–13, 462
Tens in addition	14	14–15
Hundreds in addition	14	16
Column addition	16–17	17–27, 56, 454, 458
Regrouping in addition	28	28–29
Estimating sums	30	31–34, 37, 55–56
Mental addition	35	35–36
Subtraction		
Subtraction combinations	7–9	9–13, 463
Tens in subtraction	14	15, 38
Hundreds in subtraction	14	15–16, 38
Regrouping in subtraction	40–41	42–47, 56, 455, 459
Expanded notation	42	42
Subtraction of fractions	48–49	49–51
Estimating differences	51	51–52, 53–56
Mental subtraction	53	53–55
Multiplication		
Multiplication combinations	57–59, 60, 62–63	59, 61, 464
Properties of multiplications	66	67
Number pairs and graphs	70–71	72–73, 76–77
Multiplying using tens	72, 74–75	72–73, 76–77, 456, 460
Multiplying using a machine	78–81	81
Mental multiplication	82, 86	82–83, 86–88
Estimating products	84	84–85, 88
Division		
Division combinations	65	65, 465
Properties of division	66	67
Division involving remainders	67	68–69, 92, 457, 461
Dividing a number by single digit	69, 92–93	68, 93, 103, 457, 461
Dividing using tens	72, 92	78, 89, 94–95, 103, 457, 461
Trial quotients	95–97	97–98
Estimating quotients	96–99	99–100, 102–103
Mental division	101	101–102

Table 9.8
Reorganizing a Table of Contents

Original Table of Contents	Sequentially Reorganized Table of Contents
Writing sentences	Learning parts of speech
Writing letters	Writing sentences
Learning parts of speech	Using correct punctuation
Writing paragraphs	Writing paragraphs
Using correct punctuation	Writing letters

ADAPTING ASSIGNMENTS

Numerous strategies are used by teachers to reinforce skills learned during class instruction. Giving assignments is one of the most traditional strategies employed. However, for many mainstreamed or at-risk students, assignments become a stepping-stone to class failure. Some students never understand the class lesson from which the assignment is developed, some do not clearly understand the assignment, and others have difficulty completing the assignment for different reasons. The following section will look at the assumptions we make regarding assignments, steps for adapting assignments, and types of assignments.

Assignment Assumptions

Most people have experienced being given a task to complete and finding it impossible to do, no matter how hard they try. Many students with disabilities feel this way frequently. When an assignment seems too difficult, teachers should check to see if they have made any assumptions regarding the assignment. These following suggestions will help avoid these problems.

1. Never assume that students with disabilities have copied the assignment from the board to their assignment pads correctly.
2. Never assume that after you have explained the assignment, all students clearly understand what to do, even if there are no questions.
3. Never assume that the assignment is not too difficult.
4. Never assume that the assignment is not too long. Always break the assignment into small sequential steps and teach the first step in the sequence first.
5. Never assume that all students will complete the same quantity of work as their peers. They may have the skills but not be able to do the same amount of work.

Steps for Adapting Assignments

When adapting assignments, teachers should consider three factors: the directions, the assignment itself, and the materials used in the assignment.

Table 9.9
Task Analysis of Dictionary Skill

TA–1	Given five books, including a dictionary, the student will point to and state the function of the dictionary.
TA–2	Given directions to say the alphabet, the student will recite it in proper sequence.
TA–3	Given a random selection of 10 letters, the student will arrange them in alphabetical order.
TA–4	Given a list of not more than 10 words, beginning with different letters, the student will write the words in alphabetical order.
TA–5	Given a list of not more than 10 words, beginning with the same first letter, the student will write the words in alphabetical order.
TA–6	Given a list of not more than 10 words beginning with the same first two letters, the student will write the words in alphabetical order.
TA–7	Shown a dictionary page, the student will point to and state the function of the guide words.
TA–8	Shown a dictionary page, the student will point to and state the function of the entry words.
TA–9	Given oral directions to state the meaning of the word *definition*, the student will do so.
TA–10	Given a list of two guide words and a list of entry words, the student will write those entry words that come between the two guide words.
TA–11	Given a list of entry words and a dictionary, the student will write the page number on which the entry word is found.
TA–12	Shown an entry word in a dictionary, the student will state the number of definitions listed for that word.
TA–13	Given a list of entry words and a dictionary, the student will find the words and write definitions for each word.
TA–14	Given a sentence containing a specific word, the student will write the definition of the word as used in that sentence.

Note. From ''Reading Comptency #6a-Gets Information From Resource Material: Dictionary'' (p. 10) in *Basic Skills Sequence in English,* Montpelier, VT: Vermont State Department of Education, Division of Special Education and Pupil Personnel Services. Copyright by Vermont State Department of Education, Division of Special Education and Pupil Personnel Services. Reprinted by permission.

Directions are often not stated clearly enough or not described in a way that the student with disabilities can understand. Teachers should never assume that the student accurately hears, sees, or understands directions. A lack of questions does not mean complete understanding. Some suggestions for assignment directions include:

1. Make directions clear and simple.
2. Present directions orally as well as visually.

3. Designate a place on the board where you will write directions each day.
4. Get the attention of the class before presenting directions.
5. Give directions one at a time.
6. If necessary, have a student repeat the directions. However, never draw unwanted attention to any student.
7. Ask students if they have any questions.
8. Give directions as to what students should do when they need help or do not understand the directions, such as raising a hand.
9. Encourage students to do a good job. Use positive statements such as "I can't wait to see all these good papers."
10. Give directions both orally and in written form.

Teachers must continually *adapt class and homework assignments* for students with disabilities as well as any student experiencing difficulty with instructions. Teachers can apply the following ongoing steps when adapting the assignment.

1. Be sure that students have the correct information on the assignment such as page numbers and date due.
2. Review the assignment and check for questions.
3. The assignment should be geared to the level of each student.
4. Structure each assignment so that all students can experience success.
5. Provide immediate feedback on all assignments.
6. If an assignment requires students to look up answers to questions, use an asterisk to distinguish implied fact from literal questions requiring a stated fact.
7. For a lengthy assignment, provide class time to complete part of it or divide it into 2 or more days of assignments.
8. Identify an "assignment buddy" for each student. The buddy may be another student in the same class or another class or a friend or parent outside of school. This provides a support system for the student who may not know how to complete the assignment.
9. Assignments may be given to groups of two or more students. In this case, give class time for the shared assignments and use split grading.
10. Teach students the concept of *grade averaging*, with and without 0s. Many students do not realize the difficulty of trying to raise an average after just one 0 on an assignment.
11. Allow students the option of dropping one or more low grades on assignments for each grading period.
12. Establish assignment passes that students may earn for good work and later "cash in" when they forget an assignment or receive a low grade.
13. Be consistent in writing all assignments for class and homework in the same place each day.
14. Provide both written and oral directions for all assignments.
15. If an assignment requires several steps or stages, such as projects, provide a checklist for the students.

16. Be sure that all assignment information is included in the assignment, such as points to be given, due date, format, and components.
17. If the assignment is to be copied from the board, provide a carbon copy for any student who has difficulty copying.
18. If the assignment is to be copied from the text, allow any student who has difficulty copying or who copies slowly to copy only the answers.
19. Be careful in the use of worksheets. Worksheets should be clear and uncluttered. Watch for the overuse of worksheets. Sometimes the reward for completing one worksheet is another worksheet. Giving a stack of worksheets can be overwhelming.
20. Have students put books that they need to take home in the locker with the spine toward the back of locker and on the right side of locker. At the end of the day, students reach into their lockers and review all spine-back books to take home.
21. Require a method for students to record assignments in the class.
22. Make copies of the assignments for a week at a time and give them to the student and the resource teacher.
23. After the class assignment is completed, tell students where to put the assignment and what they should do next.
24. Do not punish students by making them finish assignments during free time, recess, or after school.
25. For in-class assignments, give a warning when it is nearly time to turn in the assignment.
26. Orient students to the major points of the assignment.
27. Begin all assignments with a planned opening and a purpose.
28. Practice for assignments should be distributed in short segments instead of concentrated in one long practice period.
29. Relate all activities within an assignment directly to its objective.
30. Assess the assignment for the appropriate instruction level.
31. Use feedback from previously completed assignments to determine the quality of the next assignment.

Finally, in adapting the assignment, teachers should *systematically observe the materials* used. Because at least 75% and as much as 99% of a student's instructional time is arranged around the materials used in the classroom (Wilson, 1978), it is important that teachers spend enough time selecting or altering the materials used with assignments. Teachers should ask themselves the following questions as they select materials for assignments:

1. Does the level of the material match the student's instructional level?
2. Does the material follow a sequential format and require little special equipment?
3. Does the material not insult the student's dignity?
4. Does the material have several evaluation steps?
5. Does the material adequately meet the instructional objectives for the student?

6. Is the material compatible with teaching methods, style, and approach?
7. Does the material suit the student's learning style?
8. Are supporting materials such as teachers' manuals and resources available?
9. Is the material on the student's interest level?

A frequently used class material for assignments is that of the worksheet. Suggestions for preparing and using teacher-made or commercially provided worksheets include:

1. Monitor the use of worksheets to avoid overuse.
2. Type all items on the worksheets, if possible. Handwritten worksheets are often hard to read, and they cannot be duplicated as well as typed worksheets.
3. Prepare worksheets so that only a few items or problems will be presented on each page. Students who easily become visually distracted find it difficult to read a crowded worksheet.
4. For commercially prepared worksheets, cut the sheet into halves or use bold colors to circle certain items that are to be completed.
5. Do not give students a stack of worksheets to be completed at one time. This procedure frustrates some students enough that they will not attempt the task.
6. Rewrite commercially prepared worksheets when necessary to meet individual needs of students.

Types of Assignments

Assignments, the learning tasks that reinforce concepts taught during class instruction, are crucial to skill acquisition. However, for various reasons, some students may not be able to complete the assignment. When teachers make assignments, there are two types, control and no-control assignments.

Control assignments include in-class assignments and other assignments over which the teacher has complete control. These assignments include class discussions, problem-solving, group experiments, group projects, and independent seatwork assignments such as reading from the text, answering questions, and completing worksheets. During the times students are working on these assignments, the teacher has the control or power to make any necessary adjustments for a student. The teacher can answer questions or observe the student's work. If an assignment is too difficult, too lengthy, or too confusing, the teacher can immediately remedy the situation. When students take assignments home, the teacher begins to lose control.

No-control assignments are those that are no longer under the supervision of the teacher. Homework falls into this category. The teacher has now lost all control or power to provide direct assistance during the students' work on the assignment to any student who may experience difficulty with it. Homework is assigned for a number of reasons:

1. Homework facilitates learning through practice and application.
2. Homework individualizes learning for all students.
3. Homework is assigned for that work not completed during the school day.
4. Homework teaches independent study skills and helps develop good work habits.
5. Homework communicates to parents which concepts and skills are taught in class (Turner, 1984).

Lee and Pruitt (1970) presented four types of homework: preparation, practice, extension, and creativity. Table 9.10 shows each of these four topics with its definition and suggested adaptations for teachers to use with students experiencing difficulty with homework.

Salend and Schliff (1988) offered several guidelines for implementing homework. These are listed in Table 9.11.

For a no-control assignment, the teacher must be absolutely sure that the student has the skills necessary to meet success. When giving assignments, ask the questions, "Do I have control over this assignment, or do I have no control?"

ADAPTED LESSON PLAN FOR FORMAT OF CONTENT

Figure 9.3 (p. 282) continues our adapted lesson plan for a lesson on how sound travels in the ear. In this plan, we have added suggestions for the teacher to use when adapting the format of content. Each step can be put in sequential order (task analysis) and the teacher can color-code the path of sound as it travels.

Table 9.10
Homework Adaptations

Type of Homework	Definition	Examples	Suggested Adaptations
Preparation	Homework assigned to assist students' preparation for the next day's lesson/class	Reading a chapter Reviewing a film	Provide recorded materials for materials to be read. Prior to the lesson, review in class to assist students who could not prepare ahead of time. Allow students to prepare with a buddy. Provide a summary of material to be read. Provide a checklist for steps on procedures to be reviewed.

Table 9.10 *continued*

Type of Homework	Definition	Examples	Suggested Adaptations
Practice	Homework assigned to reinforce the skills taught during the day's lesson	Working on math problems Answering questions over class lecture	Be sure that the student understands the assignment. Review assignment directions. Review the assignment. Provide a model. Provide guided practice prior to independent practice. Check for student's functional level and match assignment to level. Provide alternative amounts of assignments to students who cannot complete the same quantity as others.
Extension	Homework assigned to extend or transfer skills taught	Book reports Practicing computer skills	Provide models for required reports. Provide a checklist of procedures. Allow buddies to work together on a shared assignment. Be sure that students have been taught for acquisition and retention prior to requiring transfer.
Creativity	Homework that requires synthesis of skills and concepts previously taught.	Projects Term papers Research assignments	Allow partners to work on projects. Provide a clearly explained checklist with examples for all projects. Do class projects that model each step prior to assigning an independent project. Remember that students who have difficulty with structure need guidance with assigned projects, papers, research projects. Consider alternative assignments for students who may not be at this level.

Table 9.11
Guidelines For Implementing Homework

Homework Practice	Guidelines
1. Selecting the type of homework	Consider the instructional purpose of the assignment as it relates to the type of homework.
	• *Practicing* material learned in class may require drill-oriented assignments.
	• *Preparing* students for future lessons should be structured to provide prerequisite information that will be necessary for a successful class lesson.
	• *Extending or transferring* types of homework takes what a student may have learned and applies it to a more complex situation.
	• *Creating* new ideas requires that students synthesize learned skills (Salend & Schliff, 1988).
2. Deciding on the content of homework	Consider the type of homework—preparation, practice, extension, creativity—in deciding on the context.
	Individualize content for each student (Salend & Schliff, 1988).
	Make sure IEP objective and content of homework are parallel (Salend & Schliff, 1988).
	Realize that preparation of homework may be difficult for a student who cannot read or traditionally has difficulty with assignments.
	Relate practice homework directly to skills taught in class.
	Evaluate the understanding level of concepts and skills taught before assigning practice homework.
3. Determining the amount of homework	Vary the amount depending on the student's age and educational placement (Salend & Schliff, 1988).
	Use homework sparingly in the early grades (Salend & Schliff, 1988).
	Avoid weekend homework (Salend & Schliff, 1988).

Table 9.11 *continued*

Homework Practice	Guidelines
	Consider the level of understanding and completion of class assignments to determine the amount of homework that can be completed.
	Consider the specific disability of a student.
	Consider the amount given in other subjects.
	Consider the amount of homework already given in subject for the week.
4. Explaining homework to students	Inform students of: • The purpose of the assignment; • The directions necessary for completion; • The date due; • The required format; • The necessary materials needed for completion; and • The source for assistance, if needed (Salend & Schliff, 1988).
	Repeat all assignments orally and visually.
	Provide a model of a completed assignment.
	Provide examples that will be duplicated.
	Check to see that students fully understand the assignment.
5. Assisting students with their assignments	Teach the value of having a selected time and place for homework.
	Review the materials that the students will need to complete the assignment.
	Provide homework folders (Salend & Schliff, 1988).
	Establish a homework hotline or class network system for answering questions when in trouble and at home.
	Help students to remember books needed for homework. Have students with lockers place all homework books with spine back on the right side of locker. At the end of the day, they pull out all books with spine back on the right side of the locker to take home.

Table 9.11 *continued*

Homework Practice	Guidelines
6. Motivating students to complete homework	Make homework assignment as interesting as possible.
	Prevent homework from being used as punishment.
	Help students to see the effects of 0s on grades by teaching the principal of averaging.
	Praise students for completed homework.
	Try to understand why a student does not do homework. Often it may be related to a lack of understanding or a problem at home.
	Consider alternatives to homework for those who routinely do not complete homework.
7. Evaluating homework	Evaluate daily and provide immediate feedback.
	Allow students to provide corrections for a grade change.
	Let students have "homework pass" grades to be used to drop low homework grades.
	Provide grade averaging based on attempting the assignment as well as correctness.
8. Involving parents in homework	Keep communication open between teacher and parents.
	Remember that many parents may not understand the homework well enough to assist their child.
	Consider the fact that after a long day's work and extended family responsibilities, parents may be too tired to monitor homework.
	Consider family-oriented activities that can serve as homework.

Note. From "The Many Dimensions of Homework" by S. J. Salend and J. Schliff, 1988, *Academic Therapy, 23,* pp. 397–403. Copyright 1988 by PRO-ED, Inc. Reprinted by permission.

OBJECTIVE	STRATEGIES/ PROCEDURES	MATERIALS/ RESOURCES	EVALUATION/ ASSIGNMENT
Date: _____ Taxonomy Level _X_ Knowledge _X_ Comprehension ____ Application ____ Analysis ____ Synthesis ____ Evaluation The student will be able to list and define the parts of the ear and the steps for the travel of sound in the ear.	Lecture on the parts of the ear and how sound travels.	Display of ear Filmstrip Chapter in text Handout of parts of ear	Fill-in-blank Test and listing
Adaptations:	Teaching Techniques: — Use acquisition outline. — Use structured organizer to show relationship of parts of ear. — Use visual of ear with lecture. Format of Content: — Develop a task analysis list of how sound travels in ear. — Color-code the path of sound as it travels within the ear and each part of the ear.	Adapted Media:	Evaluation Test: Student Assignment:

Figure 9.3
Format For An Adapted Lesson Plan: Format of Content

SUMMARY

Adapting the format of content, the third step in the model for planning and teaching, assists educators in providing structure to the content being presented within the class. The next step within the model, adapting media, will provide alternative ways of working with the media used in presenting content.

CHAPTER TEN
Adapting Media

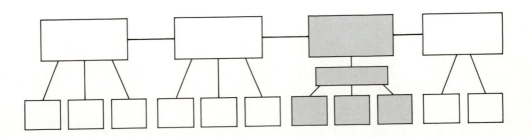

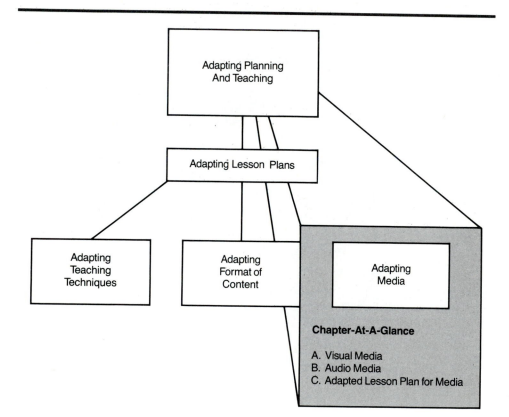

Adapting Planning
And Teaching

Adapting Lesson Plans

Adapting
Teaching
Techniques

Adapting
Format of
Content

Adapting
Media

Chapter-At-A-Glance

A. Visual Media
B. Audio Media
C. Adapted Lesson Plan for Media

The last phase of Part Three, Adapting Planning and Teaching, of the model is that of Adapting Media. Frequently, the intervention point for a student with disabilities may involve media. For example, if the teacher is presenting a lecture and the student is unable to grasp the points, the addition of an overhead projector to the class may be helpful. Adding or adapting media enhances teaching.

This chapter covers (a) uses of visual media including classroom equipment and materials; and (b) adapting audio media.

VISUAL MEDIA

Presenting information visually is beneficial to all students, but this method is particularly helpful to the student who has difficulty grasping information that is delivered auditorily. Teachers use a variety of visual media during the instructional day, including overhead projectors, computers, videotapes, movies, and filmstrips.

Overhead Projectors

The overhead projector is the most common type of equipment used in the class by regular education teachers (Wood, 1989). This section presents uses and adaptations for overhead projectors, suggestions for making transparencies more effective, teaching with transparencies, and ideas for using the overhead by subject areas.

Uses and Adaptations for Overhead Projectors

There are numerous ways teachers can affectively use the overhead projector. They can use the overhead projector to make visuals of main points in a lecture. Encourage student participation in math by presenting math problems on a transparency, with students writing answers on the transparency or on a blackboard as the teacher projects the image on the blackboard instead of a screen. Orient students to new material by using colored grease pencils to underline, circle, or otherwise emphasize the main points of a lecture written on transparencies. Encourage class discussions or stimulate interest by placing objects such as flowers or other shapes on transparencies; and visually reinforce directions by writing on the transparency while giving directions orally.

Making Transparencies More Effective

Fuhrmann and Grasha (1983) suggest numerous ways to make transparencies more effective. Orient transparencies horizontally rather than vertically so that they won't become distorted when projected and lower portions won't fall below eye level. Use fine-tipped, water-based felt pens or wax-based audiovisual (AV) pencils, or grease pencils. Place a clear plastic sheet on top of frequently used transparencies and use the sheet to highlight or emphasize parts of the permanent transparency. Use several transparencies in an overlay fashion to build an idea or concept. Use a variety of colors to highlight related concepts. Use only boldface or primary type when typing on transparencies. Show only a few points on each transparency, because too much information on a transparency reduces its effectiveness. Reveal only one item on a transparency at a time. Onionskin paper makes an especially good screen, because the teacher can see through it but the students cannot. Use colored plastic for permanent shapes—arrows, brackets, and geometric shapes that are used repeatedly. Use a thermofax copier to transfer original printed materials to transparencies. Use the media center to learn about more complex methods for making transparencies (Fuhrmann & Grasha, 1983, pp. 234–235).

Teaching with Transparencies

Brown, Lewis, and Harcleroad (1977) suggest that when teaching with transparencies, the lettering on the transparencies be printed or typed, with each character $\frac{1}{4}$-inch high. Keep a file for transparencies, and organize and label them under subject headings, titles, or lesson topics. Use an index card to describe the transparency contents and any accompanying activities.

Another tip for teaching with transparencies is to frame them for easier use. The frames keep the transparencies from sticking together. On the frame, you can write notes as follows: (a) on the top margin, write information that relates directly to the transparency and would serve as a lead-in to discussion of the transparency; (b) on the side margins, list examples or other information you will need to bring into the class discussion as you reveal the transparency; and (c) on the bottom margin, write information that provides closure for the discussion or introduces the next transparency. This process provides a smoother class discussion and reminds the teacher of vital information to be presented. Prior to the class discussion, develop a transparency that presents the major points of the lesson. Review each point and suggest that the students list each and leave a space on their papers for class notes. If you have a transparency which contains detailed information, such as a diagram, a map, or parts of the digestive system, give the students a matching copy on which to record notes. It may be impossible for some students to copy all the details. When the class discussion is completed, review the first transparency covering the major topics for class closure. Whenever the discussion is not focusing on the transparency, be sure to turn off the overhead projector to focus the students' attention back on the teacher, rather than the screen. Table 10.1 presents this information in three phases: (a) getting ready to teach with transparencies; (b) during the teaching process; and (c) after teaching.

A mask can be made to cover sections of the transparency prior to or after showing a section. Each section of the mask is progressively lifted for disclosure. Table 10.2 presents steps in making overlay transparencies.

The Chalkboard

The chalkboard is a common type of support item found in almost every classroom. When using the chalkboard, be sure that the board is clean and that the color of chalk shows up from all angles of the classroom. Organize your ideas and keep writing to a minimum. For example, if you are discussing

Table 10.1
Teaching with Transparencies

GETTING READY TO TEACH

1. Use fine-tipped felt pens or waxed-based pencils for lettering.
2. Be sure that the lettering is large, whether typed or handwritten. If handwritten, it should be printed.
3. Each character should be at least $\frac{1}{4}$-inch high (Brown, Lewis, & Harcleroad, 1977).
4. Frame each transparency with a cardboard border for easier handling.
5. Prepare transparencies so that each step of the discussion has an accompanying visual.
6. Be sure that the transparencies are in the correct order prior to class.
7. Develop masks for transparencies that need certain sections covered to avoid distraction.

DURING THE TEACHING PROCESS

1. Develop your first transparency with a listing of the major topics for discussion.
2. Instruct the students to copy down each point and leave a space for note-taking.
3. Divide the frame of the transparency into four sections. In the top margin, write an introduction to the transparency; in the left margin, list important information to be included in the class discussion; in the right margin, list activities or additional references; and on the bottom margin, write information that provides closure for the discussion or introduces the next transparency.
4. If you are using one transparency repeatedly, place a clear transparency on top of the original before marking with the felt-tipped pen (Brown, Lewis, & Harcleroad, 1977).
5. Use onionskin paper to conceal parts of the transparency (Brown, Lewis, & Harcleroad, 1977).
6. Use colored pencils to highlight major concepts or ideas.
7. Use overlays when presenting detailed information to avoid information overload.
8. If the transparency has a lot of detail, provide each student with a copy to ensure that the information is written down correctly.
9. Turn the overhead projector off when not referring to the transparency.
10. When the class discussion is completed, return to the first transparency of major points for a class review and closure.

AFTER TEACHING

1. Return the transparencies to the correct order.
2. File and label each class set by subject heading, title, or lesson topic (Brown, Lewis, & Harcleroad, 1977).
3. On an index card, describe the transparency content and any activities used.

Table 10.2
Directions for Making Overlay Transparencies

1. Draw a sketch of the whole concept for the transparency. Decide what will be the base and which parts will be the overlays.
2. Make a master drawing for each of the separate parts.
3. To line up the sheets for each overlay, put an X or some other mark outside the projection area in the same place on each master drawing. Be sure each transparency is aligned with the corners of the original drawing.
4. Prepare a transparency for each drawing.
5. Mount each sheet of the transparency in exact correspondence. The base should be under the frame and the overlays on top. All transparencies should be applied to the frame with masking tape.

Note. From *Technology, Media, and Methods* (5th ed.) by J. Brown, R. Lewis, and F. Harcleroad, 1977, New York: Macmillan. Copyright 1977 by Macmillan. Adapted by permission.

explorers, what they discovered, and important dates, develop a table with three headings (explorers, what was discovered, important dates) and write it on the chalkboard. After the class discussion, each student will have a clear, organized picture of the day's lesson. Divide the board into three sections. On the left, list the agenda for the day's class; in the middle, leave space for the day's notes; on the right, list the next day's assignments and future assignments or tests. Figure 10.1 presents a sample chalkboard design. The topics or procedures may vary. The idea is to provide continued structure for each class. Students will develop a pattern for the class details.

Computer Instruction for Mainstreamed Students

A 1981 survey conducted by the U. S. Department of Education determined that approximately half of the nation's school districts provided students with

Figure 10.1
Sample Chalkboard Design

Day's Schedule	Notes for Today	Tomorrow's Assignment

1. Check homework
2. Turn in homework
3. Class discussion
   Topics:
   _____
   _____
4. Class activity
5. Independent practice
6. Lesson review
7. Tomorrow's assignment
		Projects/Tests

access to a microcomputer or computer terminal (Coburn, Kelman, Roberts, Snyder, Watt, & Weiner, 1982). Over a decade later, the availability of microcomputers in the schools has increased; however, "the anticipated benefits of the technology are not being realized" (Cosden & Abernathy, 1990, p. 31). Cosden and Abernathy point out further that the future of microcomputers depends greatly on teacher time and assistance and that these factors must be considered when establishing goals for activities. In their longitudinal investigation of the use of microcomputers among elementary school students, the authors describe the challenges for teachers when using and integrating computer technology into the curriculum. Two models of computer use emerged, classroom-based and lab-based. Table 10.3 presents observations from this study regarding the use of each approach.

From their study, Cosden and Abernathy (1990) identified four roles for teachers in the utilization of microcomputer technology. These roles focus on defining a place for microcomputers within the curriculum. Table 10.4 lists the four roles with a brief description, strengths, and weaknesses of each.

To implement computer technology in elementary and secondary schools effectively, teachers and administrators must learn about the educational

Table 10.3
Classroom-based vs. Lab-based Microcomputer Use

Classroom-based	Lab-based
• Number of computers available to teachers is limited	• Alleviates problems of limited student access
• Supports educational philosophy that equal access to computers must be provided to all students	• Students may participate in the same activities and simultaneous use of the technology
• Must develop computer activities that can be integrated into noncomputer-based activities	• Raises a broader issue about whether lab activities are integrated into the curriculum
• Allows computer-based activities to be used that are segregated from ongoing tasks	• Problems may occur because teachers often have a choice in participating in the microcomputer lab
• Teachers usually select the segregated option, so that students find their assigned computer-based activities totally segregated from those of classmates	• When teachers do not attend labs, they have limited communication with the lab specialist, thus presenting problems for special students who have academic problems and need more instructional precision
• Students with disabilities may miss vital information in content areas during their microcomputer activities	

Note. From "Microcomputer Use in the Schools: Teacher Roles and Instructional Options" by M.A. Cosden and T. V. Abernathy, 1990, *Remedial and Special Education, 11*, pp. 31–38. Copyright 1990 by PRO-ED, Inc.

applications currently available. Aiken and Brown (1980) identified several applications, such as computer-assisted instruction (CAI), experimental learning, programming and algorithmic formulation, problem-solving, word processing, and computer literacy or awareness.

Perhaps the most widely recognized application to date, especially for students with mild disabilities, is computer-assisted instruction. Definitions vary slightly from authority to authority, but generally computer-assisted instruction can be subdivided into five major categories (Coburn et al., 1982; Watkins & Webb, 1981), including:

1. Drill and Practice—designed to give students feedback and supplement regular instruction
2. Tutorial—designed to instruct students by using a programmed format instead of regular instruction
3. Demonstration—designed to assist teachers in demonstrating concepts, relationships, and processes

Table 10.4
Approaches to Microcomputer Use

Approach to Microcomputer Use	Definition	Strengths	Weaknesses
Classroom-based microcomputer use	"Computer instruction within a class is configured so that one or two students at a time are engaged with the software while the rest of the students are assigned to other activities" (p. 36)	• Allows teachers to select activities they think are best for students • Enables teacher to be present if help is needed • Assists in providing individualization for students	• Content area integration between computer users and nonusers is low • Individualized planning is of great importance • Direct monitoring of student progress is difficult
Lab-based microcomputer use: Teacher-supervised	"The teacher assumes major responsibility for the microcomputer activities of his or her class during the scheduled lab period" (p. 36)	• Allows for integration of computer into curriculum, thus eliminating the problem of computer-based activity for some students and not for others • Allows for direct instruction	• Teacher must have interest and time for training in computer technology

Table 10.4 *continued*

Approach to Microcomputer Use	Definition	Strengths	Weaknesses
Lab-based micro-computer use: Computer specialist and teacher cooperation	"Responsibilities for instruction are shared by the computer specialist and the teacher; the specialist has the major responsibility for implementation of computer instruction, while the teacher maintains responsibility for planning the instruction" (pp. 36–37)	• Allows planning and monitoring time during the computer session • Allows teacher to rely on the specialist for technology knowledge • Enables both specialist and teacher to utilize their individual expertise	• Problems may arise if communication between lab specialist and teacher does not remain open • Specialist does not have time to learn specific information about special students
Lab-based micro-computer instruction: Computer specialist-supervised	"Instructional responsibilities are assigned to the computer specialist" (p. 37)		• Specialists need training as educators, but frequently do not have such training • Computer activities are separated from curriculum

Note. From "Microcomputer Use in the Schools: Teacher Roles and Instructional Options" by M. A. Cosden and T. V. Abernathy, 1990, *Remedial and Special Education, 11,* pp. 31–38. Copyright 1990 by PRO-ED, Inc. Reprinted by permission.

4. Simulations—designed to enable students to experiment with various solutions to real problems, such as the nuclear arms race
5. Instructional Games—designed to develop student's problem-solving abilities, reinforce previously learned concepts, and maintain high interest and motivation, such as with the spelling game, Hangman.

Brown (1988) provided suggestions that are helpful in using computers with students with learning disabilities. Specific computer-related problems according to deficit areas are presented in Table 10.5.

Computers and computer-assisted instruction are becoming commonplace in the mainstream and in the resource room because they help teachers to acknowledge individual differences among students.

Table 10.5
Suggestions for Microcomputer Use for Specific Disabilities

Perceptual Problem	Characteristics	Computer Difficulty	General Teaching Suggestions
Visual figure ground problems	Difficulty seeing visual material from a computer background	Reading one line of type in single-speed copy Locating the cursor Finding a particular menu command Locating a key on the keyboard Tracking back and forth between the keyboard and screen (Bley, 1987, p. 96)	Use sense of touch to teach Use verbal explanations for commands Explain each step and observe as the student practices Color-code keyboard Keep work area clear Record commands to go with written directions
Visual sequencing problems	Difficulty seeing items that occur in sequence	Difficulty typing Difficulty reading	
Visual discrimination problems	Difficulty seeing distinctive characters and differences	Problems distinguishing between : and ;	
Auditory figure ground problems	Difficulty receiving or processing information heard against a competing background	May not hear sounds of computer in a noisy area	Give directions visually and orally
Auditory sequencing problems	Difficulty hearing sounds that occur in sequence	Problem if commands are given orally in sequence	Have students repeat directions
Auditory discrimination problems	Difficulty distinguishing differences in sounds		Provide a written sheet of directions or instructions

Note. From "Be a Computer Tutor for People with Learning Disabilities" (pp. 91–104) by C. J. Brown in *Proceedings of the Fourth Annual Conference: Technology and Persons with Disabilities* by H. J. Murphy (Ed.), 1988, Northridge, CA: California State University. Copyright 1988 by H. J. Murphy. Reprinted by permission.

Audiovisual Media

Videotapes, movies, and filmstrips are used daily in many classes to support class instruction. For each of these types of visual presentations, teachers should provide a checklist with points from the videotape, movie, or filmstrip. The checklist should be reviewed prior to the presentation, followed during the presentation, and used as a summary after the presentation. Table 10.6 presents a framework for a sample checklist to be used by the teacher.

Using the format in Table 10.6 to plan for the use of audiovisual or AV equipment, the teacher would supply the title, length, and purpose of the AV. The teacher would list the major points prior to the presentation and review them with the class. During the presentation, students would take notes under each point. After the presentation, the teacher would review each point listed on the left and the student would take additional notes or work with a buddy and complete the section under class follow-up notes on the right. The class and the teacher would then summarize the presentation. A point to remember is that even adults have difficulty sitting in workshops and viewing videotapes,

Table 10.6
Checklist for Videotapes, Movies, and Filmstrips

Title: (completed by teacher)

Length: (completed by teacher)

Purpose: (completed by teacher)

Major Points Covered

Notes Before/During Presentation (completed by teacher, with space under each point for taking notes)	Class Follow-up Notes

1.

2.

3.

4.

Summary/Discussion

movies, and filmstrips. Keep this in mind when asking children to do the same. Additional tips for videotapes, movies, and filmstrips include:

For Videotapes

- Tape class demonstrations to be played back at a later date.
- Tape the visual explanations to math problems for review.
- Allow students to develop their own videotapes.
- Let students videotape their explanations of class lessons for use with peers.

For Movies

- Be sure that the movie is not too long.
- Use to reinforce lectures or present additional information.

For Filmstrips:

- Students can view on individual filmstrip viewers.
- Students can make their own filmstrips.
- If there is no audio with the filmstrip, be sure to read to the class.

Class Materials: Adapting Textbooks

Among the numerous materials used daily in classrooms, textbooks are the most common. This section looks at ways to adapt textbooks.

For many classrooms, assigned textbooks are the media of focus. In many secondary-level classrooms, class instruction is based on a single textbook (Hayes, 1981). Teachers issue a class textbook written for that specific grade level and require students to read the text and complete the appropriate activities. Many students never complete this task, and teachers wonder why they are not trying. Reading becomes increasingly difficult for students with disabilities as they grow older. Specifically, in the upper grades, reading the textbook is an impossible task for many at-risk youth and students with mild disabilities. Of course we want all students to develop as many skills for reading as possible. However, the reality is that we expect students with disabilities and those at-risk to "maintain the regular classroom pace." If this is our expectation, then educators must begin to implement modifications for the material to be read. Reading instruction should continue, but student support must be implemented as well.

Several years ago, a secondary-level teacher was approached about modifying the text for an 11th-grade young man. The teacher's reply was, "Oh, he reads on 2nd-grade level and must continue to learn to read. Modifying the text would provide a crutch for the student, and he would not learn to read." At a certain time in the educational sequence, we must begin to introduce to students ways in which to open doors to printed materials. When using textbooks as a tool for teaching, we must provide structure to this material, just as we have provided structure to instruction.

The following suggestions for adapting textbooks or printed matter apply to all students. Some ideas should be used regularly to introduce new text and all new chapters. Many ideas may only be necessary to use in an extreme case such as an inability to read. The ideas are presented in the same sequence a teacher would use to present the text and each chapter. Figure 10.2 graphically presents the model for presenting and adapting textbooks.

First, teachers should review the organization and structure of the textbook. Tell the students the purpose or objective of the text and how this text and the course relate to the sequence of courses. For example, if the social studies text covers a specific period in history, explain this to the class. Relate how this section in history begins with the time period where last year's course ended. Present a visual of the sequence of social studies texts for several grades. This process helps students to begin to tie together their educational sequence.

All sections of the text should be introduced at this time. Many students do not realize that their text contains a glossary of terms or an index, which they can use to trace subjects within the text. After the section review, focus on the table of contents, pointing out the parts of the texts. Provide a graphic organizer for the table of contents. An example is the graphic organizer that appears at the beginning of each part of this text, providing the reader an overview of how all the parts fit together to work as a whole. This organizer is repeated at the beginning of each part and each chapter. When students have a mental picture of the structure of the text, it is time to move to the chapters.

The organization of each chapter should be explained prior to teaching the content. Several suggestions for providing structure within the chapters include stating the purpose and using graphic organizers, chapter outlines, vocabulary, chapter questions, and focus checklists.

First, present the purpose or objective of the chapter, just as with the overall text. What will this chapter cover? Second, present a graphic organizer that shows the chapter within the total picture of the text by simply revising the organizer for the total text. Next, develop a graphic organizer to display each major and minor part of the chapter. Figure 10.3 provides a sample graphic organizer for this chapter.

Provide an outline of the chapter that includes and extends the parts of the graphic organizer. The chapter outline could serve as a lecture outline (formative study guide) as discussed in Chapter 7. Allow space for note-taking and place the page numbers for the text for each part in the left margin by each section. For each major part of the chapter, provide a brief summary outline to give a short overview of the section. These steps will help when the sentences in a text are too long, increasing reading difficulty.

The next step in the model in Figure 10.2 is to introduce chapter vocabulary. Assisting students with disabilities in learning vocabulary provides for better acquisition of learning as well as for retention of new words. Table 10.7 presents suggestions for adapting vocabulary for the text.

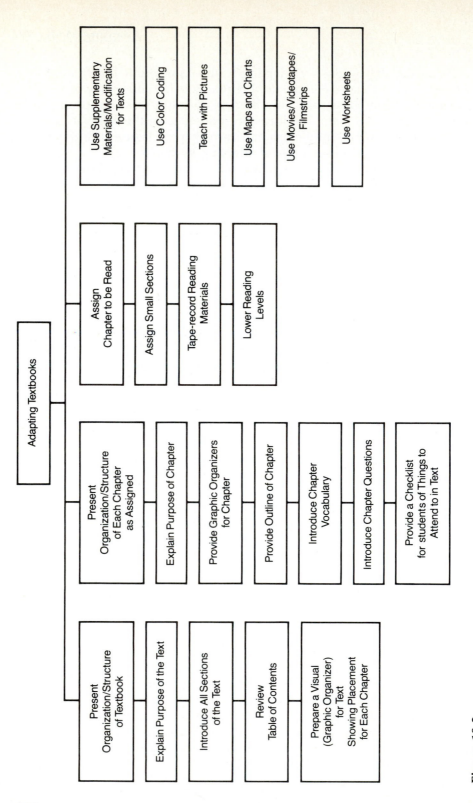

Figure 10.2
Model for Presenting and Adapting Textbooks

The figure shows a hierarchical chart with "Adapting Textbooks" at the top, branching into four main columns:

Present Organization/Structure of Textbook
- Explain Purpose of the Text
- Introduce All Sections of the Text
- Review Table of Contents
- Prepare a Visual (Graphic Organizer) for Text Showing Placement for Each Chapter

Present Organization/Structure of Each Chapter as Assigned
- Explain Purpose of Chapter
- Provide Graphic Organizers for Chapter
- Provide Outline of Chapter
- Introduce Chapter Vocabulary
- Introduce Chapter Questions
- Provide a Checklist for students of Things to Attend to in Text

Assign Chapter to be Read
- Assign Small Sections
- Tape-record Reading Materials
- Lower Reading Levels

Use Supplementary Materials/Modification for Texts
- Use Color Coding
- Teach with Pictures
- Use Maps and Charts
- Use Movies/Videotapes/Filmstrips
- Use Worksheets

298

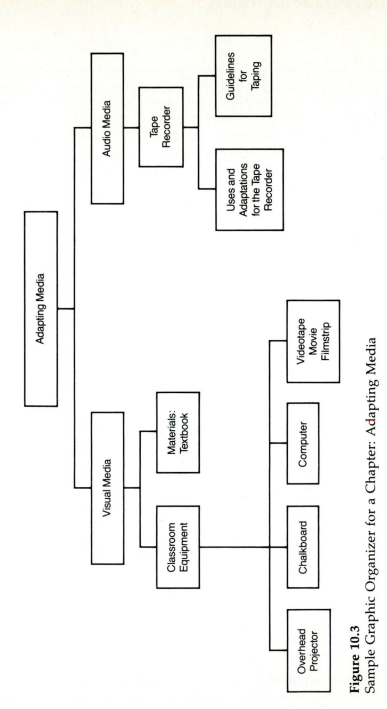

Figure 10.3
Sample Graphic Organizer for a Chapter: Adapting Media

Table 10.7
Adapting Vocabulary

1. Make a list of all bold-faced and italicized words and those presenting new concepts from the chapter. List the words in the order they occur within the chapter. Record the corresponding page number to the left of each word.

2. Beside each vocabulary word, provide a synonym or simplified definition.

3. Provide all students with the list of new vocabulary words prior to introducing the content of the chapter.

4. If students have difficulty looking up definitions or key words, provide the definition. This will cut down on the amount of work so they can spend time learning the definition of the word, which is the task we are asking them to do.

5. Instead of having the student copy vocabulary words and their definitions on notebook paper, have them write each word on the front of a 3-by-5-inch card and the corresponding definition on the back of the card. On each card, write the page number where the definition can be found. These steps save time and will produce a set of flash cards for reinforcement activities.

6. The cards can be filed in a box in order by chapter numbers.

7. When working with the flash cards, follow these steps:
   - The student holds the flash card and looks at the word.
   - Another student, a teacher, or a parent holds a list of the words and their definitions.
   - The student looks at the word while the helper pronounces the word.
   - The student repeats the word and supplies the definition.
   - The student immediately flips the card over to check the definition on the card for correct response.
   - Only work on 5 words at a time, adding another 5 after the first 5 are mastered. After learning the second 5 words, review all 10 words. Now add 5 more words. Then review all 15. This type of distributed practice is much better for memory load.

8. Be sure that the student knows what type of test you will use for vocabulary. For example, if the test will be a fill-in-the-blank without a word bank, the study process will be different than if a word bank was provided.

9. Tape-record the words for each chapter with each definition. This process will help students who cannot read the words initially to learn the words and their definitions. Be sure to number the words and read the number on the test.

The process of completing answers to chapter questions poses a major difficulty in working with reading material in many subjects. You may want to try one or more of the options found in Table 10.8.

A checklist for following the sequence of events in a story or chapter is especially helpful for students who have difficulty reading for specific details.

Table 10.8
Adapting Chapter Questions

1. Do not require that all questions be answered.

2. Reword questions to simplify vocabulary or sentence structure.

3. Avoid questions that require lengthy responses.

4. Allow students to answer questions without writing down the questions.

5. For students who have difficulty reading, make a study list of all questions as they occur, either within the context of the chapter or at the end of the chapter. Provide the correct answer and the page number where the answer can be found within the chapter.

6. Some students may need the questions and answers recorded on tape, allowing them to read along with the tape. With the recording, they would learn some information, rather than no information, as in the case of a poor reader.

7. Some students will benefit from having the page number where the answer can be found. This step will reduce busy work for the student and will help the slow reader focus on the question.

8. Remember to teach all students that the answers to questions usually occur sequentially within the text. For example, the answer to question 1 will appear in the text before the answer to question 2.

9. Allow students to copy each chapter question on a 3-by-5- or 5-by-8-inch card and number each question. As the students read the chapter, place the card with question 1 on the table beside the text. Tell them to read, looking for the answer to question 1. When they find the answer, they flip the card over and write the answer on the card, along with the page number in the text where the answer is found. They return to the text with the flash card for question 2 in front, again looking for the answer. This process assists slow readers by allowing them to read the text one time and finish with the answers to all the chapter questions. The set of cards can be used individually or with a buddy for review. This is a time-saving idea and also results in a set of flash cards. If you want to grade the questions, have the students turn in the cards.

The checklist will also provide an outline of events. You may write page numbers beside each step on the checklist. You also may provide study questions for each step. Students may check off each step as they read the section. This will help students focus on what they are reading.

The third phase of the model in Figure 10.2 includes adaptations to make when assigning the chapter to be read. First, review the chapter graphic organizer to show students how the chapter fits into the whole. Assign only small sections to be read at a time. If you assign too much to students who have difficulty reading or who track slowly, some will choose not even to attempt the assignment. Some may begin, but find the assignment too laborious to continue.

The teacher may *record the text* or sections of the text. When students follow in the text while listening to the same material recorded, they are using both the visual and auditory channels, thereby increasing their chances of retention. Teachers can record their text. Be sure to follow these suggestions:

1. Put each chapter on a separate tape.
2. Label each tape with the chapter and page numbers.
3. When recording, read the page number first, then read the text on the page. Tell the listener about any figures or tables by stating the page number and the table or figure number.
4. After referring to a table or figure, say, "return to text."
5. When moving to a new page, state the page number.
6. When the selection is completed, state "end of selection."
7. Read the table of contents for each chapter along with the chapter title and page numbers.
8. File all tapes in large tape boxes. Label each row of tapes by text title. These file boxes may be purchased at most record or videotape stores.

Companies that prepare commercially recorded texts are excellent resources, and they usually carry large inventories. For example, Recordings for the Blind, Inc., carries an inventory of 90,000 recorded texts. If a text is not in stock, they will record it free of charge. This service is available to students who are visually impaired, blind, physically disabled, or learning-disabled, and continues for life. College texts and work materials may also be recorded. A student must apply to receive the service.

Lowering reading levels is another step in the model in Figure 10.2. Common sense tells us that a large percentage of students in classes will not read on grade level. Three factors to consider when reducing the reading level of printed material are vocabulary, structure and paragraph construction, and physical format. Tables 10.9 through 10.11 present suggestions for each of these areas.

The fourth phase in the model in Figure 10.2 involves supplementary materials and modification for texts. Other modifications that can be made to printed materials include color coding, teaching with pictures, and using maps and charts, movies, videotapes, and filmstrips, and worksheets.

Color coding helps students organize what they are about to learn and helps them prioritize the learning. Using three different colors, mark key words and concepts with one color, important facts and information with another, and definitions with a third. Colors should be standardized throughout the school to avoid confusion and a color-code key posted at the front of the coded text.

Teaching with pictures is an excellent way to help poor readers or nonreaders follow a lesson or discuss ideas for a project. Many libraries contain books of pictures on history, science, and other subjects. Have students look through a sequence of pictures to focus on the clothes of different periods. Specific details in old pictures can show the way people's lives change over time and give

Table 10.9
Adapting Reading Levels through Vocabulary

Prefixes and suffixes add to complexity. Latin roots increase abstraction. To increase readability:

1. Introduce new terms and concepts slowly and allow lots of practice before introducing the next new term.
   Example: An atom contains particles of matter called electrons, protons, and neutrons.
   Modification: An atom is often described as "the smallest particle of an element." You know that an atom is matter. It has mass and takes up space . . .

2. Use synonyms of a lower order in place of complex words. Care should be taken to avoid losing the writer's intent.
   Example: We should not adjudicate the theological praxis of aught categorizations of homo sapiens to be factious.
   Modification: We should not judge the religious customs of any group of humans to be silly.

3. Make a slight revision, add an insertion, or completely rewrite. Again, care should be taken to avoid losing the writer's intent. It may be necessary to add an extra phrase, sentence, or even a paragraph to make an abstract concept more clear.
   Example: Milk that has been pasteurized is considered safer for you.
   Modification: Milk that has been pasteurized or heated to 140–155 degrees is considered safer for you. Heating kills the bacteria in the milk.

4. Nominalization should be avoided. Nominalization transforms verbs and modifiers into nouns, usually resulting in abstract meanings.
   Example: The praising of his song made him happy.
   Modification: He was happy that they praised his song.

5. Avoid overdirecting.
   Example: When you see an asterisk, stop the tape, for this is going to act as a stop sign for you, and you know that a stop sign or a red light means you have to stop.
   Modification: Stop the tape when you see an asterisk.

students a look at specific events during the period. Students could focus on a sequence of events or on cultural changes.

Maps and charts are useful in teaching students who cannot read at all or on their grade level. Maps may be enlarged, with picture clues posted on them. For example, when studying Mexico, pictures clues might include posting pictures of crops in the appropriate areas on a map, illustrating types of clothing, or demonstrating transportation on the map visually.

Movies, videotapes, and filmstrips may be used for reinforcement activities or supplementary assignments. Students who have difficulty reading can get vital details of an assignment through these media. For example, prior to assigning a novel to be read, the class may watch a movie that gives an overview of the book.

Table 10.10
Adapting Reading Levels through Sentence and Paragraph Construction

Excess punctuation, such as commas, semicolons, and slashes, indicates complexity in sentences and paragraphs. To increase readability:

1. Break long or complex sentences into smaller units of thought.
   Example: In ancient Egypt, similar tastes for cool beverages developed, but a different solution was forthcoming since a more temperate climate kept Egypt ice-free even in winter.
   Modification: The people of ancient Egypt also liked cool beverages. However, the warmer climate kept Egypt ice-free even in winter. A different solution was needed.

2. Use conversational narrative.
   Example: The dearth of leadership exhibited in this project was reflected in the tendency of the managers to address implementation problems in an ad hoc manner.
   Modification: The lack of leadership in this project was shown by the way the managers did not plan for possible problems.

3. Avoid irrelevant words, phrases, and sentences.
   Example: Lincoln was shot in the head at the Ford Theatre in Washington, D.C., by John Wilkes Booth, an out-of-work actor.
   Modification: Lincoln was shot at the Ford Theatre by John Wilkes Booth.

4. A slight revision may lead to clarity.
   Example: In the upper atmosphere, great numbers of ions are present, hence the name *ionosphere*.
   Modification: The name *ionosphere* comes from the presence of great numbers of ions in the upper atmosphere.

5. Retain grammatical markers. Words such as *because, if, before,* and *after* imply a cause-and-effect relationship and should not be deleted.
   Example: The engine failed. The plane crashed.
   Modification: Because the engine failed, the plane crashed.

6. Increase readability by making the topic sentence the initial sentence in a paragraph.
   Example: The issue of slavery was important to the South, but there were other factors involved including states' rights vs. federal rights, the commercial interests of the plantation vs. manufacturing concerns, and international vs. intranational trade. All contributed to the friction between the North and South. The Civil War was brought about by many factors.
   Modifications: There were many reasons for the Civil War. The issue of slavery was important to the South, but there were other factors involved, including states' rights vs. federal rights, the commercial interests of the plantation vs. manufacturing concerns, and international vs. intranational trade. All contributed to the friction between the North and South.

Table 10.11
Adapting Reading Levels through Physical Format

There is no formula for measuring the effect of format on readability, but it should be taken into consideration. To increase readability:

1. Use large type or lettering with adequate spacing.
   Example: How now brown cow.
   Modification: HOW NOW BROWN COW.

2. Use illustrations that teach and do not distract.
   Keep them simple.

3. Notice the quality of copies. Many children cannot see purple, so avoid this type of copy.

4. If it won't fly, don't hand it out. Extensive handouts and/or heavy textbooks can overwhelm a student before the lesson ever begins.

Worksheets are frequently used in classes for assignments and practice. When students have difficulty reading the text, they will also have difficulty reading the worksheets. Chapter 8 presents suggestions for modifying worksheets.

Resources for Implementing Textbook Adaptations

A great concern of educators is how to prepare adapted material. The following resources may assist educators in preparing and implementing textbook adaptations:

- Check to see if any of your school's clubs will take on textbook adaptations as a yearly project.
- If several teachers are using the same textbook, divide up the techniques so that each will have to prepare only a small proportion. For example, one teacher may adapt the vocabulary, another the questions.
- After students complete the answers to chapter questions, use their papers to prepare study guides.
- In faculty meetings, share ideas on ways the adaptations may be completed.
- Assign aides to the task.
- Ask local parent volunteers and/or support groups to assist in the project.
- Consult your special education teacher about groups that are willing to assist with projects for special students. (Wood & Wooley, 1986, p. 335.)

AUDIO MEDIA

Tape recorders are invaluable sources for supplementing visual work (see Table 10.12). Teachers can use tape recorders to reinforce the correct pronunciation of words; record the correct pronunciation of sounds the speech therapist is working on; help students who are easily distracted by giving them earphones; reward students by letting them record for pleasure; help students evaluate

Table 10.12
Uses and Adaptations for the Tape Recorder

1. Students may work at their own pace.

2. Teachers can prepare tapes of spelling words, math facts, and science lessons, along with worksheets or other activities to provide sequential instruction.

3. Teachers can make tapes of directions for complicated activities or textbook assignments.

4. Class discussions may be taped and later evaluated by class members or the teacher.

5. Classroom lectures can be taped for students who cannot take notes or those who are absent.

6. Students can listen to a taped story or play while following in their books, using a pointer or their finger to equate the printed word with the sound.

7. Tape recorders can be used to reinforce correct pronunciation of words in English class.

8. For students receiving speech therapy, teachers may record the correct pronunciation of sounds the therapist is working on.

9. Teachers may record study questions at the end of each chapter, pausing to allow time for student response.

10. Teachers may record chapters and activities in books for slow learners.

themselves in reading by having them record stories; reinforce lectures by recording them; give students immediate feedback by recording study questions at the end of a chapter, pausing for student response, and then recording the correct response; encourage student participation in class by having students record their own experiences to use in language experience exercises. In addition, the teacher can record every other page of a text for slow readers; this technique reduces the reader's frustration level. Finally, mainstreamed students in social studies and science classes often can learn the concepts but have difficulty reading the texts. The teacher can record social studies and science chapters for these students to listen to as they follow along in the text. Peer tutors can help with this recording.

Another use for tape recorders is for teachers to record comments intended for the student. For example, instead of written comments on a paper, record the suggestions. Project grading may be done in the same way. This allows the teacher to personalize the comments and provide suggestions for correcting or improving their work in the future.

ADAPTED LESSON PLAN FOR MEDIA

Figure 10.4 continues the adapted lesson plan, adding suggestions for adapting the material section of the lesson plan. In Figure 10.4, specific adaptations are

OBJECTIVE	STRATEGIES/ PROCEDURES	MATERIALS/ RESOURCES	EVALUATION/ ASSIGNMENT

Date: ___
Taxonomy Level
  X Knowledge
  X Comprehension
____ Application
____ Analysis
____ Synthesis
____ Evaluation
 	
The student will be able to list and define the parts of the ear and the steps for the travel of sound in the ear.
	Lecture on the parts of the ear and how sound travels.	Display of ear
		Filmstrip
		Chapter in text
		Handout of parts of ear
			Fill-in-blank Test and listing

Adaptations:	Teaching Techniques: — Use acquisition outline — Use structured organizer to show relationship of parts of ear — Use visual of ear with lecture Format of Content: — Develop a task analysis list of how sound travels in ear. — Color-code the path of sound as it travels within the ear and each part of the ear.	Adapted Media: — Label each ear part on the display. — Use a checklist for viewing film strip. — Record reading materials. — Put ear parts & definitions on 3-by-5-inch cards. — Use overhead transparency for practicing ear parts. — Project ear on chalkboard and practice drawing sound track. — Provide study guide.	Evaluation Test: Student Assignment:

Figure 10.4
Format for an Adapted Lesson Plan: Media

provided for the model of the ear, the chapter assigned and for the handout of the parts of the ear. Using these adaptations, the teacher will give random learners structure and a better opportunity for success.

SUMMARY

Using media to supplement a student's learning or adapting media to meet specific learning styles is helpful in assisting students in attaining their objectives. Making slight changes in printed material, adding a movie to the class lesson, allowing the student to record the lecture, or providing individualized comments on tape are small modifications that can make large differences in learning outcomes. Many times, students can learn the content if media are adjusted to assist in the process.

After the teacher has carefully adapted the planning and teaching process, Step 4, Evaluation and Alternative Grading Procedures, can be adapted.

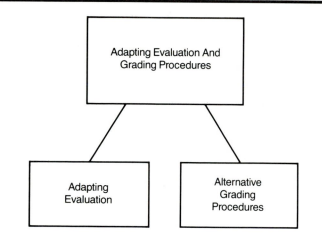

— PART FOUR —

Adapting Evaluation and Alternative Grading Procedures

Part Four includes two chapters: "Adapting Education" and "Alternative Grading Procedures." Each of these chapters extends structure in the classroom and presents ideas for classroom use.

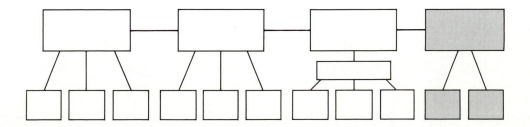

— CHAPTER ELEVEN —
Adapting Evaluation

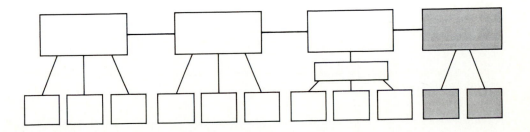

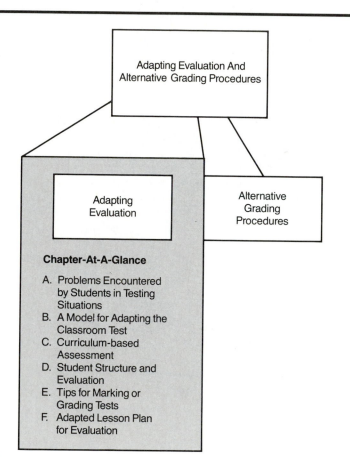

Adapting Evaluation And Alternative Grading Procedures

Adapting Evaluation

Alternative Grading Procedures

Chapter-At-A-Glance

A. Problems Encountered by Students in Testing Situations
B. A Model for Adapting the Classroom Test
C. Curriculum-based Assessment
D. Student Structure and Evaluation
E. Tips for Marking or Grading Tests
F. Adapted Lesson Plan for Evaluation

Since the passage of P.L. 94–142, regular and special educators have been working together to modify curricula, adapt lesson plans, and alter classroom environments to meet the needs of students with mild disabilities. But considerably less attention has been given to the evaluation of such students. The term *evaluation* can cover test questions, grading systems, or graduation requirements and competency testing.

Special education aims to foster student ability and potential by individualizing educational programming. As a result, both regular and special educators need to recognize the impact that testing, grading, and graduation have on the achievement and self-concept of students. Students need rewards for effort and for attaining goals; therefore, teachers must use evaluation methods that enable students to demonstrate mastery. Mastery must be based on individual student ability or potential, not on the norm. If a student with disabilities could achieve at standard levels, educators would not be providing special services. Robbins and Harway, (1977) point out that "the school-age period is crucial in the development of a child's view of himself" (p. 356). They further explain that the student with disabilities experiences a wide variety of successes and failures that tend to interfere with the development of a sense of identity. In particular, Robbins and Harvey demonstrate that if teachers give students with learning disabilities positive feedback, those students gradually set more realistic goals for themselves. But since they have encountered a great many failures in school, students with learning disabilities may need constant reinforcement before they become convinced that they can achieve.

Therefore, as teachers evaluate the progress of the student with mild disabilities in the regular classroom, they need to consider the student's cognitive and affective development. To ensure student progress, teachers should select the most appropriate and nondiscriminatory method of evaluation. Educators can meet the needs of students by using alternative evaluation techniques. This chapter looks at ways of adapting tests for students, and Chapter 12 closes our text with a discussion of alternative grading procedures.

If the primary goal for most students is mastery of concepts, teachers must find ways to give students with mild disabilities opportunities to demonstrate proficiency to regular classroom teachers, doubting and unaccepting peers, and themselves. If teachers persist in using traditional testing techniques, they further disable the very students that the law attempts to protect. While modifications in curricula and instructional procedures are more prevalent today in regular elementary and secondary classrooms, many teachers still resist changing the construction, administration, or site of a test. Many teachers consider the traditional test sacred and thus the only appropriate instrument of evaluation. The same teachers often believe that if the student with mild disabilities cannot demonstrate mastery via this one instrument under the same conditions as everyone else in the classroom, then that student has not achieved and does not deserve a passing grade. However, these teachers do not realize that frequently the student may indeed have mastered the concept, but is simply unable to demonstrate that mastery unless certain modifications are made in the test. What the student lacks are the skills necessary to succeed in a traditional setting. Although some students with disabilities may not reach the same goals as their nondisabled peers, others will surpass these same peers through hard work, determination, and perseverance. As John Dewey commented in 1937, each child is "equally an individual and entitled to equal opportunities of development of his own capacity, be they large or small in range" (Dewey, 1937, pp. 458–459)

Before adapting a test, the teacher should evaluate test objectives to see if the test is appropriate. To evaluate test objectives, the teacher should ask the following questions. Is content validity present in the test? Does the test measure what it is intended to measure? Does the test evaluate the skills taught, rather than more complex skills or concepts that were not? Is the test designed to reflect student knowledge rather than speed, ability to follow complicated directions, or vocabulary? Does the test tap knowledge in the same way retention was taught?

PROBLEMS ENCOUNTERED BY STUDENTS IN TESTING SITUATIONS

Many students have already encountered problems that could result in test failure before they even put pen to paper. The teacher needs to understand the problems often encountered by students with mild disabilities or at risk before and during a testing situation. Once aware of these problems, the teacher can move equitably to evaluate students and assist them with solutions.

Poor Comprehension

Comprehension means the ability to clearly understand what is said or explained. Students with mild disabilities often do not understand verbal directions. When the teacher gives a series of directions, they cannot recall each step correctly. Without a clear understanding of what to do or how to proceed, they might either proceed incorrectly or turn papers in with only their names on the page. Certainly, such responses obtained do not accurately indicate the full extent of the student's knowledge. Similarly, written directions are often too lengthy or complicated for the student with mild disabilities. The reading level alone may be above the student's instructional level. Directions may contain words or phrases that the student does not know, may instruct the student to perform several operations, or may ask the student to follow more than one procedure. For example, a student with poor comprehension would have difficulty following and understanding these directions:

1. Write a sentence containing a gerund.
2. Draw a circle around the gerund.
3. Indicate whether the gerund is the subject, direct object, predicate nominative, or object of the preposition by writing S., D.O., P.N., or O.P. above the gerund.

A related difficulty involves abstractions. Some students with mild disabilities can recall facts and deal with concrete ideas but do not respond well to evaluative questions or those requiring inferences or deductive reasoning. For example, the student may understand how to write a paragraph, but would have trouble writing several paragraphs on an abstract topic such as "Ecology in Action in Our Community."

Auditory Perceptual Problems: Teacher Variables

Students with auditory perceptual problems cannot process auditory information quickly and easily. The students can hear, but problems in learning occur when they try to process what is heard. Auditory problems associated with teacher variables, however, can be avoided. The teacher who administers tests orally, for example, greatly penalizes students with auditory deficits. Even simple spelling tests pose problems. Some teachers proceed too fast, not allowing the student enough time to sound out the word and transfer the sounds into their written forms. Some teachers simply call out the words without clearly delineating each syllable or sound.

Some students may experience only minor difficulty with spelling tests, but have major problems when the teacher administers quizzes or chapter tests orally. The student must not only process the question through the auditory system—a giant undertaking—but also transfer the information to paper. Sometimes this task is virtually impossible. In addition, the auditorally disabled student simply cannot recall previously asked questions. Thus, a good traditional technique prevents the student from demonstrating concept mastery.

Auditory Perceptual Problems: Environmental Variables

While teachers can adjust the amount of information they present verbally or the number of tests they administer orally, they may have little control over certain environmental auditory distractions both inside and outside the classroom. Frequently, teachers grow accustomed to a reasonable amount of background noise or sounds and become oblivious to these distractions. Students with auditory problems, however, are not as fortunate. A variety of environmental variables may distract these students from their classwork or from verbal information the teacher is presenting. These distractions include noise outside a window, conversations in an adjoining classroom, learning module distractions, announcements on the P.A. system, and incidental noise arising from peers, such as students asking questions, students whispering among themselves, and teachers reprimanding students for talking at unauthorized times. Since many of these auditory distractions cannot be eliminated or modified, the teacher should realize that, even for a few seconds, these conditions create an environment hostile to learning and not ideal for testing. The teacher must guard against assuming that if students would just pay attention, they would be able to understand or if they would just concentrate more, they could complete the assigned task or test. Students with auditory perceptual problems often find it difficult to discriminate the sounds coming from the front of the classroom, such as instructions from the teacher, from sounds filtering into the room from elsewhere. For some, concentrating and remaining focused on the task becomes virtually impossible in a classroom with normal environmental sounds. For students experiencing auditory difficulties, alternative instructional methods may be needed or alternative testing sites may prove helpful.

Visual Perceptual Problems: Teacher Variables

Many students experience problems when they receive information visually. Again, the problem for the student is not an inability to see, but an inability to process information received visually. Teacher variables often contribute to the student's visual problem.

For example, most teachers use the chalkboard as an instructional tool. Teachers invariably post spelling words, homework assignments, and other reminders on the board for students to copy into their notebooks. A number of teachers even write tests on the board, while others require students to work math problems, diagram sentences, or complete other tasks at the chalkboard. Many teachers assume that information they write correctly on the board will be copied correctly into notebooks. The majority of students in the class may succeed with ease, but any students with visual perceptual difficulties may experience a variety of problems. Primarily, they have trouble transferring information from the board to their paper or notebook. They may transpose numbers, as in page numbers assigned for homework, or interchange letters, as in spelling words or key terms for a new unit. Students then memorize the information they copied incorrectly, leading to a misrepresentation of their abilities and poor test scores. Similarly, copying homework assignments incorrectly leads to additional confusion. At night, students open their books to unfamiliar pages and problems they may not know how to solve; the following day, the teacher may be suspicious of the student's explanation for not completing the assignment. The student with visual perceptual problems encounters some of the same difficulties when attempting to take a test written on the board: difficulty transferring information to paper, understanding written directions or questions, and copying correctly. As if these problems were not enough, visual distractions on or near the chalkboard clutter the student's field of vision—homework assignments on the same board as the test, spelling words in another corner, and bulletin boards adjacent to the chalkboard, for example. The majority of teachers keep a clean chalkboard, but not all of them do.

The teacher's handwriting also affects how a student responds to any test. Although most teachers' printing or cursive handwriting ranges from average to excellent, not all teachers can claim such a distinction. Of course, typed tests are better than handwritten ones, but teachers cannot always have their tests typed. A good test does not require typing, but legibility is a must. Teachers with unusual cursive styles should print. If printing also presents problems, the teacher should ask someone else to write the test. The teacher also must ensure that all copies are legible. Not all schools possess the newest or most efficient duplicating equipment, but unreadable copies are inexcusable. Students must be able to decipher the questions to pass the test.

Most teachers use written tests in one form or another—multiple-choice, true-false, matching, fill-in-the-blank or completion, essay, and others. The student with visual perceptual problems will encounter many obstacles with such tests. For example, a teacher may give students a matching test with a long column of descriptive statements and an equally lengthy column of answer choices. Although students may know the answer to the first descriptive statement, they must peruse the entire column of answer choices, from top to bottom, to locate the correct answer. Students spend unnecessary time searching for letter equivalents to answers, sometimes to the extent that they are unable to complete the test. Even more common, some students may be oblivious to time and consequently spend the allotted period on just the matching section, not even attempting the remaining sections.

Length can also become a psychological barrier to success on written tests. At-risk students usually have failed repeatedly. The majority of such students equate tests with unpleasantness. If these students were asked about previous tests or their ability to pass tests, their responses probably would be negative. A lengthy test of three or more pages may discourage students, especially those with visual problems. They may attempt the first page and stop when they realize they cannot finish, or they may feel defeated upon first examining the test. Teachers may overhear remarks such as, "I know I don't know the answers to that many questions," or "I know I'll never finish, so why should I even begin?" The number of questions or problems per page may visually overwhelm other students. Their eyes may busily scan and rescan the page; as a result, they cannot focus on individual questions or problems and thus cannot proceed.

Some students with visual problems have difficulty identifying, recognizing, or decoding symbols and abbreviations. Simple mathematical symbols, such as $+$, $-$, $>$, $<$, or $=$, may cause visual turmoil for students with visual perceptual problems. They may confuse one symbol with another, or they may have trouble associating the symbol with its written equivalent, for example, $+$ with *plus*. Students with pronounced visual difficulties usually experience extreme anxiety when attempting to solve algebraic equations:

$$\frac{(2x + 4)}{2} - 4 = (2x + 6) + 3(2x + 3x)$$

Of course, not all students with disabilities will take algebra, but some will need to complete the course if their goal includes a college degree. Others may not take algebra but will encounter basic mathematical symbols throughout their academic and postacademic years.

Visual Perceptual Problems: Environmental Variables

Visual distractions and stimuli abound, both inside and outside the classroom. The degree of distraction varies from student to student. For some students, most visual distractions are momentary. For others, a single distraction can completely disrupt their present visual field, their ability to concentrate, and their ability to keep working. The distraction may originate outside a classroom window or inside, as a result of students moving at their desks or turning in their papers, peers making motions or gestures, or visitors entering the classroom. Whatever the source, these disruptions cause students with minor visual problems to become temporarily nonfunctional and those with more serious visual problems to remain nonfunctional indefinitely.

Time Constraints

Teachers generally strive to develop a test to fit the time frame available for giving it. Most teachers attempt to allow extra time for students who work more slowly than others. For students with disabilities, time often plays a major role in taking a test. Within the group of students with disabilities, individuals may have auditory or visual perceptual problems, motor coordination difficulties, and, frequently, reading problems. Generally, these students are not intentionally slow or lazy, and they do not mean to aggravate the teacher or disrupt the test. Rather, they have real problems caused by identified learning modality deficits. The teacher needs to remember that students with auditory problems may not be able to answer oral questions in the same time frame as students without such a disability. Similarly, students with visual perceptual, motor coordination or reading problems probably will not be able to complete most tests designed for the regular student. Teachers must try to avoid discriminating against students with recognized exceptionalities, penalizing them, not for lacking knowledge, but by not giving them an opportunity to demonstrate their proficiency.

Anxiety

Most teachers have experienced test anxiety at least once during their academic lives. Most can admit that test anxiety exists and is very real to the individual experiencing it. Teachers need to understand further that the degree of test anxiety varies considerably from student to student. When anxiety makes a student nonfunctional, the teacher should recognize it as a disability similar to those in comprehension, visual and auditory perception, and motor coordination. Anxiety differs from other disabilities, however, because it is usually temporary. Years of failure and negative responses from teachers, peers, and parents result in measurably lower self-concepts for students with mild disabilities. Because many students automatically associate taking a test with failure, they become fearful and anxiety-ridden even at the thought. Fear and anxiety, along with a history of previous failures, may even cause test phobias for a few students. For all practical purposes, these students, simply cannot function in a traditional test setting. Others feel anxiety, but not to the same extent. For example, they be extremely hesitant at the beginning of a test because they lack self-confidence, or they may stop midway through the test because they encounter one or two questions they do not know. Others stop working when they realize that their peers have finished and are turning in their papers. Such students want to be or at least appear "normal." They do not want to be the last ones working or be called *dummies*. Still other students allow their initial impression of the length or scope of the test to overwhelm them, and, like students with test phobias, become nonfunctional for a while. Anxiety, although difficult to measure, influences a student's ability to take and pass a test. Teachers should consider the anxiety level when evaluating a student's performance and attempt to reduce that level as much as possible by adapting the test.

Embarrassment

Perhaps what most students with disabilities want is to be like everyone else. Identifying with and being accepted by peers is important to any student, but it becomes essential for the student with mild disabilities. As students mature into adolescence and young adulthood, this desire for peer acceptance and approval becomes even more pronounced. Students with disabilities, who are acutely aware of their academic inabilities, will sometimes sacrifice a passing grade rather than ask the teacher a question and risk embarrassment in front of their peers. Over the years, students learn to hide or disguise their disabilities. They become specialists in looking busy or presenting an attitude that says, "I don't care," rather than admitting they do not understand how to do the work. In addition, a high percentage of students with disabilities will turn in their test papers simply because nearly everyone else in the class has done so—they cannot risk the embarrassment of being the last ones working. When teachers grade their papers and see very few questions answered, they often incorrectly assume that the student did not study.

Mainstreamed students are also sensitive about taking tests that differ from those of their peers. They may realize that they are receiving individualized programming, but they understandably want to maintain the appearance of doing the same work as their peers. Some high school students with mild disabilities insist on taking the "regular" test along with their friends, although they know it will not be scored and an individualized test will be administered in their resource class. Other students willingly take a modified test in the regular classroom as long as it closely resembles the one being taken by everyone else. The regular teacher must remember that even though students with mild disabilities need to receive praise from parents and special education teachers, they also need to maintain their pride and self-esteem in the presence of peers.

A MODEL FOR ADAPTING THE CLASSROOM TEST

Adapting classroom tests for students in the mainstream requires following a three-part model, as shown in Figure 11.1. Adaptations can be made during (a) test construction or (b) test administration or (c) by providing an alternative test site.

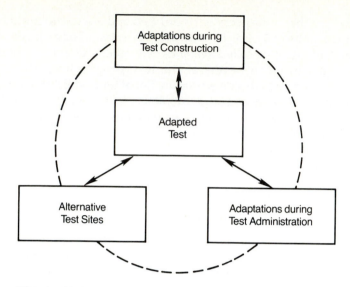

Figure 11.1
Model for Adapting the Classroom Test

Adaptations During Test Construction

Test construction may be divided into three separate components: test directions, test items, and test design. The following sections present adaptations for each of these components.

Test Directions

Directions are a critical aspect of test construction. Test directions that are not clear and understandable may cause failure for students before they even try to complete the test. Consider the following suggestions for making test directions clearer for all students.

1. Keep directions short.
2. Keep directions simple; avoid unnecessary words.
3. Type directions.
4. If directions are not typed, print neatly.
5. Place all directions at the beginning of each separate test section.
6. When giving more than one direction, list vertically.
7. List only one direction in each sentence.
8. Underline the word *Directions* to focus the student's attention.
9. Avoid using words such as *never, not, always, except*. If you must use these, underline and capitalize them.
10. Define any unfamiliar or abstract words.
11. Color-code directions.

12. Avoid making oral directions the only means of communicating the purpose of the test to students. Read directions orally as well as clearly writing them on the test.
13. Tell students the reason or purpose of the test.
14. Go over each direction before the test. Be sure that students understand what they should do.
15. Remember that students who do not clearly understand the directions will be the last to raise their hand and ask for clarification.
16. While the test is in progress, walk around the room and check to see that students are following directions.
17. Teach students that if points are to be lost, they may lose them for not knowing items on the test. But they should avoid losing additional points for not following or understanding the test directions.

Adapting Test Items

The second part of the test construction model is adapting test items. These adaptations do not invalidate or "water down" the test, but simply make test items more appropriate for students experiencing difficulty with the test process. The following suggestions are divided into two types: test items that require simple recognition and those that require structured recall. Remember that a mismatch in testing can occur when we use a type of item that is inappropriate for a student. For example, if a student has difficulty remembering information from recall, a recognition test may be more appropriate.

The five types of test items to be discussed are: multiple-choice, matching, true-false, fill-in-the-blank, and short-answer or essay. The first three types, multiple-choice, matching, and true-false, require simple recognition; the latter two require structured recall.

Multiple-Choice. The multiple-choice items is recognized as one of the most useful types of objective test questions. The following suggestions may prove helpful in constructing this item type.

1. Avoid frequent use of *fillers*.
   Example: a) Either. . .or
   b) All of the above
   c) None of the above
2. Let the student circle the correct answer rather than placing the answer on an answer sheet or blank form. This reduces the possibility of copying errors when transferring letters to the blanks.
3. Arrange the correct answer and the distractors, or incorrect answers, vertically on the page.
   Example: 1. You have a board *48 inches long*. If you cut off a *6-inch piece*, how much is left?
   a. 38 inches
   b. 42 inches
   c. 48 inches

4. Be sure all choices are grammatically consistent.
   Example: 1. Because of poor land and a short growing season, the New England colonies were forced into the economic choice of:
   a. Exporting food
   b. Trading and ship building
   c. Growing and exporting cotton
5. Avoid using more than 10 multiple choice questions per test.

Matching. The matching exercise is designed to measure factual information based on simple association. It is a compact and efficient method of measuring simple relationships. These suggestions may be helpful when selecting matching items for tests.

1. Place all matching items and choice selections on the same page.
2. Leave extra space between items in columns to be matched.
3. Use homogeneous material for each matching exercise.
4. Use small groups of matching questions. Avoid long matching lists.
5. Have one extra response in one of the columns. For example, if you have 10 items in column A, place 11 choices in column B. This statistically puts the question in the student's favor.
6. Have only one correct answer for each item.
7. Avoid having students draw lines to the correct answer. This may be visually confusing.
8. Keep all matching items brief. The student who has comprehension and reading problems may not be able to process long, wordy items.
9. Place the responses, such as names of explorers, on 3-by-5-inch cards. These become a manipulative exercise. Students can match answers to the correct answer by placing the card next to the item.[1]
10. Place the list with more lengthy items, usually the descriptive items, in the left column. This makes for less reading and will assist the slow reader.
11. Teach students who take tests that do not have the columns reversed to begin the test working from column B to column A.
12. Make a *mini-letter bank* under the blank to reduce the number of choices (see item 8 in example).
13. Place the blank for the response after each item in column A.

Example for #10, 11, 12:

Column A		Column B
1. The island continent	_____	a. North America
2. Bordered by the Atlantic	_____	b. Pacific Ocean
3. Located north of the Mediterranean Sea	_____	c. Africa
		d. Indian Ocean

[1]Special thanks to Janice Mael for suggestion 9.

4. Bordered by Africa and Asia   _____   e. Asia
5. The largest ocean   _____   f. Europe
6. Bordered by the Atlantic and Pacific,   g. Atlantic Ocean
    north of the equator   _____   h. South America
7. The largest continent   _____   i. Australia
8. Bordered by the Atlantic and Pacific,
    south of the equator   _____

                     a, c, h

True-False. The most common use of the true-false item is to measure the student's ability to identify the correctness of statements of fact or definition. The following suggestions for modifications may help in constructing these items.

1. Avoid stating questions negatively.
2. Avoid long, wordy sentences.
3. Avoid statements that are trivial or do not assess student knowledge.
4. Allow students to circle the correct answer.
5. Avoid using too many true-false questions at one time. The suggested number is no more than 10 items per test.
6. Avoid using *never, not, always,* and *except.* If you must use these words, underline and capitalize them.
7. Avoid having students change false statements to true statements unless you have taught this skill.
8. Place the words *true* and *false* at the end of the sentence.

Example:

Imperialism was a cause of World War I. True   False

Fill-in-the-Blank or Completion. This type of question is suitable for measuring knowledge of items, specific facts, methods or procedures, and simple interpretation of data. Since this type of test items requires structured recall, it is difficult for many mainstreamed students and should be used sparingly, if at all. In many cases, a multiple-choice items would be more appropriate. If teachers still want to use completion or fill-in-the-blank items, they can attempt to reduce the complexity of the item by using the following suggestions.

1. Write simple and clear tests items.
2. Avoid the use of statements taken directly from the textbook. Taken out of context, they are frequently too general and ambiguous to be used as test questions.
3. Provide large blanks for students with poor handwriting or motor control problems.
4. Be sure that the blank size matches the response. If the blank is too long or too short, students may think that their response is incorrect.

5. Place the blank at the end of the sentence.
6. Provide *word banks* for the test.
7. Provide a *mini-word bank* immediately under the response blank. This reduces memory load and can be implemented on a test that is already constructed.
8. Allow students to circle the correct choice in the *mini-word bank*.
9. Prior to the test, tell students whether they will have a *word bank* on the test.
10. Use a *floating word bank* that is detached from the test. The student can move the *word bank* up and down the right side of the page to check for the correct word, placing the words close to the blanks.
11. Have another teacher read your test to check for clear understanding of each item.
12. Place one extra word in the *word bank*. This works just as with matching items, statistically putting the test in the student's favor.
13. If a word will be used as a response more than once, list it the appropriate number of times in the *word bank*.

Example:

One of the Scandinavian countries is _____.
(Germany, Norway, Greece)

Short-Answer or Essay. Teachers use these types of test items to measure learning that cannot be evaluated by objective test items. Most essay or short-answer questions require the student to recall relevant factual information, mentally organize ideas, and write an extensive response. These responses may require skills that are extremely difficult for students with poor organization abilities or deficient writing skills. For these reasons, essay questions should be used sparingly, and with some students, not at all. Suggestions for using essay questions more effectively with mainstreamed students include:

1. Use items that can be answered briefly.
2. Be sure that students know the meaning of clue words, such as *discuss, describe, list*.
3. Underline clue words.
4. Write questions using clue words that correspond to the domain level of the student. For example, *define* is on the knowledge level, *predict* is on the application level.
5. Allow students to outline answers or provide an outline for them.
6. Use structured organizers to organize answers.
7. Make sure that the question is written on the student's independent reading level.
8. Define any unclear items.
9. Word your questions so that the student's task is clearly stated.

10. Use a limited number of essay questions on the test.
11. Always list the point value of each question.
12. Provide space for the response immediately under the question.
13. Allow the student to record the answers rather than write them.
14. Allow extra time to write answers. Remember that some students do not write as quickly as others.
15. Always allow the student to omit one or two essay questions. This reduces anxiety.
16. Provide an answer check sheet that lists the components requested in the response.
17. Indicate on the test whether you expect students' responses to include factual information, inferences, and/or applications.
18. Always provide study questions for the essay items on the test study guide.

Example:

Compare and *contrast* life in Germany and the United States. Use this outline to help organize your answer.

  I. Similarities (compare how they are alike)
    A. How is daily life the same in the United States and Germany?
    B. Give two examples
 II. Differences (contrast how they are different)
    A. How is daily life different in the United States and Germany?
    B. Give two examples

OR

Use this structured organizer to organize your answer.

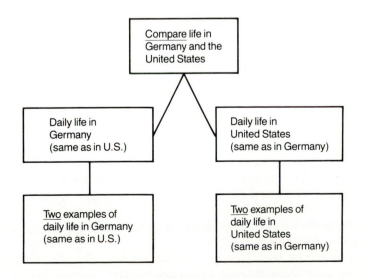

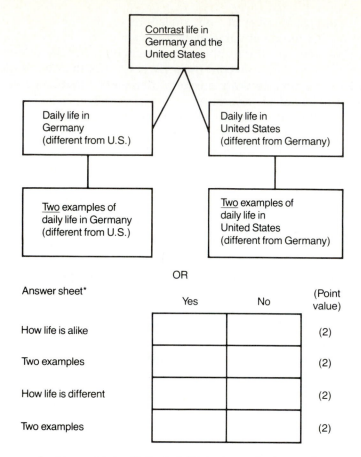

OR

Answer sheet*	Yes	No	(Point value)
How life is alike			(2)
Two examples			(2)
How life is different			(2)
Two examples			(2)

*Note. The answer sheet is provided with the test. Students can clearly see what components in the question they must address in their answer. They may check off the *yes/no* boxes when they have answered each component. The point value is listed to the right of the boxes. The teacher uses the answer sheet for grading purposes or for comments. The students can check their own papers to know specifically what they need to do to improve or restudy.

Other Test-Item Adaptations. In some academic areas, the test item may vary according to subject. For example, in math, computational problems and word problems occur on tests. In science, lab practicals may be used. The following provide suggestions for adapting for such items.

Computation problems usually require the student to apply an algorithm or a formula to find a numerical answer. Consider the suggestions found in Table 11.1.

Word problems can be very difficult for students with disabilities. The items in Table 11.2 are helpful in evaluation.

Lab practicals can be used to assess students with mild disabilities. If you've been teaching your students how to operate Bunsen burners, for example, test

Table 11.1
Adaptations for Computation Problems

1. Provide manipulative objects that make the problems more concrete.

2. Avoid mixing different problem formats in the same section. For example, a student with organizational or visual tracking difficulties may be able to solve problem A but may not be able to align the numbers in problem B.

Problem A	Problem B
4 6 8	
3 1	670 + 40 + 2861 =
+1 8 9 4	

3. Avoid mixing vertical and horizontal problems in the same section. For example, the student with visual tracking problems or for a student who has difficulty "changing gears" from one process to another, this shift in presentation from Problem C to Problem D may be confusing. It would be better to test the student's knowledge of the two processes in two separate sections of the test.

Problem C		Problem D
8	and	5 × 6 = _____.
×5		

4. Give formulas and meanings of symbols:
   $<$ means *less than*

5. Give a set of written steps for applying algorithms:

   Example: Long division
   1. Divide
   2. Multiply
   3. Subtract
   4. Check
   5. Bring down

Note. From "Adapting Test Construction for Mainstreamed Mathematics Students" by J. W. Wood and J. W. Miederhoff, 1988, *Mathematics Teacher*, pp. 388–392. Copyright 1988 by Mathematics Teacher. Adapted by permission.

the students by giving them a checklist to work through the lab (Figure 11.2). Let students who need individual help work with a lab partner or in a small group. Follow up with more specific questions. Students should complete these questions with the burner turned off. Teachers can write similar checklist tests for the use of other lab equipment, such as balances, graduated cylinders, and microscopes.

Many students can answer questions better orally than in writing. To test students' safety knowledge, you can make slides of people using improper safety procedures. You can then show these slides and ask students to describe orally which rules are being broken. Another adaptation is to read tests aloud to students with reading disabilities.

Table 11.2
Adaptations for Word Problems

1. Use simple sentences. Avoid unnecessary words that may cause confusion.

2. Use a context for the problem that is relevant to the student's personal experience.

3. Underline or circle key words, for example: *less, more.*

4. Use no more than five word problems per test, since these require greater effort to read and understand.

5. Give formulas as reminders of operations to be used.

6. Be sure that the reasoning skills being tested are appropriate to the student's comprehension level. Avoid the use of word problems with some students, as this use may be testing language and measuring skills above the student's level. For example, a student with a mild disability who has poor reading and comprehension skills may not be able to understand a complex word problem without assistance.
   Example:

   John lives 3 7/10 miles from Fair Oaks Elementary School. Trish lives 2 3/4 miles from school. Which one lives *farther* from school? _____ *How much farther?* _____

For students who learn best through hands-on experiences, you can design tests that evaluate students in a hands-on manner. For example, instead of asking students to label a diagram of an atom on a test, allow them to construct a three-dimensional model of an atom using plastic foam balls. The students can indicate on the model the location and charge of neutrons, protons, and electrons.

Test Design

Test design is the third aspect of test construction that can easily be adapted. Some adaptations in test design include:

1. Use test items that reflect techniques you used in teaching. For example, if the students were taught only to recall facts, avoid essay questions.
2. Type or print legibly. Use large type when available. If you prepare the test in longhand, be sure to list items clearly, concisely, and neatly.
3. Prepare a study guide that matches the design of the test.
4. Adjust readability level of the test to meet the students' needs.
5. Prepare the test in short sections that you can administer individually if necessary.
6. Place one type of question on each page. For example, use one page for multiple-choice questions and another for essay questions.
7. After consulting students privately about personal testing needs, adapt the test to meet those needs.

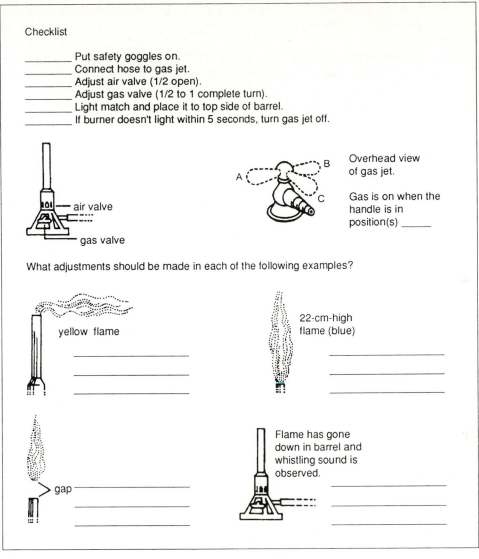

Checklist

_____ Put safety goggles on.
_____ Connect hose to gas jet.
_____ Adjust air valve (1/2 open).
_____ Adjust gas valve (1/2 to 1 complete turn).
_____ Light match and place it to top side of barrel.
_____ If burner doesn't light within 5 seconds, turn gas jet off.

air valve
gas valve

B
A
C

Overhead view of gas jet.

Gas is on when the handle is in position(s) _____

What adjustments should be made in each of the following examples?

yellow flame

_____
_____
_____

22-cm-high flame (blue)

_____
_____
_____

gap

_____
_____
_____

Flame has gone down in barrel and whistling sound is observed.

_____
_____
_____

Figure 11.2
A Lab Practical for the Bunsen Burner
Note. From "Stress the Knowledge, Not the Student: Testing the Mildly Handicapped" by J. W. Wood, J. W. Miederhoff, and J. C. Bishop, 1988, *The Science Teacher*, pp. 22–25. Copyright 1988 by The Science Teacher. Reprinted by permission.

8. If you use the chalkboard for a test, clear other material from the board, then print or write in large, legible letters. Avoid lengthy tests for students with copying difficulties.
9. Avoid using only oral tests and quizzes.

10. Plan to allow students with disabilities to take tests in the special classroom to overcome problems with time, reading ability, or embarrassment.
11. Clearly duplicate the test using black ink, if available. Avoid using faded purple copies from a duplicating machine for any students, but especially for those with visual acuity and visual perception difficulties.
12. Use a large sheet of dark construction paper under the test to act as a border. Provide a sheet of paper with a "window frame" cut in it to help in reading the test. This helps students with visual acuity and visual perception problems.
13. If the student has difficulty finishing on time, administer an adapted, shortened version of the test. Another option is *split-halves* testing, where half of the test is administered one day, and the other half, the next day.
14. If a modified test is necessary for a mainstreamed student, design it to resemble the regular test to avoid embarrassment.
15. Arrange tests so that questions that count the most come first. Some students generally work in order and may not finish the test.
16. If possible, use canary yellow paper with black print for the test.
17. Write the point value for each section on the test.
18. Place a heading for each test section with directions if they differ from section to section.
19. Handwriting should be neat and legible.
20. If typing is not possible, print the test.
21. All pages of the test should be numbered.[2]

Adaptations During Test Administration

The second component of the model for adapting the classroom test in Figure 11.1 (page 322) involves the administration of the test. Many students with disabilities may need alternative modes of administration when taking the test. Adapting during administration of tests relates directly to the problems that students encounter in the test situation as discussed at the beginning of this chapter. Each problem is listed in Table 11.3 along with suggestions for test administration.

Alternative Test Sites

Allowing students to take their tests in an alternate environment, such as the resource room, is a viable option during the testing situation for students with disabilities. Table 11.4 presents some advantages of testing in the resource room.

Modifying tests for resource students is primarily the responsibility of the regular classroom teacher because they are more familiar with the material presented to the student. However, since the special education teacher knows the individual student's unique strengths and weaknesses, it is best if the regular and special education teachers combine their efforts.

[2] Special thanks to Dave Meadows for adaptation 21.

Table 11.3
Adaptations during Test Administration

Problem	Adaptations
A. Poor comprehension	1. Give test directions both orally and in written form. Make sure all students clearly understand.
	2. Avoid long talks before test.
	3. Allow students to tape-record responses to essay questions or entire test.
	4. Allow students to take the test in an alternate test site, usually the resource classroom.
	5. Correct for content only and not for spelling or grammar.
	6. Provide an example of the expected correct response.
	7. Remind students to check tests for unanswered questions.
	8. When the test deals with problem-solving skills, allow use of multiplication tables and/or calculators during math tests.
	9. Read test aloud for students who have difficulty reading.
	10. Give a written outline for essay questions.
	11. Record instructions and questions for a test on an audio cassette tape.
	12. Use objective rather than essay tests.
B. Poor auditory perception	1. For oral spelling tests, go slowly, enunciating each syllable and sound distinctly.
	2. Avoid oral tests.
	3. Seat student in a quiet place for testing.
	4. Allow students to take tests in an alternate test site, such as the resource classroom.
	5. Place a "TESTING" sign on the classroom door to discourage interruptions.
C. Poor visual perception	1. Give directions orally as well as in written form.
	2. Check students discretely to see if they are "on track."
	3. Give exam orally or tape-record on audio cassette.
	4. Allow students to take entire test orally in class or the resource room.
	5. Seat students away from distractions (e.g., windows, door). Use a carrel or put desk facing wall.
	6. Avoid having other students turn in papers during test.

Table 11.3 *continued*

Problem	Adaptations
	7. Meet visitors at door and talk in hallway.
	8. Hang a "DO NOT DISTURB— TESTING" sign on the door.
	9. Use alternate test site if student requests it.
D. Student works poorly with time constraints	1. Allow enough time for students to complete the test. Mainstreamed students may require longer periods of time.
	2. Provide breaks during lengthy tests.
	3. Allow *split-halves* testing. Give half of the test one day and the remaining half the second day.
	4. Allow student to take the test in the resource room if necessary.
	5. Allow students to complete only the odd- or even-numbered questions. Circle the appropriate questions for students who may not understand the concept of odd and even.
	6. Use untimed tests.
	7. Give oral or tape-recorded tests. Students with slow writing skills can answer orally to the teacher or on tape.
E. Anxiety/Embarrassment	1. Avoid adding pressure to the test setting by admonishing students to "Hurry and get finished," or "Do your best, as this counts for half of your 6-weeks grade."
	2. Avoid threatening to use a test to punish students for poor behavior.
	3. Give a practice test.
	4. Give a retest if needed.
	5. Don't threaten dire consequences for failure.
	6. Grade on percentage of items completed.
	7. Have students take regular test with class and adapted test in resource room.
	8. Make modified test closely resemble regular test to avoid embarrassing self-conscious students.
	9. Avoid calling attention to mainstreamed students as you help them.
	10. Confer with students privately to work out accommodations for testing.

Table 11.4
Advantages of Testing in the Resource Room

Specific Problem	Potential Solution
Reading difficulties Slow reader Low vocabulary Low comprehension	For oral tests, student can have: More time Questions clarified New vocabulary explained Less pressure Test recorded on tape recorder
Student embarrassed by taking a test different from one given to peers in regular class	Student has acceptable setting for completing test
Student easily confused by verbal or written directions	Student has more opportunity to ask questions and may feel less frustrated
Student distracted by activity within regular classroom	Student has a more structured setting that contains fewer distractions
Student experiencing test anxiety, frustration	Anxiety is reduced No longer competing with peers Can work at own pace Has support of resource teacher

Note. From "Mainstreaming Minimanual" by J. Wood and B. Englebert, *Instructor*, 1982, *91*, pp. 63–66. Copyright 1982 by The Instructor Publications, Inc. Adapted by permission.

To work together to modify any test, regular and special education teachers must find opportunities to meet, either during the day or after school. Elementary teachers generally do not have planning periods, so their only option is usually after school. However well-intentioned the regular and special teachers may be, faculty meetings, school activities, family commitments, and parent conferences frequently prevent such joint work sessions. Similarly, regular and special teachers on the secondary level rarely share identical planning periods. And planning periods and after-school hours often fill up with conferences and other school and family responsibilities. Alternatives to meeting after school might include the following:

1. Regular and special teacher work together to familiarize the regular teacher with each student's needs, with the ultimate goal of having the regular teacher assume major responsibility for intervention.
2. Regular and special teacher work together to familiarize the regular teacher with ways the special education teacher modifies tests.
3. Regular and special education teacher work together for a longer period of time, with the ultimate goal of creating a bank of tests from which both could draw throughout the year, and then make minor modifications depending on the amount of material covered.

Regular teachers often fear that regular students may resent mainstreamed students for making better grades when they take tests in the resource room. This fear is based on the false assumption that students with mild disabilities will always make better grades because their tests are "easier." However, some students with disabilities may score significantly higher, but many are fortunate if they pass. In addition, regular students usually do not resent their peers who take their tests in a resource setting. Instead, regular students exhibit compassion—they are pleased when their friends can pass and do well; they realize that their friends have problems in school; and they often understand that their peers function below grade level, take different tests, and have reasons for being tested in the resource setting. Usually, when teachers handle resource programming and testing appropriately, both regular and special students view the program positively. Even average and above-average students sometimes ask to attend resource classes for temporary assistance or to complete a test, and the majority of slow learners not eligible for special education services would gladly attend resource classes.

The dilemma revolves around equality of evaluation. Just as teachers evaluate by traditional testing methods, they express the results of their evaluation via the use of traditional letter (A, B, C, D, F) or numerical (95, 90, 85, 80) grades. To teachers, students, parents, and the general public, these symbols generally represent a certain standard. When some students take different tests but still receive traditional grades, some teachers believe a standard has been violated. This issue has not been resolved; however, the following points should be noted:

1. Students with mild disabilities have definite learning problems, as their placement in special education attests.
2. Authorities recommend alternate site testing.
3. School systems across the nation use alternate grading systems.

For the present, regular and special educators should strive to develop equitable grading policies that will reward students with disabilities for their efforts and encourage all students to work toward their potential.

CURRICULUM-BASED ASSESSMENT

Teachers are discovering that the most useful way to assess students' needs and progress is to measure their performance in the context of the curriculum requirements of their classroom setting (Durkin, 1984; Hargis, 1982; Samuels, 1984; Thompson, 1981). Since curriculum requirements vary from school to school, it would not be feasible to compare a student's progress to the performance of students everywhere on standardized tests (Jenkins & Pany, 1978; Ysseldyke & Algozzine, 1982). A more general type of assessment, referred to as curriculum-based assessment (CBA), has emerged to fill the need for an assessment process based on the student's progress through an individual curriculum.

A major goal of CBA is to eliminate the mismatch that exists between low-achieving students and the sometimes unreasonable demands of the curriculum. For example, a student who is unable to master the second-grade math curriculum may advance to third grade with an incomplete set of skills, facing an even more difficult set of requirements (Bloom, 1976). Such students can succeed if the curriculum is adjusted. CBA allows teachers to determine what skills have been mastered, what skills need to be retaught or reviewed, and what adjustments need to be made in the curriculum.

CBA is "the practice of obtaining direct and frequent measures of a student's performance on a series of sequentially arranged objectives derived from the curriculum used in the classroom" (Blankenship & Lilly, 1981, p. 81). The essential quality of this assessment approach is the coupling of assessment with the curriculum and instruction of the classroom. The term *CBA* is also used to refer to the assessment instrument itself. Using CBA provides an objective measurement of a student's achievement based on specific classroom objectives. The teacher then uses the results to make instructional decisions (Blankenship, 1985).

According to Blankenship (1985), CBA can be given at various times during the school year. At the school year's beginning, teachers may use CBA to place students into appropriate curriculum materials, form instructional groups, and identify specific skills that students need to master. They may also use CBA immediately following instruction on a specific topic or skill to assess skill mastery and determine if reteaching is necessary. Following skill mastery, CBA can be utilized to measure long-term retention.

When developing and using CBA, the goal is to make an instrument to measure the student's present performance and develop a plan to interpret and use the results in educational decision-making. Steps for using CBA are listed in Table 11.5.

The benefits of CBA over other types of assessment include:

1. It is useful for planning instruction.
2. It focuses attention on the relevant skills students need to learn.
3. Teachers become the primary assessors rather than receiving second-hand test results.
4. Students are not retaught material they have mastered.
5. Data can be used at IEP meetings to:
    a. Summarize present levels of performance.
    b. Suggest appropriate goals and objectives.
    c. Document student progress (Blankenship, 1985).

Teachers are urged to start slowly by developing a CBA on one topic or unit. After becoming familiar with the process, they can develop CBAs for other topics and exchange CBAs with other teachers (Blankenship, 1985).

Table 11.5
Steps for Using Curriculum-based Assessment (CBA)

1. List the skills presented in the selected material.
2. Make sure all important skills are presented.
3. Decide if the skills are in logical order.
4. Write an objective for each skill on the list.
5. Prepare items to test each objective.
6. Prepare the test.
7. Plan how the CBA will be given.
8. Give the CBA immediately before instruction on a topic.
9. Study the results to determine:
   a. Which students have already mastered the skills?
   b. Which students have the prerequisite skills to begin instruction?
   c. Which students don't have prerequisite skills?
10. Readminister the CBA after instruction to determine:
    a. Which students have mastered the skills and are ready to move to a new topic?
    b. Which students need more practice?
    c. Which students need additional instruction?
    d. Which students need modifications in the curriculum?
11. Readminister the CBA throughout the year to test for long-term mastery.

Note. From "Using Curriculum-based Assessment Data to Make Instructional Decisions" by C. S. Blankenship, 1985, *Exceptional Children, 52,* p. 234. Copyright 1985 by The Council for Exceptional Children. Adapted by permission. Original Source: Blankenship, C. S. (1985). "Assessment, Curriculum, and Instruction." In J. F. Cawley (Ed.), *Practical Mathematics Appraisal of the Learning Disabled* (pp. 59–79). Rockville, MD: Aspen Systems. Blankenship, C., & Lilly, M. S. (1981). *Mainstreaming Students with Learning and Behavior Problems: Techniques for the Classroom Teacher.* New York: Holt, Rinehart & Winston.

STUDENT STRUCTURE AND EVALUATION

The last three chapters, "Adapting Teaching Techniques," "Adapting Format of Content," and "Adapting Media" discussed the importance of imposing structure for students. During the evaluation process, students can continue to have structure imposed and learn how to develop structure for themselves. During this phase, students need to know (a) the category of test; (b) the specific test item; and (c) how to study for each.

Category of Tests

As mentioned, tests will fall into one of two basic groups, based on whether they require (a) simple recognition or (b) structured recall. Students must first be taught what each group means to their study effort and which of the test item types fall into each category.

Recognition tests require students to examine a group of items or choices and select the correct answer. Because the correct answer is presented within a list of distractors, recall can be prodded. The student may recall after seeing the correct choice. Test items within this category include true-false, multiple-choice, and matching. Class instruction should focus on retention of specific information such as facts and data. Study guides should require students to focus on specific ideas and the ability to select a correct choice when presented.

Structured recall requires the student to recall the answer to a question without a visual prompt. This type of recall is heavy on memory load. Class instruction should focus on general information such as broad topics or ideas. Study guides should include focus questions designed to help students organize the study process around the "general ballpark" of the questions. Test items include fill-in-the-blank or completion, short-answer, and essay.

Tips for Specific Test Items

Specific test-taking tips for students on each of the item selections are listed in Table 11.6.

TIPS FOR MARKING OR GRADING TESTS

Teachers may use the following suggestions in marking or grading papers for students with disabilities or at risk for school success.

Tips for Marking Tests

1. When students make low grades, let them tell you why. Give extra points if they can tell you where they need to improve.
2. Give extra points on tests when students include information that you taught but did not cover in test questions.
3. Be careful in letting students check one another's papers. This procedure can prove to be embarrassing.
4. Let students keep a graph of their grades.
5. Return all graded papers folded to respect privacy.
6. Place the grade on the second page of the test or at the bottom of the front page. This also allows for privacy.
7. Write "see me" instead of a grade on papers with low marks.
8. Allow students to turn in projects early for teacher review prior to the due date. This practice encourages students to complete work early and provides the reward of teacher feedback prior to final grading.
9. If the grade on a project is low, allow the student to rewrite it for a higher grade.
10. If the test is a short quiz, let the student retake it for a higher grade. Students who receive a low grade will learn that they still need to learn the material.
11. If students can justify an answer on a test, give full or partial credit.
12. If a test question is worth 3 points and a student misses 1 point, write the score as $+2$ instead of -1.

Table 11.6
Test-Taking Tips for Students

Type of Test Item	Test-taking Strategy
Test Directions	1. Underline important words in the directions such as *list, discuss, define.*
	2. If there are several directions given, number each direction.
	3. Make a checklist (vertically) of the directions.
	4. Check off each direction as you complete it.
	5. Put the directions on a card so that you can move them from page to page.
	6. If you do not understand written directions, ask the teacher to repeat them.
	7. If directions are given orally, ask for a written copy.
	8. Be sure that you understand the directions. If not, ask for help.
	9. Remember, if you lose points on a test, lose them for not knowing the content, not for missing a direction.
	10. Draw a thin line through anything in the directions that does not relate specifically to the test.
Multiple-Choice	1. Read the question and try to answer it before reading the answers.
	2. Draw a line through each answer that could not possibly be correct.
	3. Use other questions on the test as cues.
	4. Use rules of grammar, such as the use of *a* vs. *an*, as cues to the answer.
	5. Read all choices and see what you think the correct response is for each. This will help you eliminate some answers.
	6. Be sure that you have read all choices before making your selection.
	7. If you have two options that you think are equal, select one and write a brief rationale in the margin. Sometimes extra credit is given for thinking.
	8. Never leave a multiple-choice question unanswered.
Matching	1. Begin with the first term in the column and scan the other column for the answer.
	2. Write the letters of possible answers next to the word to narrow down the choices.
	3. After you choose the answer, cross it off in the answer column.
	4. Skip any question you are not sure of and come back to it after you have answered all the other questions.
	5. If the columns are not reversed, begin with column B and work to A.

Table 11.6
continued

Type of Test Item	Test-taking Strategy
True-False	1. Circle important words, such as *never*, *always*, and *not*.
	2. Don't bother looking for a "pattern" to the answers (e.g., 2 true, 1 false, 2 true, 1 false). There probably is no pattern.
	3. Statements are usually false when the clue words indicate absoluteness (*all*, *every*, *none*, *never*).
	4. Statements usually are true when the clue words modify the absoluteness (*Many*, *most*, *fewer*, *seldom*, *sometimes*).
	5. Do not try to read into a true-false item what is not stated.
	6. Remember that *all parts* must be true or false to be completely true or false.
Completion/Fill-in-the-Blank	1. Use words from the rest of the test as cues to possible answers.
	2. If you are not sure of a question, jot down possible answers to it and return to it later.
	3. Prior to the test, check to see if this type item will be used.
	4. Ask if a *word bank* will be provided.
	5. If you have a *word bank*, mark off answers used.
Essay/Short-Answer	1. Circle key words, such as *opinion*, *three examples*, *evaluate*. Then structure your response to answer these questions.
	2. Make a rough outline of the major points asked for in the question. Organize your answer around the major points, filling in the facts.
	3. Verbalize quietly as you write if it helps.
	4. Use a structured organizer to plan your answers.
	5. Learn the seven most common clue words used: *discuss*, *contrast*, *compare*, *criticize*, *define*, *describe*, *list*.
	6. Other common essay clue words include: *review*, *analyze*, *diagram*, *summarize*, *evaluate*, *justify*, *enumerate*, *prove*, *interpret*, *state*, *outline*, *relate*, *trace*, *comment on*, *illustrate*.

ADAPTED LESSON PLAN FOR EVALUATION

Figure 11.3 presents the final and completed adapted lesson plan. In the figure the traditional plan simply stated that the teacher would use fill-in-the-blank test and listing items. Suggested adaptations include discussing the type of test item prior to the test, providing a word bank for the fill-in-the-blank items and modification for the student assignment. This lesson plan provides an overview of applications of Chapters 8, 9, 10 and 11.

OBJECTIVE	STRATEGIES/ PROCEDURES	MATERIALS/ RESOURCES	EVALUATION/ ASSIGNMENTS
Date: ___ Taxonomy Level X_ Knowledge X_ Comprehension ___ Application ___ Analysis ___ Synthesis ___ Evaluation			
The student will be able to list and define the parts of the ear and the steps for the travel of sound in the ear.	Lecture on the parts of the ear and how sound travels.	Display of ear Filmstrip Chapter in text Handout of parts of ear	Fill-in-blank Test and listing
Adaptations:	Teaching Techniques: —Use acquisition outline. —Use structured organizer to show relationship of parts of ear. —Use visual of ear with lecture. Format of Content: —Develop a task analysis list of how sound travels in ear. —Color-code the path of sound as it travels within the ear and each part of the ear.	Adapted Media: —Label each ear part on the display —Use a checklist for viewing film strip —Record reading materials —Put ear parts & definitions on 3-by-5-inch cards —Use overhead transparency for practicing ear parts —Project ear on chalkboard and practice drawing sound track —Provide study guide	Evaluation Test: —Prior to class, tell students what type of test items will be used. —Provide word bank. —Refer to evaluation chapter for specific item adaptations. Student Assignment: —Be sure that the assignment is on the appropriate cognitive levels. —Modify assignment based on each student's ability.

Figure 11.3

Format for an Adapted Lesson Plan: Evaluation

SUMMARY

This chapter provided suggestions for adapting tests and placed an emphasis on student structure and testing. The last chapter in the text, "Alternative Grading Procedures," will look in detail at grade-related issues. The text will close with a look at this last phase of evaluation.

CHAPTER TWELVE

Alternative Grading Procedures

Andrea M. Lazzari

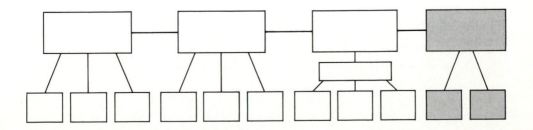

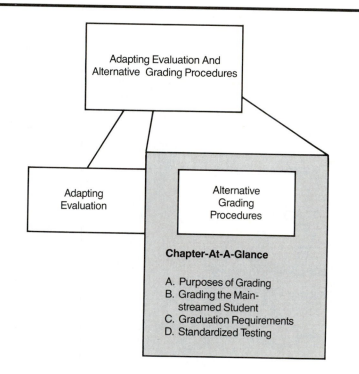

Adapting Evaluation And
Alternative Grading Procedures

Adapting
Evaluation

Alternative
Grading
Procedures

Chapter-At-A-Glance

A. Purposes of Grading
B. Grading the Main-
streamed Student
C. Graduation Requirements
D. Standardized Testing

Teachers are constantly making evaluations of their students' performance. Assigning grades is perhaps the most common and readily observable form of student evaluation, whereby a teacher makes a decision about a student's performance or ability. When assigning a grade, the teacher uses a combination of objective data, such as tests and quizzes, assignments, and class participation, and subjective measures of certain values, such as hard work, perseverance, and creativity, to derive the final grade (Jacobsen, Eggen, & Kauchak, 1989). It is the subjective aspect of the grading process that causes many teachers to feel uncomfortable with the task. Grades are frequently viewed as a necessary evil imposed on teachers by outside forces, such as district-wide policies and building-level procedures. For many teachers, assigning grades is a job responsibility for which they received little training during teacher preparation programs (Cohen, 1983).

This chapter presents (a) purposes of grading, (b) a variety of approaches to grading, (c) issues in assigning grades to mainstreamed students, (d) awarding course credit and diplomas to students completing alternative curricula, and (e) having them participate in standardized tests such as minimum competency testing.

PURPOSES OF GRADING

Even though the assignment of grades may not be a favorite task of many teachers, grades can serve several useful functions. Ideally, grades serve the purpose of providing feedback to students that will help them achieve their learning objectives. In practice, grades serve several other functions, including (a) providing feedback to parents as an indicator of their children's achievement; (b) providing data for grouping of students; (c) guiding decisions regarding promotion and graduation; (d) providing a basis for making awards and scholarships; (e) determining a student's eligibility for extracurricular activities; and (f) helping determine college eligibility and participation in collegiate athletics (Jacobsen, Eggen, & Kauchak, 1989).

The traditional practice of assigning grades may today serve primarily as an administrative function to differentiate among groups of students rather than as a mechanism to provide useful information to students. Yet, as Marsh and Price (1980) point out, an estimated 82% of junior high schools and 84% of senior high schools continue to use a letter grading system to evaluate student performance, citing letter grades as good predictors of college performance. A fallacy of viewing grades solely as a ticket to higher education is that this practice does not give equal consideration to the needs of students who will enter the workplace upon leaving high school. For such students, feedback that more closely resembles the type of evaluations they will receive on the job may be more valid and useful. It is important for educators to strive to develop alternative grading procedures that can more appropriately meet the needs of all students.

GRADING THE MAINSTREAMED STUDENT

The problems inherent in evaluating students and assigning grades can become even more complex for mainstreamed students. The integration of students with disabilities in regular education classes has created a dilemma for teachers in terms of assigning grades fairly and objectively (Hess, Miller, Reese, & Robinson, 1987). On one hand, questions arise about the equity of using different standards to evaluate students in the same classroom. For example, is it fair to the other students in the classroom to award the same letter grades and course credit to an individual who has not met the class performance standards? On the other hand, proponents of individualized grading point out that to do otherwise places an added burden on students already at a disadvantage for competing fairly with their peers and does not serve to provide useful information to students and parents. For example, a grade of "Satisfactory" or C does not reveal what new knowledge students have gained or how they have performed relative to their individual strengths and weaknesses; nor does it provide information on the effectiveness of instructional adaptations. Other questions arise over who should assume responsibility for grade assignment, which criteria should be used for grading, and what grading process should be used (Cohen, 1983).

A preliminary question to answer when considering the issue of grading a mainstreamed student is whether alternative grading procedures are necessary for that individual. In many cases, making appropriate adaptations of the learning environment, format of content, teaching techniques, and testing procedures will enable the student with special needs to be graded by the same methods used for other students in the classroom. In instances where accommodations in grading procedures are needed, they should be noted on the student's IEP along with any other adaptations that are necessary. In addition to identifying the grading procedures, the IEP should specify if a grade reporting schedule other than the standard school schedule is to be used and should identify which teacher will be responsible for determining the student's grades.

A generally accepted practice in many schools is for the teacher with primary responsibility for the content area to assign grades to students in special education (Bauer & Shea, 1989). For example, for students who are mainstreamed for all academic subjects, the regular teachers of the respective subjects would assign the grades. For others who receive most of their instruction in a specific subject in the resource room, the resource teacher would assign the grade. If the special and regular educators are teaching cooperatively, they may choose to collaborate when assigning grades to mainstreamed students. In some school districts, this decision will be predetermined as a result of system-wide policies (Cohen, 1983). Regardless of the approach chosen, the issue of which teacher will be responsible for assigning grades to mainstreamed students should be resolved at the outset of the school year or grading period, and the decision should be shared with the students and their parents.

The debate over criteria for assigning grades is not as easily resolved. As summarized by Hess et al. (1987):

> No single best practice has been identified to resolve the problems inherent in assigning grades to students with disabilities who make a sincere effort, but because of their disabilities simply cannot measure up to either the teacher's standard or the school's standard in terms of meeting all the criteria for a given course or class when traditional methods of assessment, instruction, and grading are used. (p. 1)

Alternative Methods of Grading

Although the development of alternative grading criteria for students with disabilities may not be an easy task, it is an extremely important adaptation which must be made if students with special needs are to have any chance of success in the mainstream environment. Table 12.1 displays 10 alternative evaluation approaches, which are discussed in detail in the following section.

A frequently used modification of traditional grade criteria is the establishment of general criteria for passing or failing an assignment or a course. Since determination of acceptable work is judged by broad-based criteria, the mainstreamed student has more chance of success in reaching the minimum course competencies. As with any measurement procedure, there are advantages and disadvantages to using a *pass/fail system*. Vasa (1981) identifies the following advantages of this approach:

- Students feel less pressure to compete;
- Students feel less anxiety;
- Students need not cheat or "butter up" the teacher;
- Students know what the teacher expects of them and work toward a goal;
- The teacher can increase a student's achievement or aspiration level;
- The teacher can carefully examine the student's relative abilities and disabilities; and
- The teacher does not have to compare students' work. (p. 26)

The disadvantages of the pass/fail system are:

- The teacher may not provide corrective feedback in weak areas;
- The passing grade does not distinguish between students of differing abilities;
- Some students do less work when freed of traditional grade pressure;
- Students close to failing feel the same pressures they do with traditional grades; and
- Teachers sometime find minimum standards arbitrary and difficult to define. (p. 26)

An alternative to establishing grading criteria in isolation is to modify the criteria as part of the grading procedure which is selected. A variety of alternate grading procedures have been used to evaluate students with mild disabilities. Kinnison, Hayes, and Acord (1981) present seven alternatives to traditional grading, which are used in both elementary and secondary classrooms. These alternatives are listed as items 3 through 9 in Table 12.1.

The *Individualized Education Program approach* bases grading on the student's attainment of the goals and objectives specified in the IEP. Since the IEP must specify target accuracy levels or minimally acceptable levels of competence for specific skills and/or knowledge, built-in criteria for grading exist. Teachers can determine grades by translating the competency levels on a student's IEP into the school district's performance standards. If, for example, the IEP requires 80% accuracy and 80 equals a letter grade of C on the local scale, then the student receives a C. Cohen (1983) raises two cautions to keep in mind when grading by IEP objectives: (a) Teachers should "avoid the tendency to minimize short-term expectations" by inadvertently writing shorter and/or easier objectives to help the student achieve better grades; and (b) While the presence of established grading procedures may appear to preclude the use of IEP objectives as a grading mechanism, an assessment report based on IEP objectives can be used to supplement standard report card grades (p. 89).

Table 12.1
Alternative Approaches to Student Evaluation

Approach	Definition	Example
1. Traditional grading	Letter grades or percentages are assigned.	Students earning 94% or greater of the total points available will earn an A.
2. Pass/fail system	Broad-based criteria are established for passing or failing.	Students who complete all assignments and pass all tests will receive a passing grade for the course.
3. IEP grading	Competency levels on student's IEP are translated into the school district's performance standards.	If students have an IEP that requires a 90% accuracy level and the range of 86–93 equals a letter grade of B on the local scale, the students receive a B if they attain target accuracy level.
4. Mastery-level or criterion grading	Content is divided into subcomponents. Students earn credit when their mastery of a certain skill reaches an acceptable level.	Students who can name 38 of the 50 state capitals will receive a passing grade on that unit of the social studies curriculum.
5. Multiple grading	The student is assessed and graded in several areas, such as ability, effort, and achievement.	Students will receive 30 points for completing the project on time, 35 points for including all of the assigned sections, and 35 points for using at least four different resources.

Table 12.1 *continued*

Approach	Definition	Example
6. Shared grading	Two or more teachers determine a student's grade.	The regular education teacher will determine 60% of the student's grade and the resource room teacher will determine 40%.
7. Point system	Points are assigned to activities or assignments that add up to the term grade.	The student's science grade will be based on a total of 300 points: 100 from weekly quizzes, 100 from lab work in class, 50 from homework, and 50 from class participation.
8. Student self-comparison	Students evaluate themselves on an individual basis.	Students who judge that they have completed the assignment on time, included the necessary sections, and worked independently assign themselves a passing grade for this assignment.
9. Contracting	The student and teacher agree on specific activities required for a certain grade.	Students who come to class regularly, volunteer information at least once during each class, and turn in all required work will receive a C.
10. Portfolio evaluation	A cumulative portfolio is maintained of each student's work, demonstrating achievement in key skill areas from Kindergarten to Grade 12.	Cumulative samples of handwriting show progress from rudimentary manuscript to legible cursive style from Grades 1 to 4.

Mastery-level or criterion systems divide content into various subcomponents, with pre- and posttest measures required for each step. Students earn credit only after their proficiency or mastery of a certain skill reaches an acceptable level. One disadvantage to this approach is that students are rewarded or passed for minimum, rather than optimum, performance.

Figure 12.1 displays a sequence of steps leading to the mastery level for the skill of word division. The criterion for each step is used as the pre- and posttest measure. A buddy system with an answer key for checking can be used for students to demonstrate their mastery of each step.

Multiple grading rewards the student in several areas, such as ability, effort, and achievement. The student's final grade usually is determined by averaging all three grades for each subject area. Some teachers use letter grades with subscript numbers to indicate level (above, on, or below grade level). Carpenter

Figure 12.1
Sample Criterion or Mastery-level System

Criteria for Word Division

Step		Criterion	Date*
A	I can separate word list A into two lists: single-syllable words and words with two or more syllables.	35/40 correct	_____
B	I can divide the compound words on list B into syllables.	35/40 correct	_____
C	I can divide the prefix words on list C into syllables.	35/40 correct	_____
D	I can divide the double-consonant words on list D into syllables.	35/40 correct	_____
E	I can divide the suffix words on list E into syllables.	35/40 correct	_____
F	I can divide the words with a single middle consonant on list F into syllables.	35/40 correct	_____
G	I can divide the words with two middle consonants on list G into syllables.	35/40 correct	_____
H	I can list five rules to follow for words that should not be divided.	5/5 correct	_____
I	I can divide the mixed words on list H into syllables and cross out those that should not be divided.	70/80 correct	_____

I mastered the skill of word division on _____

Signed, _____   _____
       (Student)   (Buddy)   (Date)

*Both student and buddy should initial each date.

(1985) suggests that the grades assigned should reflect both progress and effort. Another approach to multiple grading is to separate the process and product when grading students who are working diligently to master a concept or process, such as arithmetic computation, but cannot complete the work accurately (Gloeckler & Simpson, 1988). By assigning a separate grade for each of these "major messages," teachers can maintain school and district standards of grading while acknowledging individual student progress that may not reach mastery level for a particular skill or subject area.

In *shared grading*, two or more teachers determine a grade, as when a student in a regular classroom receives assistance from the resource room teacher. When using the *point system*, teachers assign points to activities or assignments that add up to the term grade. Because teachers can give equal weights to activities other than tests, they are able to individualize their instruction and evaluation much more easily than with traditional grading systems.

In *student self-comparison*, students evaluate themselves on a strictly individual basis as to whether they have met the goals and objectives of their instructional program. *Contracting* is a process whereby the student and teacher agree on specified activities or assignments required for a certain grade. Contracts allow teachers to individualize both grading requirements and assignments. Since student self-comparison and contracting are two techniques that are frequently used, the following sections offer some practical suggestions for carrying out these methods.

Many students with disabilities and students at risk have a history of academic failure. This often results in low self-esteem and inability to recognize their own strengths and achievements. For this reason, it is helpful to give all students opportunities to evaluate their own work, enabling them to recognize their individual progress as well as target areas for improvement. Self-evaluation can help students notice error patterns that they can later strive to avoid, a valuable skill to acquire prior to exiting school for the workplace. In addition to the benefits of self-comparison for the students, the technique can also free more of the teacher's time for planning and instruction.

Self-comparison can be used with even the youngest students. Kindergarten and primary-level students can be asked to compare three or four of their own projects or papers done during the school week and then tell which one they like the best and why. In lieu of letter grades, upper elementary students can be asked to apply one of several descriptive statements to their work (e.g., "terrific," "good try," and "oops!"). More in-depth evaluations, such as the one shown in Figure 12.2, can be used with middle- and secondary-level students, changing the criteria to match the type of assignment.

If a decision is made to let students evaluate their own work, the teacher must be prepared to accept the students' judgments, even if they do not correspond with the teacher's own evaluation of their work. Most often, if a discrepancy exists, it will be in the direction of the students underestimating their own merits in comparison to the teacher's evaluation.

A number-line or Likert-scale approach can be used to let students compare their evaluation of an assignment to that of the teacher. After the teacher has evaluated the assignment on the graph, students are given a chance to mark their own evaluation on the same graph, or the judgments can be made independently and compared later. The final grade on the assignment is then derived from averaging the two scores. As illustrated in Figure 12.3, the notations on the graph should be geared to student's level.

Contracting is a special education technique that has been successfully adopted by many regular educators. A contract is a written agreement between student and teacher about the quantity, quality, and time lines required to earn a specific grade (Hess et al., 1987). A good contract also includes statements about the types of work to be completed and statements as to how the student's grade will be determined. Often, a contract is a direct extension of the IEP, reflecting the performance outcomes for the specific objectives written in the IEP.

One of the distinct advantages of contracting is that a well-written contract leaves little question as to what is expected of the student to earn a passing

Figure 12.2
Sample Form for Student Self-Assessment

Self-Evaluation

Assignment:_____   Date:_____

Check *all* that apply:
_____ I completed the assignment on time.
_____ I included all of the required sections.
_____ I met the page limit for this assignment.

Three things I did well on this assignment are:
1._____
2._____
3._____

One thing I could do to improve my work on this assignment is:

My overall rating of my work on this assignment is (check *one*):
_____ My best effort   _____ Some room for improvement
_____A good effort   _____ Needs a lot more work

Signed, _____
Student Evaluator

Figure 12.3
Sample Graphs for Two Levels of Student Self-Evaluation

Suggested format for primary-level students:

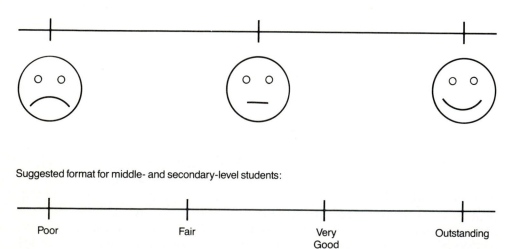

Suggested format for middle- and secondary-level students:

Poor	Fair	Very Good	Outstanding

354

grade. Another advantage of contracting is that it helps students prepare for the expectations of the workplace—if they perform specified job tasks meeting a certain standard within a given amount of time, they will receive a reward in the form of wages. A disadvantage is that, if the contract is not carefully written, the quality of students' work can be overshadowed by the quantity.

Contracts should be written in language that is easy for the student to understand. Figure 12.4 displays a hierarchy of contractual conditions that may be agreed upon by student and teacher. Some teachers prefer not to offer the alternative of a D or F to students, believing it gives them the opportunity to choose noncompliance. Others feel that if a contractual approach is to be effective, the students should be aware of the consequences of all possible levels of performance. Contracts for younger students should be simpler, with broader-based outcomes, as illustrated in Figure 12.5.

A promising alternative to traditional grading, which is now in the development stage in the West Des Moines, Iowa, Community School District, is a *portfolio evaluation system*. In this method, cumulative samples of students' work based on specific educational program goals are gathered periodically. At the end of each school year, approximately four pieces of the student's work representing key skills are selected for inclusion in the student's portfolio. The teacher and the student serve as decision-makers regarding which pieces they will put in the portfolio. The remaining pieces could be compiled in booklet form and given to the student's parents as a permanent record. For each key subject area, the portfolio provides evidence of a student's growth and achievement. For example, for the skill area of writing, a student's portfolio

Figure 12.4
Hierarchy of Contractual Statements

If (student) comes to class regularly, turns in all the required work which is completed with 90% or greater accuracy, and does one extra-credit assignment/project, he/she will receive an A.

If (student) comes to class regularly and turns in all the required work with 80% or greater accuracy, he/she will receive a B.

If (student) comes to class regularly and turns in all the required work, he/she will receive a C.

If (student) comes to class regularly or turns in 80% of the required work, he/she will receive a D.

If (student) does not come to class regularly and turns in less than 80% of the required work, he/she will receive an F.

Note. From "*Grading-Credit-Diploma: Accommodation Practices for Students with Mild Disabilities*" by R. Hess, A. Miller, J. Reese, and G. A. Robinson. Des Moines, IA: Iowa State Department of Education, Bureau of Special Education. 1987. Copyright 1987 by Iowa State Department of Education. Reprinted by permission.

Figure 12.5
Sample Contract for Primary-level Students

MY CONTRACT

If I. . .

- Take my belongings from my backpack and put them in my desk without being asked,
- Come to my reading group the first time it is called,
- Clean off my desk after snack and put all the garbage in the trash can,
- Raise my hand each time I want to answer, and
- Put all my finished papers in the "done" basket before lunch

. . .then I will receive a "plus" for the morning's work.

If I. . .

- Line up on the playground the first time the whistle is blown,
- Put all the classroom supplies back in the supply boxes after project time,
- Put all my finished papers in the "done" basket before I go home,
- Put my homework papers in my portfolio to take home, and
- Put my belongings in my backpack, get my coat from the cubby, and line up before my bus is called

. . .then I will receive a "plus" for the afternoon's work.

_____   _____
Student   Teacher

                    _____
                    Date

---

might include samples of descriptive, persuasive, and expository writing developed over the course of several years. Because portfolio evaluation provides a comparison of students' current work to their work in previous years, it eliminates the need to use letter grades in comparing students to others. This makes portfolio evaluation especially useful for those students who have unique talents or strengths in particular skill areas, yet do not perform well on graded tasks. (D. Wilkin, personal communication, December 17, 1990).

Providing Feedback to Students and Parents

Regardless of the criteria or procedure selected for awarding grades, the final step in grading any student's work should be to provide feedback to the student and parents. Many teachers are required to report student progress using traditional report card formats. Report cards, by their nature, are concerned with general expectations for the whole class (Spodek, Saracho, & Lee, 1984). For this reason, some schools may recommend or require that a notation be made to indicate those grades for which the program content has been adjusted to meet an individual student's ability. Teachers may choose to supplement report cards with narrative reports or checklists that more accurately reveal information about the student's progress and current status, such as skills that have or have not been mastered, the student's ability to work with others, readiness for future units of instruction, and success of adaptations that have been made in format, content, or classroom environment. This practice may be more widespread at the elementary level, where most report cards continue to be hand-written, as opposed to the middle- and high-school levels, where students usually receive computer-generated report statements that do not provide space for teacher narratives.

Another helpful means of sharing child-specific information with parents is a narrative letter. This format enables teachers to communicate more of the qualitative aspects of a student's work than in report cards or checklists. Used more widely in early childhood and elementary programs, narrative letters can include a description of a student's learning style and pattern of interaction with others, as well as lists of books read, projects completed, or materials used. The letter may also include descriptions of specific incidents that reflect an individual student's progress (Spodek et al., 1984).

On the secondary level, grading practices for students with mild disabilities may vary from school to school. In a survey of junior and senior high schools, Vasa (1981) identified 30 different grading practices or variations which are used. Table 12.2 present six of the most common of these practices.

In addition to report card grades or other standard reporting formats, feedback should be provided to the students in terms that have direct application to their classroom behavior, participation, and study habits. If the only type of feedback given to students is a quantitative reporting of a score or a letter grade, they may not be able to realize the error patterns in their work or generalize a successful approach to a problem from one situation to another. Without understanding what their grade means in terms of the way they approached a problem or assignment, the students may continue to repeat the same erroneous pattern of problem-solving in future work. Another disadvantage of presenting only scores or letter grades without constructive or supportive feedback is that it trains students to focus only on the end result of an assignment—the grade— rather than on the learning process.

A final consideration for educators to keep in mind when reporting grades is the meaning that grades take on when they are entered in a student's permanent record. Teachers in subsequent years use grades as an indication of a student's ability levels. For this reason, if grades are based on individual ability, a note to this effect should be made on the student's permanent record so that teachers will not hold unrealistic expectations for students. As Gloeckler and Simpson (1988) explain, "Then if a sixth-grader on a fourth-grade level is given a B, the junior high school teacher will not expect B work on a seventh-grade level the following year." (p. 62)

Table 12.2
Six Common Grading Practices in Secondary Schools

Grading Practice	Description
Letter or Numerical	Traditional system of giving the student a mark of A, B, C, D, or F or 1, 2, 3, 4, or 5 to demonstrate relative level of performance on unit or course of study.
Pass/Fail Credit/No Credit	Criterion-based measurement system that permits the individual teacher to indicate whether or not the student has met previously determined standards.
Checklists	Criterion-based measurement system that has the instructor check the student's progress against a predetermined list of needed skills or completion of specific tasks.
Contracts	Students and teacher agree to assign a mark based on predetermined goals and objectives that the student will reach during the instructional period. Such goals may be written in conjunction with the special education teacher/consultant.
Letters to Parents	A written report provided to student or parents to give narrative information about a student's performance.
Blanket Grades	All students receive a predetermined grade at the end of the marking period.

Note. From "Alternative Procedures for Grading Handicapped Students in the Secondary Schools" by S.F. Vasa. In *Integrating Secondary Handicapped Students in General and Vocational Curriculum.* Des Moines, Iowa: Midwest Regional Resource Center, Drake University, 1980, 2. Copyright 1981 by S. F. Vasa. Reprinted by permission.

GRADUATION REQUIREMENTS

Prior to the passage of P.L. 94–142 and Section 504 of the Rehabilitation Act of 1973, a limited number of options existed for the education of students with disabilities at the secondary level. Unable to meet the demands of the regular curriculum, many students with disabilities or at risk dropped out of high school and joined the work force or, more likely, the ranks of the unemployed. While more secondary-level special education programs began to be developed in response to the mandates of the legislation, many states increased the number of credits required for graduation in an effort to improve the quality of secondary education. Educators faced new dilemmas about awarding diplomas to students with disabilities.

The questions that surround this issue are similar to those on the issue of grading. The basic argument against awarding diplomas to students in special education programs is that a diploma represents a certain level of achievement to the community and to prospective employers, certifying that any student who holds a diploma has met minimum standards in the approved course of study. Opponents view the awarding of diplomas to special education students, who may have completed an adapted or modified version of the approved course of study, as a misrepresentation of a long-standing symbol of accomplishment. Proponents of awarding diplomas to students with disabilities and students at risk point out that participants in a number of different courses of study such as college preparatory, vocational education, and general education traditionally have been awarded the same diplomas and that this practice has been readily accepted by the community and prospective employers alike. Completion of a course of study in special education would represent yet another variation in the courses of study represented by the diploma. Another compelling argument in favor of awarding diplomas to all students without regard to the nature of their individual course of study is that to do otherwise discriminates against students with disabilities, denying them the same recognition for their efforts that is provided to their nondisabled peers.

Types of Diplomas

Regardless of the arguments for or against the awarding of uniform diplomas to all students, states have developed a variety of types of diplomas. Depending on state or local policy, one of three types of diplomas may be awarded to special education students. *Regular diplomas* are awarded to students in special education if they have earned the required units of credit, passed a literacy test or minimum competency test, and met other regulations prescribed by the local school board. Typically, participation in a literacy test or minimum competency testing program is an opt-out rather than opt-in program. That is, it is assumed that all students will take the test unless a decision is made to the contrary and is clearly spelled out on the student's IEP. *Special diplomas* or *modified diplomas* are awarded to students in special education who may not have earned the necessary units of credit or passed a literacy test or minimum competency test, but who have satisfactorily met the requirements of their IEPs. *Certificates of attendance* are awarded to students who have not earned units of credit or completed the requirements of their IEPs but who have completed a prescribed course of study as defined by the local school board. In many districts, the certificate of attendance signifies merely that a student has attended school and does not indicate the level of attendance or amount of participation (Hess et al., 1987; Virginia Department of Education, 1989).

Variations in the requirements for diplomas exist from state to state. In a survey of all 50 states regarding state policies that regulate graduation requirements, Bodner, Clark, and Mellard (1987) found that 17 states require different exit documents for students in special education who do not meet regular graduation requirements, 14 states require the use of the same exit document—a regular diploma—for all students, while 19 states delegate the decision on the type of document to local districts. Regardless of state or local requirements, the IEP should clearly specify the type of diploma the student is working toward, and the implications of the diploma should be discussed with the student and parents as well. This is especially critical if a nonstandard diploma is to be awarded.

Curricular Approaches to Diplomas

Weintraub and Ross (1980) point out that, unless all students have access to a program of study that leads to a diploma, equal educational access is denied to students in special education. One means of minimizing discrimination against mainstreamed students is the use of a curricular approach to the awarding of diplomas. In this method, all students are provided with curricula to meet their individual needs. Teachers then can tailor the requirements for graduation to each curriculum, developing minimum competency tests or setting other standards of achievement as needed. One advantage of this approach is that students with disabilities can realistically be expected to earn a diploma upon successful completion of their curriculum. A drawback is that educators have to develop and validate competencies for each curriculum. Another concern is that IEP teams might funnel students into existing curricula, a practice that is contradictory with the P.L. 94–142 requirement of developing individualized education programs to meet each student's unique needs.

The possible misuse of the curricular approach is cause for concern among some educators. For example, Wimmer (1981) notes that entire portions of some curricula are inappropriate for students with disabilities. She recommends that an alternative curriculum should be available for some students with mild disabilities and should include social and vocational preparation with an emphasis on career development.

Several viable options exist to the broad-scale adoption of standardized curricula for students with disabilities. The majority of these students can participate successfully in the regular education curriculum if the necessary adaptations and accommodations are made. One such option is an approach whereby *special education parallels the general curriculum*, in which alternate special education courses are developed that parallel courses in the regular curriculum in terms of course content, but have adaptations in the pace of instruction, level of details presented, and materials used. Another option involves using an *alternate special education curriculum*. In this approach, a special education curriculum is developed that departs from the academic orientation of the regular curriculum, focusing instead on functional life skills. Another approach is the *work-study program*, which allows students to earn credits while they explore various career options. This has been a traditional curricular option for students in general education. It may be an ideal approach for many students with disabilities or at risk, as it enables them to earn credits while focusing on functional skills pertinent to their lives after high school (Hess et al., 1987).

Some professionals advocate a practice of waiving units of credit for some students, favoring the awarding of equivalent high school diplomas for all students (Wimmer, 1981). Many educators do not, however, support waiving credits for any student, instead supporting a policy of "equivalent credit for equivalent time." For example, if a local district policy dictates that 120 hours of instruction generates one credit unit, then students in special education programs should be expected to meet the same standard, with course and/or curriculum adaptations being made as necessary to enable them to complete the required number of hours (Hess et al., 1987).

The many controversial issues surrounding the awarding of credits and diplomas underscore the need for careful, long-range planning for students with disabilities. Many states require that issues related to a student's graduation be addressed on the student's IEP, which must state the anticipated date of graduation, the criteria that the student must meet to qualify for graduation, and whether the student's right to participate in the minimum competency testing program is to be exercised or waived. The requirement of the Individuals with Disabilities Education Act (PL 101–476) that transition services be addressed on each secondary student's IEP also supports the need for advance planning to promote a student's movement from school to post-school activities.

STANDARDIZED TESTING

Minimum Competency Testing

Minimum competency testing in most cases consists of a standardized test administered in accordance with specific testing protocols. As indicated in the discussion on diplomas, it is widely used as a criterion for awarding diplomas. Minimum competency testing as a requirement for high school graduation is a critical issue for students with disabilities, especially since a student's performance on the test can be the deciding factor in awarding or denying a regular diploma. That decision, in turn, can have a direct influence on the student's future job placement and earning potential.

The relationship between minimum competency testing and employability of adolescents with learning disabilities was explored by Algozzine, Crews, and Stoddard (1986) in a statewide study of the effects of Florida's minimum competency testing program. The results of the study indicated that students with learning disabilities demonstrated competence on fewer communications and mathematics skills than their regular class peers and that, as a group, the students with learning disabilities performed better on certain types of tasks, such as the literal use of words, symbols, and numbers; literal recall of facts and whole number operations. A second area of inquiry was that of whether the test measured skills required by employers. Employers' ratings supported the importance of competence in basic skills and functional literacy, with 92% indicating that reading, writing, and solving number problems are important skills for the jobs available for high school graduates within their businesses.

The results of this study support the importance of basic skill instruction for students with disabilities and provide further justification for linking curriculum and course content with employment goals. However, the differential performance of one group of students with disabilities (i.e., learning disabilities) on this standardized measure once again raises questions about the use of such instruments in graduation decisions. In spite of ongoing concerns about the capacity of minimum competency tests to accurately reflect a student's ability, achievement, or potential for successful vocational performance after completion of high school, many states continue to rely on such tests as a criterion for graduation. In a survey of state directors of special education (Bodner et al., 1987), 21 of 50 states reported requiring a minimum competency test for graduation. Other states reported requiring the test, but used it for other purposes. Of the 21 states requiring a minimum competency test, 15 determined the student's exit document or type of diploma on the basis of the test scores.

An encouraging finding of the survey by Bodner et al. was that 22 states reported specific policies permitting modification in administration of the tests for students in special education. Modifications such as allowing the test to be administered individually, in small groups, or by the special education teacher or permitting extended time limits serve to ensure that the results of the testing accurately reflect a student's level of competency, rather than the effect of the student's disability.

Scholastic Aptitude Test

Another standardized test that may be of concern to some students at the secondary level is the Scholastic Aptitude Test (SAT). Students, educators, and parents should be aware that students with documented disabilities (i.e., visual, hearing, physical, or learning disabilities) may register for special versions of the SAT (e.g., in large type, in Braille, or on cassette tape). For some students, the use of certain aids such as a reader, a recorder, or a magnifying glass is allowed. Extended testing time is another available option. Eligible students also may choose to take the test at their home schools instead of a central testing site. A more limited option is available for students with documented learning disabilities. The only accommodation offered with this option is an additional 90 minutes of testing time using the regular SAT test booklet and a machine-scored answer form. Score reports for any students who test through one of these two options will indicate that a "nonstandard administration" was used. Students in need of any of these options should contact their counselor or write to the ATP Services for Handicapped Students, P.O. Box 6226, Princeton, NJ 08541-6226 (College Entrance Examination Board, 1990).

SUMMARY

Questions surrounding the awarding of grades, course credit, and high school diplomas are emotionally charged and continue to be issues of concern with respect to students with disabilities and those at risk for school failure. While questions will continue to surface, one overriding conclusion is clear—if fair and equitable outcomes in grading, minimum competency testing, and awarding of course credit and diplomas are desired, parents, teachers, and administrators at the state and local levels must continue to work cooperatively to develop policy and procedures that provide equal educational opportunities for all students. In addition, both special and regular educators must develop or upgrade the skills necessary for not only accommodating students with special needs in the mainstream, but also provide them equal opportunities for success during their school years and thereafter.

Appendices

APPENDIX A

Intervention/Transition Checklist

Student being evaluated _____

Transition Checklist

Teacher: _____ Subject: _____
Grade or type of class: _____ Date: _____
Educator completing the observation: _____

Directions: Check all that apply.
Indicate the date of completion in the space at the top of each column. Include pertinent comments. The following sources may be used to complete this form: 1. Student Interview 2. Teacher Interview 3. Parent Interview 4. Information from records 5. Other appropriate sources.

Characteristics of Mainstream Setting	Check if it Applies	Student's Present Performance Level	Has Mastered Skills	Is Working on Skills	Is Unable to Perform Skills
Section 1 - ASSESSMENT OF CONTENT AREA CLASSROOMS					
I - EMOTIONAL/SOCIAL/ BEHAVIORAL/ENVIRONMENT					
A. Regular students have positive attitudes toward students with disabilities.		Has positive attitude toward self			
		Has positive attitude toward regular students			
B. Student Interaction		Can interact appropriately in the following ways:			
1. Individual		Individual			
2. Cooperative		Cooperative			
3. Competitive		Competitive			
C. Counseling		Is able to seek guidance as needed			
1. Teacher frequently counsels students					
2. Little time provided for student counseling		Is able to express personal and/or academic problems appropriately			
D. Classroom Management System		Student works best under the following management system:			
1. Teacher's management style					
a) Behavior Modification		Behavior modification			
b) Authoritarian		Authoritarian			
c) Laissez-faire		Laissez-faire			
d) Democratic		Democratic			
e) Other (list)		Other (list)			

	Date: Date: Date:				
Characteristics of Mainstream Setting	**Check if it Applies**	**Student's Present Performance Level**	**Has Mastered Skills**	**Is Working on Skills**	**Is Unable to Perform Skills**

Section 1 - ASSESSMENT OF CONTENT AREA CLASSROOMS (cont'd)

Characteristics of Mainstream Setting	Check	Student's Present Performance Level	Has	Is	Is Unable
I - EMOTIONAL/SOCIAL/ BEHAVIORAL/ENVIRONMENT					
2. Classroom Rules		Student adapts to any management system			
a) Rules explained/posted					
b) Adherence to unstated rules required		Understands orally presented rules			
c) Student involved in rule making		Understands written rules			
		Follows unstated rules			
d) Consequences for non-compliance		Participates in rule making process			
e) Reinforcement provided for rule following		Understands consequences for non-compliance			
		Requires external reinforcement to follow rules			
E. Dress/Appearance					
1. Dress code applied		Dresses appropriately			
2. Concern given to appearance by most students		Follows dress code			
		Presents neat appearance			
F. Student requests help within the regular classroom		Student requests help from regular teacher as needed			
		Student requests help from teacher's aide as needed			
II-PHYSICAL ENVIRONMENT		Student requests help from special education teacher as needed			
A. Grouping for instruction					
1. Large group		Works well in large group			
2. Small group		Works well in a small group			
3. One-to-one		Works well one-to-one			
		Adapts to various group settings			
B. Seating Arrangement					
1. Traditional seating		Works in traditional arrangement			
2. Circular or horseshoe		Works in circular arrangement			
3. Cubicles/Carrels		Works in cubicle/carrel			
4. Other		Adapts to varied seating arrangements			
C. Sound					
1. No talking allowed		Works silently			
2. Minor distractions (some interaction)		Works with minor distractions			
3. Noisy environment (open interaction)		Works with many distractions			
4. Provisions for individual study space with reduced auditory distractions		Works in individual study space			
		Adapts to various degrees of noise			

	Check if it Applies	Student's Present Performance Level	Has Mastered Skills	Is Working on Skills	Is Unable to Perform Skills
Characteristics of Mainstream Setting			Date:	Date:	Date:

Section 1 - ASSESSMENT OF CONTENT AREA CLASSROOMS (cont'd)

Characteristics of Mainstream Setting	Check if it Applies	Student's Present Performance Level	Has Mastered Skills	Is Working on Skills	Is Unable to Perform Skills
III- TEACHING TECHNIQUES					
A. Instructional Variables					
1. Lecture		Retains material from lectures			
2. Explanation		Comprehends group explanations			
3. Audio-visual Presentation		Retains audio-visual presentations			
4. Discussion		Participates in class discussion			
5. Asking Questions		Responds to questioning adequately			
6. Self-Directed Study		Works on independent projects			
7. Experiments		Performs lab experiments			
8. Constructing		Builds projects independently			
9. Group Work		Works in small groups			
10. Other		Adapts to varied teaching methods			
IV- MEDIA					
A. Note Taking Technique Used					
1. Copied from board		Can copy notes from chalkboard			
2. Prepared by teacher		Can read teacher-written notes			
3. From lecture		Can take organized lecture notes			
4. From textbook		Can take notes from textbook			
5. Lecture outline provided by teacher		Takes notes with outline as guide			
6. Carbon copy of notes available		Reads notes taken by other student			
B. Equipment Used		Student learns from varied media:			
1. Overhead projector		Overhead projector			
2. Filmstrip projector		Filmstrip projector			
3. Tape recorder		Tape recorder			
4. Computer		Computer			
5. Videotape Recorder		Videotape Recorder			
6. Film/Movies		Film/Movies			
7. Television		Television			
8. Slide Projector		Slide Projector			
9. Other		Other			

		Date:	Date:	Date:

Characteristics of Mainstream Setting	Check if it Applies	Student's Present Performance Level	Has Mastered Skills	Is Working on Skills	Is Unable to Perform Skills
Section 1 - ASSESSMENT OF CONTENT AREA CLASSROOMS (cont'd)					
V- CONTENT					
A. Adaptations of Assignments					
1. No modifications made in subject matter		Needs no modifications			
2. Some modifications made: (list)		Requires some modifications (list)			
3. Peer tutors used		Requires assistance of peer tutor			
B. Class procedure					
1. Students read aloud		Reads text aloud			
2. Students present projects/ reports orally		Presents materials orally			
3. Student panel discussions		Participates in oral discussions			
4. Other (list)		Adapts to varied class procedures			
C. Materials					
1. Textbooks used Grade level of text		Can read textbooks at grade level			
2. Supplementary handouts		Needs text adapted to _ level			
3. Lab work required		Reads most handouts			
		Works in laboratory setting			
		Completes lab reports			
		Assembles and stores equipment			
4. Notebook required		Can organize and keep notebook			
5. Other (list)		Adapts to variety of materials			
D. Homework					
1. Assignments copied from chalkboard		Copies accurately from chalkboard			
2. Written assignments provided		Reads written assignments accurately			
3. Oral assignments provided		Can follow directions			
		Can keep homework in notebook			
4. Kept in notebook		Can complete homework independently			
5. Other requirements (specify)					

			Date:	Date:	Date:
Characteristics of Mainstream Setting	Check if it Applies	Student's Present Performance Level	Has Mastered Skills	Is Working on Skills	Is Unable to Perform Skills
Section 1 - ASSESSMENT OF CONTENT AREA CLASSROOMS (cont'd)					
VI- EVALUATION					
A. Test format used		Can take tests in these formats:			
1. True-False		True-False			
2. Matching		Matching			
3. Fill-in-the-blank		Fill-in-the-blank			
4. Multiple choice		Multiple choice			
5. Essay		Essay			
6. Open book		Open book			
7. Other (list)					
B. Tests given orally		Can take oral tests			
C. Tests copied from board		Copies tests accurately from board			
D. Tests are timed		Works under time pressure			
E. Study guide provided prior to test		Utilizes study guide effectively			
F. Allows resource teacher to administer tests		Needs test administered by resource teacher			
G. Tests are handwritten		Reads handwritten tests			
H. Tests are typed		Reads typed tests			
		Other test modifications needed: (list)			
I. Grading systems		Student works under these systems:			
a. Letter grades		Letter grade			
b. Checklist		Checklist			
c. Contract		Contract			
d. Point System		Point System			
e. Pass/Fail		Pass/Fail			
f. Other		Student adapts to varied grading systems			
Section 2 - ASSESSMENT OF RELATED ENVIRONMENTS					
I- CAFETERIA					
A. Procedures for purchasing lunch ticket/token posted or explained		Follows correct procedures for ticket/token			
B. Lunchroom routine explained/posted		Follows lunch routine: Purchases lunch Finds assigned table Returns tray			
C. Students enter cafeteria unsupervised		Finds cafeteria independently			

			Date:	Date:	Date:
Characteristics of Mainstream Setting	Check if it Applies	Student's Present Performance Level	Has Mastered Skills	Is Working on Skills	Is Unable to Perform Skills

Section 2 - ASSESSMENT OF RELATED ENVIRONMENTS (cont'd)

Characteristics of Mainstream Setting	Check if it Applies	Student's Present Performance Level	Has Mastered Skills	Is Working on Skills	Is Unable to Perform Skills
D. Rules for lunchroom conduct explained/posted		Understands rules of conduct and follows them independently			
E. Appropriate after lunch activities explained/posted		Finds appropriate activity after eating lunch			
II-PHYSICAL EDUCATION A. Uniform required		Purchases appropriate uniform			
		Brings clean uniform once/week			
		Changes uniform under time pressure			
B. Showering required		Showers independently			
C. Gym locker assigned		Memorizes lock combination			
		Works under time pressure			
D. Rules of game given orally		Follows oral game rules			
E. Notetaking required of class procedures, rules		Takes notes adequately			
F. Activities organized into large groups		Participates in large group play			
III-MUSIC/ART A. Students move to class independently		Moves to nonacademic classes independently			
B. Rules of classroom explained/posted		Follows orally presented rules			
		Follows written rules			
C. Grading system used		Works best under following system:			
1. Letter grade		Letter grade			
2. Pass/fail		Pass/fail			
3. Other		Adapts to various grading systems			
IV-ASSEMBLIES/ SCHOOL PROGRAMS A. No talking allowed		Can sit quietly during programs			
B. Assigned seating area		Finds appropriate seat			
C. Irregular scheduling of programs followed		Adapts to interruptions in daily schedule			

			Date:	Date:	Date:
Characteristics of Mainstream Setting	**Check if it Applies**	**Student's Present Performance Level**	**Has Mastered Skills**	**Is Working on Skills**	**Is Unable to Perform Skills**
Section 2 - ASSESSMENT OF RELATED ENVIRONMENTS (cont'd)					
V-Between Classes (secondary) A. Lockers 1. Assigned locker number 2. Lock required		Knows location of locker Memorizes lock combination Can work lock combination under time pressure			
B. Movement 1. Rules for hallway conduct explained/posted 2. Students move from class to class following written schedule		Understands oral rules Understands written rules Student requires map of school Student copies schedule accurately Student memorizes schedule			
VI-LIBRARY A. Procedures for checking out books explained/posted B. Finds appropriate books independently C. No talking allowed		Follows check out procedures independently Finds fiction, non-fiction, and major Dewey Decimal system sections without assistance Works quietly			

Wood, J.W. (1991) Project SHARE. Richmond, VA; Virginia Commonwealth University. With Permission

APPENDIX B

Associations & Publishers

Associations

Name of Resource Address and Phone Number	Information Regarding Resource
The Alexander Graham Bell Association/DEA 2417 Volta Place, NW Washington, DC 20007 (202) 337–5220	Provides both services and support for persons with hearing impairment. Established in 1890 to encourage the use of residual hearing and teaching of speech and speech-reading.
The American Association for Counseling and Development 5999 Stevenson Avenue Alexandria, VA 22304 (703) 823–9800	A nonprofit organization with members in all disciplines, ranging from elementary to college level. Members include guidance counselors, counselors, and human development specialists.
The American Association on Mental Retardation 1719 Kalorama Road, NW Washington, DC 20009 (202) 387–1968	Represents individuals with mental retardation and their families. Publishes two journals, *American Journal on Mental Retardation* and *Mental Retardation*.
The American Council of the Blind 1010 Vermont Avenue, NW Suite 1100 Washington, DC 20005 (202) 393–3666	A national consumer and advocacy organization composed primarily of individuals who are blind or visually impaired.
The American Foundation for the Blind 15 West 16th Street New York, NY 10011 (800) 232–5463	Provides a continuum of services to help meet the needs of professionals in the blindness and low-vision fields as well as individuals who are blind or visually impaired.

Associations *continued*

Name of Resource Address and Phone Number	Information Regarding Resource
The American Humane Association Children's Division 63 Inverness Drive E Englewood, CO 80112 (303) 792–9900	A national nonprofit organization providing research, consultation, technical assistance, and program assistance to public and private child protective agencies.
The American Occupational Therapy Association 1381 Piccard Drive Rockville, MD 20852	In collaboration with the committee on Allied Health Education and Accreditation of the American Medical Association, officially recognized as the accrediting agency for entry-level educational programs for occupational therapists.
The American Personnel and Guidance Association 5999 Stevenson Avenue Alexandria, VA 22304 (703) 823–9800	Serves counselors and produces books and journals. Has a lobbying division and an information services division.
The American Physical Therapy Association 1111 N. Fairfax Street Alexandria, VA 23314 (703) 684–2782	With more than 50,000 members, the largest association of physical therapists, physical therapist assistants, and physical therapy students in the U.S. Founded 60 years ago.
The American Printing House for the Blind P.O. Box 6085 Louisville, KY 40206 (502) 895–2405	Provides Braille, talking books, educational aids, and large print for persons who are visually impaired or disabled.
The American Psychological Association 1200 17th Street, NW Washington, DC 20036 (202) 955–7600	The major organization representing psychology in the U.S. Since its founding, has been working toward the advancement of psychology as a science, a profession, and a means of promoting human welfare.
The American Speech-Language-Hearing Association 10801 Rockville Pike Rockville, MD 20852 (301) 897–5700	An association at the forefront of fostering scientific study of the processes of individual communication and stimulating the exchange of information among persons and organizations thus engaged.
The American Vocational Association 1410 King Street Alexandria, VA 22314 (703) 683–3111	The only national professional association representing all components of the field of vocational technical education.

Associations *continued*

Name of Resource Address and Phone Number	Information Regarding Resource
The Association for Retarded Citizens of the US P.O. Box 6109–2501 Avenue Arlington, TX 76005 (817) 640–0204	The nations's largest volunteer organization devoted solely to improving the welfare of children and adults with mental retardation and their families. Also provides services to parents and other individuals, organizations, and communities for jointly meeting the needs of persons with mental retardation.
Center for Special Needs 700 Ackerman Road Columbus, OH 43202 (614) 447-0844	Provides a synopsis of projects throughout Ohio, Illinois, Indiana, Michigan, Minnesota, Pennsylvania, and Wisconsin.
The Clearinghouse on Child Abuse and Neglect P.O. Box 1182 Washington, DC 20013 (703) 821-2086	Maintains a database of documents, audiovisual materials, service programs, excerpts of state statutes, and ongoing research projects concerning child abuse and neglect.
The Council of State Administrators of Vocational Rehabilitation 1055 Thomas Jefferson Street, NW Washington, DC 20007 (202) 638-4634	A membership organization of the state directors of vocational rehabilitation programs. Refers callers to the appropriate state office for further assistance.
The Council for Exceptional Children 1920 Association Drive Reston, VA 22091 (703) 620-3660	A professional organization dedicated to improving the quality of education for all exceptional children and youth and supporting the professionals who serve them.
The Epilepsy Foundation of America 4351 Garden City Drive, Suite 406 Landover, MD 20785 (301) 459-3700	Committed to the prevention and eventual cure of epilepsy and improving the lives of individuals with epilepsy.
The Gifted Child Society 190 Rock Road Glen Rock, NJ 07452 (201) 444-6530	Founded in 1957 to further the cause of gifted children. Provides assistance to parents of these children and professional training to encourage educators of all types to meet the special needs of these youngsters.
The International Reading Association 800 Barksdale Road Newark, DE 19714 (302) 731-1600	A 90,000-member nonprofit education organization devoted to the improvement of reading instruction and the promotion of the lifetime habit of reading.

Associations *continued*

Name of Resource Address and Phone Number	Information Regarding Resource
Learning Disability Association 4156 Library Road Pittsburgh, PA 15234 (412) 341-1515	The national organization devoted to defining and finding solutions for the broad spectrum of learning problems.
March of Dimes Birth Defects Foundation 1275 Mamaroneck Avenue White Plains, NY (914) 428-7100	With some 300 chapters nationwide and a special network of volunteers, scientists, and medical professionals, fights a broad range of birth defects.
The Muscular Dystrophy Association 801 Seventh Avenue New York, NY 10010 (212) 586-0808	Supports scientific investigations seeking the causes of and effective treatments for muscular dystrophy and related neuromuscular disorders and sponsors a broad program of selected patient and community services in addition to research.
The National Association for Creative Children/Adults 8080 Springvalley Drive Cincinnati, OH 45236 (513) 631-1777	Aids gifted and creative children and adults in understanding themselves better so that they can achieve positive self-concepts and provides the opportunity for individuals and groups to benefit from research on creativity.
The National Association for the Visually Handicapped 3201 Balboa Street San Francisco, CA 94121 (415) 221-3201	Provides counseling, education, and referrals for persons with partial eyesight.
The National Association of Private Residential Resources 6400 HT Corners Place Falls Church, VA 22044 (703) 642-6614	Represents providers of private residential services that are members of the organization.
The National Association of State Directors of Special Education (NASDSE) 2021 K Street, NW Washington, DC 20006 (202) 296-1800	A national team working together to improve the education of exceptional children.
The National Black Child Development Institute 1463 Rhode Island Avenue, NW Washington, DC 20005 (202) 387-1281	A nonprofit organization dedicated to improving the quality of life for black children and youth by enabling the black community to participate in the development of children's programs.

Associations *continued*

Name of Resource Address and Phone Number	Information Regarding Resource
The National Diffusion Network, US Dept of Education 555 New Jersey Avenue, NW Washington, DC 20208-5645 (202) 357-6134	A federally funded dissemination system that helps public and private schools, colleges, and other educational institutions improve by sharing successful education programs, products, and processes.
National Mental Health Association 1021 Prince Street Alexandria, VA 22314 (703) 684-7722/(800) 969-NMHA	The nation's only citizen's volunteer advocacy organization concerned with all aspects of mental health and mental illness.
The National Library Service for the Blind and Physically Handicapped Library of Congress Washington, DC 20542 (202) 707-5100	Provides a free library service to persons who are unable to use standard printed material because of visual or physical disabilities.
The National Heart Institute 9000 Rockville Pike Building 31, Rm 4A21 Bethesda, MD 20892 (301) 496-4000	A principal biomedical research agency of the federal government. Composed of 13 institutes, a hospital, and a library.
Autism Society of America 8601 Georgia Avenue Suite 503 Silver Spring, MD 20910 (301) 565-0433	Founded by parents of children with autism. Provides information, referrals, and printed materials to members.
The National Amputation Foundation 12-45 150th Street Whitstone, NY 11357 (718) 767-3103	Provides services such as legal counsel, vocational guidance, placements, social activities, liaison with outside groups, psychological aid, and training in the use of prosthetic devices.
The National Association of the Deaf 814 Thayer Avenue Silver Spring, MD 20919 (301) 587-1788	Recommends and supports legislation in such areas as education, rehabilitation, and civil rights on behalf of Americans who are deaf or hard of hearing.
The National Braille Press, Inc. 88 St. Stephen Street Boston, MA 02115 (617) 266-6160	Offers Braille printing and is a publishing house that also offers various publications for sale.
The National Council for Social Studies 3501 Newark Street, NW Washington, DC 20016 (202) 966-7840	A professional membership organization for social studies educators at all levels.

Associations *continued*

Name of Resource Address and Phone Number	Information Regarding Resource
The National Easter Seal Society 70 E. Lake Street Chicago, IL 60601 (312) 726-6200	Promotes the equality, dignity, and independence of persons with disabilities by providing a wide range of high-quality direct services to meet varied rehabilitation needs nationwide.
The National Education Association 1201 16th Street, NW Washington, DC 20036-3290	With more than 2 million members, leads the effort for effective educational reform. Continues to call for higher standards and for change that meets the needs of all students.
The National Hemophilia Association 110 Greene Street New York, NY 10012 (212) 431-8541	A nonprofit organization founded in 1948 dedicated to the treatment and cure of hemophilia.
The National Kidney Foundation 30 E 33rd Street New York, NY 10016	The major voluntary health agency seeking the answer to diseases of the kidney and urinary tracts in prevention, treatment, and cure.
The National Multiple Sclerosis Society 205 East 42nd Street New York, NY 10017-5706 (212) 986-3240	Established in 1946, is the national voluntary health agency that supports an international program of scientific research aimed at finding effective means of preventing and arresting multiple sclerosis.
Orthotic and Prosthetic Specialities, Inc. 14228 Cherry Lane Court Laurel, MD 20707 (301) 470-3344	Specializes in custom seating for persons with disabilities.
The President's Committee on Employment of People With Disabilities 1111 20th Street, NW Washington, DC 20036-5044 (202) 653-5044	A public-private partnership of national and state organizations and individuals working together to improve the lives of individuals with physical, mental, or sensory disabilities by increasing their opportunities for employment.
The President's Committee on Mental Retardation Regional Office Bldg., #3 7th and D Streets, SW, Rm 2614 Washington, DC 20201 (202) 619-0634	An advisory committee to the President and the Secretary of Human Services on matters related to mental retardation.

Associations *continued*

Name of Resource Address and Phone Number	Information Regarding Resource
Recordings for the Blind, Inc. 215 E 58th Street New York, NY 10022 (212) 557-5720	A national nonprofit organization providing recorded textbooks, library services, and other educational resources to individuals who cannot read standard print because of a visual, physical, or perceptual disability.
The Social Science Education Consortium 3300 Mitchell Lane Boulder, CO 80501-2272 (303) 492-8154	Provides publications in the area of social studies and gives workshops related to social studies.
The Spina Bifida Association of America 1700 Rockville Pike Rockville, MD 20852 (301) 770-SBA4	Since 1975, has served as the national office representing approximately 100 local chapters of parents and adults with spina bifida, the medical and allied health professionals who work with them, and family members.
The United Cerebral Palsy of New York City 120 E 23rd Street New York, NY 10010 (212) 677-7400	Provides information for individuals and parents of persons with cerebral palsy. Also supports research on cerebral palsy. There are local chapters throughout the country.

Publishers

Name of Resource Address and Phone Number		
The American Guidance Service Publisher's Building Circle Pines, MN 55014-1796 (800) 328-2580	Braille Circulating Library 2700 Stuart Avenue Richmond, VA 23220 (804) 359-3743	Development Learning Materials 1 DLM Park Allen, TX 75002 (800) 527-4747
Barnett-Loft P.O. Box 5380 Chicago, IL 60780	Careers, Inc. 1211 10th Street, SW Largo, IL 34640 (813) 584-7333	Educational Activities P.O. Box 392 Freeport, NY 11520 (516) 223-4666
Bell and Howell 6800 McCormick Road Chicago, IL 60645 (708) 675-7600	The Cuisenaire Co of America 12 Church Street, Box D New Rochelle, NY 10802 (800) 237-3142	Fearon Publishers 500 Harbor Blvd Belmont, CA 94002 (415) 594-7810

Publishers *continued*

	Name of Resource Address and Phone Number	

Follett Publishing
  Company
1000 West Washington
  Blvd
Chicago, IL 60607
(312) 668-6097

George Wahr Publishing
  Co.
304-½ S State Street
Ann Arbor, MI 48104
(313) 688-6097

Glencoe-McGraw-Hill
  Merrill
936 Eastwind Drive
Westerville, OH 43081
(614) 890-1111

Holt, Rinehart, and
  Winston
Orlando, FL 32887
(407) 345-2500

Houghton Mifflin
  Company
1 Beacon Street
Boston, MA 02108
(617) 725-5000

Incentive Publications
3835 Cleghorn
Nashville, TN 37215
(615) 385-2934

J. H. Pence Company
5107 Lakeside Avenue
Richmond, VA 23228
(804) 262-8609

Kimbo
10 N 3rd Avenue, B
Denver, CO 80222
(303) 757-2579

Mosby
11830 Westline Industrial
  Drive
St. Louis, MO 63145
(314) 872-8370

Newbridge Book Club
900 Chester Avenue
Delran, NJ 08370
(609) 461-9339

News Readers Press
P.O. Box 131
Syracuse, NY 13210
(315) 422-9121

Prentice-Hall Publishing
  Co
Rte 9, West
Englewood Cliffs, NJ
  07632
(201) 592-2000

Research Press
Box 3177
Champaign, IL 61826
(217) 352-3273

Science Research Associates,
  Inc.
155 N. Wacker Drive
Chicago, IL 60606-1780
(800) 621-0476

Scott, Foresman Company
1900 E. Lake Avenue
Glenview, IL 60026
(312) 729-3000

Silver Burdett Company
250 James Street
Morristown, NJ 07960
(210) 285-7700

Special Education Materials
540 Nepperhen Avenue
Yonkers, NY 10701
(914) 963-9060

Steck-Vaughn
P.O. Box 26015
Austin, TX 78755
(412) 343-8227

Sterling Publishing Co, Inc.
387 Park Avenue South
New York, NY 10016
(212) 532-7150

Zaner-Bloser
1459 King Avenue
Columbus, OH 43216
(800) 421-3018

References

Affleck, J. Q., Lowenbraun, S., & Archer, A. (1980). *Teaching the mildly handicapped in the regular classroom.* Columbus, OH: Merrill.

Aiken, R. M., & Brown, L. (1980). Into the 80s with microcomputer-based learning. *Computer, 13*(7), 11–16.

Algozzine, B., Crews, W. B., & Stoddard, K. (1986). *Analysis of basic skill competencies of learning disabled adolescents.* (ERIC Document Reproduction Service No. ED 191 775)

Anderegg, M. L., & Vergason, G. A. (1988). An analysis of one of the cornerstones of the regular education initiative. *Focus on Exceptional Children, 20*(8), 1–8.

Anderson, R. M., Greer, J. G., & Odle, S. J. (1978). *Individualizing educational materials for special children in the mainstream.* Baltimore, MD: University Park Press.

Anderson, W., Chitwood, S., & Hayden, D. (1990). *Negotiating the special education maze.* Rockville, MD: Woodbine House.

Baker, J. L., & Gottlieb, J. (1980). Attitudes of teachers toward mainstreaming retarded children. In J. Gottlieb (Ed.), *Educating mentally retarded persons in the mainstream.* Baltimore, MD: University Park Press.

Barnett, D., Zins, J., & Wise, L. (1984). An analysis of parental participation as a means of reducing bias in the education of handicapped children. *Special Services in the Schools, 1,* 71–84.

Barngrover, E. A. (1975). A study of educators' preferences in special education programs. *Exceptional Children, 37,* 754–755.

Bateman, B. (1962). Sighted children's perceptions of blind children's abilities. *Exceptional Children, 29,* 42–46.

Bauer, A. M., & Shea, T. M. (1989). *Teaching exceptional students in your classroom.* Boston, MA: Allyn & Bacon.

Bauwens, J., Hourcade, J. J., & Friend, M. (1989). Cooperative teaching: A model for general and special education integration. *Remedial and Special Education, 10*(2), 17–22.

Billings, H. K. (1963). An exploratory study of the attitudes of noncrippled children toward crippled children in three selected elementary schools. *Journal of Experimental Education, 31,* 381–387.

Blake, K. A. (1974). *Teaching the retarded.* Englewood Cliffs, NJ: Prentice-Hall.

Blankenship, C. (1985). Using curriculum-based assessment data to make instructional decisions. *Exceptional Children, 52*(3), 234.

Blankenship, C., & Lilly, M. S. (1981). *Mainstreaming students with learning and behavior problems: Techniques for the classroom teacher.* New York: Holt, Rinehart, & Winston.

Bloom, B. S. (1968). Learning for mastery. (UCLA-CSEIP) *Evaluation Comment, 1*(2).

Bloom, B. S. (Ed.) (1956). *Taxonomy of educational objectives: The classification of educational goals. Handbook I. Cognitive domain.* New York: Longman.

Bodner, J. R., Clark, G. M., & Mellard, D. F. (1987). *State graduation policies and program practices related to high school special education programs.* Lawrence, KS: Kansas University, Department of Special Education. (ERIC Document Reproduction Service No. ED 294 347)

Brantlinger, E. (1987). Making decisions about special education placement: Do low income parents have the information they need? *Journal of Learning Disabilities, 20,* 94–101.

Brown, D. (1988). Be a computer tutor for people with learning disabilities. In H. J. Murphy (Ed.), *Proceedings of the Fourth Annual Conference on technology and persons with disabilities.* (pp. 91–104). Pacific Telesis: California State University, Northridge.

Brown, J., Lewis, R., & Harcleroad, F. (1977). *AV Instruction: Technology, media, and methods* (5th ed.). New York: Macmillan.

Bruner, J. S., & Tajfel, H. (1961). Cognitive risks and environmental change. *Journal of Abnormal Psychology, 62,* 231–241.

Bryk, A. S. (1983). Editor's notes. In A. S. Bryk (Ed.), *New directions for program evaluation: Stakeholder-based evaluation.* Washington, DC: Jossey-Bass.

Carbo, M. (1982). *Reading style inventory.* Roslyn Heights, NY: Learning Research Associates.

Carbo, M., & Hodges, H. (1988, Summer). Learning style strategies can help students at risk. *Teaching Exceptional Children,* 55–58.

Carpenter, D. (1985). Grading handicapped pupils: Review and position statements. *Remedial and Special Education, 6*(4), 54–59.

Cartwright, C. A., Cartwright, G. P., Ward, M., & Willoughby-Herb, S. (1981). *Teachers of special learners.* Belmont, CA: Wadsworth.

Chalfant, J. C., & Pysh, M. (1989). Teacher assistance teams: Five descriptive studies on 96 teams. *Remedial and Special Education, 10*(6), 49–58.

Charles, C. M. (1980). *Individualizing instruction* (2nd ed.). St. Louis, MO: C. V. Mosby.

Coburn, P., Kelman, P., Roberts, N., Snyder, T. F., Watt, D. H., & Weiner, C. (1982). *Practical guide to computers in education.* Reading, MA: Addison-Wesley.

Cohen, S. B. (1983). Assigning report card grades to the mainstreamed child. *Teaching Exceptional Children, 15*(2), 86–89.

College Entrance Examination Board. (1990). SAT and Achievement Tests Registration Bulletin 1990–91. Princeton, NJ: Author.

Cooper, J., Hansen, J., Martorella, P., Morine-Dershimer, G., Sadker, M., Sokolove, S., Shostak, R., TenBrink, T., & Weber, W. (1977). *Classroom teaching skills: A workbook.* Lexington, MA: D. C. Heath.

Cosden, M. A., & Abernathy, T. V. (1990). Microcomputer use in the schools: Teacher roles and instructional options. *Remedial and Special Education, 11*(5), 31–38.

Council for Exceptional Children (1989). Update: Survey of CEC members' professional development needs. *Teaching Exceptional Children, 21*(3), 78–79.

Council for Exceptional Children (1990). Education of the handicapped act amendments of 1990: Summary of major changes to current law. *Office of Governmental Relations Information Item,* 1–20. Reston, VA: Author.

Council of the Great City Schools (1988). *Special education in America's cities.* Washington, DC: Author.

Courtnage, L., & Healy, H. (1984). Interdisciplinary team training: A competency- and procedure-based approach. *Teacher Education and Special Education, 7,* 3–11.

Courtnage, L., & Smith-Davis, J. (1987). Interdisciplinary team training: A national survey of special education teacher training programs. *Exceptional Children, 53*(5), 451–458.

D'Alonzo, B. J., D'Alonzo, R. L., & Mauser, A. J. (1979). Developing resource rooms for the handicapped. *Teaching Exceptional Children, 11*(3), 91–96.

Dardig, J. (1981). Helping teachers integrate handicapped students into the regular classroom. *Educational Horizons, 59,* 124–129.

Dave, R. H. (1970). *Taxonomy of educational objectives: Psychomotor domain*. New Delhi, India: National Institute of Education.

Davies, I. K. (1981). *Instructional techniques*. New York: McGraw-Hill.

Department of Special Services and Special Education, Fairfax County Public Schools. (1990). *Social competency curriculum: Communication school-related (Vol. 3)*. Fairfax, VA: Author.

Dewey, J. (April, 1937). Democracy and educational administration. *School and Society*, 458–459.

Donaldson, J. (1980). Changing attitudes toward handicapped persons: A review and analysis of research. *Exceptional Children, 46*(7), 504–514.

Doris, S., & Brown, R. (1980). *Toleration of maladaptive classroom behaviors by regular and special educators*. Fresno, CA: California State University. (ERIC Document Reproduction Service No. ED 211 456)

Dunn, R., Dunn, K., & Price, G. E. (1979). *Learning styles inventory manual*. Lawrence, KA: Price Systems.

Durkin, D. (1984). Is there a match between what elementary teachers do and what basal reader manuals recommend? *The Reading Teacher, 37*, 734–745.

Federal Register. Washington, DC: Department of Health, Education, and Welfare, Office of Education, August 23, 1977.

Ferrara, S. F. (1984). *Modifications, support, and mainstreaming: Excellence in mainstreaming practices and evaluation*. Paper presented at the Annual Meeting of the Evaluation Research Society, San Francisco, CA. (ERIC Document Reproduction Service No. ED 257 254)

Final, M. J. (1967). Attitudes of regular and special class teachers toward the educable mentally retarded child. *Exceptional Children, 33*, 429–430.

Flynn, J., Gack, R., & Sundean, D. (1978). Are classroom teachers prepared for mainstreaming? *Phi Delta Kappa, 59*, 562.

Frymier, J. (1989). *A study of students at-risk: Collaborating to do research*. Bloomington, IN: Phi Delta Kappa Educational Foundation.

Fuchs, L. S., Butterworth, J. R., & Fuchs, D. (1989). Effects of ongoing curriculum-based measurement on student awareness of goals and progress. *Education and Treatment of Children, 12*, 41–47.

Fuchs, L. S., Fuchs, D., & Hamlett, C. L. (1989). Effects of alternative goal structures within curriculum-based measurement. *Exceptional Children, 55*, 429–438.

Fuhrmann, B. S. (1980, August). *Models and methods of assessing learning styles*. Paper presented at a meeting of the Virginia Educational Research Association.

Fuhrmann, B. S., & Grasha, A. F. (1983). *A practical handbook for college teachers*. Boston, MA: Little, Brown.

Gardner, R. W. (1959). Cognitive control: A study of individual consistencies in cognitive behavior. *Psychological issues*. 1.

Gersten, R., Darch, C., Davis, G., & George, N. (1991). Apprenticeship and intensive training of consulting teachers: A naturalistic study. *Exceptional Children, 57*(3), 226–236.

Gersten, R., & Woodward, J. (1990). Rethinking the regular education initiative: Focus on the classroom teacher. *Remedial and Special Education, 11*(3), 7–16.

Gloeckler, T., & Simpson, C. (1988). *Exceptional students in regular classrooms*. Mountain View, CA: Mayfield.

Goldstein, S., Strickland, B., Turnbull, A., & Curry, L. (1980). An observational analysis of the IEP conference. *Exceptional Children, 46*, 278–286.

Goldstein, S., & Turnbull, A. (1982). Strategies to increase parent participation in IEP conferences. *Exceptional Children, 48*, 360–361.

Good, T. L. (1987). Two decades of research on teacher expectations: Findings and future directions. *Journal of Teacher Education, 38*(4), 32–47.

Good, T., & Brophy, J. (1987). *Looking in classrooms* (4th ed.). New York: Harper & Row.

Goodman, H., Gottlieb, J., & Harrison, R. (1972). Social acceptance of EMR's integrated into a non-graded elementary school. *American Journal of Mental Deficiency, 76*, 412–417.

Graden, J., Casey, A., & Bonstrom, O. (1985). Implementing a prereferral intervention system: Part II. The data. *Exceptional Children, 51*, 487–496.

Greenburg, D. E. (1987). *A special educator's perspective on interfacing special and regular education: A review for administrators*. Reston, VA: The Council for Exceptional Children.

Greer, J. G., Friedman, I., & Laycock, V. (1978). Instructional games. In R. M. Anderson, J. G. Greer, & S. Odle (Eds.), *Individualizing educational materials for special children in the mainstream* (pp. 267–293). Baltimore, MD: University Park Press.

Grossman, H. J. (Ed.). (1983). *Classification in mental retardation*. Washington, DC: American Association on Mental Deficiency.

Guetzloe, E. (1989). *Youth suicide: What the educator should know. A special educator's perspective*. Reston, VA: The Council for Exceptional Children. (ERIC Document Reproduction Service No. ED 316 963)

Guskey, T. R. (1981). Individualizing instruction in the mainstream classroom: A mastery learning approach. *Educational Unlimited, 3*(1), 12–15.

Hancox, D., & Zinpoli, T. J. (1990). Federal law gives families control of services to their young children. *Impact, 3*(2), p. 4217.

Hargis, C. H. (1982). *Teaching reading to handicapped children.* Denver, CO: Love.

Haring, W. C. (Ed.). (1978). *Behavior of exceptional children.* Columbus, OH: Merrill.

Hart, V. (1981). *Mainstreaming children with special needs.* New York: Longman.

Harvey, D. J., Hunt, D. E., & Schroder, H. M. (1961). *Conceptual systems and personality organization.* New York: John Wiley.

Hawisher, M. F., & Calhoun, M. L. (1978). *The resource room.* Columbus, OH: Merrill.

Hayes, D. (1981). Secondary-level disabled readers: Let them read and learn—all of them. *Journal of Research and Development in Education, 14*(4), 85–89.

Helge, D. (1989a). Concerns regarding "at-risk" students. In *Hearing before the Subcommittee on the Handicapped of the Committee on Labor and Human Resources on the Reauthorization of the EHA Discretionary Programs* (pp. 237–238). Washington, DC: U.S. Government Printing Office.

Helge, D. (1989b). Rural "at-risk" students—Directions for policy and intervention. *Rural Special Education Quarterly, 10*(1), 3–16.

Heron, T. E., & Harris, K. C. (1987). *The educational consultant.* Austin, TX: Pro-Ed.

Hess, R., Miller, A., Reese, J., & Robinson, G. A. (1987). *Grading-credit-diploma: Accommodation practices for students with mild disabilities.* Des Moines, IA: Iowa State Department of Education, Bureau of Special Education.

Hoover, K. H., & Hollingsworth, P. M. (1975). *Learning and teaching in the elementary school.* Boston, MA: Allyn & Bacon.

Hudson, F., & Graham, S. (1978). An approach to operationalizing the IEP. *Learning Disability Quarterly, 1*(1), 13–32.

Hupp, S., Able, H., & Conroy-Gunter. (1984). Assessment of sensorimotor abilities of severely retarded children and adolescents. *Diagnostique, 9,* 208–217.

Idol, L. (1988). A rationale and guidelines for establishing special education consultation programs. *Remedial and Special Education, 9*(6), 48–58.

Idol, L., Paolucci-Whitcomb, P., & Nevin, A. (1987). *Collaborative consultation.* Austin, TX: Pro-Ed.

Idol-Maestas, L., & Ritter, S. (1985). A follow-up study of resource/consulting teachers: Factors that facilitate and inhibit teacher consultation. *Teacher Education and Special Education, 8*(3), 121–131.

Idol, L., & West, J. F. (1987). Consultation in special education: 2. Training and practice. *Journal of Learning Disabilities*, 20(8), 474–494.

Iowa Department of Education (1989). *Guidelines for serving at-risk students*. Des Moines, IA: Author.

Jacobsen, D., Eggen, D., & Kauchak, D. (1989). *Methods for Teaching*. Columbus, OH: Merrill.

Jaffee, J. (1966). Attitudes of adolescents toward the mentally retarded. *American Journal of Mental Deficiency*, 70, 907–912.

Jarolimek, J., & Foster, C. (1981). *Teaching and learning in the elementary school* (2nd ed.) New York: Macmillan.

Jenkins, J. R., & Pany, D. (1978). Standardized achievement tests: How useful for special education? *Exceptional Children*, 44, 448–453.

Johnson, A., & Cartwright, C. (1977). The roles of information and experience in improving teachers' knowledge and attitudes about mainstreaming. *Journal of Special Education*, 13, 453–462.

Johnson, D. W., & Johnson, R. T. (1986, April). Mainstreaming and cooperative learning strategies. *Exceptional Children*, 52(6), 553–561.

Johnson, G. R. (1976). *Analyzing college teaching*. Manchaca, TX: Sterling Swift.

Johnson, R. T., Johnson, D. W., & Holubec, E. J. (Eds.). (1987). *Structuring cooperative learning: Lesson plans for teachers* (pp. 55–56). Edina, MN: Interaction Book Company.

Kagan, J. (1966). Reflection-impulsivity: The generality and dynamics of conceptual tempo. *Journal of Abnormal Psychology*, 71, 17–24.

Kaplan, S. W., Kaplan, J. A. B., Madsen, S. K. & Taylor, B. K. (1973). *Change for children*. Pacific Palisades, CA: Goodyear.

Kauffman, J. M. (1989). *The regular education initiative as Reagan-Bush education policy: A trickle-down theory of education of the hard-to-teach*. Charlottesville, VA: University of Virginia, Curry School of Education.

Kauffman, J. M., & Pullen, P. L. (1989). An historical perspective: A personal perspective on our history of service to mildly handicapped and at-risk students. *Remedial and Special Education*, 10(6), 12–14.

Kauffman, J. M., Pullen, P. L., & Akers, E. (1986). Classroom management: Teacher-child-peer relationships. *Focus on Exceptional Children*, 19(1).

Kavale, K., & Forness, S. (1987). Substance over style: Assessing the efficacy of modality testing and teaching. *Exceptional Children*, 54, 228–239.

Keefe, J. W. (1979). *Student learning styles: Diagnosing and prescribing programs*. Reston, VA: National Association of Secondary School Principals.

Kelly, D. (1990, June 26). A call to cut school class size. *USA Today*, p. 1D.

Kelly, G. A. (1955). *The psychology of personal constructs*. New York: Norton.

Kelly, L. K. (1979). Student self-scheduling: Is it worth the risks? *NAASP Bulletin*, 63(424), 84–91.

Kindsvatter, R., Wilen, W., & Ishler, M. (1988). *Dynamics of effective teaching*. New York: Longman.

Kinnison, L. R., Hayes, C., & Acord, J. (1981). Evaluating student progress in mainstreamed classes. *Teaching Exceptional Children*, 13(3), 97–99.

Kjerland, L., Neiss, J., Franke, B., Verdon, C., & Westman, E. (1988). Team membership: Who's on first? *Impact Newsletter*. Minneapolis, MN: University of Minnesota Institute on Community Integration.

Krathwohl, D. R. (Ed.). (1964). *Taxonomy of educational objectives. The classification of educational goals. Handbook II: Affective domain*. New York: Longman.

Kurpius, D. (1978). Introduction to the special issue: An overview on consultation. *Personnel and Guidance Journal*, 56, 320–323.

Lazar, A. L., Houghton, D., & Orpet, R. E. (1977). A study of attitude acceptance and social adjustment. *Behavior Disorders*, 2(2), 85–88.

Lee, Jr., J. F., & Pruitt, K. W. (1970). Homework assignments: Classroom games or teaching tools? *Clearing House*, 1, 31–35.

Lewis, R. B., & Doorlag, D. H. (1987). *Teaching special students in the mainstream*. Columbus, OH: Merrill.

Leyser, Y., & Lessen, E. (1985). The efficiency of two training approaches on attitudes of prospective teachers toward mainstreaming. *The Exceptional Child*, 32, 175–183.

Locher, P. (1988). The usefulness of psychoeducational evaluation of preassessment screening for sensory-motor and perceptual encoding deficits. *Psychology in the Schools*, 25, 244–251.

Locher, P., & Worms, P. (1981). Visual scanning strategies of perceptually impaired and normal children viewing the motor-free visual perception test. *Journal of Learning Disabilities*, 14, 416–419.

Long, N. J., & Newman, R. (1980). Managing surface behaviors of children in schools. In N. J. Long, W. Morse, & R. Newman (Eds.), *Conflict in the classroom: The education of emotionally disturbed children* (4th ed.). Belmont, CA: Wadsworth.

Loucks-Horsley, S., & Roody, D. (1990). Using what is known about change to inform the regular education initiative. *Remedial and Special Education*, 11(3), 51–61.

Lovitt, T. (1989). Constructing graphic organizers. *Graphic organizer interactive video packet*. Salt Lake City, UT: Utah Learning Resource Center.

MacMillan, D. L., Meyers, C., & Yoshida, R. (1978). Regular class teachers' perceptions of transition programs for EMR students and their impact on the students. *Psychology in the Schools, 15*, 9–103.

Maher, C. A. (1981). Decision analysis: An approach for multidisciplinary teams on planning special service programs. *Journal of School Psychology, 19*, 340–349.

Marsh, G. E., & Price, B. J. (1980). *Methods for teaching the mildly handicapped adolescent*. St. Louis, MO: C. V. Mosby.

Marston, R., & Leslie, D. (1983). Teacher perceptions from mainstreamed versus nonmainstreamed teaching environments. *Physical Educator, 40*, 8–15.

Maryland State Department of Education, Division of Instructional Television. *Teaching children with special needs: Elementary level*. Owings Mills, MD: Author.

Mather, N., & Kirk, S. (1985). The type III error and other concerns in learning disability research. *Learning Disabilities Research, 1*, 56–64.

McKenney, J., & Keen, P. (1974). How managers' minds work. *Harvard Business Review, 53*(3), 79–90.

McKenzie, H., Egner, A. N., Knight, M. F., Perelman, P. F., Schneider, B. M., & Garvin, J. S. (1970). Training consulting teachers to assist elementary teachers in the management and education of handicapped children. *Exceptional Children, 37*, 137–143.

Mercer, C. D. (1987). *Students with learning disabilities* (3rd ed.), (p. 44). Columbus, OH: Merrill.

Middleton, E., Morsink, C., & Cohen, S. (1979). Program graduates: Perceptions of need for training in mainstreaming. *Exceptional Children, 45*, 256–263.

Miller, L. (1990). The regular education initiative and school reform: Lessons from the mainstream. *Remedial and Special Education, 11*(3), 17–22.

Mitchell, A. (1989). Old baggage, new visions: Shaping policy for early childhood programs. *Phi Delta Kappan, 70*(9), 664–672.

Morine-Dershimer, G. (1978—79). Planning in classroom reality: An in-depth look. *Educational Research Quarterly, 3*(4), B3–99.

Morsink, C. V. (1984). *Teaching special needs students in regular classrooms*. Boston: Little, Brown.

National Association of State Directors of Special Education (1990a). *Office of special education programs issues: 12th report to Congress*. Liaison Bulletin, *16*(2), 1–3.

National Association of State Directors of Special Education (1990b). *Education of the Handicapped Act Amendments of 1990 (P.L. 101–476): Summary of major changes in Parts A through H of the Act*. Washington, DC: Author.

National Coalition for the Homeless (1989). *American nightmare: A decade of homelessness in the United States*. Washington, DC: Author. (ERIC Document Reproduction Service No. ED 371 645)

National Council on Disability (1989). *The education of students with disabilities: Where do we stand? A report to the President and Congress of the United States*. Washington, DC: Author.

Nelson, C. M., & Stevens, K. B. (1981). An accountable consultation model for mainstreaming behaviorally disordered children. *Behavior Disorders, 6*(12), 82–91.

Newman, R. K. (1978). *The effects of informational and experimental activities on the attitudes of regular classroom students toward severely handicapped children and youth*. Unpublished doctoral dissertation, University of Kansas.

Olson, L. (1987). Chiefs urge that states "guarantee" school quality for those "at risk." *Education Week, 7*(11), 1.

Overton, T. (1992). *Assessment in special education: An applied approach*. Columbus, OH: Merrill.

Peterson, N. L. (1987). *Early intervention for handicapped and at-risk children*. Denver, CO: Love.

Piechowiak, A. B., & Cook, M. B. (1976). *Complete guide to the elementary learning center*. West Nyack, NY: Parker.

Polloway, E., Patton, J., Payne, J., & Payne, R. (1989). *Strategies for teaching learners with special needs*. Columbus, OH: Merrill.

Post, L., & Roy, W. (1985). Mainstreaming in secondary schools: How successful are plans to implement the concept? *NASSP Bulletin, 69*, 71–79.

Powers, D. A. (1979). Mainstreaming EMR pupils at the secondary level: A consideration of the issues. *The High School Journal, 63*(3), 102–108.

Presseisen, B. Z. (1988). Teaching thinking and at-risk students: Defining a population. In B. Z. Presseisen (Ed.), *At-risk students and thinking: Perspectives from research* (p. 19–37). Philadelphia, PA: NEA/RBS.

Purkey, W. (1978). *Inviting school success*. Belmont, CA: Wadsworth.

Public Law 94–142, Section 504, and Public Law 99–457: Understanding what they are and are not. (1989). Reston, VA: The Council for Exceptional Children.

Raphael, T. E. (1982). Question-answering strategies for children. *Reading Teacher, 36*, 186–190.

Raphael, T. E. (1986). Teaching question-answer relationships revisited. *Reading Teacher, 39*, 516–523.

Reed, S., & Sautter, R. (1990). Children of poverty—The status of 12 million young Americans. *Phi Delta Kappan, 71*(10), K1–K12.

Relic, P. D., Cavallaro, A., Borrelli, M., & Currie, J. H. (1986). *Special education/ regular education*. West Hartford, CT: West Hartford Public Schools.

Reschly, D. J. (1988). Minority mild mental retardation overrepresentation: Legal issues, research findings, and reform trends. In M. C. Wang, M. C. Reynolds, & H. J. Walberg (Eds.), *Handbook of special education: Research and practice: Vol. 2. Mildly handicapping conditions* (pp. 23–41). New York: Pergamon Press.

Reynolds, B., Martin-Reynolds, J., & Mark, F. (1982). Elementary teachers' attitudes toward mainstreaming educable mentally retarded students. *Education and Training of the Mentally Retarded, 17*, 171–176.

Reynolds, M. C. (1989). An historical perspective: The delivery of special education to mildly disabled and at-risk students. *Remedial and Special Education, 10*(6), 7–11.

Reynolds, M. C., Wang, M. C., & Walberg, H. J. (1987). The necessary restructuring of special and regular education. *Exceptional Children, 53*(5), 391–398.

Rich, H. C. (1982). *Disturbed students: Characteristics and educational strategies.* Baltimore, MD: University Park Press.

Rist, M. C. (1990, July). The shadow children: Preparing for the arrival of crack babies in school. *Research Bulletin.* Bloomington, IN: Phi Delta Kappa Center for Evaluation, Development, and Research.

Robbins, R. L., & Harway, N. I. (1977). Goal setting and reactions to success and failure in children with learning disabilities. *Journal of Learning Disabilities, 10*(6), 356–362.

Robinson, V. (1990, Fall). Regular education initiative: Debate on the current state and future promise of a new approach to educating children with disabilities. *Counterpoint*, p. 5.

Rocha, R. M., Wiley, D., & Watson, M. J. (1982). Special subject teachers and the special educator work to mainstream. *Teaching Exceptional Children, 14*(4), 141–145.

Roit, M., & Pfohl, W. (1984). The readability of P.L. 94–142 parent materials: Are parents truly informed? *Exceptional Children, 50*, 496–505.

Rosenthal, R. (1974). *On the social psychology of the self-fulfilling prophecy: Further evidence of Pygmalion effects and their mediating mechanisms.* New York: MSS Modular.

Rosenthal, R., & Jacobson, L. (1968). *Pygmalion in the classroom: Teacher expectation and pupil's intellectual development.* New York: Holt, Rinehart, & Winston.

Rowe, M. B. (1974). Wait time and reward as instructional variables, their influence on language, logic, and fate control: Part 1. Wait time. *Journal of Research on Science Teaching, 11*, 81–94.

Ryor, J. (1978). The perspective of regular education. *Learning Disability Quarterly, 1,* 6–14.

Safran, J., & Safran, S. P. (1985). Organizing communication for the LD teacher. *Academic Therapy, 20*(4), 427–435.

Salend, S. J., & Salend, S. M. (1986). Competencies for mainstreaming secondary level learning disabled students. *Journal of Learning Disabilities, 19,* 91–94.

Salend, S. J., & Schliff, J. (1978). The many dimensions of homework. *Academic Therapy, 23*(4), 397–403.

Salvia, J. S., & Hughes, C. (1990). *Curriculum-based assessment: Testing what is taught.* New York: Macmillan.

Salvia, J., & Ysseldyke, J. (1988). *Assessment in special and remedial education* (4th ed.). Boston, MA: Houghton Mifflin.

Samuels, S. J. (1984). Basic academic skills. In J. E. Ysseldyke (Ed.), *School psychology: The state of the art.* Minneapolis: National School Psychology Inservice Training Network, University of Minnesota.

Schlesinger, H. J. (1954). Cognitive attitudes in relation to susceptibility to interference. *Journal of Personality, 22,* 354–374.

Schmelkin, L. P. (1981). Teachers' and nonteachers' attitudes toward mainstreaming. *Exceptional Children, 48*(1), 42–47.

Schniedewind, N. & Salend, S. J. (1987, Winter). Cooperative learning works. *Teaching Exceptional Children, 19*(2), 22–25.

Showers, B. (1985). Teachers coaching teachers. *Educational Leadership, 42*(7), 63–68.

Schulte, A. C., Osborne, S. S., & McKinney, J. D. (1990). Academic outcomes for students with learning disabilities in consultation and resource programs. *Exceptional Children, 57*(2), 162–172.

Schumaker, J. B., & Deshler, D. D. (1988). Implementing the regular education initiative. *Journal of Learning Disabilities, 21*(1), 36–42.

Schweinhart, L. J., & Weikart, D. P. (1980). Young children grow up: The effects of the Perry Preschool Program on youths through age 15. *Monographs of the High/Scope Educational Research Foundation,* No. 7.

Shapiro, E. S. (1988). Preventing academic failure. *School Psychology Review, 17,* 601–613.

Shapiro, E. S. (1989). *Academic skills problems: Direct assessment and intervention.* New York: The Guilford Press.

Simpson, R. L. (1980). Modifying the attitudes of regular class students toward the handicapped. *Focus on Exceptional Children, 13*(3), 1–11.

Spodek, B. (1982). What special educators need to know about regular classrooms. *The Educational Forum*, *XLVI*(3), 295–307.

Spodek, B. Saracho, O. N., & Lee, R. C. (1984). *Mainstreaming young children.* Belmont, CA: Wadsworth.

Stainback, W., Stainback, S., Courtnage, L., & Jaben, T. (1985). Facilitating mainstreaming by modifying the mainstream. *Exceptional Children*, *52*(2), 144–152.

Student teaching handbook. (1982). Richmond, VA: Virginia Commonwealth University, Division of Teacher Education, School of Education.

Sulzer-Azaroff, B., & Mayer, G. R. (1977). *Applying behavioral analysis procedures with children and youth.* New York: Holt, Rinehart, & Winston.

Suydam, M. N. (1985, April). Individualizing for cooperative learning. *Arithmetic Teacher*, *32*(8), 39.

Taylor, P. (1970). *How teachers plan their courses.* New York: National Foundation for Educational Research.

Tenbrink, T. (1977). Writing instructional objectives. In J. Cooper, J. Hansen, P. Martorella, G. Morine-Dershimer, D. Sadker, M. Sadker, R. Shostak, S. Sokolove, T. Tenbrink, & W. Weber (Eds.), *Classroom teaching skills: A handbook.* Lexington, MA: D. C. Heath.

Thompson, A. C. (1981). Some counterthinking about learning disabilities. *Journal of Learning Disabilities*, *14*, 394–396.

Thousand, J. S., & Villa, R. A. (1990). Sharing expertise and responsibilities through teaching teams. In W. Stainback & S. Stainback (Eds.), *Support systems for educating all students in the mainstream.* Baltimore, MD: Paul H. Brookes.

Tucker, J. (1980). Ethnic proportions in classes for the learning disabled: Issues in nonbiased assessment. *The Journal of Special Education*, *14*, 93–105.

Turnbull, A. P., & Turnbull, H. R. (1986). *Families, professionals, and exceptionality.* Columbus, OH: Merrill.

Turner, T. (1984). The joy of homework. *Tennessee Education*, *14*, 25–33.

Vasa, S. F. (1981a). Alternative procedures for grading handicapped students in the secondary schools. *Education Unlimited*, *3*(1), 16–23.

Vasa, S. F. (1981b). Alternative procedures for grading handicapped students in the secondary schools. In S. F. Vasa, *Integrating secondary handicapped students in general and vocational curriculum.* Des Moines, IA: Drake University, Midwest Regional Resource Center.

Vaughn, S., Bos, C., Harrell, J., & Lasky, B. (1988). Parent participation in the initial placement/IEP conference 10 years after mandated involvement. *Journal of Learning Disabilities*, *21*, 82–89.

Vermont State Department of Education, Division of Special Education and Pupil Personnel Services. Reading competency #6a—Gets information from resource material: Dictionary. *Basic Skills Sequence in English*. Montpelier, VT: Author.

Virginia Department of Education (1989). *Issues related to graduation and students receiving special education services* (Supts. Memo No. 126). Richmond, VA: Author.

Visual News. (Fall, 1990 4[4]) Richmond, Virginia: Virginia State Library for the Visually and Physically Handicapped, p. 1.

Voight, B. C. (1973). *Invitation to learning*. Washington, DC: Acropolis Books.

Watkins, M. W., & Webb, C. (1981). Computer-assisted instruction with learning disabled students. *Educational Computer, 1*(3), 24–27.

Weber, W. A. (1977). Classroom management. In J. M. Cooper (Ed.), *Classroom teaching skills: A workbook* (pp. 237–239). Lexington, MA: D. C. Heath.

Weber, J., & Stoneman, Z. (1986). Parental nonparticipation as a means of reducing bias in the education of handicapped children. *Special Services in the Schools, 1*, 71–84.

Wehman, P., & McLaughlin, P. J. (1981). *Program development in special education*. New York: McGraw-Hill.

Weintraub, F. J., & Ross, J. W. (1980). Policy approaches regarding the impact of graduation requirements on handicapped students. *Exceptional Children, 47*(3), 200–203.

West, E. (1975). *Leading discussions*. Unpublished. Minneapolis, MN: University of Minnesota.

West, J. F., & Brown, P. (1987). State departments of education policies on consultation in special education: The state of the states. *Remedial and Special Education, 8*(3), 45–51.

West, J. F., & Idol, L. (1990). Collaborative consultation in the education of mildly handicapped and at-risk students. *Remedial and Special Education, 11*(1), 22–31.

Wiederholt, J. L., & Chamberlain, S. P. (1990). A critical analysis of resource programs. *Remedial and Special Education, 10*(6), 15–37.

Wilson, J. (1978). Selecting education materials and resources. In D. Hammil & W. Bartel (Eds.), *Teaching children with learning and behavior problems*. Boston, MA: Allyn & Bacon.

Wimmer, D. (1981). Functional learning curricula in the secondary schools. *Exceptional Children, 47*(8), 610–616.

Winters, R. (1985). *Child abuse digest* (p. 3). Tampa, FL: Winters Communications.

Witkin, H. A., Moore, C. A., Oltman, P. K., Goodenough, D. R., Friedman, F., Owen, D. R., & Raskin, E. C. (1977). Role of field-dependent and field-independent cognitive styles in academic evolution: A longitudinal study. *Journal of Educational Psychology, 69*(3), 197–211.

Wood, J. W. (1989). *Mainstreaming: A practical approach for teachers.* Columbus, OH: Merrill.

Wood, J. W. (1991a). *Instructional adaptations for mainstreamed and at-risk students.* Richmond, VA: Virginia Commonwealth University.

Wood, J. W. (1991b). Project SHARE. Richmond, VA: Virginia Commonwealth University.

Wood, J. W., Davis, E., Lazzari, A., Sugai, G., & Carte, J. (1990) National status of the prereferral process: An issue for regular education. *Action in Teacher Education, 12*(3), 50–56.

Wood, J. W., & Englebert, B. (1982). Mainstreaming minimanual. *Instructor, 91*(7), 63–66.

Wood, J. W., & Miederhoff, J. W. (1988). Adapting test construction for mainstreamed mathematics students. *Mathematic Teacher,* 388–392.

Wood, J. W., Miederhoff, J. W., & Bishop, J. C. (1988). Stress the knowledge, not the student: Testing the mildly handicapped. *The Science Teacher,* 22–25.

Wood, J. W., & Reeves, C. K. (1989). Mainstreaming: An overview. In J. W. Wood, *Mainstreaming: A practical approach for teachers.* Columbus, OH: Merrill.

Wood, J. W. & Wooley. J. A. (1986). Adapting textbooks. *The Clearing House, 59,* 332–335.

Yinger, R. (1980). A study of teacher planning. *The Elementary School Journal, 80*(3), 107–127.

Ysseldyke, J. E., & Algozzine, D. (1982). *Critical issues in special and remedial education.* Boston, MA: Houghton Mifflin.

Ysseldyke, J. E., & Algozzine, D. (1990). *Introduction to special education* (2nd ed.). Geneva, IL: Houghton Mifflin.

Ysseldyke, J., Algozzine, B., & Epps, S. (1983). A logical and empirical analysis of current practice in classifying students as handicapped. *Exceptional Children, 50,* 160–166.

Young, J. L., & Shepherd, M. L. (1983). *The adjustment of the educable mentally retarded to the regular classroom: The teacher's perspective.* Hattiesburg, MS: University of Southern Mississippi. (ERIC Document Reproduction Service No. ED 258 372)

Index

About the Author

Judy W. Wood is Professor of Special Education at Virginia Commonwealth University in Richmond, Virginia. A native of Center, Texas, Dr. Wood received a B.S. degree in English and mental retardation at the University of Southern Mississippi in Hattiesburg, Mississippi. She holds master's and Ph.D. degrees in special education from the same university. Her interests lie in assisting regular and special education teachers in providing appropriate instruction for students with disabilities and children and youth at risk for success within our schools.